DATE DUE

NO 29 00			
DE 20 02 JE 10 02			
AP 25 03			
MY 20 03			

DEMCO 38-296

ART WITHOUT BOUNDARIES

The World of

MODERN DANCE

ART
WITHOUT
BOUNDARIES

by Jack Anderson

UNIVERSITY OF IOWA PRESS Ψ IOWA CITY

University of Iowa Press, Iowa City 52242
Copyright © 1997 by the University of Iowa Press
All rights reserved
Printed in the United States of America

Design by Martha Farlow

http://www.uiowa.edu/~uipress

Printed on acid-free paper

LIBRARY OF CONGRESS CATALOGING-IN-PUBLICATION DATA
Anderson, Jack, 1935 –
    Art without boundaries: the world of modern dance / by Jack Anderson.
        p.   cm.
    Includes bibliographical references (p.   ) and index.
    ISBN 0-87745-583-X
    1. Modern dance—History.   I. Title.
    GV1783.A53   1997
    792.8—dc21   96-52226

02 01 00 99 98 97 C 5 4 3 2 1

To George

The foregoing generations beheld God and nature face to face; we, through their eyes. Why should not we also enjoy an original relation to the universe? Why should not we have a poetry and philosophy of insight and not of tradition, and a religion by revelation to us, and not the history of theirs?

RALPH WALDO EMERSON, *NATURE*, 1836

I am glad to hear that you propose to take the bit in your teeth and buck for freedom. There is little use in painting—in living in fact—unless you let yourself grow your natural course.

You will have a wonderful time. Others (those who wish to dictate) will not be satisfied perhaps—but they are never satisfied anyway—and you will give them better than they know. At any rate what you will give will be news from your country.

ROBERT HENRI, *THE ART SPIRIT*, 1930

CONTENTS

INTRODUCTION AND
ACKNOWLEDGMENTS

MODERN DANCE REMAINS A MYSTERY. IT IS KNOWN THE world over and, in some form or other, has existed since the late nineteenth century. Yet no one has ever been able to say precisely what it is. Nevertheless, if modern dance is mysterious, it is also glorious, and it has proved to be miraculously self-renewing. Therefore anyone trying to describe its historical development can only revel in its diversity. My own research has been one adventure after another.

Because many accounts of modern dance now exist, a few words should be said about the nature and purpose of this one. It is primarily intended for the general reader. I hope it will be of interest both to dancegoers curious about the art they have enjoyed onstage and to dance students who wonder about the origins and development of the craft they are perfecting in the studio.

This is a chronicle, rather than a theoretical treatise. It advances no all-encompassing concept of what constitutes "modernism" in modern dance. Indeed, given the historical evidence, I suspect that the unabashed eclecticism of the art makes it impossible to formulate any such concept. To a great extent, dancers are described here because, for one reason or another, critics and dancegoers in their time considered them "modern"—whatever "modern" meant to them or may now mean to us.

I have also directed attention to some unclassifiable dancers who, if unlike other moderns of their era, are also dissimilar to ballet dancers or exponents of national dance or musical-theatre styles. Finally, as a lover of eccentricity, I must confess that a few dancers are mentioned here because I found them so unusual that I could not ignore them. Through their very idiosyncrasies, they contributed something to the dance of their time.

This book attempts to be panoramic and internationalist in scope. American books on modern dance often focus almost entirely on American dancers. Although this is understandable enough, such an emphasis gives a somewhat distorted view of the scene. Ever since there was anything that could be termed modern dance, it has been an international art. Therefore I have ranged widely, not out of any "revisionist" desire to minimalize established giants, but to place them among their contemporaries.

Material is arranged historically, rather than biographically. Some long-lived and important leaders (for instance, Martha Graham and Mary Wigman) will of necessity reappear in various parts of the book. As a result, information about them is scattered rather than neatly gathered together; I thought readers might find it interesting to compare their achievements with those of other choreographers in a given period.

Suspecting that the general reader may know more about the contemporary scene than about modern dance's past, I have stressed the far away and long ago. Also, I have been cautious about admitting too many younger choreographers into these pages because these artists are still developing and anything that can be said about them today may be totally out of date tomorrow.

I hope my discussions of celebrated and obscure figures alike will prompt further research into their careers and achievements. I also know that other dancers I have been unable to mention because of lack of space remain worthy of serious study.

Many people have aided me in the writing of this book. I am especially grateful for the assistance given me by Madeleine Nichols, curator, and her staff at the Dance Collection of the New York Public Library for the Performing Arts at Lincoln Center. The "morgue" at the *New York Times* has also been a splendid source of information.

If it had not been for the late David Voss, not a page of this book might exist. At a time when I was filling note card after note card with information, but without transferring any of it into coherent prose, it was David who repeatedly badgered me with requests to *see* some of the material he had heard me talk about. So I got down to the business of writing. David was the first reader of many of these chapters; I regret that he was unable to live to read the finished book.

So, too, I regret that Robin Howard—surely one of the most admirable figures in modern-dance history—is not alive to read this account of the art to which he devoted himself so wholeheartedly. I consider myself fortunate that I was able to interview him shortly before his untimely death.

Advice, reminiscences, suggestions, and information have come from Keith Bain, Ann Barzel, Roger Beck, Shelley C. Berg, Selma Jeanne Cohen, Valda Craig, Agnes de Mille, Gedeon Dienes, Eiko and Koma, Annabel Farjeon, Joanne Ferguson, Claudia Gitelman, Lotte Goslar, Hellmut Gottschild, Ann Hutchinson Guest, Judith Brin Ingber, George Jackson, Claudia Jeschke, Lydia Joel, Mildred Kaeser, Horst Koegler, Pauline Koner, Susan Manning, Aurel Milloss, Nancy Moore, Erik Naslund, Genevieve Oswald, Ou Jian-Ping, Barbara Palfy, Charles and Stephanie Reinhart, Jacqueline Robinson, José Sasportes, Christena L. Schlundt, Josephine Schwarz, Jane Sherman, Julia Smith, Kathrine Sorley Walker, Emma Lewis Thomas, Pauline Tish, Patrizia Veroli, and Bert Wechsler. Susannah Keagle has patiently assisted by putting my manuscript on the computer.

In addition to providing me with information, Pia Gilbert was gracious enough to translate long passages of German for me. Translations from the French, unless otherwise credited, are by myself.

Once again, George Dorris has been a pillar of strength in his encouragement and enthusiasm.

PART *1*

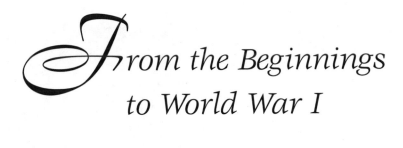

*From the Beginnings
to World War I*

$\mathscr{J}$NDELIBLE EPHEMERAL

Modern dance as term and reality

MODERN DANCE IS AN ART AS ELUSIVE AS IT IS GREAT. NO one has ever offered an all-inclusive, totally satisfying definition of it. No one can point to its date or place of origin. Yet something known as modern dance does exist and, despite periodic attempts to pronounce it dead, modern dance continues to flourish.

The American choreographer Paul Taylor once asked himself, "Modern dance? To me, modern dance is a license to do what I feel is worth doing without somebody saying that I can't do it because it does not fit into a category." And, with oxymoronic accuracy, Dominique Dupuy, a French choreographer, has defined modern dance as "L'Indélébile Ephémère": the indelible ephemeral.[1]

Modern dance has been an art of such disparate manifestations that it is hard to determine what they have in common. Even the stage attire of modern dancers has been bewilderingly varied. They have worn Grecian tunics, as if to evoke a Hellenic golden age. They have let tights or costumes resembling gymnasium outfits emphasize the physical robustness of movement. Austere skirts or robes have made modern dancers seem priests and priestesses. On other occasions, modern dancers have totally concealed their bodies so that they become pieces of moving sculpture. They have also worn ordinary street clothes or the latest examples of high fashion. And although some of the modern-dance pioneers were labeled "barefoot dancers," modern dancers have worn sandals, shoes, and boots, as well.

Establishing precise parallels between modern dance and modern painting, modern music, and modern literature proves difficult.

Modern dancers have tended to use "modern" as a synonym for "new" or "creative," and they have prized experimentation. Yet they have never subscribed for long to any ideology.

Modern dance has often been said to involve a point of view, rather than a specific esthetic program. The dancers who have labeled themselves—or who have allowed themselves to be labeled—modern have prized the freedom to present whatever is important to them in whatever manner they consider appropriate. Choreographers have offered dances with specific plots or philosophical or political messages, dances that are expressions of emotions, and dances that are studies in sheer energy. Modern dance is a provisional art, one which the choreographer José Limón has said is "in essence, non-academic; in principle, experimental; in practice, eclectic and inclusive." [2]

But eclecticism does not make it rootless. Dancers do not live in vacuums. They study with teachers, work with older choreographers, and absorb, reject, or transform the artistic developments occurring around them. Modern dance exists in a web of cultural influences.

Modern dance is frequently referred to as an American art. The critic Clive Barnes called it that in 1978 when he said that modern dance "is one of the only, possibly apart from jazz *the* only indigenous American art form." About a decade later, Paul Taylor employed similar language when he declared modern dance to be "the one art form other than jazz that can be called truly American." [3]

Modern dance has undeniably flourished in America. But it has never been exclusively American. Some of the earliest American modern dancers were stirred by European theories. Europe may have been inspired by the example of these Americans, but it soon produced its own modern dance. Four great American dancers—Loïe Fuller, Isadora Duncan, Maud Allan, and Ruth St. Denis—achieved real acclaim in America only after they had triumphed in Europe and only St. Denis spent most of her creative life in America. The others, in effect, became citizens of the world, traveling from country to country as if they believed that art recognized no borders.

Over the years, the art we now generally know as modern dance has been called many things: rhythmic dance, interpretative (or interpretive) dance, natural dance, Expressionist (or expressive) dance, free dance, barefoot dance, and art dance, to name only a few; also, to name a few more, *danse libre, Absoluter Tanz, Freier Tanz, Tanz-*

kunst, Bewegungskunst, and *Ausdruckstanz.*[4] The terms are not entirely synonymous, for each emphasizes a different aspect of the art.

"Modern dance" has become the term that now encompasses all these choreographic manifestations. Yet it has never totally pleased anyone. "Modern dance" can imply something merely transient. Nevertheless, the term has stuck. And attempts by some recent critics to devise a separate category for a type of dance that has developed from it have resulted in nothing more than a new and even more awkward term: "postmodern dance."

"Modern dance" appears to have acquired its multitude of meanings by a process of evolution. During the early twentieth century, perceptive writers and sensitive dancers began to feel that significant changes were occurring in dance. In *Der Moderne Tanz,* a book of 1910, Ernst Schur asserted that, although the old ballet was dead, dance had nevertheless become an important part of modern culture; among the dancers he cited as evidence of choreographic rejuvenation were Isadora Duncan, Elizabeth Duncan, Rita Sacchetto, Ruth St. Denis, the Wiesenthal Sisters, and the exponents of the new Russian ballet. On 16 May 1911 at the Teatro dell'Accademia dei Filodrammatici in Milan, Rita Sacchetto — as much of a modern dancer as her now more famous contemporaries Duncan and St. Denis — offered a recital which the printed program announced as an example of "sue creazioni mimo-drammatiche di danze moderne" (her mimo-dramatic creations of modern dance).[5]

J. E. Crawford Flitch's *Modern Dancing and Dancers* (1912, revised in 1913) surveys many of the dance forms of the time from ballet to Apache and cancan dancing. Flitch also discusses Duncan, St. Denis, Loïe Fuller, and Maud Allan, and he predicts, "It is not unlikely that when the art historian of the future comes to treat of the artistic activity of the first decade of the twentieth century, he will remark as one of its most notable accomplishments a renaissance of the art of Dance." Equally comprehensive in scope is an American book of the same year, Caroline Caffin and Charles H. Caffin's *Dances and Dancers of Today,* which examines everything from ballet and folk dancing to Duncan, Allan, St. Denis, Sacchetto, and the Wiesenthals. Like Flitch, the Caffins speak prophetically: "Today, in America, we have awakened to the consciousness that dancing may be something more than a form of social amusements in ballrooms, or of geometric exercise on the stage. We are taking a keen interest in the Art of the Dance."[6]

Hans Brandenburg's often reprinted *Der Moderne Tanz* of 1913 is almost entirely devoted to creators we would now classify as modern dancers: Duncan (and her sister's school), St. Denis, the Wiesenthals, Sent M'Ahesa, Emile Jaques-Dalcroze, the Sakharoffs, Gertrud Leistikow, and Ellen Tels. That Brandenburg also includes a chapter on Russian ballet is a sign that early-twentieth-century critics perceived that the Russians—particularly, the companies of Anna Pavlova and Sergei Diaghilev—were offering a type of dance far more vivid and, in Diaghilev's case, far more adventurous than the anemic ballet that prevailed in some Western European opera houses.

Over the years, writers began to separate ballet and modern dance, possibly because all ballet dancers, however conservative or avant-garde they may be in their taste, receive an essentially similar form of training. Modern dance has been more heterogeneous, in pedagogy and esthetics alike. That is one reason why it resists definition. Yet critics and audiences in any given time tend to perceive certain types of dance productions as being "modern." Thus in 1931, when John Martin, the dance critic of the *New York Times*, gave a much-publicized series of lectures called "The Modern Dance," the entire audience surely knew what he meant, although they may not have shared his opinions.

So, too, dancegoers today have their own views of the "modern." Modern dance can seem an art of infinite variety; it certainly sprang from varied sources.

ƎETTING THE STAGE

American society · European World's Fairs ·
Developments in the arts · Gymnastics ·
Educational reform · Dress reform

"CERTAIN IDEAS ARE IN THE AIR. WE ARE ALL IMPRESSION-able, for we are made of them; all impressionable, but some more than others, and these first express them. This explains the curious contemporaneousness of inventions and discoveries. The truth is in the air, and the most impressionable brain will announce it first, but all will announce it a few minutes later. So women, as most suscep-tible, are the best index of the coming hour." [1] So wrote Ralph Waldo Emerson in 1852 in his essay "Fate." Cultivated Americans read Emerson. So did Europeans. These words may very well have been read and pondered by the visionaries—most of them women—who, working separately yet often in a remarkable community of spirit, helped create modern dance.

Living in later, more troubled times, it is easy to sentimentalize the past and to sigh nostalgically over the prosperous farms and cozy parlors of a hundred years ago. But nineteenth-century America was not invariably pleasant. It could be crude and rough, and very vio-lent. There were bloody frontier battles between white settlers and Native Americans. During the 1860s, the entire nation was shaken by a monstrous Civil War. Child labor and industrial exploitation were common.

Dour evangelists warned that the flesh was evil and that sinners would be damned. Other thinkers disagreed. The Transcendental-ists believed that humanity and the universe were spiritual and good. The Universalists and Unitarians preached universal salvation. Utopian thinkers established such communities as Brook Farm in

Massachusetts, Oneida in New York, and New Harmony in Indiana. And when the Boston intellectuals—Emerson among them—argued that the facts of nature are signs of spiritual facts and that artists must seek spiritual truths beyond outward appearances, sensitive Americans listened.

If America yearned for illumination, Europe, despite its own political upheavals, seemed ablaze with light. Thanks to Thomas A. Edison's invention of the incandescent lamp, lights literally shone through the night at the Paris Universal Exposition of 1889. The London Crystal Palace Exhibition of 1851 had been the first of what have come to be known as world's fairs. The nineteenth century loved them. They were signs of technological progress, commercial prosperity, and artistic achievement. The 1889 exposition gave Paris the Eiffel Tower, that remarkable combination of engineering and whimsy, and a now-demolished Palace of Machines crammed with inventions. The fair's Palace of Fine Arts offered, among other attractions, the largest display of American painting that had ever been seen in Europe. There were also pavilions devoted to the cultures of such nations as Egypt, Siam, Morocco, Persia, and Japan. There were comparable revelations at the Paris Exposition of 1900, a fair that put at least a few examples of modern dance on view.

"I would rather go to Europe than to heaven," said the American painter William Merritt Chase. Isadora Duncan, the iconoclastic American dancer, agreed. "America is the land where they drink lemonade," she said. "And how can one dance on lemonade?"[2] To American writers, artists, and dancers, Europe may have seemed livelier than heaven, more intoxicating than lemonade. Europe seethed with cultural ferment.

During the nineteenth century reformist educators stressed the importance of personal growth and creativity and, increasingly, schools offered instruction in art and music. There was physical education, as well. Influenced, in part, by European theories of gymnastic training, America developed its own interest in physical culture. Thus, during the 1890s, Melvin Ballou Gilbert and Dudley A. Sargent advocated "aesthetic calisthenics," which was based upon the five traditional balletic positions of the feet and which made use of such balletic poses as attitude and arabesque.[3]

The champions of physical education helped prepare the way for modern dance, and gymnastic exercises often served as technical starting points for young women who longed to dance.

Women were shaking off constraints. They needed to, for they were being stifled—mentally, physically, neurologically. In the decade after the Civil War, ill health mysteriously plagued American women. Disease accounted for some of this malaise. So did clothing. Long skirts dragged in the mud and were therefore unhygienic. And clothes could be so tight and binding as to threaten the normal development of bones and internal organs.

But much of the ill health may have had psychological or psychosomatic causes. Genevieve Stebbins, a movement teacher, quotes a letter from a woman identified as a Mrs. Botta: "Few of us in New York can deny that we live in a high state of nervous tension. This chronic constriction of nerves, never relaxed, involves such expenditure of vital force as often precludes possibilities of rest." No wonder determined women campaigned for fresh air, simple clothing, and improved hygiene.[4]

Restless children in Europe and America have often dreamed of running off to join the circus or the Gypsies. Some rebellious young women did something even more daring: they ran off and became dancers. And they made their dancing a declaration of independence.[5]

O PIONEERS!

Art Nouveau • Loïe Fuller • Skirt dancing • François Delsarte • American Delsartians • Steele Mackaye • William Rounseville Alger • Genevieve Stebbins

FROM THE 1890S TO THE OUTBREAK OF WORLD WAR I, European and American crafts, architecture, and interior design were influenced by what has come to be known as Art Nouveau. It was a style that flourished in many cities simultaneously—Paris, New York, Glasgow, Vienna, and Budapest, among them—and its practitioners designed everything from lamps and glassware to buildings and subway stations.

Although the product of an urban culture, Art Nouveau proclaimed the importance of nature by favoring sinuous, flowing lines and shapes inspired by vines, flowers, tendrils, windblown grass, and swirling waves. Its artistic products were often fanciful and extravagant. Two Americans rank among its major figures: Louis Comfort Tiffany, a glassmaker famous for his iridescent colors, and Loïe Fuller, a dancer whose works glowed and shimmered with a magic all her own.

Fuller was the first American pioneer of modern dance to achieve international acclaim. She spent much of her artistic life in Europe, where enraptured audiences dubbed her "The Painter with Light," "The Fairy of Light," and "The Magic Princess of Pearly Tints."

Born in rural Illinois in 1862, she came from a musical family. Her father was a fiddler and square dance caller; her mother had studied to be an opera singer. Mary Louise Fuller (her name soon shortened to Loie and turned by the French into Loïe) was a child temperance lecturer and, later, a singer and actress. In 1892, when she was thirty, she created her first sensation as a dancer.

Precisely what led to this breakthrough remains shadowy, for Fuller offered several versions of how she came to invent the type of dance that made her famous. However, she seems to have been entranced by the play of sunlight on a piece of silk she was draping about herself. From her observations came a new form of movement and stage illusion. After Brooklyn performances in 1892, she went to Paris where, on 4 November 1892, she created a sensation at the Folies-Bergère. The Parisians adored her and called her "La Loïe." Fuller, in turn, loved Paris and made it her home.

Her dances owed much to changing stage effects. In her solos, Fuller stood wrapped in a glowing mass of drapery, which she manipulated, often with the aid of concealed sticks and wires, so that it rose and fell and cascaded about her while rays of light streamed upon the fabric. Offstage, Fuller was said to be physically plain and pudgy; onstage, she was bewitching.

The costume for her *Serpentine Dance* consisted of hundreds of yards of China silk which she let billow about her while lighting effects suggested that it was catching fire and taking shapes reminiscent of flowers, clouds, birds, and butterflies. Fuller performed her *Fire Dance* standing on a pane of glass that was lighted from below, giving the impression that flames were rising upward. *Mirror Dance* was also a solo, yet reflecting surfaces on the stage made it seem as if eight women were dancing. Fuller's skirt resembled an enormous flower in *Lily Dance*, and in *Rose Dance* she sank to the stage covered with crimson petals.

Occasionally during her career, which extended into the 1920s, Fuller appeared as the head of a company, and she used other performers to intensify her effects. The arms of otherwise totally hidden dancers became writhing serpents in *Arabian Nights*. No human beings at all were visible onstage in *The Sea*. Instead, the audience beheld the wavelike motions of an enormous cloth controlled by unseen dancers.[1]

Artists fell under Fuller's spell, and such major poets as Stéphane Mallarmé and William Butler Yeats wrote about her. La Loïe may even have been the inspiration for a character in one of L. Frank Baum's Oz books for children. In *The Road to Oz*, published in 1909 and the fifth volume in the series, Baum introduces Dorothy, his heroine, to Polychrome the Rainbow's Daughter, who appears "clad in flowing, fluffy robes of soft material that reminded Dorothy of woven cobwebs"; when she entertains her friends by dancing,

Polychrome "whirled until her fleecy draperies of rainbow hues enveloped her like a cloud."[2]

Baum, whose fictional creations included a tin woodman and a clockwork man, loved to combine fantasy with gadgetry. So did Fuller. She presented magical visions of beauty which, with their flowing lines and imagery drawn from nature, owed much to Art Nouveau. But she achieved her effects with modern technology. A lover of nature, Fuller was also a child of the age of science.

Fuller did not derive all her ideas from lofty sources. A seasoned trouper who appealed to the general public as well as to intellectuals, she achieved her first success in a music-hall, the Folies-Bergère. Many early modern dancers—and ballet dancers, as well—appeared in music-halls, variety theatres, and vaudeville houses. Turn-of-the-century audiences liked such theatres for the diversity of their offerings. Just as people today settle down for an evening of television-watching that may include comedies, dramas, musicals, and documentaries, so audiences at variety theatres could enjoy singers, dancers, actors, comedians, and acrobats. Serious dance attractions and short plays or abbreviated dramatic classics presented by famous stars added novelty to a bill and gave theatres the reputation for being "high class."

Fuller may have borrowed the idea for her distinctive costuming from the variety theatres. From the 1870s onward, "skirt dancers" were popular in English music-halls. Skirt dancing—a form of dancing in which a woman manipulated a long skirt as she moved—was especially associated with Kate Vaughan, whose solos emphasized the rushing and whirling of her ankle-length gown.[3] But whereas skirt dancers remained content to charm, Fuller's effects were grander. Of the various tendencies that have influenced modern dance, Fuller's works can be considered early examples of abstraction. She rarely portrayed specific characters, and although her dances may have derived from strong feelings, they were not confessional outpourings. Despite the frequent comparisons of her dances with fire, flowers, and waves, her works were not studies in physics or botany. Instead, she used nature imagery to create designs in space.

Through artistry, Fuller may have transcended her own personal limitations as a dancer. "And yet they say she did not dance!" exclaimed the *American Dancer* in its obituary for Fuller in 1928.[4] Opponents of modern dance have frequently accused modern dancers of not being able to dance. Fuller's success is a reminder that what matters onstage is not necessarily the number or difficulty of steps, but the imagination with which those steps are employed. She knew how to make her esthetic visions theatrically credible.

Nevertheless, Fuller left behind no school of dance or carefully thought out theory of stagecraft. In time, the dance world did acquire mentors—among them, a man who, during his lifetime, devoted virtually no attention to dance whatsoever.

The audiences that flocked to *Madam Sherry*, Otto Harbach's musical comedy hit of 1910, were soon singing one of its songs: "Every little movement has a meaning all its own, / Every thought and feeling by some posture may be shown." And most theatregoers of 1910 knew what that song was about: Delsarte.

Delsarte was a theory, a philosophy, and, ultimately, something of a cult. But before it became a way of thinking about movement and life, it was simply a man's surname.

François Delsarte was the son of a French physician and became the uncle of the composer Georges Bizet.[5] As a young man, he possessed an attractive tenor voice and enrolled at the Paris Conservatory in 1825, when he was fourteen. Faulty training soon caused him to lose his voice. He then attempted to become a teacher of singing and elocution. But he found that his teachers contradicted one another: the method that one upheld, another would scorn. Delsarte therefore decided to devote himself to the formulation of the basic laws of artistic expression. He did so not by theorizing alone, but through firsthand research. He went out and looked at people.

He watched adults walking in the street and children playing in the parks—and the different ways children reacted when they were touched by their parents and when they were touched by their nannies. He studied rich and poor, beggars and businessmen. He visited hospitals, morgues, insane asylums, and prisons. He observed the work of rescue crews after a mine disaster. He attended dissections and stood beside the beds of dying patients.

Beginning in 1839, Delsarte taught the theories of posture and gesture he had developed. Yet at his death in 1871 it was discovered that he had organized few of his notes and ideas in a publishable form. That task fell to his disciples, who promulgated a system remarkable for its union of science and spirituality. Delsarte contended that "to each spiritual function corresponds a function of the body; to each grand function of the body corresponds a spiritual act."[6]

What is controversial in Delsarte's teaching is the way he combined his rigorous observations with his conception of the Christian Trinity. "Take from me the Trinity," he confessed, "and I no longer understand God, all becomes obscure and shadowy, and I no longer have reason for hope." [7]

Neither Delsarte nor his wife Rosine had a conventional religious upbringing. One day in Paris, however, Rosine, feeling weary and exhausted, stepped inside the Church of Saint-Etienne du Mont to rest. There, she said, a vision of Sainte Geneviève, the patron saint of Paris, came to her and filled her with religious faith. Rosine, in turn, converted her husband.

Delsarte came to view all existence in terms of Trinities. Just as the One God of Christianity was made up of Three Persons, Father, Son, and Holy Spirit, so the world, as God's creation, abounded with its own Trinities. Delsarte defined a Trinity as "the unity of three things, each of which is essential to the other two." [8] Thus, divine qualities are expressed in life in beauty, truth, and goodness, and the basic human faculties are the physical, the emotional, and the intellectual. Music consists of rhythm, harmony, and melody, and dance involves ease, coordination, and precision.

Analyzing movement, Delsarte divided the body into three zones: the head (intellectual), the torso (emotional), and the lower limbs (physical). All actions involve attitude (a term Genevieve Stebbins, one of his disciples, clarified by explaining that "positive assertion rises, negative assertion falls"), force, and motion. [9] There are three "Great Orders of Movement": oppositions (any two bodily parts moving in opposite directions), parallelisms (any two bodily parts moving in the same direction), and successions (any movements passing through the entire body—or any part of the body—that cause each muscle or joint to move one after the other in the path of this progression). And gestures can be of three kinds: away from the center of the body, balanced, and toward the center of the body.

Delsarte had begun by rebelling against rigid systems. But what he produced was a system which, with its plethora of Trinities, might have flabbergasted even some pious Christians. Nevertheless, Delsarte pointed to fundamental kinetic truths. If his triune division of the body is something of an oversimplification (after all, the head—the intellectual zone—is associated with emotional grimacing as well as cerebration), the concept of three zones is not foolish. We speak of having an idea "in mind." Our hearts stir, ache, thrill, or throb with emotion. And the lower body contains both the limbs responsible for locomotion and those bodily parts prudes have called "dirty." Finally, Delsarte's theory is important because it proclaimed outward actions signs of inward states. Most early modern dancers were aware of this teaching.

Steele Mackaye (1842–1894), an American actor, director, and playwright, studied with Delsarte shortly before the theoretician's death. Mackaye returned to America excited by Delsarte's ideas, which he enthusiastically propagated. Like other American Delsartians, he also expanded upon them, developing a system of expression based upon principles of relaxation that came to be known as harmonic (or esthetic) gymnastics. In Boston, Mackaye was encouraged in his promulgation of Delsartianism by Lewis B. Monroe, director of the Boston University School of Oratory, and the Reverend William Rounseville Alger, a Unitarian clergyman and a cousin of the novelist Horatio Alger, Jr.

William Alger, who had been an outspoken opponent of slavery, was a popular figure on the lecture circuit, and his published works include both a *Critical History of the Doctrine of a Future Life* and a *Life of Edwin Forrest, the American Tragedian.* He may well be one of the first American clergymen to exert some influence upon dance—or, more accurately in this case, dancelike movement. Although, as the denomination's very name implied, the Unitarians were skeptical of the doctrine of the Trinity, Alger may have regarded Delsarte's Trinities as poetic metaphors. At any rate, he was impressed by Delsarte's mysticism.

"Delsarte," Alger said, "begins with God, it descends to nothing, and turns and reascends to God, and interprets everything that lies between." [10] Alger even thought harmonic gymnastics could be the basis of a new form of religious education derived from the idea that a person's physical nature is a manifestation of (rather than a sinful antithesis to) that person's spiritual nature.

Delsarte took North America by storm. Delsartian theories found their way into schools of elocution and expression. Elocution (or oratory) was often studied by clergymen, lawyers, and politicians, who, in turn, lent respectability to Delsartian notions. "Expression" was a loose term that applied to institutions offering courses in physical culture, pantomime, and dramatics; such schools also sought to develop grace in young women. Delsartian ideas spread through the middle and upper classes until by the late 1880s some Delsarte teachers sought to influence all aspects of daily life.

The most important of the American Delsartians was Genevieve Stebbins (1857 to at least 1915), an actress who became fascinated by the teachings of Delsarte and Mackaye and from them devised her own movement principles. Like Mackaye, she stressed relaxation (or "decomposing," as she termed it). But, as a complement to relaxing, she invented "energizing" techniques: exercises in which one set of muscles would be contracted while the rest of the body remained relaxed. Such exercises controlled tension and taught people how to use bodily energy efficiently. She also emphasized flexibility of the joints, deep breathing, and the clothing reforms—especially the discarding of corsets—that would make such flexibility and breathing possible.

Stebbins developed the theatrical aspects of Delsarte by staging two types of productions: pantomimic interpretations of stories, poems, or ideas and "statue posing." Contrary to what that term may suggest, statue posing was not static. Rather, the performer would slowly and gracefully move from one pose to another, letting each pose melt into the next. Statue posing demanded muscular control and sensitivity to dynamics; it was certainly an art.

But was it dance? Many people today might not call it that; others, familiar with the array of activities that can take place at what are billed as dance concerts, might well consider it dancing.

Yet it was not professional dancing. Delsartian performances were, for the most part, amateur activities that appealed primarily to women. They did no one any harm. Indeed, they may have done much good in the late nineteenth and early twentieth centuries when women often led sedentary lives. Delsartian exercises stimulated them; Delsartian idealism inspired them.

Out of such idealism and a welter of other influences a woman would emerge who was unquestionably a dancer by anyone's definition and a professional dancer at that: Isadora Duncan.

$\mathcal{J}$SADORA DUNCAN, HELLENISM, AND BEAUTY

Isadora Duncan and her family • *Sada Yacco* •
The Wiesenthal Sisters • *Margaret Morris* • *Ruby*
Ginner • *Irene Mawer* • *Paul Swan* • *Maud Allan* •
Rita Sacchetto

IN THE VERY FIRST PARAGRAPH OF HER AUTOBIOGRAPHY, *My Life,* Isadora Duncan confesses, "Before I was born my mother . . . could take no food except iced oysters and iced champagne. If people ask me when I began to dance I reply, 'In my mother's womb, probably as a result of the oysters and champagne—the food of Aphrodite.'" A few paragraphs later, she writes, "I was born by the sea, and I have noticed that all the great events of my life have taken place by the sea. My first idea of movement, of the dance, certainly came from the rhythm of the waves." [1]

Isadora—like Loïe Fuller before her, Duncan was known throughout the world by her first name—discloses much about herself in those passages. Whether or not her statements about her birth are literally true, they suggest her flamboyance, the outrageousness that made her the talk of two continents. But Duncan did more than shock. When she speaks of the waves, she is acknowledging the importance of natural rhythms in her dances. Duncan built her choreography upon such motions as those of winds and waves. But she was not content to create charming nature sketches. The rhythms of her dances seem those of all life and of the universe itself.

Duncan was born in San Francisco—a city by the sea—in 1878. She grew up to become the most celebrated American dancer of her time. Yet most of the audiences she amazed were not American. She regularly performed in her native land only from 1895 to 1899, and although she made later visits to it, she, like Fuller, spent most of her time in Europe. One can understand why. Many European theatregoers revered her. Some Americans did, too; others, however, accused her of exerting a subversive influence upon art, politics, and morals.

The youngest child in her family, Isadora had a sister, Elizabeth, and two brothers, Augustin and Raymond—all destined to have careers in the arts. Elizabeth taught dance. Augustin became an actor and director. Raymond grew up to become a Renaissance man of the arts whose life was as colorful as that of Isadora.

The Gold Rush of 1849 had prompted the Duncans' father, Joseph Charles Duncan, to wander west from his native Philadelphia. But he found no fortune and became involved with several unsuccessful business schemes. He eventually deserted his wife, Mary Dora, and their children. Mary Dora divorced him and in the process divorced herself from Roman Catholicism to become a follower of Robert Ingersoll, an eloquent orator who defied orthodoxy and advocated atheism.

Perpetually short of money, the Duncans moved often to escape their creditors. Mary Dora, who made her living as a piano teacher, passed on her love of music to her children. She also read Shakespeare and the Romantic and Victorian poets to them. Isadora's formal education was haphazard. Yet she did acquire a love of art and literature from her mother—and, from somewhere, a love of dance.

Isadora says in her autobiography that when she was still a little girl she would gather together all the babies in her neighborhood and teach them to wave their arms. Later, to earn extra money for her family, she gave dancing lessons. But where did she herself learn to dance? "In my mother's womb" may well be part of the answer. It is believed that the Duncans had some contact with Delsartian theories, and Isadora may have been exposed to dancelike gymnastics in school. She says she took a few ballet lessons in San Francisco, but denounced ballet as unnatural when she was asked to stand on her toes. Sometime before 1899, she studied with two ballerinas, Katti Lanner and Marie Bonfanti. But her antipathy to ballet only increased. In any case, by 1899 she had already been dancing professionally.[2]

In 1895, Isadora considered herself adept enough to seek a job as a dancer. She and her mother traveled east to find theatrical work. One day in Chicago, she barged into the office of the noted theatrical manager Augustin Daly and proclaimed, "I have discovered the dance. I have discovered the art which has been lost for two thousand years." She then announced, "I am indeed the spiritual daughter of Walt Whitman."

Daly kept sputtering, "That's quite enough! That's *quite* enough!" But nothing could stop her. Daly ended up by offering Duncan a role in a pantomime he was producing.[3] She continued to work in Daly's shows until 1897, when she decided to strike out on her own.

Isadora did not find things easy. She gave concerts in New York. Assisted by other members of her family, she also performed in the drawing rooms of wealthy society ladies in the mansions of the fashionable summer resort of Newport, Rhode Island. On such occasions, Isadora danced while her mother accompanied her on the piano and Augustin or Elizabeth recited poetry. But being a "society pet" did not make her happy.

After vainly trying to raise money from millionaires' wives, Isadora had a hunch—a good one, it proved—that she might be better appreciated abroad. Therefore, in 1899, she, Elizabeth, Raymond, and their mother sailed off to Europe, in a cattle boat because they could not afford a fancier vessel. It was a dreary voyage, and the sight of the poor beasts cramped in the hold helped make Raymond a confirmed vegetarian. The Duncans arrived in London penniless, but wily. Once, Isadora recalled in her autobiography, they registered at a deluxe hotel, claiming that their baggage would be arriving later from Liverpool. They ordered a huge meal from room service, spent the night in luxury, and sneaked out early the next morning.[4] Did this really happen? Isadora says it did. But she was known to embroider facts. At any rate, it makes a good story.

London was not entirely new to Isadora. She had been there in 1897 in one of Daly's productions. As she had in New York, she danced in society drawing rooms, then gave her first public London concert on 16 March 1900. From the outset, Duncan attracted artists and intellectuals.

She went on to Paris. There the artists applauded her even more fervently than their British counterparts did, and she was accompanied on a few occasions by such composers as André Messager and Maurice Ravel. She posed for the sculptor Auguste Rodin. But when he propositioned her, she resisted his advances.

There was a great world's fair in Paris, the Universal Exposition of 1900, and its attractions included Javanese and Cambodian dancers, as well as performances by Loïe Fuller and Sada Yacco, a Japanese actress and dancer praised for her gestural subtlety who was the star of a troupe of Japanese players directed by her husband, Otojiro Kawakami. Duncan admired Fuller and Yacco.

Yacco was something of a revolutionary. At a time when Japanese theatrical companies were either all-male or all-female, she dared to set foot on the same stage with men. Fuller and Duncan applauded her; so did such writers as Max Beerbohm and André Gide. But Edward Gordon Craig, the controversial English director and designer, was appalled, calling Yacco's innovation "a pity. . . . The introduction of women upon the stage is held by some to have caused the downfall of the European theatre, and it is feared that it is destined to bring the same disaster to Japan." Although he was the son of the actress Ellen Terry and for a time Isadora's lover, Craig believed that only the masculine mind is fitted for the theatre, and he thundered in italics, "*Before the art of the stage can revive women must have passed off the boards.*"[5]

Fuller invited Duncan to perform under her auspices. But Isadora was startled to find La Loïe surrounded by an entourage of women who were extremely affectionate toward one another—much too affectionate to make her feel at ease with them.

Duncan traveled throughout Europe. She made her first Russian visit in 1904 and deeply impressed Konstantin Stanislavsky, the stage director who headed the Moscow Art Theatre, and Michel Fokine, the rebellious young ballet choreographer. Both Stanislavsky and Fokine were trying to free their arts from outworn conventions and considered Duncan a kindred spirit.

She returned to perform in the United States in 1908, the same year that a group of artists, among them John Sloan, mounted an exhibition that startled conservatives because of the painters' fondness for everyday urban subject matter. Sloan admired Isadora, as did Robert Henri, a painter and art teacher who exerted considerable influence upon younger artists. Henri wrote, "Isadora Duncan, who is perhaps one of the greatest masters of gesture the world has ever seen, carries through a universe in a single movement of her body. Her hand alone held aloft becomes a shape of infinite significance."[6]

A typical solo program by Duncan lasted about two hours.[7] It was a demanding occasion that required considerable strength and endurance. Even when Duncan appeared with her pupils, the group offered only one or two items and the rest of the program would, as usual, be solos with musical interludes during costume changes. Duncan disdained elaborate scenery and performed on a bare stage hung with blue curtains. Her programs were akin to lieder concerts or piano recitals, and any emotional or dramatic effects in them were created entirely by her choreography and by the way it harmonized with the music she chose.

To the horror of purists, Duncan danced to the music of such composers as Christoph Gluck, Ludwig van Beethoven, Frédéric Chopin, Richard Wagner, Johannes Brahms, and Aleksandr Scriabin. Great music stirred great passions in her, and because she managed to create distinguished choreography to undisputed musical masterpieces, she demonstrated that dance was not a trivial or merely decorative art.

Duncan amazed audiences with her very appearance. She wore simple robes or tunics and, like most of the other modern dance pioneers, usually danced barefoot. She and other early modern dancers considered the bare foot more sensitive to degrees of touch and weight than the shod foot and believed that it was easier for a bare foot both to secure a firm grasp on the ground and to touch the earth delicately. Just as no potters would cover their hands when shaping vases, why, the modern dancers wondered, should dancers cover their feet?[8]

Because her robes and tunics suggested Hellenic attire, Duncan was often called a Greek dancer. Occasionally, she objected, pointing out that she was no Athenian from the fifth century B.C. but a "Scottish-Irish-American" dancer.[9] She insisted that, although she often drew upon Greek myths and vase paintings for inspiration, she was making no attempt to reconstruct any actual ancient Greek dance. Nevertheless, like many of her contemporaries, she idealized ancient Greece as a golden age in which humanity's material and spiritual powers were united.

Intensely idealistic, Duncan was not always practical. She once tried to build a palatial art center in Greece, not realizing that the property she had acquired was totally devoid of drinking water. A woman of infinite contradictions, she pronounced herself a Socialist, yet was charmed by European high society and praised British servants for their docility.

On certain matters she spoke loudly and clearly. She constantly attacked the lingering traces of puritanism in America. She advocated women's rights, including their right to have professional careers as dancers. She also declared that women should be free to bear children as they pleased. Believing that no woman should be afraid of her body, she continued to perform when she was noticeably pregnant. Duncan distrusted the institution of matrimony, viewing it as a form of bondage. Curiously, however, she often had affairs with men who wished her to give up her career, and she quarreled with virtually all her lovers.

In 1904, she fell in love with Gordon Craig, who became the father of her daughter Deirdre, born in 1906. Later, she had an affair with Paris Singer, heir to the sewing machine fortune, who was the father of her son Patrick, born in 1910.

Both children died in a freak accident in 1913. The children and their nurse had gone out for an automobile ride. When the car stalled, the chauffeur got out to crank up the engine. Instead of putting the gear in neutral, he left it engaged. The car rolled over an embankment into the river Seine and the children and their nurse drowned. A year later, Isadora gave birth to another son, but he died in her arms. The deaths of her children plunged her into despair, and some of her friends speculated that she never fully recovered from their loss.

Duncan, who loved children, dreamed of a world in which they could dance happily. Whereas Walt Whitman wrote that he could hear America singing, Duncan prophesied that she could see America dancing.[10] She made several attempts to start schools—none of them in America, however.

The first, in 1904, was in Germany. It lasted about four years. In 1914, she founded another school, near Paris. But it was abandoned at the beginning of World War I. Both were a financial drain on Isadora, for she charged no tuition. Believing that children should spend all their time in a wholesome environment, she separated students from their parents; in effect, she orphaned them. She even adopted six girls—Irma, Lise, Margot, Erica, Ann, and Maria Theresa—and gave them the surname Duncan. They occasionally appeared with her on programs, toured America on their own (1918–1920), and were nicknamed the Isadorables.

Duncan subjected her pupils to a rigorous curriculum that included dancing, singing, gymnastics, and music theory, as well as academic subjects. A charismatic presence, she was not necessarily a well-organized pedagogue. At times, she was not even present among her students, for she was dancing elsewhere, both to raise money for the school and to satisfy her own creative impulses.

Although Duncan never developed a comprehensive pedagogical system, she had clear ideas about the art of dance. Just as Walt Whitman proclaimed "I Sing the Body Electric," so Duncan conceived the body as a dynamo and devoted hours of study to discovering how its power worked. Speaking of this process, she wrote, "I was seeking and finally discovered the central spring of all movement, the crater of motor power, the unity from which all diversities of movements are born."[11] Duncan located the source of movement in the solar plexus and sought to have movement radiate into the extremities not as a succession of isolated steps and poses, but in a continually expressive flow of energy.

Duncan choreographed at least 223 dances, a figure that can be raised as high as 250 if certain composite entities—for instance, her suites based on episodes from Gluck's operas—are considered separate pieces, rather than parts of a single work. Duncan created 47 dances for her students; the rest are solos.[12] Thematically, many of her compositions express idealistic strivings and a search for beauty; there are also dances of sorrow, courage, liberation, and joy.

Duncan impressed audiences with her apparent spontaneity. She thereby caused some viewers to misinterpret the nature of her choreography. It began to be said—and it is occasionally still said—that her works were improvised.

An unpredictable performer, Duncan was indeed able to improvise and was known to interrupt concerts by lecturing her audience on art or politics. Nevertheless, such outbursts were atypical. Her dances were carefully constructed. That is one reason why some have been preserved and revived. Moreover, she performed dances over a long period. Even if these pieces had their origins in improvisation, constant repetition would have caused them to become essentially fixed in choreographic structure.[13]

Duncan's technique was based upon such fundamental physical actions as walks, skips, runs, gallops, and low jumps. What made her riveting to watch was her sense of dynamics, the way she could arrange seemingly simple movements into kinetic crescendos and diminuendos. Duncan's dances abounded in contrasts between stillness and movement, and their ebb and flow of motion recalls such natural phenomena as the tides of the ocean, the swaying of grass in the wind, and the inhalation and exhalation of the breath itself.

Duncan was capable of fervor as well as delicacy. During World War I, she danced the *Marseillaise*, the French national anthem, as a tribute to her adopted country. Wearing a blood-colored robe, she created the illusion that she first beheld and then was crushed by enemy armies. Yet she managed to rise up in triumph against them. In *Marche Slave*, to the music of Peter Tchaikovsky, Duncan portrayed an oppressed serf. Holding her hands as if bound behind her back, she stumbled forward. But this victim also achieved liberation. Freed of her invisible chains, she brought her hands slowly and painfully forward as if to indicate that, during her oppression, they had forgotten how to move.[14] By means of the body, Duncan revealed the soul. This, in its day, was rightfully considered revolutionary.

She also survived several artistic revolutions. The Salon d'Automne exhibition of 1905 introduced Parisians to such painters as Henri Matisse and André Derain, who, because of their fondness for vibrant colors, were nicknamed Fauves, wild beasts. Around 1907, Pablo Picasso and Georges Braque began to paint canvases in which the shapes of ordinary objects were broken down into a multitude of geometric angles; the artistic movement that resulted from their experiments became Cubism. Also in 1907, Filippo Marinetti, an Italian theorist, published the *Futurist Manifesto*, in which he called for an art that embodied the speed and violent energy of the twentieth century. During World War I, iconoclastic artists known as Dadaists made strident and often bizarre protests against social hypocrisy. And the Surrealist painters and poets of the 1920s preoccupied themselves with the irrational world of dreams and the subconscious.

Duncan lived until 1927. Yet her dances reflect little of these developments. Her approach to choreography may have been innovative, but her artistic taste—and that includes her Hellenism—remained that of the turn of the century.

W. R. Titterton, one of Duncan's British admirers, made a shrewd appraisal of her art: "As the walls of Jericho before the trump of Joshua, so before her the factory walls fell down, the festering slums and ugly places of London crumbled to dust, and away to Arcady we danced to the sound of her shepherd's piping."[15] Conceivably, such choreography could be dismissed as escapist. But Duncan did not simply ignore reality. She envisioned a realm of noble emotion and endeavor in which truth and beauty were linked. And no matter what audiences or critics thought, Duncan followed her own course. "I have never waited to do as I wished," she said. "This has frequently brought me disaster and calamity, but at least I have had the satisfaction of getting my own way."[16]

Isadora's sister Elizabeth and brother Raymond also made contributions to dance. To Elizabeth fell the task of trying to keep Isadora's schools going, and during the 1920s and 1930s she directed

schools of her own. Unlike her capricious sister, Elizabeth was a me-
thodical pedagogue, and it was she who managed to bring order to
Duncanism.[17]

Raymond was as unpredictable as Isadora. He embraced ancient
Greek culture with an ardor that surpassed that of his sister. He studied Greek art and developed his own form of Greek dance. Letting
his hair grow long, he discarded ordinary street wear in favor of robes
and sandals. Around 1910, he could be seen traveling about with an
entourage of female admirers—some of them the mothers of his
children—and a flock of smelly goats that provided milk for the
children.[18]

In 1911, he founded his Akademia, a Parisian school that promoted
vegetarianism and teetotalism and offered courses in arts, crafts, philosophy, oratory, music, theatre, gymnastics, and dance.[19] A painter,
sculptor, fabric designer, and printmaker as well as a dancer, Raymond put into practice his theory that everyone should be self-
sufficient.

Raymond and his wife visited Albania during the Balkan War of
1912. They took over a community there, established their own republic, printed their own money, and organized their own militia,
returning to Western Europe only after an opposing faction blew up
the town.[20]

Raymond Duncan, who died in 1966 at the age of ninety-one, was
still giving solo dance and dramatic performances in the 1950s and
1960s. A program of 1953 referred to him as "the greatest bard of all
times" and for a 1961 concert he billed himself as "Self Woven—Self
Shod and Self Liberated—One Man Against the World."[21] Raymond
knew he was a "character," and he once admitted, "Wonderful are
the fruits of publicity."[22] But he also possessed a real sense of design
and craftsmanship and, like Isadora, he inspired people to dance.

Isadora's influence was incalculable. Scores of dancers tried to imitate her. The simplicity of her staging and the emotional candor of
her movements seemed an antidote to the superficiality and stuffiness of polite society and academic art. Isadora reminded people of
the beauty and dignity of nature. As J. E. Crawford Flitch observed,
"When an art grows infirm, there always comes a time when the
practitioners hold council over the failing body and prescribe the
remedy. And the remedy is always the same—they recommend a return to Nature." But Flitch perceived the impossibility of such a
return: "The difficulty of applying this precept to the dance lay in the

fact that there was no nature to return to, or rather that nature itself had become corrupt and sophisticated." Therefore, he noted, another inspiration was proposed: "the art of the antique world."[23]

Across the stages of Europe and America flitted dancers in works inspired by brooks or breezes or the glories of Greece. The sight of them alarmed Flitch: "We are threatened with performances in which naive young creatures in tenuous classic drapery amuse themselves by capering on bare feet, gathering and scattering make-believe roses, splashing in imaginary rivers, undulating snaky arms. Shooting arrows, playing ball, butterfly catching. The dance cannot return to nature in the sense which Isadora Duncan intended, by returning to this rather kindergarten Arcadia."[24] Some of Isadora's imitators produced appallingly sentimental works. Yet a concern for nature and Hellenic ideals prompted other choreographers to employ such source materials in fruitful ways.

By mixing Strauss waltzes with the lightness of ballet and the directness of "Greek" dancing, the Wiesenthal Sisters—Grete, Elsa, and Berta—created a style that was uniquely their own and, at the same time, unmistakably Viennese.

Of the balletically trained sisters, it was Grete, the eldest, who became the most important choreographer. In 1902—a year in which Isadora appeared in Vienna—Grete and Elsa were named coryphées in the ballet company attached to the Vienna Opera.[25]

They became increasingly dissatisfied with the restrictions of classical ballet. In 1908, Grete, Elsa, and Berta gave a performance at the Fledermaus cabaret that included dances to the music of Chopin, Beethoven, Jules Massenet, Joseph Lanner, and Franz Schubert and to the Johann Strauss waltz *Roses from the South.* The Wiesenthals offered dances to many composers, but they were most famous for their interpretations of such Strauss waltzes as *Wiener Blut, Voices of Spring,* and *The Blue Danube* (a composition to which Duncan created a much-praised solo of her own).

The Wiesenthals favored flowing movements to lyrical music, impetuous steps and sweeping turns to allegros. Their freshness of presence led critics to compare them with the *Jugendstil,* a Viennese artistic movement akin to Art Nouveau. Among their admirers was the poet Rainer Maria Rilke. The Caffins wrote that Grete's dancing is "cool, fragrant, and soothing. But it is not cold or insipid. . . . She touches the emotions more than moves them, like the light sweep of the harp strings after the variety and complexity of the orchestra."[26]

Because of their charm and fondness for waltzes, it is easy to classify the Wiesenthals as purveyors of light entertainment. But they should not be underestimated. They removed the waltz from the intrigues, ostentatious finery, social climbing, and rigid etiquette of the ballroom until what remained was joy in three-quarter time.

For Margaret Morris (1891–1980), "Greek" dance was only the first step toward a technique of her own.[27] The London-born Morris received dancing lessons, including ballet, as a child and made her professional stage debut at the age of eight as a fairy in a pantomime.

When she was eighteen, she studied with Raymond Duncan, who had come to London to lecture on Greek music and dance. Although she valued Duncan's teaching and staged a production of Gluck's opera *Orfeo ed Euridice* in the Greek style in 1910, she did not consider her choreography a form of archeology. "To tell the truth," she confessed to the *Dancing Times* in 1917, "I do not claim to be reviving Greek dancing, but to be introducing a method that I think allows of unlimited development in the future. It is really immaterial to me if it was used by the Greeks or Egyptians or any other ancient nation."[28]

Morris became acquainted with the novelist John Galsworthy and immediately fell in love with him, although, as she points out in her autobiography, "our relationship remained entirely innocent."[29] Galsworthy gave her financial assistance to open a London school and organize a company in 1910. The school attracted aspiring actors—among them, Elsa Lanchester—as well as dancers; unlike Isadora, Morris sought male students, claiming, "The system of dancing is vigorous and athletic and is invaluable as a training for every kind of game and sport."[30]

In 1913, Morris took a troupe to Paris, where she danced a Felix Mendelssohn nocturne, excerpts from Edvard Grieg's "Holberg Suite," a Claude Debussy arabesque, and a Spanish solo to Domenico Scarlatti. It was in Paris that she met J. D. Fergusson, the Scottish painter she later married.[31]

Gradually, her interests widened. She developed a system of dance notation, which she published in 1928, the same year Rudolf Laban introduced his own more famous notation system. As Morris grew increasingly interested in movement as a therapeutic tool that could aid the physically and mentally disabled, she placed less emphasis upon theatrical productions. However, she again choreographed for the stage after 1939 when she and her husband settled in Glasgow.

Morris eventually found herself torn between dance as theatre, therapy, and pedagogy. Many dancers after her have struggled with comparable claims. Ruby Ginner (1886–1978) turned from choreography to pedagogy. Like Morris, she studied ballet and rejected it and, again like Morris, she admired Greek art. But whereas Morris sought to transcend Greek influences, Ginner spent her life studying vases, sculptures, and bas-reliefs to develop what she called the Revived Greek Dance. It was while appearing as a dancer in Morris's production of *Orfeo* that Ginner fully became aware of the majesty of Greek art and the soundness of Isadora Duncan's principles. Organizing a little company, the Grecian Dancers, in 1911, she began to perform everywhere, including music-halls in rough parts of cities, before audiences who came to jeer but remained to applaud. In 1915, Ginner met Irene Mawer, a mime who became her artistic associate; together they opened a school.[32]

Ginner and Mawer often presented students in public programs. Typically, one of 1917 included a Greek spear dance, a Dionysian revel, a ritualistic funeral dance, a Spartan boy's solo, and a scene inspired by the Olympic Games. The bill also included Spanish dances, Russian dances, dances to poems by Elizabeth Barrett Browning and Rupert Brooke (read by Mawer), and two narrative compositions: *The Poke Bonnet*, a comic mime, and *The Unveiling*, an Egyptian dance-drama about a goddess who claims the soul of a priestess.[33]

The Revived Greek Dance became a form for students and amateurs, rather than professionals. Ginner considered it to possess spiritual as well as physical value. She regarded Greek culture almost with idolatry. "In ancient Greece the dance was prayer," she said, "it was praise, it was ecstasy, it was sorrow, it was tragedy, it was comedy."[34]

Ginner's Greek dances were performed barefoot, and their technique derived from walking, running, leaping, and skipping. Both during her lifetime and after her death skeptics charged that the Revived Greek Dance is technically limited. Nevertheless, it helps children move freely and lyrically, and it continues to be taught in schools throughout Great Britain, including the Royal Ballet School.

Ancient Greece also enraptured Paul Swan, an extremely handsome young American artist who, after studying at the Art Institute of Chicago, came to New York, where he earned so much money painting portraits of the actress Alla Nazimova that he was able to travel to Egypt and Greece. Somehow, he emerged from his wandering as a dancer in the Greek manner who also ventured into other lyrical and exotic styles, choreographing dances with such titles as *Pierrot's Serenade, A Greek Phantasy, Chinese Idol, Syrian Dance, Narcissus*, and *The Quest of the Soul.* Swan also offered his own male version of *Le Cygne*, a solo associated with the ballerina Anna Pavlova that was often popularly known as *The Dying Swan.*

Swan, who died at eighty-nine in 1972, was never considered a major dancer. Nevertheless, he was a persistent one who appeared throughout Europe and America. Settling permanently in New York when World War II loomed, he gave a Sunday night dance recital every week—except during the summer—from 1939 to 1965.[35]

Of all early-twentieth-century dancers, it was Maud Allan who was most frequently compared with Isadora Duncan. Both specialized in solo programs in which they danced barefoot in simple costumes to classical music. Offstage, they were similar in some ways, as well. Both had affairs with numerous men; Allan, it is thought, was also the lover of several women. But whereas Duncan flaunted her nonconformity, Allan desperately tried to keep all personal details about herself from being known.[36]

Allan lied outrageously, telling people that her parents were doctors in Toronto. She was indeed born in that city—and then was raised in San Francisco—but both her parents worked in a shoe factory. She concocted stories about other aspects of her life and surely thought she was justified in doing so. In her vague and effusive autobiography, Allan admits, "I have had many sorrows in my short life, sorrows too great and deep to mention in this little volume. . . . An episode in my life has left its deep imprint upon my work."[37]

Unwary readers might suspect her of talking about a love affair. Instead, she is referring to a murder. In 1898, when she was twenty-five, her brother Theo was convicted and hanged for having killed two young women, after which he allegedly hid their bodies in the belfry of the Baptist church, for which he was the assistant Sunday school superintendent. Allan never recovered from the horror of this case, and she felt its notoriety followed and plagued her, even though she was in Europe at the time of the trial. She therefore changed her surname from Durrant to Allan.

A talented pianist, she studied music in Berlin. Later, in Weimar, her teacher—and lover—was the composer Ferrucio Busoni. However, somewhere around the turn of the century, Allan's interest shifted to dance. She claimed that it was seeing Sandro Botticelli's *Primavera* (a painting also admired by Isadora) in the Uffizi Gallery in Florence that inspired her to explore the expressive qualities of dancing. Guided by a friend, Marcel Remy, a Belgian journalist and musician who later composed for her, she began to analyze the figures in Greek vase painting.

In her autobiography, Allan says she used to do exercises every morning—not mechanical drill-like routines, but graceful fluid movements—and admits to being impressed by the theories of Delsarte.[38] Yet the exact process by which she made herself into a dancer is unknown.

By 1903, she considered herself ready to appear in public, and on 24 November she made her debut in Vienna, offering a program of solos to Mendelssohn's *Spring Song*, the adagio from Beethoven's "Moonlight Sonata," a Bach gavotte and musette, Robert Schumann's *Träumerei*, Schubert's *Ave Maria*, Anton Rubinstein's *Valse Caprice*, and two mazurkas, the *Funeral March*, and a waltz by Chopin.[39] She was thirty years old at the time.

Critics constantly likened Allan to Duncan, a comparison that rankled her, even though some observers pronounced Allan superior to Duncan in musicality. J. E. Crawford Flitch thought Allan able to suggest changes from major to minor keys by changes in movement qualities.[40] She also possessed the mimetic ability to people a stage with presences which, though invisible to the audience, were so real to her that when she bent to gather flowers she convinced her viewers that they were there, and when she extended a hand it was clearly to pluck blossoms from a branch. Essentially, Allan was a lyrical dancer. At her worst, she was bland. W. R. Titterton went so far as to call her "the English Miss in art."[41] One dance, however, was anything but genteel: *The Vision of Salomé*, which she presented in Vienna in 1906 and with which she scandalized Europe and America for years afterward. The hallucinatory solo depicted Salome dancing before King Herod and calling for the death of John the Baptist; she then danced in perverse ecstasy with the prophet's head.

Salome seems to have bewitched an extraordinary number of painters, writers, composers, and choreographers in the late nineteenth and early twentieth centuries. The most notorious works about her, other than Allan's dance, were the play by Oscar Wilde and the opera based on it by Richard Strauss. Wilde's *Salomé*, which was published first in French in 1893 and a year later in English with illustrations by Aubrey Beardsley, could not be performed on the London stage until 1905, because of opposition from the lord chamberlain, the British government's censor. Strauss's *Salome* received its premiere in Dresden in 1905 and subsequently created a furor in cultural capitals throughout the world. Its Paris premiere in 1907 coincided with a season by Maud Allan and many theatregoers, confused by the presence of two Salomes in the same city, mistakenly thought that Allan's was set to excerpts from the opera, whereas it had a score by Remy.

That same year, Strauss's *Salome* so outraged the patrons of New York City's Metropolitan Opera Company that it was yanked from the repertoire after a single performance. But that was not the end of Salome in New York. The opera requires Salome to dance as well as sing. Usually, the work's star both sings and performs the dance. At the Met, however, Olive Fremstad, the singer, had a dancing "double," Bianca Froehlich, and when *Salome* was banned from the Met, Froehlich performed her dance in a variety theatre. Later that year, someone who called herself Mlle Dazie did a Salome dance in the *Ziegfeld Follies*. By the next year, Salome had become so much the rage that Mlle Dazie (whose real name was Daisy Peterkin) was teaching Salome routines that dancers could perform in vaudeville houses across the country. Gertrude Hoffman also got in on the Salome act. Hoffman was a dancer who occasionally had the disconcerting habit of presenting other people's dances—among them, the ballets of Michel Fokine—without giving them credit. She danced a *Salomé*, modeled upon Allan's, at Hammerstein's Victoria, a leading New York vaudeville theatre, in 1908. And in 1909, Mary Garden caused a sensation by both singing and dancing Strauss's *Salome* for Hammerstein's Manhattan Opera.

The world was gripped by what more than one journalist termed "Salomania."[42] The mania was real enough. What is not so clear is its cause. Turn-of-the-century audiences did like the exotic—a taste that would be capitalized upon by Diaghilev in ballet and Ruth St. Denis in modern dance. But that still does not explain why people should have been so taken by a story about a nasty young woman who wishes to have a saint's head cut off. Some fashions remain essentially inexplicable: strange fads have come and gone in art, clothes, popular music, and cooking.

Yet there may be reasons why Salome was a woman people loved to hate. Salome is glamorous, forceful, and sensual. In various ways, she destroys both a lascivious king and an ascetic saint. Rebels against the stiff moral code of Allan's time may have taken delight in her antics, and women who felt themselves oppressed may have relished her attacks upon masculine tyranny. Of course, Salome is eventually killed; conventional virtue does triumph. If it did not, the story of Salome might have been found totally unacceptable. But what made it titillating was the way Salome managed to work quite a lot of mischief before being punished.

Although Isadora Duncan occasionally introduced mimetic gestures and hints of dramatic situations into compositions, her solos were essentially emotional evocations. And although Maud Allan was considered a gifted mime, many of her solos were similarly evocative. Other dancers, however, created both mood-pieces and solos depicting specific characters or historical eras.

One such dancer was Rita Sacchetto (1880–1959). The daughter of an Austrian mother and an Italian father, Sacchetto studied ballet in Munich, but traditional classicism did not appeal to her. She became a concert dancer who toured until an accident forced her to stop performing in 1918. She appeared in New York, during the 1909 and 1910 seasons with the Metropolitan Opera, performing with the Metropolitan Opera Ballet, as well as incorporating some of her solos into the dance sequences of operas in the repertoire. Sacchetto also taught, and on 5 April 1910 she and her pupils gave a concert at the Plaza Hotel.[43]

Sacchetto was known for choreographic vignettes based upon paintings or styles in art history. Thus her *Minuetto*, to the music of Wolfgang Amadeus Mozart, derived from a Thomas Gainsborough painting of the Duchess of Devonshire. And *Caprice Espagnol*, in which Sacchetto played castanets, was inspired by Diego Velázquez.

Sacchetto's most famous solo was variously listed on programs as *Crinoline Dance*, *Krinoline*, and *Loin du Bal*. At times, certain ideas do seem to be "in the air." Just as there was a "Salomania," so *Loin du Bal*, which Sacchetto performed in New York in 1910, was not the only dance of its type. In this choreographic sketch to music by Ernest Gillet, Sacchetto portrayed a young woman who, sitting alone, dreams of the joys of a ball. Rising to her feet, she moves about the stage as if dancing with an imaginary partner.[44] Ballet lovers may find this scenario akin to that of *Le Spectre de la Rose*, which Michel Fokine choreographed for Diaghilev's Ballets Russes in 1911, except that, in Fokine's ballet, the young woman's partner is a real male dancer—none other than the legendary Vaslav Nijinsky at the pre-miere—who represents the spirit of the rose she has brought home from the ball. It cannot be ascertained if Diaghilev and Fokine were familiar with Sacchetto. Youthful longing, of course, is a perpetual choreographic theme.

The Caffins said that Sacchetto's dancing possessed "a dainty ele-gance and a high-bred deliberateness."[45] They also observed that a recurrent theme in Sacchetto's choreography was woman's aspiring toward some ideal goal. One of her most ambitious creations was *The Intellectual Awakening of Woman*, an allegory for a cast of thirty to Grieg's *Peer Gynt Suite* that showed the striving of the soul of woman upward from the darkness of submission into the light of emancipation.[46]

Although best known as a choreographic portraitist, Sacchetto had theories about what today would be called plotless or abstract dance. She dreamed of choreographic interpretations of symphonic scores in which the leading dancer would represent "the one leit-motif which is the backbone of the symphonic structure,"[47] while other dancers represented secondary themes. Sacchetto's works, there-fore, exemplify some of the principal concerns of the modern dance of her time: the theatrical incarnation of moods and ideas, the depic-tion of specific characters, and the kinetic interpretation of music.

RUTH ST. DENIS AND THE EXOTIC

Ruth St. Denis • *Sent M'Ahesa* •
Magdeleine • *Adorée Villany*

JUST AS ISADORA DUNCAN WAS OFTEN TYPED AS A "GREEK" dancer, so Ruth St. Denis, her great American contemporary, was popularly known as an "exotic" or "mystic" dancer. She was both. Yet her exoticism involved giving impressions, rather than reconstructions, of the dances of other cultures. Her works were secular as well as sacred in theme and, although she was religious, she resisted easy categorization in denominational terms.

St. Denis's career paralleled Duncan's in many ways.[1] Both were influenced by Delsarte. Both studied and rejected ballet. Both toured in commercial theatrical productions before breaking away to devise a dance form of their own. Both were idolized in Europe.

St. Denis and Duncan were similar in still another way. Each was the daughter of a strong-minded mother and a comparatively weak father. Ruth's mother, Ruth Emma Hull, had graduated from the University of Michigan Medical School, but a nervous collapse prevented her from practicing medicine. While she was a patient at a sanitarium, she was given dancing lessons by one of her physicians. She also studied with Aurilla Colcord Poté, a pupil of Delsarte. Although her precarious health made it impossible for her to be a doctor, Ruth Emma Hull devoted herself to worthy causes, including women's clothing reforms and the abolition of corsets.

She met and fell in love with Thomas Dennis, a machinist and inventor, at an artists' colony in Perth Amboy, New Jersey, and they were married, without license or clergy, in a marriage by contract on

4 December 1878. Only slightly more than a month later, on 20 January 1879, their daughter Ruth was born.[2]

Whereas Ruth Emma Hull, despite ill health, persevered through sheer strength of will, Thomas Dennis never accomplished much, and his inventions usually failed. Unlike Isadora Duncan's mother, who became a freethinker, Ruth Emma Hull was deeply religious. Her husband, however, was an agnostic influenced by Thomas Paine and Robert Ingersoll. Unfortunately, in times of stress he turned not to philosophy, but to dreaming and drink. This aspect of her family life made Ruth Dennis, while still a girl, devise an epigram: "A man who does not believe in God generally leans on somebody who does."[3]

Not the least peculiarity of the Dennis family was the fact that Ruth's younger brother had no first name. Ruth Emma and Thomas never got around to giving him one. As a child, he was nicknamed Buzz. When he grew up, he was officially known as Brother Dennis and, still later, as Brother St. Denis or simply B. St. Denis.[4]

To raise money, the family turned Pin Oaks, the farm they acquired near Somerville, New Jersey, into a boardinghouse. It attracted something of an arty crowd, and its residents nightly gathered to discuss everything from the latest play to Theosophy and Christian Science. Young Ruth's tastes in reading were equally far-ranging. She loved sentimental novels, yet she also tried to puzzle out philosophical texts and was drawn to Christian Science because of the way Mary Baker Eddy, the denomination's founder, regarded everything as spiritual in nature.

Like Isadora, Ruth appears to have been an intuitive dancer. Her mother encouraged her theatrical interests. Horrified at this, some prim relatives sent Ruth to a school run by the evangelist Dwight Moody. But after one argument with the straitlaced preacher about the morality of dance and theatre, she called him a bigot and left the place, never to return.

Ruth was deeply impressed by a performance she saw Genevieve Stebbins give in 1892. Her mother gave her some Delsarte lessons, and she was also sent to local dancing schools, where she learned to do kicks, cartwheels, backbends, and splits.

During the week of 29 January 1894, Ruth Dennis made her New York debut as an act on the bill of Worth's Family Theatre and Museum. Worth's was what was known as a "dime museum," a peculiar sort of institution that offered displays of curios—old coins, historical relics, three-headed calves pickled in alcohol—along with variety-show attractions. Ruth shared the bill with an equilibrist-juggler, an albino musician, and Lillie the Trick Dog.[5] Physically supple and mentally alert, Ruth copied what other dancers of the time were doing, and her specialties came to include skirt dances and slow splits. She also studied ballet and had a few lessons with Marie Bonfanti. But she and the Italian ballerina did not get along. As she told the critic Walter Terry, "I learned three of the five possible positions of the feet and was asked to leave."[6]

Like Isadora, Ruth was employed by Augustin Daly. Then she had the good fortune to work for another celebrated producer and director: David Belasco. In 1900, she appeared in London as an actress in his production of *Zaza*, and when the play's engagement ended she found time to visit Paris and stroll through the exhibition, where, again like Isadora, she admired Loïe Fuller and Sada Yacco.

Belasco was a master of realism, and the settings for his productions were often painstakingly detailed. Ruth may have learned much from him: for instance, how to manipulate props and wear costumes with authority and, even more important, how to pace productions and build them to climaxes.

It was Belasco who, as she liked to say, "canonized" her by calling her "Saint Dennis." The nickname was a sly reference to her propriety. Ruth Dennis was tall and beautiful—but romantically unapproachable. So, for Belasco, she was a "saint." Later, when searching for a striking stage name, she became St. Denis.

One of her admirers was the architect Stanford White. But he too could accept "no" for an answer from Ruth and, in an avuncular fashion, encouraged her, often providing her with money. When she became a famous dancer, St. Denis, like Duncan before her, was propositioned by Rodin; she, too, fled his studio.

St. Denis was justifiably concerned with her reputation. Moralists unsympathetic to nontraditional marital arrangements would have said that she had been born out of wedlock, and she had entered a profession that some people virtually equated with prostitution. Moreover, she was a proud, independent woman determined to have a career of her own without the aid of a "protector."[7]

St. Denis continued to work for Belasco, and 1904 found her touring the country in his production of *Madame DuBarry*. In later years, she never tired of talking about something that happened during that tour. One day in Buffalo, New York, she and another member of the company were sipping ice cream sodas in a drugstore when she looked up and beheld a poster. What she saw changed her life and American dance, as well.

The poster advertised a brand of cigarettes called Egyptian Deities and showed the goddess Isis enthroned in a pillared temple. As an example of graphic art and archaeological accuracy, it was not much. Nevertheless, it cast a spell on Ruth. She had to have it for her own. Then she realized she had to create dances that fully expressed the mysticism implicit in the depiction of the goddess. The psychological effect of the poster far surpassed its esthetic value and, looking back on the incident, St. Denis remarked, "If such a vision had happened within the church, I should have been a candidate for sainthood."[8]

The poster may have been Egyptian, but the first works it inspired were Indian. St. Denis immersed herself in Oriental philosophy, and she discovered a troupe of Indians at a Coney Island sideshow who provided her with information about Indian dances and costumes. What resulted was *Radha*, which she presented on 28 January 1906 and which then became part of a two-performance-a-day music-hall show at Proctor's 23rd St. Theatre. "The entire dance is done in bare feet," the advertisements announced.[9] On 22 March 1906, St. Denis offered a special matinee of *Radha* and two other Indian dances, *Incense* and *The Cobras*, that was attended by many socially prominent New Yorkers. She was now a dancer to be taken seriously.

The Indian dances are typical of the pieces for which St. Denis became famous. Each was visually arresting. *Radha* and *Incense* also attempted to cloak spiritual messages in exotic trappings. In *The Cobras*, the secular exception, St. Denis portrayed a snake charmer and wore glittering emerald rings on the first and fourth fingers of each hand. As she twisted her long arms, the rings resembled snakes' eyes while her arms became serpents slithering and writhing about her neck and body. The solo was based on a gimmick. But it was one that worked magnificently, for the "snakes" seemed infinitely evil. *The Cobras* was also a kinetic experiment. Lacking fancy kicks and turns, it employed only a few carefully chosen movements. St. Denis achieved the maximum effect from minimal means.

That can also be said of *Incense*, in which she played a woman scattering incense on a brazier. As she watched the smoke curl upward, she let her arms ripple in imitation. On one level, *Incense* could be enjoyed merely as a study in fluid arm movements. At the same time, it could be interpreted as a dance of religious contemplation.

Radha, the most ambitious of the Indian creations, combined sensuality, spirituality, and spectacle. St. Denis cast herself as Radha, a goddess first glimpsed seated in meditation. Gradually, she stirred to life, tempted by the appeals of the five senses, each of which was represented by symbolic props and actions. Finally, she burst into a delirious sensual dance, only to pause, contrite, and return to her meditations.

The choreography contained little that was authentically Oriental and the accompaniment was taken from *Lakmé,* Léo Delibes's French opera on an Indian theme. But literal authenticity did not matter here. Not the least of the things that made *Radha* remarkable was the way it presented its theme. Ostensibly, it advocated the renunciation of worldliness—a message preached by the saints of many religions. But it did so in a sensually beguiling manner. *Radha* may have ultimately concerned asceticism; nevertheless, some theatregoers surely attended it to see the dancer's exotically clad body and to discover for themselves that "the entire dance is done in bare feet."

Personally, St. Denis was acutely aware of the rival claims of flesh and spirit. She sought religious enlightenment and often created dances about people engaged in a mystic search. But St. Denis was acquainted with secular as well as sacred joys. Typically, she once told Walter Terry that she had made "a pilgrimage . . . I went to the place where I was conceived. Where you were born is unimportant. You're born in labor, in pain, in considerable messiness. What is there to celebrate about that? But you are conceived in love, in passion, and in ecstasy. *That* is when it all begins." [10]

St. Denis often cast herself as goddesses. She looked like one, offstage as well as on. Tall, slender, and beautifully proportioned, she combined grace with strength. Before she was thirty, her hair had started to turn white. Somehow, this only added to her allure. She knew how to present herself well onstage. *Kwan Yin* was one sculptural pose after another, and in *White Jade* she was a figurine that descended exquisitely from a pedestal. All of her dances were notable for their flow of movement, and, like Loïe Fuller, she could make any fabric she held seem an extension of herself.

Her physical beauty was often perceived as having a mystic aura. Hugo von Hofmannsthal, the poet and playwright, wrote of her, "In her motionless eyes stands a mysterious smile: the smile of the Buddha statue. It is a smile which is not of this world." [11] The dance historian Mark E. Perugini noted that in St. Denis there is "always the glamour of the East, but the East without its menace, without its material vice; the East exalted and austere."[12]

St. Denis's Orientalism was decidedly idiosyncratic. She based many dances upon Asian myths and symbols, yet they seldom expressed any specific Asian philosophy, and she was part of a nineteenth-century American spiritual tradition that includes Unitarianism, Universalis41

m, and Christian Science. These religious groups differ in many ways. Yet they all insist that the divine spark can be found in everyone and emphasize a God of Love rather than a God of Wrath.[13]

Like Fuller, Duncan, and Allan before her, St. Denis triumphed in Europe. She arrived there in 1906, the year of *Radha*, achieving a mild success in London, a greater success in Paris, and a wild success in Berlin. Central Europe loved her, and for two years she overwhelmed audiences in Germany, Austria, and Hungary. Her admirers included Max Reinhardt, the great stage director, and such prominent writers as Hugo von Hofmannsthal, Frank Wedekind, and Gerhart Hauptmann. Her most ardent fans vowed to build a theatre just for her.

However, unlike the other dancing expatriates, St. Denis longed for her homeland, and she returned to America in 1909.

Ancient Greece had been idealized in Western culture as a society dedicated to reason and enlightenment; ancient Egypt and Asia, in contrast, have often been viewed as realms of mystery—lands of strange rituals, yet lands that may also guard spiritual secrets. Several European dancers emphasized the mysterious and uncanny.

Among them was Sent M'Ahesa, who was born Elsa Margarethe Luisa von Carlberg in Latvia around 1893. Largely forgotten today, she was taken very seriously by audiences earlier in the century, and in 1913 she was included by Hans Brandenburg in *Der Moderne Tanz*, his influential survey of modern dance.[14] M'Ahesa's repertoire ranged from the biblical (*At Belshazzar's Feast*) to *Yardvi*, a dance to a South American song. However, she specialized in Egyptian dances performed in elaborate costumes that were often adorned with metal and stone ornaments, and the instruments she employed for accompaniment included tambourines, cymbals, and triangles. The most famous of her Egyptian creations was *Bird of Death* (a piece also known as *Demon of Death*), in which she portrayed a sinister birdlike creature with enormous wings who was said to live in caves beneath the earth.

In 1927, a critic for the *Dancing Times* said that M'Ahesa represented an "impersonal" art because she weaves "exotic figures and fantasies into cool, clearly cut forms, and never allows herself to be carried away." Karl Ettlinger, a German critic, also called attention to M'Ahesa's essential sobriety in a review of 1910:

> She won't allow any of the stereotypical techniques of the ballet to enter her realm: eyes toward heaven, hand in the general vicinity of the bosom where one suspects the heart to be, arms flailing in all directions, legs in every possible gymnastic distortion, so that one must ask willy-nilly: where *did* the flea bite? . . .
>
> Her movements are angular, geometric, exactly as they are seen in the ancient Egyptian paintings and reliefs. Her weapons are not "softness of line" or "playful grace"—quite the contrary, they are almost unnaturally broken lines, with occasionally almost doll-like stiffly executed positionings. . . . Naturally, the way Sent M'Ahesa dances is not the way one ever danced during the reign of the Pharaohs. But she found the answer to her questions in the style of ancient Egyptian dances.[15]

M'Ahesa settled in Stockholm in 1938 and for some years worked in the Dance Museum there; she died in 1970.

Whereas M'Ahesa was simultaneously strange and serious, it is difficult to say just how serious two other strange dancers of her time were. Each arose virtually out of nowhere to enjoy a moment of fame.

Around 1903, a dancer variously known as Magdeleine, Madeleine, Madelaine, and Magdeleine G. began to turn up on European stages.[16] Although she was first heard of in Munich, no one can say what her origins were. Magdeleine, who was sometimes referred to as a "sleep dancer" or a "dream dancer," had to be hypnotized before she could perform. Once she had entered a state of trance, she reportedly burst into dances of great complexity and beauty, even though she claimed to have had no previous formal training. She would appear on stage with her hypnotist, who would take about a minute to throw her into a trance. Afterward, he restored her to normalcy in about fifteen seconds.

Once hypnotized, her features grew rigid. When music sounded, she rose up and danced. Should the music be interrupted, she remained frozen in her last pose. Her repertoire included Georg Friedrich Handel's *Largo*, a Chopin waltz, a Boccherini minuet, Franz Lehár's *Merry Widow Waltz*, and the *Marseillaise*, which she was said to perform with astonishing passion. Critics likened her choreographic style to that of Maud Allan. Curiously, however, there is no indication that anyone ever tried to determine if she always performed the same steps to the same music or if each new performance was a fresh improvisation.

What is one to make of Magdeleine? One's first impulse is to cry, "Fraud!" She might very well have been one. If so, she was up-to-date in her charlatanry, for her performances reflect the fascination with the workings of the unconscious or subconscious mind that led to a preoccupation with hypnotism in the nineteenth century and that was being intensified by the researches of Sigmund Freud and other early-twentieth-century psychoanalysts.

Magdeleine was last heard of in 1912.

The next year, Adorée Villany caused an uproar in Paris. Her programs purported to trace the history of civilization and included Egyptian, Babylonian, and Assyrian dances, as well as a choreographic portrait of Salome and a dance of a persecuted Christian. What created the fuss were dances in which Villany appeared nude. Because of them she was fined by a French court in 1913. (She had previously been arrested for nudity in Munich in 1911.)

Because, in our own times, attention-getting journalists still use "nude" simply to mean "flimsily" or "scantily" clad, one wonders what "nude" meant back in 1913. The *London Sunday Chronicle* for 7 May 1913 seems to leave no doubt. Villany, its correspondent reported, "appeared on the stage naked — not 'almost,' or 'practically,' or 'good as naked,' but naked *tout court.*"

Villany continued to perform into the 1920s, although she no longer inspired scandals. A young American living abroad made his stage debut at one of her Viennese performances of the 1920s: he eventually became the distinguished dance critic and poet Edwin Denby. Like Magdeleine, Villany makes dance lovers of another era wonder whether she was a serious artist or only a sensationalist. Denby took her seriously enough that, looking back late in his life, he could describe Villany as "ahead of her time, behind Isadora's." [17]

DANCING INTO THE FUTURE

*Ted Shawn • Norma Gould • Denishawn • Gertrude
Colby • Emile Jaques-Dalcroze • Hellerau • Rudolf
Steiner • Rudolf Laban • Ascona*

AS FAR AS AMERICAN MODERN DANCE IS CONCERNED, TED Shawn is the father of his country. The first great American male modern dancer and choreographer, Shawn organized companies, schools, and festivals and convinced thousands of Americans that dancing was an honorable profession for men. No wonder several generations of dancers called him Papa.

The son of a newspaperman, Edwin Myers ("Ted") Shawn was born in Kansas City in 1891. Initially, he thought of becoming a minister. In a sense he did: he was an evangelist for dance. As a young man, Shawn was deeply impressed by the Reverend Dr. Christian F. Reisner,[1] a Methodist clergyman he encountered first in Kansas City and then in Denver, where Shawn attended the University of Denver.

Dr. Reisner was a clerical showman. His services—in Kansas City, Denver, and, later, in New York City—resembled vaudeville bills, combining prayers and scripture readings with such attractions as magicians, acrobats, mandolin players, and birdcall imitators. Dr. Reisner's churches attracted standing-room-only crowds. He was especially famous for his annual "snow service," a July event during which he preached from atop a hill made of cracked ice. Shawn could sometimes be equally flamboyant in his dance presentations.

Shawn might well have become a preacher himself if he had not been stricken with diphtheria while still a university student. The serum that saved his life temporarily paralyzed him and, during his period of enforced quiet, he said, "I had time to think deeply, and I thought myself out of the ministry, out of the Methodist church and free from all previous moorings."[2] The theatre, which he had loved all his life, claimed him and, daringly, he decided to be a dancer, even though his aghast fraternity brothers protested, "But, Ted, *men* don't dance."[3]

All too many people believed that. Shawn proved them wrong. One way he did so was to make comparisons between dance and athletics. As he once told a reporter, "Dancing is a manly sport, more strenuous than golf or tennis, more exciting than boxing or wrestling and more beneficial than gymnastics."[4] Dancers of a later day might find Shawn's rhetoric self-consciously macho. But when Shawn was young he had reason to feel that this was the best way to persuade the unconverted, and dance teachers seeking male students continue to compare their art with athletics.

Shawn further insisted that dance was spiritual, as well as manly. In 1917, he presented his "Church Service in Dance Form" at the International Church of San Francisco, and he repeated this choreographic ceremony in other houses of worship, much to the alarm of pastors of congregations opposed to liturgical dance.

Shawn began to study dance in Denver with Hazel Wallack, a former member of the Metropolitan Opera Ballet. Then he set out for Los Angeles, curious about that lively young far western city. There he met Norma Gould, who had been running a dance school since 1908.[5] They formed a partnership.

Both dancers were ambitious and were convinced of the seriousness of dance as an art form. Nevertheless, they started out modestly and practically as entertainers: they became a ballroom dance team. At hotel "tango teas" they demonstrated that sultry Latin American fad, then danced with members of the audience. Shawn, Gould, and a small company of dancers and musicians toured in 1914, performing for employees of the Santa Fe Railroad and their families in stations along its route.

That same year, perhaps as an antidote to the rowdiness of the railroad audiences, Gould and Shawn took courses at the Unitrinian School of Personal Harmonizing and Self-Development in New Canaan, Connecticut. The institution, which had been founded by Mary Perry King and the poet Bliss Carman in 1911, taught Delsarte, gymnastics, and exercises designed to develop vocal and bodily expressiveness. The school's ideals were reflected in a speech of 1911 in which Carman called his students "seers and prophets of a new day, taking part in the creation of that better world which is to be."[6]

Gould and Shawn may have had to present tango teas. But their minds and hearts were elsewhere.

Gould eventually returned to her flourishing school in Los Angeles. She also taught dance at the University of California Southern Branch (now UCLA) in 1919 and began teaching at the University of Southern California in 1920. Teaching at both universities until 1924, she was one of the first professional dancers to become involved with higher education. Gould, who died in 1980, remained active in the Los Angeles dance scene through the early 1940s.

Shawn stayed in the East. And he met Ruth St. Denis.

He had seen her perform in Denver in 1911. Artistically, it was love at first sight. "Never before or since have I known so true a religious experience or so poignant a revelation of perfect beauty. I date my own artistic birth from that night," he recalled.[7]

Shawn applied to study with her in 1914. At their initial meeting, the two dancers found themselves kindred spirits. They talked from teatime to dinner and then past midnight, when they made arrangements to meet the next day. Instead of becoming St. Denis's student, Shawn became her partner and on 13 August 1914 her husband. However, St. Denis, who was twelve years his senior, demanded that the word "obey" be removed from the marriage service and refused to wear a wedding ring, considering it a sign of bondage. St. Denis and Shawn tried to keep their marriage secret because, at the time, married stars were not considered glamorous. But during an interview St. Denis told a reporter, supposedly off the record, that she had married "the most beautiful man in the world." The next day, several newspapers announced that she had married Paul Swan—because that dancer had let himself be billed as "The Most Beautiful Man in the World."[8]

Once the news of St. Denis's marriage had become known and her true husband had been identified, the dancers realized that the fact that they were married constituted evidence that dancers did not necessarily lead dissolute lives. Then a publicity stunt helped link their names together. When they were appearing in Portland, Oregon, in 1915, their theatre manager announced that he would send free seats to the person who devised the best title for a mazurka the couple performed. The winner was a Margaret Ayer, who called the dance *The Denishawn Rose Mazurka*. As Portland's nickname is "The City of Roses," her title had local appeal. But "Denishawn" proved to have universal appeal, and it served as the name of a school, a company, and a style of dance production. Curiously, no one knows if Margaret Ayer used her tickets, for she never stopped backstage to introduce herself. Having made her one great contribution to dance history, she thereupon vanished from it.[9]

Also in 1915, St. Denis and Shawn founded their Denishawn School in Los Angeles. It was the most important American dance school at the time. An eclectic institution, it affirmed, in a statement drawn up by Shawn, that "the art of the dance is too big to be encompassed by any one system."[10] Instead, Shawn proposed to include all systems in his curriculum. It was a revolutionary concept; even today, few schools have such far-ranging ambitions. Out of Denishawn would come, in the 1920s, some of the great American modern dancers.

The opening of Denishawn and the efforts of Norma Gould are signs of a growing interest in the devising of systematic programs of dance instruction for both amateurs and aspiring professionals. Among the pioneers of dance education was Gertrude Colby,[11] a native of Minneapolis who in 1910 entered the Sargent School of Gymnastics at Harvard University, which was under the direction of Dudley Sargent. There she learned a form of dance that combined elements of ballet and social dancing. In 1913, Colby began to teach at the Speyer School, the demonstration school of Columbia University Teachers College; when the Speyer School closed in 1916, she joined the faculty of Teachers College itself, remaining until 1931. By that time, she had trained hundred of teachers.

Inspired, in part, by the example of Isadora Duncan, Colby developed a form called Natural Dance based upon what she considered to be children's natural rhythmic activities—including walking, running, skipping, ball playing, hoop rolling, and kite flying. Although Natural Dance was sometimes called technically amorphous, it was important for its emphasis on creativity. "I wanted each girl to work out a philosophy and understanding of dance for herself," Colby said.[12] That statement's implicit assumption that dance is essentially an activity for girls is a sign of the time in which it was made. But its equally implicit affirmation of the value of questing, questioning, and experimentation remains valid.

One major system of movement training was founded by a man who, like Delsarte before him, never intended to have anything to do with dance. Emile Jaques-Dalcroze, a Swiss composer and movement theorist, was born in 1865 in Vienna. He was the son of a representative of a Swiss watch firm, and the family was living in Austria at the time. The family later moved back to Geneva. Jaques-Dalcroze returned to Vienna as a music student to study with Anton Bruckner; he also studied with Léo Delibes in Paris. Although his original family name was Jaques, he altered it to Jaques-Dalcroze in honor of a friend. However, despite the fact that his official surname is Jaques-Dalcroze, that hyphenated name is often reduced to Dalcroze when speaking of him.[13]

A small, rotund man who was unexpectedly light on his feet, Dalcroze was blessed with a gift for mimicry and delighted in amateur theatricals. Yet he did not aspire to be an actor. And he was certainly not a dancer.

Nevertheless, as the Viennese modern dancer Gertrud Bodenwieser remarked, "Dalcroze may be likened to one of those great mariners who sailed out to discover another route to some land, and discovered a whole unknown continent."[14] Dalcroze sought to reform music education. In the process, he made an incalculable contribution to movement training.

As professor of harmony at the Geneva Conservatory, Dalcroze was shocked to find that many students, after years of diligent study, failed to grasp some of the basic principles of music and were incapable of relating the concepts taught in theory classes to their own performances as singers or instrumentalists. Believing that what the body has learned it never totally forgets, Dalcroze developed a system of rhythmic training which he called *rhythmique*. However, because that word is difficult for people unfamiliar with French to pronounce, John Harvey and Percy Ingham, two of Dalcroze's British supporters, popularized the term eurhythmics, which is derived from Greek words meaning "good rhythm."[15] The system is sometimes also known as "Dalcroze eurhythmics" or, simply, "Dalcroze."

When conservatory officials refused to give Dalcroze studio space for his exercises, which they dubbed *singeries* (monkeyshines), the undaunted teacher rented halls and continued his classes elsewhere. He and his disciples eventually devised complex sequences of movement assignments.

Although Dalcroze insisted in 1926 that "eurhythmics is *not* a school of dancing,"[16] exercises for his advanced students were often kinetically demanding and the rhythmic training they provided was valuable for dancers, as well as musicians. Students learned such things as how to clap hands in a crescendo while moving their feet in a diminuendo, how to beat four beats with their arms while walking three beats to a bar, and how to make two movements with the head while making three with the left arm, four with the right arm, and five with the feet. (The *Dancing Times* of London wondered if all this might be "trying to the nerves.")[17] As the movements grew more elaborate, they sometimes turned dancelike. And when Dalcroze had students represent each voice in a fugue with movement, he came close to creating dance compositions.[18]

Thanks to Wolf and Harald Dohrn, two German brothers who were successful manufacturers, Dalcroze in 1910 was provided with a new school in Hellerau, a suburb of Dresden, Germany. It was an exciting place. Hellerau was a planned community, a "garden city." Dresden was simultaneously a ravishingly beautiful city of Baroque buildings (most of which would be destroyed in World War II) and a major center of modern German painting and music. The Dohrns were generous patrons, Wolf proving especially idealistic. A former economics student at the University of Munich and an active member of the Christian Socialist movement, Wolf believed that rhythm was an important part of all human work, play, and art, yet felt that the natural rhythms of life were being destroyed by industrialization. However, instead of rejecting technology, he sought to reform it.[19]

In addition to a school the Dohrns provided Dalcroze with an auditorium, the Festspielhaus, which was completed in 1912. Its nonproscenium "open" stage was the site of many theatrical events, one of them created by the experimental stage and lighting designer Adolphe Appia. It was there in 1913 that Dalcroze and Appia presented a production of Gluck's *Orfeo ed Euridice* in which large groups of people moved in response to the formal and emotional qualities of the music on a set that was a nonrealistic arrangement of steps, platforms, and draperies.[20]

By 1913, there were more than 600 students—adults and children alike—from sixteen countries at Hellerau.[21] In addition to musicians, they included people whose primary interest was dance. Among Dalcroze's teaching assistants was Suzanne Perrottet, who was considered an exquisitely musical dancer.

Branch Dalcroze schools began to spring up in many cities, including New York, where a school was founded in 1915. But whereas eurhythmics flourished throughout the world, the Hellerau school came to an abrupt end in 1914 when, upon the outbreak of World War I, Dalcroze in effect banished himself from Germany by signing a statement protesting Germany's military policy and the bombing of Reims cathedral in France. He returned to Switzerland, and the Hellerau school was used as a hospital.

More than a school, Hellerau in its time was a gathering-place of visionaries. "There," wrote Alfred Schlee (a Hellerau student who later edited *Schrifttanz*, an important dance magazine), "an inspired way of life was born, shared by teachers and students alike. . . . In this atmosphere my international outlook and tolerant nature were strengthened."[22] The implications of Hellerau extended beyond music and dance.

So did those of eurythmy[23]—a word just similar enough to eurhythmics that the two are sometimes confused. A form of visible speech, eurythmy is the invention of Rudolf Steiner, a philosopher who sought to unite science, art, and religion in a metaphysical teaching called Anthroposophy. The first public performances of eurythmy occurred in Munich in 1912. Two years later, Steiner established a cultural and philosophical center called the Goetheanum in the Swiss town of Dornach.

Steiner believed that all theatre is a revelation of the divine Word, that every speech sound is an invisible gesture, that poetry is a dance of sounds, and that each sound is associated with a specific inner feeling and a specific movement. More controversially, Steiner argued that these correspondences among sounds, feelings, and movements are identical in all languages.

Thus, for Steiner, a broad A ("ah") represented wonder, amazement, or admiration, and was indicated by a wide stretching movement of the arms. In general, vowels (and their gestural equivalents) express inner feelings, whereas consonantal sounds and gestures refer to the outer world. Punctuation was made visible by pauses and frozen gestures.

What one thinks of eurythmy probably depends upon one's opinion of Steiner's metaphysical and linguistic theories. Nevertheless, it can be employed theatrically. Followers of Steiner in Europe and America still band together in eurythmy groups to perform works choreographed to poetry and classical music.

Denishawn, Hellerau, and the Goetheanum may have differed in their specific aims and methodologies. But all three centers valued movement for its esthetic and spiritual significance, and all provided students with some sort of systematic training.

Another such center was Ascona, an idyllic village in the southern Swiss Alps which around the turn of the century became a summer colony for artists and intellectuals. There, in 1913, Rudolf Laban, a Hungarian teacher, choreographer, and theorist, offered a summer dance course on premises that had once belonged to a vegetarian group. Laban and his associates lived in huts, and when they were not studying or dancing they did farm work, weaving, and baking. He urged students to throw off the constraints of materialist society and to devote themselves wholeheartedly to nature and art.[24]

Laban eventually became one of the most important figures in modern dance. But before that came about, World War I intervened.

From 1914 to 1918, much of Europe was a bloody battlefield. The war simultaneously horrified and fascinated artists. Many regarded it as the destiny to which Western civilization was fated. An old era was ending, and no one could predict what might come next. Whereas Isadora Duncan, Ruth St. Denis, and other dancers before the war rhapsodically equated beauty and truth, postwar dancers often derived an awesome new kind of beauty from the world's harshest truths.

Loïe Fuller in her *Serpentine Dance.*

Isadora Duncan in her fervent solo *Le Marseillaise*. Photograph by Arnold Genthe, 1916, courtesy of the Dance Collection of the New York Public Library for the Performing Arts.

Maud Allan and the head of John the Baptist in *The Vision of Salomé*. Photograph courtesy of the Dance Collection of the New York Public Library for the Performing Arts.

Rita Sacchetto in *Minuetto*, inspired by Thomas Gainsborough's portrait of the Duchess of Devonshire. Photograph by Lützel-München, courtesy of the Dance Collection of the New York Public Library for the Performing Arts.

Ruth St. Denis as a Japanese goddess in *Kwan Yin*. Photograph courtesy of Jane Sherman.

Ted Shawn in *Osage-Pawnee Dance of Greeting,* representing the meeting of two friendly Native American tribes. Photograph courtesy of Jane Sherman.

Sent M'Ahesa in *Bird of Death* (also known as *Demon of Death*). Photograph courtesy of the Dance Collection of the New York Public Library for the Performing Arts.

Mary Wigman in *Witch Dance* (*Hexentanz*). Photograph courtesy of the Dance Collection of the New York Public Library for the Performing Arts.

Harald Kreutzberg in *Night* (*Gesang der Nacht*). Photograph courtesy of the
Dance Collection of the New York Public Library for the Performing Arts.

Valeska Gert in *Canaille* (*Scum*), one of her portraits of the dregs of society. Photograph courtesy of the Dance Collection of the New York Public Library for the Performing Arts.

Gret Palucca leaping. Photograph courtesy of the Dance Collection of the
New York Public Library for the Performing Arts.

Oskar Schlemmer's *Stick Dance*. Photograph courtesy of the Dance Collection of the New York Public Library for the Performing Arts.

Rosalia Chladek in "Dance with Pole" ("Tanz mit dem Stab") from her *Rhythms* cycle. Photograph courtesy of the Dance Collection of the New York Public Library for the Performing Arts.

Michio Ito in *Pizzicatti*. Photograph courtesy of the Dance Collection of the New York Public Library for the Performing Arts.

Gertrud Bodenwieser Dancers in *The Demon Machine*. Photograph by Benda, courtesy of the Dance Collection of the New York Public Library for the Performing Arts.

Helen Tamiris in *Adelante,* her dance about the Spanish Civil War. Photograph courtesy of Pauline Tish.

Martha Graham and Company in *Primitive Mysteries*. Photograph by Barbara Morgan, courtesy of Lloyd Morgan.

Pauline Koner and Lucas Hoving as an early twentieth-century mother and son in Doris Humphrey's *Ruins and Visions*. Photograph by Peter Basch, courtesy of Pauline Koner.

The diplomats arguing in Kurt Jooss's *The Green Table*. Photograph by Renger-Patzsch, courtesy of the Dance Collection of the New York Public Library for the Performing Arts.

Hanya Holm's concern for stage space and group movement as revealed in her *Orestes and the Furies*. Photograph by Fritz Kaeser, courtesy of Mildred Kaeser and Claudia Gitelman.

Bella Lewitzky and Herman Boden in *The Beloved*, Lester Horton's dance-drama about a husband's suspicions of marital infidelity. Photograph courtesy of the Dance Collection of the New York Public Library for the Performing Arts.

Ted Shawn's Ensemble of Men Dancers in the heroic *Kinetic Molpai*. Photograph courtesy of the Dance Collection of the New York Public Library for the Performing Arts.

Roger Ohardiene and Katherine Dunham in Dunham's *Barrelhouse Blues*. Photograph by Alfredo Valente, courtesy of the Dance Collection of the New York Public Library for the Performing Arts.

Betty Jones and José Limón in Limón's *The Moor's Pavane*, based on Shakespeare's *Othello*. Photograph by Walter Strate.

The Alvin Ailey American Dance Theatre in Ailey's *Revelations*. Photograph by Bill Hilton.

Sara Yarborough, Dudley Williams, and members of the Alvin Ailey American Dance Theatre in Donald McKayle's *Rainbow 'Round My Shoulder*, concerning the dreams and memories of chain-gang convicts. Photograph by Fred Fehl.

Dore Hoyer in *Ophelia.* Photograph courtesy of the Dance Collection of
the New York Public Library for the Performing Arts.

Alwin Nikolais's *Imago*.

The Merce Cunningham Dance Company in Cunningham's *Sounddance.*
Photograph by Johan Elbers.

The Paul Taylor Dance Company in Taylor's *Insects and Heroes.*

Trisha Brown and Stephen Petronio in Brown's *Set and Reset*.

Meredith Monk's *Education of the Girlchild*. Photograph by Peter Moore.

Pina Bausch's *Arien*. Photograph by Ulli Weiss.

Members of the Butoh company Dai Rakuda Kan in Akaji Moro's *Sea-Dappled Horse*. Photograph by Jay Anderson, © 1982.

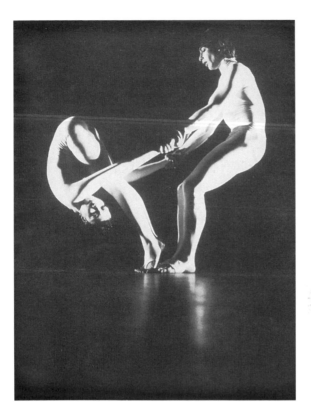

Cathy Lewis and Anthony Van Laast in the London Contemporary Dance Theatre's production of Siobhan Davies's *Diary*. Photograph by Anthony Crickmay.

Rambert Dance Company in Richard Alston's *Roughcut*. Photograph by
Catherine Ashmore.

PART 2

From World War I to the Great Depression

$\mathcal{N}$EW TIMES, NEW ARTS

Aftermath of World War I • Ausdruckstanz •
Expressionism • Rudolf Laban • Grace Cornell •
Movement Choirs

WHEN WORLD WAR I ENDED IN 1918, MUCH OF EUROPE LAY in ruins. Many of the world's philosophic and artistic assumptions had also shattered. The next decade would be a time of questioning and rebuilding.

Germany experienced economic chaos. Two revolutions in Russia in 1917 eventually resulted in the establishment of the Union of Soviet Socialist Republics, and some people thought communism the hope of the future. At the same time, advocates of fascism were also influential: Benito Mussolini assumed power in Italy in 1922, and Adolph Hitler founded the National Socialist (or Nazi) Party in Germany in 1925. Liberals and conservatives, radicals and reactionaries, argued about how to put the world back together.

Disillusioned members of the postwar generation were outspokenly skeptical. Whereas some debated all night, others caroused. There were times when the 1920s seemed a perpetual party. The war was over, so it was time to celebrate, especially to the irresistible rhythms of jazz. If no one knew what the future might bring, why not at least revel in the present?

The decade following the war came to be known in the United States as the "Roaring Twenties." It roared with artistic energy, as well as with high spirits and political rhetoric. The beauty and exotica of prewar choreography were no longer enough. As one dancer of the time was heard to exclaim, "What have we to do with harmony when the whole world stands afire?"[1]

Whereas some of the most innovative modern dancers before the war were Americans, immediately after the war and on into the late 1920s it was the European dancers—especially those of Germany and Austria—who proved daring. And they dared sooner and more boldly than many of their American counterparts did.

During World War I, some artists known as Dadaists gathered in neutral Switzerland, where they gazed at the carnage about them with undisguised scorn. Prizing intuition above reason and desiring to destroy traditional social norms, the Dadaists engaged in savage mockery and staged raucous multimedia events that sometimes combined poetic declamation with music and movement. These manifestations were seen by Rudolf Laban, who had opened a Zurich school in 1915, and some of his students participated in Dadaist activities.

By 1919, most of the Dadaists had left Switzerland. But a new spirit of irreverence prevailed throughout Central Europe. After the war, Germany was plagued by unemployment and a sense of national powerlessness which, even though inflation slowed in 1923 and economic recovery seemed underway by 1928, remained pervasive and encouraged the rise of Hitler. Nevertheless, despite economic and political woes, German arts flourished.

German dance between the two world wars is often known in English as "Expressionist dance." That term is misleading. To some dance lovers today, it may imply that all German dance was emotionally turbulent—which was not the case. German choreographers did indeed express raw personal feelings, but they also produced lyrical mood-pieces, satirical sketches, and dances of social and political commentary.

The Germans called their modern dance *Ausdruckstanz*, which means "expressive" rather than "Expressionist" dance. Like "modern dance" in English, it was a term that some dancers considered inadequate. Nevertheless, again like "modern dance," it stuck because no one managed to think of anything better.

Whatever they sought to express, the advocates of *Ausdruckstanz* emphasized the dancer's ability to shape space and control time. As Mary Wigman, perhaps the greatest of all the German dancers, proclaimed, "Dancing . . . is a living language which speaks directly to all mankind without any intellectual detours. The mediator of this language is the human body, the instrument of the dance."[2]

Writing in 1930 about dances and artworks she had seen in recent years, Dorothee Günther, a Munich dance teacher, remarked, "One senses that something is expressed from within man, that it comes into existence as long as man allows room for these intuitive forces."[3] Her statement suggests that even though *Ausdruckstanz* was not always specifically "Expressionist," it probably could not have developed as it did had it not been for the precedent of the art movement known as Expressionism.[4]

German Expressionism, which began to attract attention around 1910, predated the major developments in *Ausdruckstanz*; by 1925, when *Ausdruckstanz* was flourishing, it was firmly established, no longer considered experimental and, for some viewers, on the wane. The painters who at one time or another were associated with the movement included Lyonel Feininger, Wassily Kandinsky, Ernst Ludwig Kirchner, Paul Klee, Emil Nolde, Max Pechstein, and Karl Schmidt-Rotluff.

Expressionist painters sought to convey the essence of people, situations, events, and emotions (which could range from joy to despair) through vivid colors and meaningful distortions of line. Like Expressionism, *Ausdruckstanz* rejected simple realism in favor of distorted lines and revelatory shapes, and many German dancers expressed both deeply personal feelings and transcendent longings.

Modern dance developed rapidly throughout Central Europe. Much of the time, dancers worked independently. Yet there were major attempts to bring factions together—notably, the three Dancers' Congresses held in Germany.[5] The first, in Magdeburg in 1927, attracted 300 participants. The second, in Essen the next year, attracted 1,000, and as many as 1,400 took part in the third, in Munich in 1930. Various types of dance, including ballet, were shown at these events. But modern dance dominated them. In 1928, Mary Wigman even declared, "There are at least in Germany no further recruits for the ballet."[6] She turned out to be wrong. Nevertheless, hers was a widely shared opinion.

The most important theorist of Central European dance, and one of the most influential thinkers in all dance history, was Rudolf Laban.[7]

Laban (or von Laban, as his name was originally rendered) was born in 1879 in Poszony, a city of the Austro-Hungarian Empire which is now known as Bratislava and which was ceded to Czechoslovakia after the breakup of the empire. Laban, who was of Hungarian descent, was the son of a military governor of the empire and traveled extensively as a boy, developing a keen interest in the customs of the empire's peoples.

Laban's increasing interest in mysticism and ritual later led him to become a Freemason. His love of art and theatre disturbed his parents, who considered an artistic career unsuitable for someone of his high social position. Indeed, when one of Laban's uncles became an actor, he so scandalized his relatives that they forced him to change his name to avoid embarrassing them.

An indifferent and rebellious student, Laban wandered off on his own around the turn of the century, leading a Bohemian existence in Paris and scraping by as best he could. He initially planned to be an artist—and all his life he was a maliciously amusing caricaturist. Instead, he became a dancer and choreographer. Although he was known to have worked with pupils of Delsarte and Dalcroze, exactly how that happened remains shadowy, just as it is hard to say how such otherwise dissimilar figures as Loïe Fuller and Maud Allan became dancers.[8]

Laban quickly gained enough expertise to direct dance activities at Ascona and run his school in Zurich. After the war, he taught and choreographed in many cities and by the end of the 1920s he was considered Germany's leading dance reformer and theorist. Few advanced dancers working in Central Europe, whether in *Ausdruckstanz* or in ballet, failed to feel his influence, directly or indirectly.

Witty, playful, sarcastic, and demanding, he was extraordinarily charismatic, personally as well as professionally. He had affairs with many women and fathered several children. "No one was safe with him," his pupil Sigurd Leeder remarked.[9] An artistic dreamer, Laban needed people to turn his visions into realities; he found them all his life. And although he consistently made money, he just as consistently spent every penny of it on new projects.

Laban's choreography ranged from light-hearted solos to ambitious allegorical "dance-plays." A ceaseless experimenter, he concerned himself with the ways in which dance productions can communicate. Sometimes, to study the possible effects that might result, he would ask his dancers to perform the same work in different costumes: those appropriate to its historical setting on one occasion, neutral or deliberately timeless costumes on another. He built some dances out of everyday gestures, including affirmative nods, negative head shakes, beckonings, and defensive hand gestures. Believing that movement should be expressive in itself without the aid of emotionally stirring music, he choreographed works in silence, as well as works for which the accompaniment was a percussion ensemble or the stamping, shuffling, and clapping sounds made by the dancers as they moved.

Laban's large-scale productions often showed masses of people struggling against other masses or against space itself. In *The Deluded* (*Die Geblendeten*), a dance of 1921, much of which was performed in silence, individuals gathered in an imposing, but deceptive, unity that kept disintegrating into separate violent, servile, dreaming, searching, raving, and paralyzing forces until true unity was established. *Fool's Mirror* (*Narrenspiegel*) (1926) viewed the world through the eyes of a fool (played by Laban himself). To emphasize the dualities of human existence, three characters wore specially designed costumes that revealed two sides of their personalities simultaneously.[10]

Laban's choreography was introduced to New York on 19 June 1932 when Grace Cornell, one of his American pupils, presented a recital of brief pieces he had created for her. They bore such titles as *Apparition* (Milhaud), *The Pretty Shepherdess* (to a *Ländler*), *Hungarian Fantasy* (Kodály), *Song of Persia* (Bantock), *The Gypsy* (unaccompanied), and *Once upon a Time* (Gluck). All were solos, except for *Romantic Waltz*, in which Cornell's partner was a young Mexican-born dancer, José Limón.

The concert disappointed John Martin, the *New York Times*'s dance critic. The solos, he said, came "as a considerable surprise, for they were dreary and empty. Indeed, it is difficult to reconcile them with the fact that their creator is one of the leading theorists of the German dance." Cornell's dancing, however, was another matter: "She revealed beautiful movement, under excellent control and with a charming youthfulness about it."[11]

Laban remains important today not as a choreographer, but as a thinker who attempted to discern and analyze fundamental principles of movement. Studying the working of the human body, he concluded that all movements involve effort and shape; moreover, patterns of effort and shape can be indicative of states of physical (and, possibly, mental and spiritual) harmony or disharmony.

Laban proceeded to scrutinize the workings of body parts and to classify basic types of human actions. As he analyzed movement progressions—which he termed movement scales—he used geometric shapes such as the tetrahedron, cube, octahedron, and icosahedron as analogies for the course of movements between points in space.

Just as musicians traditionally divide singers into such specific types of voices as soprano, alto, tenor, and bass, so Laban believed that, as a result of physique and artistic temperament, there were three types of dancer. The *Hochtänzer* (high dancer) is especially adept at leaping, moving lightly, and defying the pull of gravity; this type of dancer is the ideal of classical ballet. The *Tieftänzer* (low dancer) is at ease in the lower parts of space; such dancers (and some of the early German modern dancers belonged to this category) favor strong, impulsive movements, including stamping and crouching. The *Mitteltänzer* (dancer of middle range) tends to move on the horizontal and is especially suited to freely flowing and swinging movements.[12]

Laban's theories have excited generations of dancers, teachers, and kinesiologists. Yet some dancers have found them intimidating. The elaborate terminology, the references to geometry—all this can seem ponderous. So can attempts to elucidate Laban. Here, for instance, is one writer defining the icosahedron as "the amount of space contained within twenty equilateral triangles formed by the assembly of thirty equal sides . . . it has twelve corners and twenty triangular surfaces."[13] Anyone left mystified by high-school geometry might find this explanation perplexing, rather than illuminating. Back in 1930, a Berlin correspondent for the *Dancing Times* complained that Laban "is too high up in the clouds, he is too much of a didactic philosopher and lacks natural simplicity."[14]

Nevertheless, Laban's analyses remain valuable for their comprehensiveness. Moreover, his analyses led to a system of dance notation which remains remarkable for its thoroughness and accuracy. Originally known as Kinetography Laban and also as *Tanzschrift*, it is now known as Labanotation.

Laban's wide-ranging interests and his categorizations of body types led him to argue that dancing can be an activity for all people and that it need not be restricted to the favored few whose bodies approach a single desired physical ideal. Furthermore, he saw no reason why artistic (as opposed to social) dancing should be done only by professionals.

He therefore organized *Bewegungschöre* (movement choirs),[15] large groups of amateurs—or mixtures of professionals and amateurs—

who performed serious works in a spirit of communal solidarity. The founding of movement choirs came at a time when social critics feared that industrialization threatened to dehumanize workers. Through collective movement, some speculated, people might be able to transcend everyday existence and attain a state of *festliches Sein* (festive being). Movement choirs—whether Laban's or those based on the approaches of other teachers—could consist of several dozen or of several hundred participants. The steps they performed were simpler than those associated with professional troupes, and the emphasis was upon groupings and patterns, rather than virtuoso feats.

Movement choirs took part in civic festivals and performed for labor unions, religious groups, and political parties. Choreographers of all ideological persuasions organized them.

In Berlin in 1929, a group called the Recitation and Movement Chorus offered a two-part program that depicted the sufferings of the working class, the struggle to defeat wars and starvation, and the enslavement of humanity by machines. For the Vienna Festival that same year, Laban himself staged a procession through the streets modeled upon the civic processionals of the medieval guilds. Wearing costumes ranging from those of the sixteenth century to those of the twentieth, the participants allegorically represented such arts as painting, sculpture, modern ballet, modern dance, and modern ballroom dancing. The procession also included military bands, the police force, and a group of electric player-pianos.

Laban tried to unite a multitude of ideas, forces, and tendencies into one grand synthesis. His immediate concern was dance. But because he regarded dancing as an expressive, rather than a decorative, art, his ultimate concern was life.

ℱORM, FEELING, PATTERN, PASSION

Mary Wigman • Harald Kreutzberg • Niddy Impekoven • Valeska Gert • Anita Berber • The Bauhaus • Vera Skoronel • Gret Palucca • Oskar Schlemmer • Absolute Dance • Dorothee Günther • Maja Lex • Spannung

LIKE THE BEST OF THE GERMAN EXPRESSIONIST PAINTERS, many German modern dancers realized that feelings could not be communicated to other people simply through emotional outpouring. The dancers and the painters alike believed that art is most powerful when form and content are inseparably joined.

Scores of dance lovers of the 1920s and early 1930s considered the works of Mary Wigman to be among the most memorable examples of such a union. Wigman loved to say, "Without ecstasy there is no dance. Without form there is no dance."[1] For Wigman, form was not merely a container for ecstasy (or for any other passion or idea), but its very embodiment, and her ability to externalize feelings made her one of the greatest choreographers of the twentieth century.

The daughter of a businessman, Wigman was born in Hanover in 1886. That she became a dancer at all is something of a miracle.[2] Looking back in wonder toward the end of her long life, Wigman wrote: "My friends, shall I tell you the story of the ugly duckling that miraculously turned into a swan? Because it could not be foreseen that the mousy little girl would be transformed into a world-famous dancer. This certainly may seem a metamorphosis bordering on the miraculous."[3] Mousy she may have been, but Mary, who was sent to boarding schools in England and Switzerland, possessed a keen intellect, was a voracious reader, and became fluent in several foreign languages.

The young Wigman did not quite know what she wanted to do with her life. With no intention of settling down as a housewife, she kept breaking off one engagement after another until, when she reached her twenties, her friends began to worry about her future. Distressed and confused, Wigman would weep through the night alone in her room, her body swaying as she sobbed.

Her curiosity was piqued by performances she saw by the Wiesenthal Sisters and by children trained in the Dalcroze method. Finally, she made a decision. To the horror of her family, she went off to Hellerau in 1910. Two years later, she received a certificate qualifying her to teach "rhythmic gymnastics." Yet even that was not enough to calm the turbulence that raged within her. Her friend the painter Emil Nolde told her about Rudolf Laban, and in 1913, when she was twenty-seven, she joined Laban's group at Ascona and embarked upon a career as a dancer. She remained with Laban for seven years, becoming his assistant at his school in Zurich, where she witnessed the irreverent performance events of the Dadaists.

Eventually, Wigman began to choreograph. At first, she found it such a struggle that she suffered a breakdown and had to retreat into temporary seclusion. By 1919, she had recovered sufficiently to present a program of dances before an audience of patients at a Swiss sanitarium. The patients applauded her; in contrast, German audiences soon afterward pronounced her "mad."

Later in 1919, she returned to Germany and settled in Dresden, where she opened a school that trained an extraordinary number of dancers. She enjoyed increasing success as a dancer and choreographer both in Germany and abroad, and she toured America three times between 1930 and 1933 under the management of the impresario Sol Hurok.

A strong, muscular woman with a large face, high cheekbones, a broad mouth, and deep eyes, Wigman was in no conventional sense pretty. Her dancing was frequently earthbound, and she favored kneeling, crouching, crawling, creeping, and falling. Her costumes were severe; indeed, some audiences found them unattractive. Nevertheless, she was a compelling presence and in her dances—especially her solos—she sought to ally herself with the powers of life, death, fate, and eternity.

She assembled many of her solos into cycles or suites, in which each dance related to or was programmed as a significant contrast to the others. She also presented excerpts from these cycles as independent entities. Among the best-known of the cycles were *Visions* (choreographed between 1925 and 1928), *Shifting Landscape* (1929), and *Sacrifice* (1931).[4] Many of Wigman's solos depicted nonrational psychic forces that shaped human destiny for good or for ill. She was especially celebrated for her *Witch Dance*. Wigman first created a solo about a witch as early as 1914, and this malevolent figure choreographically haunted her for more than a decade. Wigman's witch was a repulsive crouching figure clad in barbaric robes. Far from being a laughable Halloween caricature, this personification of evil symbolized unrestrained, naked instincts. As Wigman herself noted, she was "beast and woman at one and the same time."[5]

Monotony (also known as *Whirl Dance*) was equally famous. In this solo, Wigman turned continuously for six or seven minutes to percussion accompaniment. Beginning slowly, she steadily gained speed, letting her silver dress whirl about her. Then she slowed, only to accelerate again; as she turned, her arms traced sinuous patterns in the air. An ecstatic vision inspired by ritualistic dervish dances, *Monotony* was often interpreted as an allegory of humanity obsessed with the riddle of life.[6]

Other works were equally striking. In *Lament*, she kept bending lower and lower under the power of some opposing will that finally conquered her. *Storm Dance* was a swirling solo in a flame-colored robe. *Song of the Sword* was as sharp and energetic as its title implied. *Dance into Death* sent Wigman dashing in frenetic diagonal patterns. Her solos were usually intense. Yet not all were somber. Thus in *Dance of Summer* she suggested the languor of a sultry day, and her *Gypsy Dances* were filled with abandoned skipping.

Because Wigman often concerned herself with struggles between conflicting powers, it was only natural that she would create group works in which opposing forces were given corporeal shape. She was as famous in Germany for her ensemble compositions as she was for her solos. Abroad, however, she was regarded primarily as a soloist. That, perhaps, is not surprising, for she did not always tour with a group. Only once — during the 1932–1933 season — did she bring her company to America, in *The Way*, a symbolic account of the process of redemption that was regarded as one of her weaker efforts. Even before she left Europe, the critic Joseph Lewitan called it disappointing because it looked as if it had been born not out of inspiration, but under the pressure of an American contract.[7]

However, German audiences admired several of Wigman's group works. For instance, *Scenes from a Dance Drama*, a suite of ten items choreographed in 1923–1924, explored states of unity and separation.

Individuals attempted to form a group, and the group attempted to form a circle, only to break apart in chaos until Wigman emerged as a leader to reunite everyone. These scenes could be formally interpreted simply as studies in patterning, but in politically divided Germany they had social significance for leftists and rightists alike.

Several aspects of Wigman's productions prompted comment. One was her use—or nonuse—of music. Some of her dances were performed in silence. Others did have music. But to assert the autonomy of dance as an art, Wigman's accompaniments were composed by musicians along with the choreography or entirely after the choreography had been created. Her scores were often spare and were intended to be of no artistic interest apart from the dances for which they were written. They also made extensive use of percussion instruments. For her 1931 American tour, Wigman brought over two Hungarian flutes, an assortment of drums, five Chinese gongs, one set of Indian bells, and a pair of cymbals.[8] The rhythms of such instruments helped call attention to or intensify the choreographic rhythms.

Wigman sometimes danced wearing masks, not merely to look fantastic or bizarre, but in an attempt to escape from or transcend her ordinary self. She made a subtle distinction between makeup and masks: "Makeup gives the dancer's features a second skin and plays along with his finest and most detailed facial expressions. Not so the rigidity of the mask. It preserves its clearly defined contours, its sculptural shape. It gives the dancer a second face, it characterizes and typifies, but can never be exploited psychologically."[9]

Possibly as a result of her training with Laban, Wigman possessed a remarkable awareness of space. She viewed the stage not as a floor to cross, but as a three-dimensional entity with which she could have emotional as well as physical relationships. Hanya Holm, one of her pupils who became a distinguished choreographer and teacher in her own right, has remarked that in Wigman's dances "she alternately grapples with space as an opponent and caresses it as though it were a living, sentient thing."[10]

Hostile critics called some of her works "a mad frenzy" and "an imbecilic dislocation of the joints."[11] But for such a passionate defender of modern dance as John Martin of the *New York Times*, Wigman was amazing: "With Wigman the dance stands for the first time fully revealed in its own stature; it is not storytelling or pantomime or moving sculpture or design in space or acrobatic virtuosity or musical illustration, but dance alone, an autonomous art exemplifying fully the ideals of modernism in its attainment of abstraction and in its utilization of the resources of its materials efficiently and with authority. This brings it, however, to no state of finality, no crystallization, but only to a complete statement of its selfhood, to a revelation of the principles upon which it may enlarge its borders and deepen its awareness of itself." [12]

The most famous European male modern dance soloist of his time was Harald Kreutzberg, who devised a form of choreographic portraiture in which he developed essentially pantomimic gestures in an idiosyncratic manner. Born in 1902 in a region ceded to Czechoslovakia after World War I, Kreutzberg was the grandson of the director of a traveling circus who also made wax figures. His father was born in Philadelphia while Kreutzberg's grandfather was exhibiting his works there. [13] Young Harald studied music and ballet and played children's roles in operetta productions. He desired to be a painter and enrolled in the Dresden Academy of Art. In Dresden, however, he encountered Mary Wigman and became her student.

Kreutzberg attracted the attention of the great stage director Max Reinhardt, who cast him as both actor and dancer in some of his productions. It was as Puck in Reinhardt's staging of *A Midsummer Night's Dream* that he made his American debut in 1927. That year, he also gave dance recitals with Tilly Losch as his partner. Later, he toured America with first Yvonne Georgi and later the American ballet dancer Ruth Page. However, during most of the 1930s and again after World War II, Kreutzberg was best known in America as a soloist.

Onstage, he was remarkable—for his looks as well as his dancing. Kreutzberg shaved his head. He did it for the first time in Berlin in 1925 to portray an unhappy and mysterious jester in a ballet called *Don Morte*. Wishing to appear suitably melancholy, he tried several kinds of masks and caps. All dissatisfied him. Then he decided to shave his head. Noticing him backstage, some of his fellow dancers complimented him on his unusual makeup. But when they touched his head, they shrieked with surprise. Reinhardt, however, praised him for his appearance, and Kreutzberg never let his hair grow back.

It was not just the look of his head that made Kreutzberg striking. As Ruth Page recalls, "Harald could evoke any mood in his great dancing. His rapport with any audience, any place, was immediate and overwhelming. He could make his public laugh or cry at his will." [14]

Kreutzberg specialized in solos — many with scores by his long-time companion Friedrich Wilckens — that ranged from the whimsical to the macabre. Everyone agreed that he could virtually hypnotize an audience. But throughout his career, Kreutzberg, who lived until 1968, was occasionally accused of being a purveyor of escapist entertainment. Thus, in 1935, Ralph Taylor, an American critic, accused him of "porcelain preciosity" and of offering audiences "treacle instead of truth." [15]

Doris Hering of *Dance Magazine* provided a balanced appraisal of Kreutzberg's artistry in 1953:

> Harald Kreutzberg is not deep, and his work is not even really of these times either in style or subject matter. Yet he is so adept at the creation of atmosphere that one's interest never flags.
>
> No matter what Mr. Kreutzberg does, whether he emphasizes dancing or mime, a tantalizing sense of another time, another place, another world is established — with ostensibly the simplest of means. [16]

Hering singled out two solos as examples of Kreutzberg's gestural economy. In the second of *Two Japanese Short Poems*, the mere flicking and dropping of a fan created a sense of nostalgia and desolation. Wearing a long black robe and cape in *Winter, the Angel of Silence*, Kreutzberg suggested, through the opening and turning of his hands and a few gentle inclinations of his head, that death could be a comforter to unfortunate people. *Winter* was one of several dances based on images of angels in medieval art. Using broad, simple legato movements in *Angel of the Annunciation*, Kreutzberg delivered divine tidings to Mary, then was stirred by her beauty and the glory of his message. Although Mary remained an invisible figure in this solo, Kreutzberg made her presence as real to the audience as it was to his angel. *The Angel of the Last Judgment*, in contrast, was a stern herald of doom.

Master of Ceremonies derived from a role Kreutzberg had played in Reinhardt's production of Carlo Gozzi's eighteenth-century play *Turandot*. Portraying a master of ceremonies at a Chinese court, Kreutzberg had moved through scene after scene with an exotic, faintly sinister grace. Walter Terry praised the dance solo based on this character for its "haughty sinuosities, its inscrutable but slightly sardonic elegance and its mercurial gestures which were reflected in the quick posture changes of the body, the shifting of body-weight and of direction." [17]

Kreutzberg was repeatedly drawn to grotesque subject matter. However, unlike Wigman, whose eeriness evoked vast irrational forces, Kreutzberg, like a medieval carver of gargoyles, took delight in creating curious shapes and strange gestures. *Hangman's Dance* depicted a ghoulish executioner cavorting on the graves of his victims. *Fantastic Waltz* showed a grizzled old man summoning enough strength to dance a final wild waltz. *Three Mad Figures* introduced audiences to a forlorn man who cares for nothing but the tiny flower he holds in his hand, a megalomaniac who imagines himself lord of the earth, and a madman convinced that he is being followed by enemies. In *The Eternal Circle*, inspired by medieval paintings of the "dance of Death," Kreutzberg portrayed Death and six of his victims, indicating the various characters through rapid changes of costumes, masks, and gestures.

Not all Kreutzberg's fancies were bizarre. He had an impish sense of humor, which he revealed in *Til Eulenspiegel*, his portrait of a medieval mischief maker. *The Gardener in Love* found him as a shy gardener who, when thinking of his beloved, treats his rake as a mandolin and his apron as a cavalier's cape. And his exuberant clowning in *Dance through the Streets* often set audiences cheering.

Dancegoers of the time were fond of such sketches. Niddy Impekoven was another dancer known for them. A child prodigy, whose father was an actor, Impekoven was born in Berlin in 1904, made her debut at the age of six, and continued to dance through the 1930s. Later in life, she liked to give the impression that she had arrived out of nowhere onto the stages of Europe in a spontaneous burst of inspiration. Joseph Lewitan chided her for this, informing his readers that she had once been a pupil of Heinrich Kröller, a prominent German ballet teacher and choreographer. Lewitan wrote, "Today, perhaps, she denies her past and does not care for ballet any more—yet she received much from it for which to be grateful"—most importantly, her lightness and delicacy.[18]

One of her most popular creations, *Munich Coffee-Warmer*, was an example of pure charm. In this solo, she turned herself into a "cozy," a knitted cover placed over a teapot or coffeepot to keep its contents warm. Wearing a flat Bavarian hat tied under the chin and a Bavarian peasant costume with a bulging skirt that did indeed resemble a "cozy" covering a pot, Impekoven glided drolly across the stage like an animated doll.[19]

In contrast to Impekoven, Valeska Gert offered theatrical vitriol. Gert broke down traditional boundaries between dance, acting, and mime and epitomized the artistic spirit of Berlin after World War I. Despite political unrest and grinding poverty, its citizens lived a devil-may-care existence. Its satirical revues were famous, many of its cabarets notorious. The city's irreverent outlook was captured in *The Three-Penny Opera*, the collaboration between the poet and playwright Bertolt Brecht and the composer Kurt Weill, which received its premiere in Berlin in 1928.

Gert acted in G. W. Pabst's film version of *The Three-Penny Opera* and performed sketches in Brecht's *Red Revue*. Fascinated by the playwright's theories of politicized and populist "epic theatre," she once asked him, "What *is* epic theatre?" His reply: "What you do."[20]

The daughter of a Jewish manufacturer, Gert was born in Berlin in 1892. When her father suffered financial reverses during World War I, she sought ways to support herself. Office work suited her not at all. The flamboyant young woman found herself attracted to the theatre, and she studied acting and dancing. She performed in classic and contemporary plays and, in addition to *The Three-Penny Opera*, appeared over the years in such films by Pabst as *Diary of a Lost Girl* and *Joyless Street* (Greta Garbo's first movie outside Sweden), as well as in Jean Renoir's *Nana*. She also ran a cabaret, the Kohlkopf (cabbage-head).

In 1916, Rita Sacchetto hired Gert to dance in one of her productions. But when the performance came, Gert found herself tired of Sacchetto's choreographic charm. "I was itching to burst in on all this sweetness," she recalled. "Full of bravado, I exploded like a bomb from the wings."[21] Wickedly exaggerating the choreography and grimacing as she performed, Gert left spectators in an uproar.

Gert amazed audiences with her own eccentric solos. She called her works *Tontänze* (sound dances) because of the way she combined movement with vocal sounds that included shrieks, squeaks, neighs, and grunts, as well as words. Fascinated by people who live on the outer edge of respectable society, she choreographed portraits of boxers, jazz musicians, and prostitutes. Thus, in *Procuress* she based her movements on those of burlesque strippers, but danced them with no sex appeal whatsoever so the audience beheld nothing but unrelieved calculated coarseness.

Wrapped in blue and white swaddling clothes in *Baby*, she transformed herself into a squalling infant who produced an astonishing array of piercing sounds until she finally quieted herself by sticking her thumbs in her mouth. Wearing a long black skirt in *Death*, she stood motionless on a glaringly lit stage. Then, slowly, her body tensed, her hands clenched into fists, her face became distorted with pain, and her mouth widened into a silent scream. As life gradually ebbed from the woman she portrayed, Gert let her body relax, her arms go limp, and her head drop like that of a doll.

Gert inspired violent critical reactions. One German critic, Fred Hildenbrandt, called her "a dreadful hussy" who "moves in a shameless, disgusting way that is depravity, nothing more nor less, it is simply depravity." As for the alleged immorality of some of her solos, Gert herself declared that one of the purposes of her art "might be to show that vicious and evil people are merely poor creatures who do not know how to free themselves from their unfortunate predicament." In 1929, an anonymous correspondent for the *Dancing Times* characterized Gert as "a laughing, squeaking demon."[22]

Among her New York admirers was the critic Grant Code, who praised her for being a "truly great vulgarian." He continued: "Call her a hefty but voluptuous female Boris Karloff with a magnificent head of shaggy black hair, a way of doing things to her hands that would scare little children into an early grave, a voice that is a caricature of all the human voices in the world, and a wicked pair of legs that can whisper tragedy or go into a type of violent activity . . . and you have some notion of the woman." For the Berlin *Vossische Zeitung*, "She is as poisonous as absinthe and just as inebriating."[23]

Gert knew she was a child of a frenzied time and wondered what might become of herself. Foreseeing her old age, she mused: "I know . . . how I will die. Only the kitty will be with me. When I'm dead, I won't be able to feed him. He's hungry. In his dire need he nibbles at me. I stink. Kitty is a gourmet, he doesn't like me any more."[24] Gert lived on until 1978. And much of her life continued to be tumultuous.

Whereas Gert, a product of Berlin, was also a commentator on it, Anita Berber succumbed to its feverishness. As one German writer, Lothar Fischer, has said: "She was the queen of the Berlin Bohemians.—A gambler.—She was bisexual, but more a lesbian.—She danced naked, a champion of the eroticism of the dance.—The star of early sex-education films, and a stage actress.—An alcoholic and a drug addict. . . . She was representative of her age, and a victim of it." [25] She also appears to have been a talented, if erratic, dancer.

Berber was born into an artistic household in 1899: her father was a classical musician, her mother a cabaret singer. She studied with Rita Sacchetto in 1915 and the next year danced works called *Rose* and *Diana with Arrow* on the same Sacchetto program during which Valeska Gert shocked the audience by grotesquely altering the choreography. [26] In 1917, Berber began giving evenings of her own works; in 1918, she acted in Fritz Lang's film *Dr. Mabuse the Gambler.*

Berber's early dances tended to be character sketches or impressions of pieces of classical music. Her style changed radically after 1922 when she met and married a dancer who was said to have once performed with a nude troupe. She started to favor the scantiest of costumes and the most lurid of themes. Her dances bore such titles as *Ecstasy, Suicide, Morphine,* and *Cocaine*—the drug to which she was addicted offstage.

When Berber remarried in 1926, her choreography grew less sensationalistic. Yet she remained such a disquieting performer that in 1927 her appearances in Vienna prompted an angry mob to storm the theatre and pelt her with eggs and bottles. Expelled from the city by the police, she went on to Budapest, where she met with another vehement reception. [27]

Her dances undeniably had impact. Today, however, it is difficult to determine how much they seriously explored and how much they merely exploited their decadent subject matter. And one can only speculate how Berber might have developed if she had not died of tuberculosis in 1928.

Although much Central European choreography was powerful, not all of it was intended to be an externalization of emotional states or a revelation of character. Choreographers interested in abstract dance emphasized form rather than feeling, pattern rather than passion.

In some ways, Mary Wigman concerned herself with all these matters. She insisted in an interview in 1933 that "it is dancing I dance. I wish people would not try to read hidden meanings into my dance." [28] This may sound like a strange remark from a choreographer known for her emotional force. However, Wigman seldom depicted specific people in specific predicaments; the kinetic portraiture of Valeska Gert was alien to her. Rather, Wigman sought to convey the essence of a state of mind or feeling. Her use of space suggested that she meticulously calculated her effects, and she proved capable of writing analytically about even her most intense creations.

Some of the choreographers interested in abstraction were influenced by the artists associated with the Bauhaus, a school and workshop of art and design founded in Weimar in 1919 by the architect Walter Gropius. He and his colleagues believed that society could be changed for the better through good design and intelligent planning and that technology could improve rather than enslave humanity. Artists associated with the Bauhaus included László Moholy-Nagy, Josef Albers, Paul Klee, and Wassily Kandinsky. Although the Bauhaus prized experimentation, many of its products tended to be more cerebral than the visceral art of the Expressionists or the strange visions of the Surrealists. Yet Bauhaus art was also capable of playfulness.

One choreographer who was said to invest geometrical forms with emotional significance was Vera Skoronel, a dancer born in Switzerland in 1906 of a Russian mother and an Austrian father. She studied with both Laban and Wigman. According to Joseph Lewitan, some of her dances were "notoriously bizarre." Yet during the 1920s she went from a preoccupation with "short, broken, and disordered rhythms" to a concern for "graceful, harmonious, womanly movements." Lewitan thought her inimitable: "Or do people here believe one can learn the art of being a volcano?"[29]

In another review,[30] Lewitan called attention to Skoronel's "intoxicating mentality," to her compositional skill in creating works based on such geometrical shapes as lines, triangles, circles, and rays, and to her ability to contrast, blend, disentangle, and dissolve groupings of dancers. Unfortunately, Skoronel died in 1932 when she was only twenty-six. Nevertheless, in his *Manuel de Danse* of 1938, Werner Schuftan called her "le plus grand génie de la danse du XXe siècle"— the greatest genius of twentieth-century dance.[31]

Even at the time, some critics would have considered Schuftan's view extreme. Many would have pronounced Wigman "the greatest genius." Yet Wigman did have a serious rival for eminence: Gret Palucca, another of her own former students. According to the art historian Rudolf Arnheim, Palucca danced with "an eminently modern variety of *joie de vivre*."[32]

Born in Munich in 1902, Palucca began ballet studies with Heinrich Kröller in 1918, only to find classical dance constricting. She then discovered Wigman, enrolled in her Dresden school in 1920, and eventually became a member of her company. Wigman soon recognized her pupil's talent: "Among my first students was a narrow-hipped, boyish-looking girl with a pert face framed by wild reddish-blond hair. Her name: Gret Palucca. An excellent dance temperament with a natural ability to jump such as I have never experienced again with any of the many dancers I have taught through the years." [33]

Palucca respected Wigman. Yet Wigman was also the model from which she would deviate. Whereas Wigman was cosmic and emotionally intense, "in Palucca," says Arnheim, "there was much youthful exuberance, the strength of stunning leaps, the smile, the sparkle." [34] That a dancer so temperamentally antithetical to Wigman could emerge from the Wigman school suggests that it did more than produce imitations of its founder.

Palucca opened her own Dresden school in 1925 and organized a company. But she attracted particular attention as a soloist. Palucca eschewed both the theatrical trappings associated with ballet and Wigman's solemn robes. She favored neutral lighting that could remain unchanged for an entire concert and adopted such simple costumes as smocks, pajamas, and plain skirts with sleeveless tight bodices.

Writing in the *Dancing Times* in 1928, a Berlin correspondent said of Palucca, "Her dancing is cheerfulness itself, and every movement of hers accentuates easiness, pleasure and delight with life." Joseph Lewitan called attention to her "vigorous recklessness." Reviewing German dance concerts in 1932, Etta Linick singled out Palucca's ability to create the illusion of "floating on space." [35] But Linick also praised Palucca for her choreographic logic.

Palucca was more than an exuberant virtuoso. Her effects were carefully plotted. She wrote in 1934 that "each dancer must independently find laws and methods for her dances. Where tradition fails, only personal experience can have weight." [36] Choreographically, Palucca concerned herself with movement qualities, rather than emotional evocations. As Linick noted, "Her subject matter is entirely abstract and does not include characterizations." [37] Not surprisingly, then, her repertoire contained works bearing such titles as *Light Beginning*, *Bright Dances*, *Dark Force*, *Apassionata*, *Distant Swinging*, and *Two Fragments: Quiet Song, Driving Rhythm*.

One of Arnheim's favorite solos was *Technical Improvisations* (1927). Based on Palucca's daily studio morning exercises, during which she began with a wriggling of the toes and methodically set her body into motion by working upward to her neck, the piece did indeed consist of limbering exercises. But Palucca performed them so that shaking, pushing, and stretching movements became signs, often comic, of haughtiness, impatience, collapse, and attack. The result was "a merry confusion of states of mind held together only by the systematic exploration of the anatomy."[38]

Palucca's logic, clarity, and love of abstraction caused her to be admired by many abstract painters. Wassily Kandinsky made a series of abstract drawings based on her dance movements. László Moholy-Nagy, of the Bauhaus, termed her "the most lucid of today's dancers. She is for us the newly found law of motion."[39]

For a Berlin critic, "this dancer represents the absolute opposite to Mary Wigman's style, and it is a clear indication of the public's taste that Palucca had a far more enthusiastic reception on the part of the younger spectators than even Mary Wigman. . . . [Palucca] has established herself as the dancer of youth."[40]

Oskar Schlemmer, a Bauhaus artist who was born in 1888, also became an important choreographer. He joined the Bauhaus faculty in Weimar in 1921 and remained with the school when it moved to Dessau in 1925. Even before his association with the Bauhaus, Schlemmer had been interested in theatre and dance; his involvement with the performing arts deepened during the 1920s when he offered dance productions that emphasized abstract and often geometric shapes in space. Like Loïe Fuller, Schlemmer encased dancers in fantastic costumes that concealed or distorted the natural line of the body, and he employed unusual lighting effects.

One of Schlemmer's most ambitious productions was the *Triadic Ballet*, which he first staged in Stuttgart in 1922 and later revived in other cities. The three-part work was inspired by a series of trinities that might have delighted Delsarte: form, color, movement; body, mind, spirit; line, plane, volume; and circles, squares, triangles.[41] Despite its complex schematization, the piece was far from solemn. One woman wore a tutu made of colored balls. Another woman's costume looked like an enormous bubble. Balls adorned one man's costume like Christmas tree ornaments. Another man seemed to be made of tubes. Still other men's costumes created the illusion that human beings had been turned into poles and disks. And a woman in a stiff, saucerlike tutu danced a duet with an apparently armless man in a costume resembling a diving suit with a fringe attached to it.

Schlemmer combined esthetic and metaphysical concerns with a love of circus, cabaret, and magic. Some of his shorter dances were simultaneously explorations of space and theatrical conjuring tricks. In *Hoop Dance*, a dancer enclosed himself in several hoops, so that he became a human astrolabe; later, he attached the hoops to his back like wings and gathered them behind him in a shape suggesting a peacock's tail. Helmeted figures paraded through *Block Play*, rearranging blocks and building them into a structure reminiscent of the Tower of Babel. A black-clad dancer with twelve white poles attached to his body performed against a black backdrop in *Pole Dance*. He manipulated these poles so that they created shape after shape in space. Because the black costume blended into the black backdrop, spectators were more conscious of the movement of the poles than of the dancer.[42]

Schlemmer's dance-theatre was in many ways that of a painter or sculptor. Movements tended to be simple and the props and costumes kept the audience's attention focused upon mass, volume, and shape, rather than upon intricacies of steps and gestures. Schlemmer meticulously categorized the basic shapes of the body: the egg shape of the head, the vase shape of the torso, the club shapes of the arms and legs, the ball shapes of the joints, the star shape of the spread hand, the infinity sign suggested by folded arms, and the cross shape of the back bone and shoulders.[43]

Schlemmer's opponents accused him of transforming dancers into robots. One critic sneered in 1926:

> Costumes, stage and human bodies become apparatus, machinery, clockwork toys. This new ballet has absolutely nothing in common with artistic dance expression, not even with marionette or doll plays. . . . Those who prefer the whistle of the underground, the lifeless mechanical shriek of engines and motors, to the sincere expression of human feelings, will no doubt become enthusiastic about this new "Ballet." In any case, it is very original.[44]

Such attacks horrified Schlemmer. Far from advocating dehumanization in life or art, he thought his productions exemplified humanity's laudable desire for "precision, instead of vagueness," a desire to "escape from chaos and a longing for form."[45] Moreover, he viewed his peculiarly costumed dancers as timeless figures capable of symbolizing joyous and tragic aspects of the human condition. And he hoped his dances could "serve the metaphysical needs of many by constructing a world of illusion and by creating the transcendental on the basis of the rational."[46]

As modern dance developed in the 1920s, choreographers devoted themselves to theoretical as well as practical matters. One idea discussed by many dancers, especially in Europe, was that of "Absolute Dance." Like many dance terms, this concept grows increasingly cloudy the more closely one examines it. But, essentially, what its proponents meant by it was a kind of dance production in which all effects were basically choreographic and in which music, stage design, costuming, and lighting were subsidiary elements serving only to enhance those choreographic effects. Some advocates of Absolute Dance also sought to abolish choreographic narrative and traditional mimetic gestures.

The theory sounded fine. But how, in actuality, could one be sure that all effects in a given work were purely choreographic? Could not even simple music and spartan décor be a theatrical distraction? As for content, could not a movement suggesting attraction, longing, or repulsion be branded as pantomimic? If so, how was a dancer to express *anything*? As Elizabeth Selden put it, "The question is, how close the dancer can get to a purely formal conception without sacrificing the possibility of communication."[47] And, of course, most of the dancers of the 1920s and 1930s, far from being concerned with pattern alone, were making urgent efforts to communicate.

"Absolute Dance" easily became a term critics and dance fans could apply to works they admired, for it gave them some sort of conceptual basis on which they could justify their feelings. Like other such broad terms, it remains important for indicating some of the major choreographic preoccupations of a given era. In popular parlance, as Selden noted,[48] Absolute Dance also became a synonym for dance without any music whatsoever or for dance accompanied by instruments—usually percussion—that served only to accentuate major choreographic changes or developments in a piece.

Many modern dancers of the 1920s struggled to prevent dance from being subservient to music. Dance, they argued, was an autonomous art and not, like opera, a form of musical theatre. Although dance undeniably involved rhythm, there was no reason why dance rhythms had to be identical to musical rhythms.

The modern dancers observed several choreographic approaches to music. Many popular ballets were performed to pretty, but unmemorable, tunes ground out by some obliging member of a theatre's musical staff. In contrast, one of the things that made the creations of Diaghilev's Ballets Russes amazing was the way they combined fine choreography with scores by distinguished composers. Diaghilev affirmed the importance of choreography by showing it could hold its own with great art and music.

Through her use of music, Isadora Duncan did something of the same thing. She danced to Gluck, Brahms, and Wagner; indeed, she presented solos to the music of these mighty composers. And because her choreography at its best refused to be overwhelmed by the music, she demonstrated how powerful dancing can be. However, during the 1920s and 1930s, dancers actively sought to free themselves from what they regarded as bondage to music. But if not music—then what? Some dancers were bold enough to create works without accompaniment: silent dances. Such dances continue to be choreographed. Many are effective. Nevertheless, choreographers usually avoid putting together programs of nothing but unaccompanied works, for they have discovered that an entire evening of silence can be monotonous.

In the 1920s and 1930s, live music of some kind was the only real option for dancers, other than silence. Just as choreographers do today, many chose existing pieces of music. Others commissioned scores. Occasionally, composer and choreographer worked side by side in the creation of a dance. Dancers also often put together works in silence and then asked musicians to compose scores for them that would either complement or serve as a deliberate contrast to the choreographic moods.

Modern dance scores of the 1920s and 1930s were frequently for chamber ensembles. Not all choreographers could afford orchestras. Some even felt that orchestras could be a distracting presence. When they commissioned scores for chamber ensembles, many dancers sought to avoid lush and all too easily beguiling string melodies, preferring instead the spare, but rhythmically vital, sounds of winds and percussion instruments.

There were teachers, dancers, and musicians who sought to combine music and dance in such a way that, both in the classroom and onstage, dancers made music and musicians danced. Among them was Dorothee Günther, a teacher in Munich who in 1924 began to collaborate with the composer Carl Orff on a training method that would unite music with dancing and gymnastics. Their efforts contributed to the formulation of Orff's *Schulwerk*, his system for developing a child's musical imagination. The *Schulwerk* included rhythmic and melodic exercises, improvisation exercises, and speech exercises that served to demonstrate the connections between sounds, words, and movements. At Günther's school, Orff also organized percussion ensembles, and instruments were often played by students as they danced.

Günther said of her aims, "I wanted to discover a method of reviving the natural unity of music and movement—music and dance; a method which would be available not only to a few natural artists but would solve the educational problem of awakening in everyone the sense of rhythmic movement, and of stimulating a love of dancing and music making—a general freedom of expression and receptivity."[49]

The pedagogical system of Günther and Orff also had its theatrical applicability. One outgrowth of it was Maja Lex's *Barbaric Suite*, presented at the Munich Dancers' Congress of 1930. The movement consisted of structured improvisations to the sound of a percussion orchestra, and performers were called upon both to dance and to make music. Gunnild Keetman, the associate of Orff who composed the score, even participated in the choreographic action during the third episode while one of the dancers took her place in the orchestra.

The five-part suite began with "Dynamic Rhythms," a steady accelerando. In "Dance with Sticks," two dancers accompanied a third dancer with the sounds of hand clapping and bamboo sticks. Then two dancers established a rhythm on kettledrums that was taken up by the full orchestra and set other dancers in motion. This "Dance with Kettledrums" gave way to a complex interplay of arms in "Canon." And the suite ended with a furioso "Leap Dance." For the admirers of *Barbaric Suite*, music became dance, dance became music, and human beings were transformed into patterns in motion.[50]

Classroom procedures may have varied from studio to studio. Nevertheless, on both sides of the Atlantic dancers tended to speak in terms of polarities. Among those most commonly employed in Germany were *Spannung* (or *Anspannung*) and *Abspannung* (or *Entspannung*). *Spannung* literally means "tension." But, to Germans, *Spannung* did not possess the unpleasant connotations that "tension" has for English speakers, who associate it with nervousness or rigidity. Rather, *Spannung* was a desirable quality associated with determination, muscular control, and dynamic struggle. However, if a dance involved nothing but *Spannung* its movements could seem intolerably jittery. Therefore *Abspannung* (relaxation) was proposed as a counterpart to *Spannung*. John Martin saw in *Spannung* and *Abspannung* "the ebb and flow of muscular impulses." American modern dancers would soon find their own terms for such states.[51]

FAMILY TREES AND HARDY GROWTHS

Loïe Fuller • Maud Allan • Isadora Duncan • Irma Duncan • Raymond Duncan • Valeria Dienes • Maggie Gripenberg • Madge Atkinson • Akarova • Emile Jaques-Dalcroze • Hellerau-Laxenburg • Rosalia Chladek • Michio Ito • Paris Opéra Ballet Eurhythmics • The Sakharoffs • Futurism • Valentine de Saint-Point • Gertrud Bodenwieser • Gertrud Kraus • Jean Weidt • Georges Pomiès • G. I. Gurdjieff • Tanzgymnastik • Aurel Milloss • Yvonne Georgi

EUROPEAN MODERN DANCE CONTINUED TO ATTRACT STUB-bornly independent performers and choreographers. Nevertheless, in examining their backgrounds it is often possible to establish lines of descent and to trace them back to the art's pioneers. Two major figures, however, exerted little direct influence: Loïe Fuller and Maud Allan. Although a prominent presence on the French cultural scene, Fuller developed no school of technique or choreography. Neither did Allan, despite the fact that she made sporadic efforts to teach. Indeed, most of her life until she died in 1956 involved a slow slipping into obscurity.

Isadora Duncan, in contrast, continued to arouse controversy. In 1921, she accepted an invitation to direct a school in the Soviet Union. Russian intellectuals had long admired her, and she had contemplated opening a Russian school as early as 1908. Moreover, many officials of the new Soviet government sought to be as revolutionary in art and education as they were in politics. No wonder, then, that Duncan arrived in Moscow with high hopes.

Duncan responded eagerly to the new society about her. Several of her dances reflected her enthusiasm. *Warshavianka*, set to a revolutionary song, was a group dance that showed revolutionists falling in battle, yet always managing to pass the banner of liberation to the next person in line. In her interpretation of the *Internationale*, the Communist anthem, Duncan gestured as if summoning the masses.

She also startled the masses watching her in the theatre by baring her left breast to symbolize a nursing mother giving strength to her children.

Like many idealists of the time, Duncan hoped that communism might free humanity from poverty and oppression. However, although she may have been starry-eyed, she was not blind to the realities she encountered. Thus she was appalled to find, at a time of economic hardship when many ordinary citizens were nearly starving, that some Soviet bureaucrats lived the same sort of luxurious life that had been associated with the deposed aristocrats.

Russian art and theatre after the revolution were often wildly experimental. Modern dance groups were formed, and some radicals wished to abolish ballet altogether, regarding it as a remnant of a decadent tsarist regime. However, such bold choreographers as Fedor Lopukhov and Kasian Goleizovsky sought to prove that ballet was capable of reform, and ballet remains Russia's leading form of theatrical dance.

Problems bedeviled Duncan as teacher and school director. For one thing, she spoke Russian badly and essentially taught by demonstrating. When she wanted to make an extended commentary, she spoke German to her assistant, Ilya Schneider, who proceeded to translate her remarks into Russian.

Duncan was now a middle-aged woman, and she had put on weight. Nevertheless, she continued to appear in flimsy costumes and without special makeup or brassiere. Alexander Rumnov, an actor who admired her, recalls that "frequently her breast fell out of the chiton. With a gesture full of chastity and grace she would replace it to the murmur of the orchestra seats and the considerable din from the gallery. She treated this as an absolutely natural thing."[1]

Duncan might have been able to cope with matters of language, art, and physical appearance. Financial difficulties proved insoluble. The Soviet government lacked sufficient funds to support her school, and officials reluctantly informed her that if she wished to keep it going she would have to do so on the profits of performances for paying audiences. So once again she set out on tour—to Western Europe and America—leaving Irma Duncan, one of the "Isadorables," to supervise the school. In the process, Irma became a gifted teacher. Until she settled in the United States in 1930, Irma directed both the Moscow school and a performing ensemble drawn from its students that toured the world. Now receiving government funds, the school continued until 1949, although it had a greater influence upon the teaching of artistic gymnastics than upon dance.[2]

When Duncan returned to Western Europe in 1922, she was accompanied by Sergei Esenin, a handsome and gifted poet. He also happened to be Isadora's husband. They were wed on 2 May 1922, much to the surprise of some of Duncan's acquaintances. For one thing, when they met in 1921 he was twenty-six and she was forty-four. Moreover, Duncan had always scorned the institution of marriage; yet now she was married. It has been suggested that the wedding was designed to avoid any scandals that might develop if Duncan and Esenin were known to be living together during her tours. Victor Seroff, Duncan's friend and biographer, has also speculated that Soviet authorities may have recommended the marriage on the theory that Duncan's famous name might serve as a protection to Esenin and discourage attacks—physical as well as political—on the militantly communist poet.[3]

Esenin was a disastrous choice for a husband. Physical attraction was possibly the only bond that held him and Isadora together. They could not even converse. Esenin knew no foreign languages; Duncan's Russian was primitive. Esenin had no interest in dance or classical music; Duncan was unaware of the new trends in Russian poetry. Worse yet, Esenin was a heavy drinker who grew violent when intoxicated, and he was known to have wrecked the furniture in more than one hotel room. The Soviet authorities were certainly correct in believing that Duncan was better known outside Russia than her husband. Indeed, he soon began to feel that he was being led about by her—and he resented it. Some of Isadora's friends also accused him of stealing from her.[4]

Duncan and Esenin arrived in the United States for what proved to be her last American tour. Beginning in October 1922 and extending through the following January, it provoked scandal after scandal. Esenin was rowdy; Duncan, outspoken. Interrupting a Boston performance to lecture her audience, she waved a red scarf above her head and shouted, "This is red! So am I!" Then she tore open her tunic to reveal her breasts and cried out, "This—this is beauty!" The mayor forbade her ever to appear in Boston again, and the evangelist Billy Sunday thundered, "That Bolshevik hussy doesn't wear enough clothes to pad a crutch."[5]

Duncan and Esenin returned to Russia in 1923 and formally separated; two years later, Esenin committed suicide. Duncan performed again in Western Europe in 1924, trying to raise money for her school, now firmly in Irma's hands.

Duncan acquired a studio in Nice in 1926 and proposed spending half the year there and the other half in Moscow. Nothing came of this scheme. But Duncan did happen to be in Nice on the evening of 14 September 1927. A lover of fast automobiles, she accepted an invitation to go for a ride in a sports car. Wrapping herself in a long shawl, she stepped into the car, proclaiming, "*Adieu, mes amis. Je vais à la gloire!*"—Goodbye, my friends, I go to glory![6] The end of the shawl became entangled in the spokes of a wheel; when the car started, her neck was broken.

Isadora's death was as flamboyantly theatrical as much of her life had been. She always provided journalists with "good copy." Her behavior was unpredictable; her private life untidy. Nevertheless, Isadora Duncan was a great artist, one who did achieve glory as a cultural prophet. If wherever she went she set gossips chattering, she also inspired young people to make their own dances.

As a creative art, Duncanism did not survive Isadora. Her most fervent disciples made an invaluable contribution to dance history by preserving some of her choreography, but most of their own original efforts were of lesser importance. Isadora was an inspiration, not a model to be copied.

Duncan affected theatregoers in surprising ways. Valeria Dienes, who was born in Hungary in 1879, studied philosophy at the University of Budapest, from which she obtained her doctorate in 1905.[7] She went to Paris in 1911 to study with the philosopher Henri Bergson. But when she saw Isadora Duncan, Dienes wanted to dance, and she began to study with Raymond Duncan.

After opening a school in Budapest in 1912, she developed a system of movement training that she called orchestics. A Budapest performance by Dienes's group on 1 April 1917 is believed to be the first public performance by a Hungarian modern dance company. The program included works in a Duncanesque style to music by Schubert, Chopin, Grieg, Schumann, and Weber, and to poems by Rabindranath Tagore and the Hungarian writer Mihály Babits. Dienes, who died in 1978, went on to choreograph works on biblical and historical themes.

Maggie Gripenberg developed modern dance in Finland.[8] Gripenberg, who was born in 1881, came from a cultivated aristocratic family. Without the support of such enlightened and socially important relatives, she might not have succeeded as a dancer at all in the strait-laced Finland of her day. A talented pianist and artist, Gripenberg also loved to dance, but her family was reluctant to provide her with lessons. Nevertheless, before she had ever seen Isadora, she made up dances in what she fancied was the Duncan style, based upon reports of the American dancer's performances. When Gripenberg at last attended a concert by Duncan—in Dresden in 1905—she was so overwhelmed that she stayed up all night improvising in her nightgown.

Back in Finland later that year, she studied with Hilma Liiman, a Helsinki dance teacher. She also worked with other teachers in Finland and Sweden and, in 1910, with Dalcroze in Geneva. His approach greatly appealed to the musically sensitive Gripenberg. Finally, on 13 November 1911—when she was thirty—Gripenberg made her professional debut in Helsinki, dancing barefoot in short chiffonlike costumes.

She continued to perform, choreograph, and teach. In 1920 –1921, she toured America with a partner, Onni Gabriel. Because she was totally unknown in the United States, she had difficulty obtaining bookings. Her programs attracted a specifically Scandinavian-American audience and were largely ignored by critics of the major newspapers. Yet Gripenberg, who lived until 1976, was a major figure in her own country.

She was especially drawn to themes of slavery and liberation, possibly finding in such subject matter parallels to the struggles of twentieth-century Scandinavian women to free themselves from restrictive social conventions. Thus, in her *Danse Macabre* (Saint-Saëns), a slave begged for freedom, only to die in her master's arms, and in *Prelude* (Rachmaninoff) a chained peasant battled for her life.

But Gripenberg did not confine herself to such issues. *Beggars' Dance*, originally choreographed for a production of S. Ansky's *The Dybbuk*, one of the classics of the Jewish theatre, emphasized contorted positions and grotesque slithering arm movements. And in *Percussion Instrument Etude* dancers moved in drill-like contrapuntal patterns while accompanying themselves on percussion instruments held in their hands.

Madge Atkinson (1885 –1970), an English dancer, was inspired by the freedom and flow of Duncan's movements and, like Ruby Ginner, traced them to Hellenic sources.[9] Atkinson believed that the ancient Greeks were eloquent dancers and that it was therefore not improper to call the dance that had developed in the early twentieth century "Greek." [10] Yet she realized that much of what was taught in the name of "Duncan dancing" was technically amorphous. She therefore developed a dance form she termed Natural Movement, which included separate exercises for each limb from the head downward.

Atkinson opened a school in Manchester in 1918, transferring it to London in 1936. She sought to train the mind as well as the body and to instill her students with a love of beauty. Again like Ginner, she appears to have become more concerned with dance as a means of achieving physical and spiritual well-being than with dance as a theatrical art.

The Belgian dancer who called herself Akarova was wholeheartedly theatrical [11]—indeed, she was often a one-woman theatre. She was born Marguerite Acarin in 1904 and, as a young woman, studied singing at the Royal Academy of Music in Brussels and dancing with Marthe Roggen, a teacher influenced by Dalcroze. Acarin was so fascinated by some performances that Raymond Duncan gave in Brussels in 1922 that she also attended his lectures and workshops. The two soon became friends. How strange they must have seemed to the solid citizens of Brussels as they strolled together through the streets! Duncan wore his usual ancient Greek outfits. But Acarin, who considered herself a modern liberated woman, clad herself in male attire.

The same year that she encountered Raymond Duncan, Acarin met Marcel Baugniet, a Belgian painter and furniture designer, and she soon realized that both men were in love with her. She married Baugniet in 1923. It was he who invented her stage name. Thanks to the charismatic performances of Anna Pavlova and Diaghilev's Ballets Russes, Russian names were fashionable. (They still are.) So Marguerite Acarin became, simply, Akarova.

She collaborated with Belgian musicians and artists, and in 1937 a studio theatre was built for her in Brussels by Jules-Jean Eggericx, an architect and city planner who was a pioneer in the design of Belgian "garden cities." Akarova occasionally appeared with a partner or small company. But, during the 1920s and 1930s, she was known for her unusual solos. She wished each of her creations to be a total synthesis of the arts. Although, despite her musical training, Akarova never composed accompaniments, she increasingly designed her own costumes and scenery, and in both the productions she devised and those created for her by painters she often interacted with the décor.

In her staging of Debussy's *La Boîte à Joujoux* (1937), the audience beheld a line of toys. One, however, came alive: it was Akarova. On other occasions, she played many characters during the course of a single work, and she devised easily convertible or superimposable costumes to make quick changes possible. Choreographing *Le Sacre du Printemps* in 1935, she divided Igor Stravinsky's score into separate scenes in which she portrayed such key figures in this ritual of human sacrifice as Ancestor, Shepherd, and Chosen Maiden. In her version of Darius Milhaud's *La Création du Monde* (1938) she danced the roles of Man, Woman, and Magician to express her view that creation is a union of natural, artistic, and erotic forces.

The theories of Emile-Jaques Dalcroze continued to be influential. Dalcroze himself remained in Geneva after the war. But Hellerau reopened in 1919 under the direction of Christine Baer-Frissell, who had been an instructor at the prewar school. The new Hellerau was never as important as its predecessor. However, it placed increased emphasis upon dance, and among its important teachers was Valeria Kratina, a dancer and choreographer.[12]

Dissension between staff and management led in 1925 to the founding, under Kratina's direction, of a new school, the Hellerau-Laxenburg School in an old castle in an idyllic 1,700-acre park on the outskirts of Vienna. Kratina passed on the direction of the school in 1930 to Rosalia Chladek, one of her pupils. Because of the pressures of creative and administrative work, Chladek relinquished direction of the school to Ernst Ferrand in 1936, yet remained associated with it as choreographer and teacher. Like the Dresden Hellerau, Hellerau-Laxenburg became a gathering-place for dancers from many nations. At the same time that Hellerau-Laxenburg was training new dancers, former students of the old Hellerau were making names for themselves as choreographers.

Among them was Michio Ito, a Japanese dancer who was born in Tokyo in 1892.[13] His family background reflects the cultural tensions of turn-of-the-century Japan. Whereas his paternal grandfather was a samurai who opposed all contact with the West, his father was an architect and a friend of Frank Lloyd Wright, and his progressive-minded mother was the daughter of a zoologist. At the age of eighteen, Ito decided he wanted to study singing in Europe. But two dance performances changed his life. When he saw Vaslav Nijinsky perform with Diaghilev's Ballets Russes in Paris in 1911, he was so excited that he walked all night in a drenching rain, and when he saw Isadora Duncan a few months later in Berlin, he presented her with a bolt of silk and begged to become her pupil. Tentative plans were made for him to study with her sister, Elizabeth. Instead, in 1912, he discovered the Dalcroze school at Hellerau.

When World War I broke out, Ito went to London, where he made his debut as a dancer in 1915. Like Duncan and St. Denis, he performed in society drawing rooms and became acquainted with people in the arts. His friends included the poets William Butler Yeats and Ezra Pound, both of whom were fascinated by the nonrealistic ritualism of Japanese theatre. Yeats wrote a play in the Noh style, *At the Hawk's Well*, a verse drama about a young man searching for the water of immortality who is bewitched by a hawk while a sacred well overflows with the precious water. At the play's London premiere in 1916, Ito portrayed the hawk. He wore an enormous headdress, painted his face to resemble a mask, and with his arm and torso movements suggested a bird's large spread wings and the hawk's flight through the air.

Ito moved to New York later in 1916. Dancegoers there found him extraordinary in appearance because of the way his luminous eyes stared out of a face framed by long shining black hair.[14] Believing that the upper body was the corporeal medium that made ideas and emotions visible, Ito based his technique upon ten basic arm gestures, which he likened to the twelve notes of the chromatic scale. Like musical notes, these gestures could be almost endlessly combined and varied. Movements for the lower body became of secondary importance. Although such a technique might have bewildered ballet fans used to elaborate footwork, followers of Delsarte would have said that Ito was choreographically emphasizing the body's emotional and intellectual zones.[15]

Ito's solos were short. He called them "dance poems." Audiences familiar with Asian literature might have likened them to Japanese haiku. Most of his dances were conceived without any concern for theatrical conventions of "masculine" or "feminine" movement and could be performed by either a man or a woman. Elizabeth Selden commented, "You can look at the dancer and no longer know whether it is man, woman, child, or angel dancing there."[16]

One possible exception to Ito's sexual neutrality was *Tango* (Albéniz).[17] Wearing tightly fitted black trousers, a short jacket, and a black hat, Ito appeared taut and pantherine. Yet he jokingly called this a "well-behaved tango," for it was essentially a study in restraint: although the person he portrayed seemed always ready to pounce, he never did. The solo conveyed a sense of the intensity of Spanish dancing without containing actual Spanish steps. So, too, in his dances on Asian subjects, Ito, like St. Denis, sought to suggest the essence of a culture, rather than to reproduce aspects of it literally.

Each of Ito's solos emphasized specific movement qualities. *Joy* (Schumann) expressed its emotions with small buoyant leaps. In *The White Peacock* (Griffes), Ito used feathery hand gestures and sweeping winglike motions to suggest a godlike bird. One of Ito's most popular creations was *Pizzicati*, to a pizzicato variation from Delibes's ballet *Sylvia*. The feet never moved in this solo. Instead, to the delicate plucking of the strings, the dancer made sharp, almost violent, arm and torso movements while his shadow loomed behind him on the backdrop.

Occasionally, Ito's solos were as interesting for what they implied as for what they actually depicted. For instance, *Ball* (Chopin) could be viewed simply as a portrait of someone throwing an invisible ball to an unseen player and catching it in return. But the curious urgency of the game made it possible to imagine that the other player was Fate.

Ito went to perform in Los Angeles in 1929; he remained there until 1942. Southern California's large outdoor theatres and arenas (or "bowls," as they came to be called) prompted this erstwhile miniaturist to stage monumentally scaled works. Thus he used 200 dancers at the Rose Bowl in 1929, when he choreographed ensembles to Tchaikovsky's *Andante Cantabile*, Grieg's *Peer Gynt Suite*, Anton Dvořák's *New World Symphony*, and two Chopin waltzes. California expanded Ito's choreographic horizons.

Another major choreographer who emerged from the Dalcroze tradition was Rosalia Chladek, an Austrian dancer born in Brno (which eventually became part of Czechoslovakia) in 1905. A pupil of Valeria Kratina at Hellerau, Chladek followed her teacher to Hellerau-Laxenburg in 1925 and became closely associated with dance activities in the Vienna area. Josephine Schwarz, an American dance teacher who studied at Hellerau-Laxenburg, admiringly recalls, "Chladek was tall, and she walked like a lynx."[18] As a performer, wrote John Martin, who visited Austria in 1932, "She is in many respects a feminine Kreutzberg. She has his type of vigor, his electrical dynamism. . . . Except for the fact that she is unusually tall she would make a superb team-mate for him."[19] (Kreutzberg, who could look tall onstage, was in reality tiny.)

Like Wigman and other choreographers of the time, Chladek was fond of dance suites or cycles of related items. Her *Mythological Suite* contained portraits of Narcissus, Penthesilea, the Pythian oracle, and the Thanatogete (Leader of the Dead). *Marches* offered festive, heroic, barbaric, and funereal marches. *Archangels* depicted Michael the Fighter and Lucifer the Outcast. *From the Life of Maria* (to excerpts from the *Marienleben*, songs written between the fourteenth and seventeenth centuries in honor of the Virgin Mary) showed Mary in the temple, the Annunciation, the Pietà, and Mary's death and Assumption. *Joan of Arc* was divided into two parts, listed in the program as "The Country Girl: Vocation; Visions of Battle; Victory and Defeat" and "The Prisoner: Awareness of the Prison; Visions of the Tribunal and of Mercy."[20]

For *Contrasts*, a group work, Chladek juxtaposed gracious music by Mozart with dissonant music by Sergei Prokofiev. In the same review in which he likened Chladek to Kreutzberg, Martin praised *Contrasts* for its beauty of form and, in the Prokofiev section, for the sense of "impersonal architectonics" created by the way dancers carried sticks and hoops. Martin also admired two sections of *Rhythms*: "Flowing," which consisted of legato movements to a melody for solo oboe, and "Bound," in which, to percussion music, Chladek used a rod to suggest inhibition. Martin noted of "Earth," an episode from another cycle, *The Elements*, that this solo, danced in silence, was "actually built without music and not merely danced without audible accompaniment."[21] This subtle distinction was relevant at that time, when many choreographers were experimenting with unusual accompaniments or with no accompaniment whatsoever.

Dalcroze's ideas continued to be taken seriously in conservatories and dance academies throughout Europe. Eurhythmics even managed to find its way into one of the shrines of ballet tradition when, in 1917, Jacques Rouché, director of the Paris Opéra, introduced eurhythmics classes into the curriculum of the Opéra's ballet school.[22]

Although several of the regular faculty members considered the Dalcrozians to be intruders, the eurhythmics teachers and their pupils were sometimes able to band together as a little troupe to offer productions of their own. Nevertheless, their activities were not considered important, and the classes were gradually abandoned.

Some European modern dancers came from thoroughly miscellaneous backgrounds.

Like Harald Kreutzberg, Alexandre and Clothilde Sakharoff emphasized pantomimic dance. Before their deaths (Alexandre in 1963, Clothilde in 1974), they had traveled widely and were enormously popular. Neither is associated with any specific pedagogical method and both set careful limits to their artistic range. Yet their admirers maintained that they worked exquisitely within them.

Alexandre was born into a bourgeois Russian family in 1886.[23] As a child he loved to paint and to improvise theatrical performances in the family garden. His mother warned him that, if the Gypsies ever spotted him, they would carry him off. He thereupon always left the garden gate open, in the hope that the Gypsies would find it easier to abduct him. At seventeen, he was sent by his father to study law in Paris. At the same time, he studied painting with William Bouguereau.

In Paris, Alexandre was overwhelmed when he saw the great actress Sarah Bernhardt in Edmond Rostand's *L'Aiglon*, her plasticity of gesture amazing him as much as her elocution. Casting aside his law books, he began to study acrobatics. He turned himself into a dancer and in 1910 performed in Paris and Munich, where, in 1913, he met Clothilde von Derp, the daughter of an aristocratic German family. Clothilde, who was born in 1895, was a sickly child who was sent to the ballet school of the Munich Opera in the hope that she would gain strength. She and Alexandre were married in 1919.

They called their art "abstract pantomime" and regarded the body as "a keyboard of the flesh" upon which choreography could play. In their own case, that keyboard could be likened to such a refined instrument as the harpsichord. The Sakharoffs were known for painstakingly detailed choreographic studies in which slow turns of the head or stretchings of the fingers could be of the utmost importance. And their dances featured sumptuous costumes designed by Alexandre.[24]

Some critics charged that such fanciness reeked of preciosity. A Parisian writer for the *American Dancer* who signed herself Nadja scorned them as being "so easy for the public to like—that is all I can say. There are many who surpass her work. . . . He is too effeminate for my taste."[25]

"But what performers they are!" insisted another Parisian writer, Edouard Szamba, in the *Dancing Times.* "Not a button on their costume that is not a work of art in its way. Needlework it may be— psychologically, artistically and choregraphically [sic]; but it reached to a summit of figurative representation that very few dancers otherwise attain." Szamba particularly praised Alexandre's *Pavane Royale,* an evocation of the era of Louis XIV, for having "the great airs of a golden peacock."[26]

Emile Vuillermoz, still another admiring critic, observed that just as the Americans had developed the "moving picture," so the Sakharoffs had invented a form of "moving sculpture." He found them so esthetically and temperamentally united that in their performances they formed "un hermaphrodisme artistique," an artistic hermaphroditism.[27]

Nevertheless, although they invariably closed their programs with a duet and sometimes offered another duet at the midpoint, the Sakharoffs specialized in solos: one of the dancers would perform, then the other, then the first would return for a new solo, and there would be occasional instrumental interludes to help both change costumes or catch their breath.

Possessing refined musical tastes, the Sakharoffs choreographed to Bach, Debussy, Gabriel Fauré, and Emmanuel Chabrier, as well as to some of the charming pieces Fritz Kreisler composed in honor of eighteenth-century composers. They drew their inspirations from periods of history and styles of art, evoking in various works the Middle Ages, the Renaissance, and the Baroque era. *D'Après Goya* was a cycle of solos derived from the Spanish painter Francisco de Goya. *Bourrée Fantasque* paid tribute to the commedia dell'arte. Although they seldom attempted tragic themes, Clothilde performed *Isolde's Death* (to music from Wagner's *Tristan und Isolde*), and several of their works were taken from the Bible. The Sakharoffs' dances resembled jeweled ornaments.

In total contrast, the artists and writers who called themselves Futurists sometimes staged wild, irreverent theatrical events to indicate their impatience with moral and esthetic norms. The dancer Valentine de Saint-Point was one of the few women associated with the Futurist movement,[28] which had been founded in Italy by the polemicist Filippo Marinetti.

The Futurists gloried in speed, energy, dynamism, and modern technology. Their love of sheer power even led some of them to praise violence and war and to ally themselves with fascism. And their adulation of the man of action was implicitly misogynistic. In a manifesto on dance of 1917, Marinetti declared he longed for a choreographic form that would be "Inharmonious—Ungraceful—Asymmetrical—Dynamic" and proposed three subjects for choreographers: *Dance of the Autocar, Dance of the Machine Gun,* and *Dance of Shrapnel.*[29]

Little is known about Saint-Point or her background, although she was variously referred to as the grandniece (or the great-grandniece) of the poet Alphonse Lamartine and the granddaughter of the poet and novelist Victor Hugo; she herself also published poetry and worked as a painter. Saint-Point cultivated an aura of mystery. For interviews, she clad herself in rich fabrics and jewels and reclined on a couch while a pet marmoset frisked at her feet. During an American visit in 1917, she said that war had destroyed art in France and that it was time for New York to become a great international art center. With Pierre Monteux as her conductor, she gave a program at the Metropolitan Opera House, 3 April 1917, which included dances of love, irony, pantheism, and war bearing such titles as *The Puppet and Death, Vegetation Fantasy, Hymn to the Sun, The Poppies of Blood,* and *The War.* A brief comment in the *New York Times* praised the "beautiful colored light effects" and Saint-Point's "shining gold armor" in the war dances, but also noted that this was a dance recital for "an invited but not wholly comprehending audience."[30]

Saint-Point called her choreography *métachorie* and wished it to be a union of dancing, music, architecture, sculpture, poetry, and painting. Although she often wore exotic costumes akin to those favored by Ruth St. Denis, Saint-Point claimed to favor intellectualism over sensualism. She veiled her face to create an effect of depersonalization, and she was fascinated by geometrical forms: for her, love was concave, hate convex, and desire oblong.

Unlike her male Futurist colleagues, who were contemptuous of women, Saint-Point insisted that the personalities of all true heroes possess both masculine and feminine components. However, convinced that she lived in a time of excessive femininity, she thought the Futurists were right to glorify virility, and she urged women to become strong and forceful.

If Saint-Point now seems an eccentric figure, she remains of interest because of the way she appears to have combined some of the exoticism and idealistic striving of prewar dance with the harsher forms of much postwar art. Her views of men and women constitute her idiosyncratic response to the battles for independence that women were waging in her time.

Gertrud Bodenwieser quietly struggled to achieve her own independence.[31] The daughter of a cultivated Viennese stockbroker, Bodenwieser, who was born in 1890, received ballet lessons as a child. But when she sought to become a professional dancer, she was forced to change her name from Bondi (her real surname) to Bodenwieser to placate members of her family who considered a stage career insufficiently respectable. She gave her first solo recital in 1919, at the age of twenty-nine, and soon acquired a reputation as a teacher as well as a dancer.

Bodenwieser's company toured extensively and on its visit to London in 1929 was twice discussed by the *Dancing Times* in "The Sitter Out" (a column usually written by the magazine's editor, Philip J. S. Richardson). In the June issue, Bodenwieser technique was said "to occupy a position midway between that of the classical ballet and the extremely modern ... Wigman school." The July issue found that she appealed to the often conservative British taste because she was "less iconoclastic and therefore more understandable" than Wigman.[32]

Bodenwieser's Viennese classes began with basic barre exercises designed to stretch and flex the muscles. Keith Bain, one of her later Australian pupils, recalls that she prized fluidity and used to speak of "breathing wrists." The barre work, however, was only a preliminary to the essential material of the class. Each lesson was built around an idea or image. All movements performed were supposed to express this theme, and classes ended with improvisations. Bodenwieser never gave a totally technique-oriented class.[33]

Some of Bodenwieser's dances explored various aspects of a single theme. *The Great Hours* was devoted to the creative hour, the hour of expectation, and the hour of fulfillment. In *Rhythms of the Subconscious*, an introduction called "Dusk Descending" was followed by images of desire, lust, and anxiety, and the finale was "Ascent into Clarity." Other dances—among them *Swinging Bells*, *Exchange of Vibrations*, and *Angular Play of Lines*—were based on movement qualities. Bodenwieser occasionally ventured into social criticism. Her *Cart Drawn by Man* paid tribute to oppressed laborers. And when she choreographed *Masks of Lucifer* in 1936, she envisioned a world plagued by intrigue, terror, and hate.

Bodenwieser also staged works that existed primarily to entertain. Her interpretations of Viennese waltzes and Austrian peasant dances were extremely popular. In choosing dancers for her company she favored women with long hair, and she incorporated the motions of sweeping hair into her choreography to make some of her dances especially attractive.

However, she remains best known for a somber piece: *The Demon Machine*, choreographed in 1923 to music by L. H. Mayer. Painters, writers, and choreographers of the 1920s and 1930s were simultaneously attracted to and repelled by machines.[34] Artists in the struggling Soviet Union often extolled them as symbols of progress, whereas intellectuals in the highly developed countries of Western Europe and North America had ambiguous responses to the machine age. The bold renderings of industrial scenes by Charles Sheeler and Charles Demuth (American painters who were accurately labeled "Precisionists" by critics) celebrated the power of industry and hinted at the possibility of a technological utopia. Mixed feelings were expressed in other works. Karel Čapek's *R.U.R.*, a play of 1920, introduced the word "robot" into the languages of the world. *The Adding Machine*, Elmer Rice's play of 1923, called attention to the dehumanization of modern urban life.

There were many dances, or *ballets mécaniques*, on industrial themes. The movements of machines fascinated choreographers and prompted them to create dances notable for their percussive attack. But, like painters and writers, choreographers also had comments to make. Bodenwieser showed human harmony and then the perils of mechanization in *The Demon Machine*. By having dancers move like pistons and turn like monstrous wheels, she showed industrialism run amok so that the machine was now the master—and not the servant—of humanity. *The Demon Machine* remained a staple of her company's repertoire for three decades.

Gertrud Kraus also began in Vienna, where she was born in 1901. A music student who planned to become a concert pianist, she worked as an accompanist for Ellinor Tordis, a modern dance teacher who encouraged students to choreograph and to present pieces during class.[35] One day, when Tordis asked if anyone had a dance to show, Kraus rose from the piano bench, walked to the center of the studio in her street attire, and, without ever having had a dance lesson, performed her first solo.

The response was a universal and astonished silence. Crestfallen and fearing she had made a fool of herself, Kraus picked up her music and headed for the door. "Wait!" Tordis shouted, having gathered her wits about her. "What you did was most interesting. I want to discuss it."

But Kraus replied, "Sorry, the silence was too long." Nevertheless, she refused to be discouraged and enrolled as a dance student of another teacher: Gertrud Bodenwieser.[36]

Kraus began to choreograph. She staged the dances for a production of Nikolaus Lenau's drama *Faust* in 1926 and created solos and group works of her own. Some of her pieces were grotesque, even macabre. In *Guignol*, a puppet came to life, jerking about as if pulled by invisible strings. *The Strange Guest* was a portrait of a demonic Paganini-like violinist. *Tired Death* showed Death wearied by four years of world war, yet still crouching, waiting for victims.

One of Kraus's most ambitious productions was *The City Waits* (1933). Inspired by Maxim Gorki's "Song of the City," it concerned a village youth (played by Kraus) who comes to a large city where he encounters the idle rich as well as homeless beggars and oppressed workers. The bodies of the dancers became the city, their arm positions suggesting steeples and roofs. *The City Waits* included Kraus's own protest against the "demon machine," a scene in which dancers imitated pistons and cogwheels. But the work ended affirmatively, to suggest that progress remained possible.

Jewish themes were present in Kraus's choreography from the outset. Some of the movements in *Songs of the Ghetto* were inspired by Hasidic dances. Several works—including *Miriam* and *Hagar in the Desert*—derived from the Bible, and Kraus portrayed a delicate youth in *The Jewish Boy*.

Vienna was a politically divided city in the 1920s, when liberals found themselves pitted against reactionary and anti-Semitic factions. Disturbed by such fascist tendencies, Kraus became a political activist who staged programs for Socialist and Zionist organizations.

Jean Weidt, a militantly political German dancer born in Hamburg in 1904, studied with Sigurd Leeder, a dancer and teacher who had worked with Laban and who became closely associated with the German choreographer Kurt Jooss. Weidt was known as "the Red dancer" and sought to adapt *Ausdruckstanz* and elements of ballet technique into vehicles for the presentation of revolutionary social content.[37]

Weidt possessed firsthand knowledge of social hardships. He came from a working-class family: his father drank away whatever money he earned; his mother did odd jobs. Weidt organized a dance group and appeared with it at the Dancers' Congress in Essen in 1928. The next year, he joined the Communist Party.

"I wanted to dance the themes of the working class, and I wanted to dance for the working class," he declared.[38] His *Lament for a Soldier* expressed antimilitarist sentiments with abrupt broken movements. *Dance with the Red Flag* was a revolutionary exhortation. *Old People's Dance* concerned the plight of the elderly. Weidt remained true to his political convictions all his life.

Although modern dance flourished in Central Europe, it failed to establish itself in ballet-loving Paris, where the Dalcrozians at the Paris Opéra were considered minor figures at best. Nevertheless, French modern dancers did struggle for recognition. Some were known primarily as teachers.

The most promising French modern dancer of the time was Georges Pomiès, who began his career as a music-hall singer before turning to dance. Although largely self-taught, he acquired a remarkable technique and made his debut as a modern dancer at the age of twenty-six in 1928. His works—including a tragic dance to Beethoven's "Moonlight Sonata"—were considered austerely eloquent. He died suddenly in 1933.[39]

Just as such earlier figures as Delsarte and Rudolf Steiner found spiritual as well as esthetic values in movement, so some thinkers of the 1920s also viewed movement philosophically or metaphysically.

Among them was George Ivanovitch Gurdjieff, a mystic born in the Caucasus sometime in the 1870s.[40] Gurdjieff, who traveled widely, settled in 1915 on an estate near Paris. Believing that every movement indicated a change in the mind or nervous system and that movements could significantly alter thought or perception, he developed a system of sacred gymnastic exercises. Although his students offered performances in Paris and New York in 1923 and 1924, his movements were not designed to entertain, but to contribute to the spiritual development of the performer. Convinced that people fall too easily into mental and physical habits, Gurdjieff invented sequences that were so deliberately strange, awkward, and angular that anyone attempting them had to be mentally as well as physically alert.

Although Gurdjieff himself gave up interest in "the movements" after he was injured in an automobile accident in 1924, his exercises continue to be taught by his disciples, and his ideas have influenced several writers and artists. Lincoln Kirstein, the co-founder (with George Balanchine) of the New York City Ballet, has frequently acknowledged his indebtedness to the mystic's teachings; in his book *Nijinsky Dancing*, he states, "As in everything I do, whatever is valid springs from the person and ideas of G. I. Gurdjieff."[41]

Before Olgivanna Milanov became the third wife of the architect Frank Lloyd Wright in 1928, she had lived on Gurdjieff's French estate and had taught and performed his movements. She retained an interest in them. When the Wright-designed Unitarian Church of Madison, Wisconsin, was completed in 1951, the opening week's festivities included a program of "Gurdjieff Movement" by members of Wright's Taliesin Fellowship under Olgivanna's direction.[42]

For all modern dance's prizing of individuality, it was still held that students should be masters of some basic technique that would permit them to dance in many styles. But what was this technique to be? As the British critic Fernau Hall remarked, it was the teacher's aim "to train the pupil in a variety of different qualities, tempi and rhythms of movement, so that he could create a variety of dances for himself and tackle any movement a choreographer might require of him." But, in actual fact, said Hall, "the 'freedom' of the free dancer proved to be illusory, for the vocabulary of movement available to him—consisting as it did of the mannerisms of his teacher—was extremely limited."[43] All too often, the pupils of a school looked like imitations of that school's guiding spirit.

Some teachers, including Mary Wigman, believed that it was possible to base a neutral, all-purpose technique upon gymnastics. This *Tanzgymnastik* sought to train a body to move in whatever way a specific choreographer demanded. But there were students and teachers who charged that *Tanzgymnastik* was not technically comprehensive enough to produce fully trained bodies.[44]

Conservative ballet lovers were quick to pounce upon this weakness of modern dance training. Arnold L. Haskell, the British critic who popularized the word "balletomania" and who evinced little sympathy for modern dance, thundered his contention that ballet dancers can do everything that modern dancers can do, whereas these other schools are so limited in range that they cannot depart from one mood. . . .

I am always open to conviction, but at the present moment I can see neither entertainment nor art in such dancing, and this being the case it seems safe to prophesy for it an early demise.[45]

Haskell's prediction of modern dance's imminent demise never came true. Even so, his remarks on technique may have rankled, for they contained a grain of truth.

To some modern dancers, ballet was anathema. But the less doctrinaire ones realized that ballet did not have to be vacuous. Diaghilev's experiments attested to that. Many modern dancers had received ballet training; they may have ultimately rejected ballet, yet they had subjected themselves to its discipline.

Choreographers and teachers began to wonder if it might be possible to harmonize ballet with modern dance. For instance, Lizzie Maudrik was a Berlin ballet teacher who was also interested in Laban's theories; Alexander von Swaine was a German ballet-trained modern dancer who appeared in productions by Rosalia Chladek as well as in his own compositions; and Max Terpis tried to combine some of the new modern ideas with traditional classical forms.[46]

Aurel Milloss (who was also known as Aurel von Milloss and Aurelio M. Milloss) was born in 1906 in a small town that was then in Hungary but became part of Yugoslavia.[47] His father was a chemist; his mother, a concert pianist, died a year after his birth. Milloss was given music lessons, but when he saw Vaslav Nijinsky dance *Le Spectre de la Rose* during a performance by Diaghilev's Ballets Russes during the winter of 1912–1913, he vowed to become a dancer.

Milloss began his training with ballet lessons. However, when he was struck by the choreographic daring of Laban's company, which he saw in 1924, he realized that another valid way of dancing existed. In 1925, he went to Paris to study with the legendary ballet teacher Olga Preobrajenska. That same year, he journeyed to Berlin to study with Laban, who made him acutely aware of the importance of weight, space, and time.

Nevertheless, Milloss still desired to increase his knowledge of ballet. Fearing that Laban might be horrified at the notion, he told him that he wished to study with Italian ballet master Enrico Cecchetti. Instead of disapproving, Laban—whose tastes were surprisingly broad—gave Milloss his blessing because, he said, Cecchetti was the best.

Cecchetti was famous for having developed a meticulously ordered series of daily classroom exercises. But because he was not verbally articulate, some students found him pedantic. Milloss, in contrast, was inspired by Cecchetti's classes because Laban had taught him how to analyze movement.

Milloss gave his first program of his own choreography in Berlin in 1928 before an audience that included Wassily Kandinsky, Oskar Schlemmer, and Max Terpis. Until his death in 1988, he worked primarily with ballet companies—first in Germany and Hungary, then in Italy through World War II, and after the war in France, Germany, Austria, and Brazil. His creations—of which *The Miraculous Mandarin, Estro Arguto,* and *Le Portrait de Don Quichotte* are among the best known—were based on classical technique, yet they possessed a gestural angularity that suggested the influence of Expressionism, and their thematic seriousness (which led critics to pronounce the weakest of them excessively cerebral) was surely a legacy of Milloss's years with Laban.

Yvonne Georgi also sought to bridge the gap between ballet and modern dance. Her roots were in the modern idiom. Born in 1903, the daughter of a French-Arabian mother and a German father, she was a musical prodigy who originally hoped to be a concert pianist. But a growing interest in dance led her to study at Hellerau and then with Wigman, with whose company she performed. She also toured as the partner of Kreutzberg. She was a fiery dancer, and her *Kassandra* was a solo of mounting frenzy. Describing Georgi in one of her New York recitals with Kreutzberg in 1929, Mary F. Watkins wrote in the *New York Herald Tribune,* "Hers is a dynamic style of almost fierce intentness, a brusque, whole-hearted, downright method, associated with a personality which is ardent and frank. There is a ruthless, steely suggestion in some of her work of the machine, of the relentlessly modern pace and tempo." [48]

Georgi was not content with being a recitalist. During her years with Kreutzberg, she also created ensemble compositions for companies in Germany and Holland. Some of her early productions bore such titles as *The Mechanical House* and *Baby in der Bar,* and she did her own versions of such Stravinsky ballets as *Pulcinella* and *Petrouchka* (with Kreutzberg in the title role).

Georgi called for a greater theatricalization of modern dance, which she warned should not grow unduly spartan. In 1928 she said, "Those who create dances for the theatre must have the ability, not only to involve themselves and their own feelings in the dance, but to arrive at a *Gesamtkunstwerk* by giving form and shape to their surroundings (stage-space, costumes, lighting, décor, movement) and their own expression."[49] This concern for theatricality increasingly led her to investigate the resources of ballet, and after World War II she worked primarily with ballet companies until her death in 1975.

Whether or not they employed actual ballet steps, some Central European modern dancers demonstrated that they could rival ballet choreographers in the creation of large-scale productions. At the same time, however, they produced the choreographic equivalents of chamber music with their solos and duets. The same tendencies are also observable in the development of American modern dance.

DENISHAWN

Ruth St. Denis • *Ted Shawn* • *Ronny Johansson* •
Margarethe Wallmann • *Doris Humphrey*

DENISHAWN WAS AMERICA'S FIRST GREAT MODERN DANCE center. It must have impressed students by its very appearance. Ruth St. Denis and Ted Shawn established their Los Angeles school in a Spanish-style stucco house on a hilltop estate. Its rooms had casement windows, and their blue-green curtains rustled in the California breezes. Classes were sometimes held outdoors on the terrace. Students ate box lunches under the pepper trees, and pet dogs and cats—and, at one time, a majestic peacock—roamed the premises.

Denishawn tried to be an inspiring place. "We wanted the school to be a stream for ideas," St. Denis said.[1] In addition to dance classes, the curriculum included lectures on dance history, art, music, and philosophy. Students also learned about lighting and makeup. There were even sessions devoted to the art of posing for photographs, something which both St. Denis and Shawn could do superlatively well.

The basic Denishawn class began with stretching exercises at the barre, followed by exercises in the center of the studio. The technical base of most of this material was ballet, but without pointe work, although elements of non-Western techniques were often included. Center exercises ended with "Arms and Body": sequences in which loose swings of the arms gradually intensified until the entire upper torso was involved in bendings, circlings, and swoopings. Then came across-the-floor exercises emphasizing turns and leaps. At the end of each class, students learned an actual dance, which could be Greek, Spanish, Gypsy, or Oriental in style. These practice pieces served to remind students that dance was a theatrical art; some were so attractive that they were even presented on Denishawn programs.[2]

St. Denis and Shawn were as much concerned with practicalities as with ideals. They made sure their pupils were capable of performing in movies and musical comedies as well as in "art" dances. They prepared and sold, through mail order, choreographic notes for dances, along with their musical scores and player-piano rolls. Such commercial schemes brought in needed cash; the popularity of these mail-order ventures also insured that, in a nation in which standards of dance training varied alarmingly, at least some teachers were coaching students in competently choreographed dances.

Denishawn exposed its students to many styles. Justifiably proud of their own achievements, St. Denis and Shawn did not always look approvingly upon some of the works they saw by other dancers. Nevertheless, they were not rigid: they introduced students to eurhythmics and occasionally imported guest teachers of European modern dance, among them Ronny Johansson and Margarethe Wallmann.

Johansson was an elfin Swedish dancer, originally trained in ballet, who began making American appearances in 1925. For St. Denis, seeing Johansson dance was "love at first sight," for Johansson possessed "a splendid trained body, a piquant face, a sensitive mind and a delicious humor."[3]

Margarethe Wallmann (whose first name was at various times spelled Margarete and Margarita) was an Austrian dancer, trained in both ballet and modern dance, who directed the Berlin branch of the Wigman School. Like Yvonne Georgi, she advocated an unabashedly theatrical dance and did not hesitate to use ballet technique. During World War II, she directed the large ballet company attached to the Teatro Colón, the opera house of Buenos Aires. After the war, she returned to Europe and increasingly devoted herself to staging operas.

Denishawn's founders dominated their school. Each was quite different in manner. Shawn—called Papa by generations of dancers—openly shared his affection for students and was genuinely paternal, while St. Denis, known as Miss Ruth, was more awesome. Denishawn students revered both. One dancer, Florence Andrews, even adopted Florence O'Denishawn as her stage name.

Both St. Denis and Shawn taught and choreographed. But whereas St. Denis could be pedagogically vague at times, Shawn was well organized. St. Denis writes in her autobiography: "The outline and organization of the Denishawn School was Ted's. My part was to supply, in the unfolding years, the color of the Orient, certain concepts of music visualization . . . and such spiritual inspiration and teaching as could be given within the close and harried activities of the school of the dance." Using less exalted language, she once admitted her faults in structuring classes. Then she added, "But I can inspire like hell."[4] Shawn, in contrast, was articulate and systematic. However, possibly because St. Denis remained so fascinatingly aloof, many former Denishawn students speak of Shawn with respect, but grow almost rapturous at the mention of St. Denis.

One reason why Denishawn thrived was its aura of respectability. Its founders were married and preached spiritual values. However, Denishawn's propriety was something of a veneer. Its founders were complex people, and their marriage foundered when St. Denis and Shawn discovered that they were both in love with the same man.[5] Yet the general public knew little of their private lives, and the very fact that they were married helped make Denishawn a well-regarded institution. During the 1920s, branch Denishawn schools were established throughout the country; a New York Denishawn opened in 1924, and the entire organization moved its headquarters there in 1929.

No one could have accused Denishawn of choreographic monotony. St. Denis and Shawn created an astonishing variety of dances and placed great emphasis upon stage spectacle.[6] In an early group venture, the entire Denishawn School participated in *A Dance Pageant of Egypt, Greece, and India,* presented in 1916 at the open-air Greek Theatre in Berkeley, California. The production included Shawn's *Pyrrhic Dance,* the first of his many all-male compositions, and *Tillers of the Soil,* a poignant duet in which St. Denis and Shawn depicted the labors of an Egyptian peasant couple.

Denishawn also had its experimental side. Shawn's *Death of Adonis (Adagio Pathétique,* 1924) was based upon a Greek myth about a handsome youth who is wounded while hunting. Formally, this sculptural piece in which poses slowly melted into one another may have recalled some of the works of Genevieve Stebbins, but it was daring because of its almost total nudity. Yet, while physically striking, the dance never seemed salacious.

Both St. Denis and Shawn experimented with what they called music visualizations: plotless dances that tried to express the structure of musical compositions in choreographic terms. St. Denis, assisted by a musically sensitive student, Doris Humphrey, was the first to attempt this sort of dance. Later, Shawn contributed music visualizations of his own and continued to choreograph them after St. Denis lost interest in the form. The choreographers claimed that they were not trying to impose any literal story or emotional situation upon the music; their concerns, they said, were entirely structural. Thus they made groups of dancers represent each section of the orchestra when they choreographed to symphonic scores; in their choreography to Bach two-part inventions, one group would correspond to the first musical "voice," and another to the second. Nevertheless, despite their stated reluctance to "interpret," St. Denis and Shawn did convey changing moods; Shawn even professed to find specifically masculine and feminine qualities in certain pieces of music.[7]

One music visualization that is still performed by modern dance groups is *Soaring*, a dance by St. Denis and Humphrey to Schumann's "Aufschwung" that was first presented in 1920. Although several variant versions of the choreography have survived, all involve a central soloist, four women, and a large billowing square of silk that constantly changes shape as it is waved and rippled. If the use of the silk suggests the influence of Loïe Fuller, *Soaring* possesses its own endearing lyricism and joyousness.

Denishawn's tours could offer everything from serious concert programs to light entertainment. In arranging them, Shawn proved a remarkable impresario. During the 1924–1925 season, Denishawn was booked for twenty-eight weeks—an unheard-of amount for a dance group at the time. Later in 1925, Denishawn embarked upon a twenty-month tour of the Orient, a journey that all who took part remembered with awe.

Despite the rigors of travel, which can cause some companies to pare down their repertoires, Denishawn prepared four different programs for Asia. A listing of the contents of one program suggests Denishawn's diversity: *Second Arabesque* (a trio in Grecian style), *Adagio Pathétique* (Shawn's *Adonis* solo), *Hoop Dance* (a solo performed by Doris Humphrey with a large hoop), *Album Leaf and Prelude* (a duet), *De Lachau Waltz* (a dance with a scarf for Humphrey and four women), *Brahms Waltz and Liebestraum* (a group work inspired by Botticelli's *La Primavera*), *Cuadro Flamenco* (Spanish dances), *Japanese Flower Arrangement* (a solo in which St. Denis portrayed a geisha), *Garland Plastique* (a piece for five women with long garlands of flowers), *Invocation to the Thunderbird* (an American Indian solo for Shawn), *Pasquinade* (a solo for Humphrey as a Creole belle), *The Crapshooter* (an Americana solo for Charles Weidman),

Around the Hall in Texas (a depiction of a cowboy dance hall), *Gringo Tango* (a cowboy version of a tango), *The Legend of Pelée* (in which St. Denis used an enormous scarf to transform herself into an active volcano), *Boston Fancy: 1854* (a stylized square dance), and *Egyptian Ballet* (a suite with episodes concerning peasants, gods, and religious ideas of rebirth).[8]

Despite Shawn's entrepreneurial skills, bookings were not always easy to find. Yet Denishawn had to keep touring in order to pay its dancers professional wages; tours also helped support the Denishawn School. During the 1927–1929 season, St. Denis and Shawn even headed a group of dancers in the touring *Ziegfeld Follies.*

Increasingly, the charge began to be raised that Denishawn promoted a glib eclecticism. Looking back on her Denishawn days, Doris Humphrey once said, "I knew how everyone moved but I didn't know how *I* moved. They [St. Denis and Shawn] thought all dance was one. But I and others wanted to know how it was to dance as an American."[9] Humphrey said this in 1956—decades after her experiences with Denishawn and decades after artistic trailblazers had developed an interest in serious dance in America. Humphrey was one of those trailblazers. So, too, in their ways, were St. Denis and Shawn.

Shawn himself described what the old tours were like:

> The general public didn't know what to make of us. We were a "road company" obviously, but nobody sang, nobody spoke lines. Those people accustomed to the stereotyped entertainment of melodrama and comedy were disappointed by our numbers designed for neither the sob nor the guffaw. Bigtime-Charlies who misinterpreted the pictures of our advance posters booed when they realized we weren't putting on a hootchy-kootchy Little Egypt sort of show. The front-row boys paid to see legs in action not legends unfold.
>
> Only a few informed people out front knew what to expect of us, how to look at a dance performance.[10]

Ruth St. Denis once said in class, "One should *think* of dance as an art although one may have to *do* it as a business."[11] By skillfully balancing art with business, Denishawn helped the "few informed people" swell into a multitude. Denishawn was a strong organization: strong enough to make its presence known and felt—and strong enough to be a force against which a new generation would rebel.

MERICAN FERMENT

*Eugene von Grona • Benjamin Zemach • Hans Wiener
(Jan Veen) • The Marmeins • Elsa Findlay • Edwin
Strawbridge • Edith Segal • Sara Mildred Strauss •
Jacques Cartier • Angna Enters • The Lewisohns •
Bird Larson • William Norman Guthrie • Margaret
H'Doubler • Nellie C. Cornish • Lucile Marsh •
Mary F. Watkins • John Martin*

NEW YORK CITY WAS EXCITING IN THE 1920S. ITS SKYLINE was known throughout the world, and for some people New York's skyscrapers symbolized twentieth-century energy and ambition. The city never seemed to sleep, nor did it ever seem to grow dark, for at night the major thoroughfares were illuminated by street lamps and the giant flashing advertising signs that caused Broadway to be nick-named "The Great White Way."

Dance developed rapidly. Theatre and jazz flourished. So did crime. During Prohibition, legislation made it illegal to purchase alcoholic beverages. As a result, Prohibition spawned undercover bars known as "speakeasies"; running these clubs and controlling the trade of "bootleg" liquor led to gangsterism.

No wonder, then, that Margaret Einert, a British dance teacher who frequently visited America, could regard New York with mixed feelings. She wrote in 1929 that

> the cultural trend seems to be toward life in the raw, in varying de-grees. One cannot exactly "dance" prize-fighters, detectives and gang-sters, but the same robustness of spirit pervades the most modern of the productions.
>
> There is an American word which seems to have grown in impor-tance each summer recently and, like the word "pep," however much one may dislike it, there come occasions when no English word can substitute [for] it: I refer to the term "hard-boiled."[1]

That same year, Ruth St. Denis declared that, because of increased public interest in dance, "the dance recitals of New York are rivaling musicals—we have at least one every week throughout the year. The dance is now definitely coming into its own!"[2] New York dancers were eager to perform. Unfortunately, they lacked space in which to do so. Not all theatres were suitable for dance. Of those that were, many regularly housed plays or musicals. New York dance events therefore tended to occur on Sunday, the legitimate theatre's traditional "dark night."

That night was "dark" not just to give actors a rest: a city law forbade all theatrical entertainments on Sunday. However, because concerts and charity benefits were not illegal, dancers found ways of getting around the law. Some billed their programs as "sacred concerts"; others donated ten percent of their box office earnings to charity.

Occasionally, dance programs were stopped. In 1930, Mary Wigman was brought before a court on the charge of dancing on Sunday. When the attorney for her and her impresario, Sol Hurok, argued that "Miss Wigman was just making motions," the judge—possibly relieved that he could find a way out of convicting one of the world's most celebrated performers—ruled that "making motions" did not constitute dancing and was therefore not in violation of the Sabbath code.[3] Eventually, as a result of sustained protests, the Sunday law was repealed in 1932.

Later critics and historians have wondered how much influence European modern dance had on American dance of the 1920s and early 1930s. "Very little" is the answer many proud American dance lovers give. John Martin has argued that the American dancers' "own prime necessity, as they were well aware, was to resist all influences from without and to find for themselves the principles that underlay the dance."[4] But Martin wrote that in 1939, the year that Hitler and his Nazi dictatorship plunged the world into war. By then, Americans were understandably loath to admit that anything about their dance could have been influenced by Germany. And American dancers were undeniably eager to travel their own creative paths.

Yet even as they did so, they may have glanced around them.[5] Because European dancers made their most radical post–World War I experiments earlier than the Americans did, reports of their efforts may have indirectly inspired the Americans to venture beyond Duncanism and Denishawn. During the 1920s and 1930s, *Dance* and

American Dancer occasionally printed articles about European dance, as did the widely read British publication *Dancing Times.* What was happening on one continent was also being imported to the other. Louis Horst, musical director first for Denishawn and later for Martha Graham and a host of other American modernists, studied in Vienna in 1925. Ronny Johansson, Harald Kreutzberg, Yvonne Georgi, and Mary Wigman performed in America, as did lesser-known European dancers. Among them was Eugene von Grona (who also billed himself as Eugene van Grona and simply as Von Grona), a German student of Wigman and Jutta Klamt (a teacher who tried to blend dance and gymnastics). Von Grona began performing in New York in 1926, appearing both in modern dance concerts and on the programs of such variety theatres as the Radio City Music Hall. Although the *New York Times* found him "more spectacular than substantial," he offered several works that were determinedly experimental. *Syncopation,* a jazz dance, was lighted so that the performers cast triple shadows. *The Spirit of Labor,* which had a factory setting, concerned the human spirit caught by the machine. The choreography emphasized hammering gestures, and the accompaniment consisted of thudding noises produced by connecting a microphone to the theatre's power plant.[6]

Although the Russian-born Benjamin Zemach studied ballet and Dalcroze eurhythmics as well as a form of dramatic dancing taught by Inna Tchernezkaia, a pupil of the Sakharoffs, his first love was theatre.[7] Between 1917 and 1924, he studied in Moscow with such innovative stage directors as Konstantin Stanislavsky, Yevgeny Vakhtangov, and Vsevolod Meyerhold. He became a member of the Habima Theatre, a Moscow Hebrew theatre; when that group experienced internal dissension during an American tour in 1927, Zemach chose to remain in New York.

As Zemach's interest in dance increased, he came to specialize in works on Jewish themes. *Ruth* retold the biblical story in flowing movements. *Farewell to Queen Sabbath* was based on Jewish rituals of welcoming and bidding farewell to the Sabbath, envisioned as a queen bringing peace, harmony, and rest. The dancers, who were dressed in long black kaftans, represented a community of Orthodox Jews, and the choreography emphasized rhythmic beating movements and increasingly ecstatic swayings.

The Viennese-born Hans Wiener was a descendant of five generations of physicians.[8] He, too, planned to become a doctor even though, as a boy, he had studied dance. But dance eventually claimed him. He received a scholarship to the Wigman School in Dresden, appeared with Yvonne Georgi's group, and also studied with Kurt Jooss and Rudolf Laban.

He made his New York debut in 1928 and remained in America. The group of students with whom he sometimes appeared was billed as a "motion choir," and the titles of certain of his works of the 1920s suggest both the analytical and the Expressionist tendencies of Central European dance: *Space Destruction*, *Tension and Swing*, *Witch Dance*, and *Cymbal Dance* (which was accompanied only by tomtom and cymbals). He was also capable of humor, and in his comic *Wedding Day—Burlesque* he costumed half of his body as a bride and the other half as a groom. Settling in Boston, Wiener became one of that city's leading dance teachers; as a protest against the Nazis, he changed his name to the less German-sounding Jan Veen.

American choreographers began to express the hectic pace of twentieth-century life—often in what may now seem self-consciously "modernistic" ways. In her 1929 New York reports for the *Dancing Times*, Margaret Einert mentions a dance in which three sisters—Miriam, Phyllis, and Irene Marmein—formed a grouping that resembled an Art Deco skyscraper. Einert also described *Men and Machines*, choreographed by Elsa Findlay, a eurhythmics teacher:

> The dancers at the back wave their arms and run up and down to the rapid beating of a drum, ever getting faster and faster, typifying the rhythm of machinery. The dancers in front circle to a slower musical accompaniment typifying the human rhythm. The latter cannot keep pace with the former and fall, apparently conquered.
>
> In the end, however, the human intellect prevails, and the machines collapse.

Appropriately, Einert titled one of her reports "Exit Romanticism."[9]

The ballet-trained Edwin Strawbridge found himself drawn to modern dance. He performed in 1929 with an all-male group (a rarity at that time) and five years later created his own "machine dance" by choreographing Prokofiev's *Le Pas d'Acier*.[10] Sponsored by the League of Composers and conducted by Leopold Stokowski, *Le Pas d'Acier* had a complicated scenario involving the problems of mechanization.

Edith Segal injected leftist politics into "machine" choreography. For a Lenin Memorial Meeting in Madison Square Garden in 1927, she offered *The Belt Goes Red*, in which dancers representing an assembly-line belt produced a bolt of bright red material, thereby indicating that these machines were now working to achieve Socialist ideals.[11]

Sara Mildred Strauss came to be known as "silent Sara." Beginning in 1928, she presented entire evenings of dance without musical accompaniment. Many audiences found these silent evenings difficult to watch. Reviewing a Strauss performance in 1928, M. E. Smith snapped in the *American Dancer*, "The idea of a silent recital does not appeal greatly to the New York audiences and therefore Sara does not come in for the serious attention of dance lovers." However, Richard L. Stokes, who covered the same concert for the *Evening World*, found the silent program a revelation: "Novel and striking was the proof that the eye has a feeling for rhythm as well as the ear."[12] In 1933, Strauss left the modern dance field to organize and train groups of women to perform — to music — in revues and other theatrical productions.

Jacques Cartier created his own accompaniment as he moved in *Congo Voodoo Dance*, a solo of 1927 in which he beat out rhythms with his feet while dancing on a huge rhinoceros-hide drum. Cartier performed versions of this piece both on the concert stage and in revues. The son of an American diplomat, Cartier lived in India and South Africa when he was young and was sent to a military school in Tennessee and from there to Vanderbilt University. Dissatisfied with formal education, he ran off to New York and found work in Broadway shows.

An eclectic, Cartier offered evenings of American Indian dances, as well as works on religious themes. He also choreographed character sketches, and for much of his career he specialized in productions that combined dance and mime with the spoken word.[13]

Many performers of the 1920s and 1930s fit no simple categories. One such artist was Angna Enters, who came to New York from Milwaukee in 1919 to study at the Art Students League. It is now believed that she was about eighteen at the time, although she usually gave 1907 as the year of her birth.[14] She found work as a freelance illustrator. But seeing Michio Ito led her to study dance with him, and she became his partner in 1921.

Enters presented her first complete choreographic program in 1926. She went on to create more than 250 solos. Most were character sketches, some of them gently serious. Thus *Moyen Age* depicted a figure on a medieval stained-glass window. Other solos were comic, among them *Oh, the Pain of It!*—a spoof of Wigman's angularities—and *Entr'acte*, which showed a flapper defying etiquette by smoking in public.

Sometimes, Enters's comedies left a bitter satiric aftertaste. In *Aphrodisiac—Green Hour*, she played a weary streetwalker out of Henri de Toulouse-Lautrec drinking absinthe in a Parisian cafe. She portrayed two women in *Time on My Hands*: a bored rich woman who fills her days with beauty treatments, reducing exercises, and cigarette smoking and an impoverished seamstress. *Feline*, which was Spanish in style, used the silhouette of a black Spanish gown and mantilla to suggest a cat's ears and torso; making her hands curl like paws and suddenly strike outward like claws, Enters evoked some of the less attractive feline aspects of a woman's personality. In *The Boy Cardinal* she was a boy raised by political intrigues to a high ecclesiastical office; although solemnly robed, the lad was still able to reveal his natural exuberance with an outburst of castanet playing.

It was hard to classify Enters. Were her portraits mime sketches or solo dances? Actors thought her a dancer; dancers often considered her an actress. She herself called her pieces "Episodes and Compositions in Dance Form," and, as she toured the United States into the 1950s, she was known as a "wordless monologist."

Interest in dance training grew. When the Neighborhood Playhouse opened in New York in 1915, its founders, Irene Lewisohn and her sister Alice, envisioned an all-inclusive organization which sought a synthesis of drama, dance, music, and design.[15] Working with young people in the neighborhood, Irene, who had studied with Genevieve Stebbins, organized a dance group, and the Playhouse became known for productions with imaginative décor. Over the years, their casts included many noted dancers, among them Michio Ito, Charles Weidman, and Martha Graham, who also taught at the Playhouse school.

The Minnesota-born Bird Larson, who received a degree from Columbia University Teachers College in 1913, tried to combine the ideas of creative expression associated with Gertrude Colby (with whom she had studied) with a concern for scientific facts about movement.[16]

Larson taught at Barnard College and also at her own school, which for a time was located in a building at the back of St. Mark's

Church-in-the-Bowery, an Episcopal church in what became known as New York's East Village. A historically important congregation—Peter Stuyvesant is buried in the churchyard—St. Mark's was also a controversial one in the 1920s because its rector, the Reverend Dr. William Norman Guthrie, occasionally incorporated dance into worship services.

Phoebe Guthrie, his daughter, was a pupil of Larson. Encouraged by Dr. Guthrie, Larson began to create dances on religious themes, presenting them outside the church and then in the sanctuary itself. A ritual dance of the Annunciation, inspired by a Luca Della Robbia plaque that hangs in the church, touched off an artistic and liturgical scandal in 1921 because some of Dr. Guthrie's fellow clergymen thought it improper for six women clad in draperies to dance in church, even on a sacred theme. A reporter for the *New York Mail* dubbed Dr. Guthrie "the Ziegfeld of the churches." [17] Nevertheless, despite the commotion, the danced ritual was repeated annually for several years.

Dr. Guthrie was so convinced of the spiritual importance of dance that in 1923 he published *The Relation of the Dance to Religion*, a small book in which he eloquently called for reforms in theology and liturgy. He deplored the tendency of people to identify religion "with more or less outgrown infantile ethics . . . and with more or less obsolete theological conceptions." Rather, he argued, the arts may help us achieve a fresh religious consciousness, and through liturgical dance "our Religion of the Incarnation might recover its sacramental power. . . . And will not the Dance itself be the living conscious rhythm, as it were, of the cosmic God, to the all-but-audible music of the spheres?" [18]

In her secular works, Larson increasingly rejected conventional musical accompaniment as a motivation for dance composition, turning instead to the direct use of emotional states as choreographic source material. But these experiments were cut short by her sudden death in 1927, following the birth of her only child.

Margaret H'Doubler was surely the most influential American dance educator to come to prominence after World War I. The daughter of a Swiss artist, photographer, and inventor, she was born in Beloit, Kansas, in 1889; her unusual surname, H'Doubler, is an American form of her original Swiss family name, Hougen-Doubler. She majored in biology and chemistry at the University of Wisconsin at Madison, but she was also active in women's sports and was asked to stay as a physical education instructor after her graduation in 1906.

When Blanche Trilling, her department head, was perceptive enough to suspect that dance could be an important part of the college curriculum, she sent H'Doubler to New York in 1916. There she studied with Gertrude Colby and came under the influence of Bird Larson. Upon her return to Madison in 1917, H'Doubler developed a system of dance education suitable for colleges. The next year, she organized a dance group called Orchesis, a name based on a Greek word for expressive gesture; in years to come, scores of other colleges would also name their own groups Orchesis. After 1921, Wisconsin broadened the comprehensiveness of its dance curriculum, and in 1927 it established a dance major program leading to a degree. H'Doubler remained on the faculty in Madison until her retirement in 1954; thereafter, she was in demand as a guest teacher until her death in 1982.

H'Doubler's conception of dance as an organized form of self-expression led her, like Larson, to stress the importance of anatomy and kinesiology. She also treated dance as a theatrical art, and not simply as an aid to self-development. An energetic, well-read woman, H'Doubler was influenced by theories of progressive education and believed that schools must prepare young Americans for life in a democracy.[19]

H'Doubler's faith in art, science, and political activism was shared by Nellie Centennial Cornish, who was born in 1876, the year of the Centennial of the American Revolution (hence her middle name).[20] A music teacher with little formal education—she never even graduated from high school—Cornish was nevertheless blessed with remarkable intuition and sensitivity. In 1914, she founded the Cornish School of Allied Arts in Seattle, an institution which soon became a major center for music, drama, and painting.

Dance found its way to the school in 1916, when Mary Ann Wells, a pioneering ballet teacher in the Pacific Northwest, began to offer classes there. After modern dance entered the curriculum in 1921, the school invited many distinguished guest teachers, including Martha Graham, Louis Horst, Michio Ito, Ronny Johansson, and Lore Deja, a fiery red-haired dancer who introduced Wigman technique to the Northwest in 1931.

Nellie Cornish was known to students and colleagues as "Miss Aunt Nellie" or "Miss A. N." Those quaint names are deceptive, for she was not simply a sweet eccentric. Let Martha Graham describe her: "She was a small, round, plump little lady with the dynamics of a rocket, and we were all terrified of her, terrified of her tongue, and, in a way, terrified of her dream."[21]

The prominence of the Cornish School in the cultural life of Seattle was a sign that American dreams of the arts were starting to come true.

Another sign that dance was growing up was an interest in dance criticism. Newspapers had almost always covered dance performances. But editors often sent music or drama critics to them. Whereas some of those critics wrote well about dance—especially Carl van Vechten, a *New York Times* music critic who covered dance events in the 1910s—others were ignorant and insensitive.

During the 1920s, dancers and writers argued that dance criticism was an independent field that demanded its own specialists. Perhaps the first New York dance columnist was Lucile Marsh, who began to write for the *World* in 1927.[22] But when the *World* was combined with the *Telegram* in 1932, the post of dance writer was not included in the merger. Later in 1927, two other New York newspapers appointed dance critics. Mary F. Watkins, who had been an ambulance driver during World War I and had served as secretary to Olive Fremstad, the soprano who created the role of Salome at the Metropolitan Opera, was a music critic at the *New York Herald Tribune* when she was named its dance critic. She wrote perceptively on dance until 1934, when she left journalism to devote herself to her family.[23]

Her appointment at the "Trib" came only a few weeks before John Martin, who had been a music student and then an actor and stage director, was chosen dance critic of the *New York Times*. He remained there until 1962, covering all forms of dance, including modern dance, of which he became a major theorist, and his influence was crucial in the development of American dance for decades.

REBELS

Helen Tamiris • *Martha Graham* • *Doris Humphrey*

BY THE LATE 1920S, THREE WOMEN HAD CHANGED THE shape of American modern dance: Helen Tamiris, Martha Graham, and Doris Humphrey.

Tamiris rebelled against ballet. She was a political rebel, as well. The daughter of Russian-Jewish immigrants who settled in New York City, she was born Helen Becker in 1902. Her father, a tailor, made policemen's overcoats in a sweatshop. As a child, Helen studied "Interpretative Dancing" with Irene Lewisohn and Blanche Talmud, and when she was fifteen she joined the Metropolitan Opera Ballet; she also studied ballet with Michel Fokine.

Helen was an outspoken young woman with a stubborn streak. Her outspokenness prevented her from graduating from high school. After she made a street-corner speech opposing America's entry into World War I, her shocked principal told her that, as punishment, her diploma would be withheld from her.[1] Her stubbornness was reflected in her dissatisfaction with both ballet and Interpretative Dancing. As she said in her unfinished memoirs, she soon concluded that "I don't want to be a Duncan dancer—or a ballet dancer—I want to be myself—But what was myself?"[2]

Many of her contemporaries asked similar questions. For them self-discovery involved esthetic exploration. Nevertheless, all had to raise money to buy food and pay the rent. Helen did so by appearing in commercial entertainments. She cast aside Becker as a surname and professionally adopted Tamiris, the name of an ancient Persian queen. At first, she billed herself simply as Tamiris; later, she was known as Helen Tamiris. When she appeared at a Sportsmen's and Outdoor Show in Cleveland early in her career, posters announced her as "Tamiris—In an Astonishing Exhibition by the Modernistic Athletic Dancer." Other attractions on the bill included log rollers, a menagerie, "Exciting Stunts in the Big Tank," and a fashion show of women's sportswear.[3]

Tamiris was not the only modern dancer forced by economic necessity to work in musical shows or nightclubs. Nevertheless, a few of Tamiris's colleagues spoke of her with slight disdain because they considered her too "commercial."[4] Conceivably, they may have been jealous. Tamiris was a glamorous woman. With her mane of thick reddish-gold hair, she certainly did not look like a priestess of dance, and she was a vibrant personality on and off the stage.[5]

Tamiris gave her first choreographic program in 1927. Her diverse offerings bore such titles as *Circus Sketches* and *Impressions of the Bull Ring*. Two items were somewhat out of the ordinary. *Subconscious*, set to Debussy, reflected America's growing fascination with psychology by showing a conflict between inhibition and liberation. *The Queen Walks in the Garden*, performed in silence, was the first of Tamiris's experiments exploring the relationship between movement and sound (or the lack of it). In this work, Tamiris portrayed a queen walking at twilight and nostalgically fancying herself a girl.

She experimented with sound again in 1928 by choreographing *Prize Fight Studies* to the beating of piano strings. To make sure her movements looked authentic, she took lessons from a professional boxer. Also that year, she choreographed *Twentieth Century Bacchante*, a portrait of a drunken flapper, and, most importantly, *Two Spirituals: Nobody Knows de Trouble I See, Joshua Fit the Battle ob Jericho*, the first of an ongoing series of pieces choreographed to spirituals. Tamiris surprised some dancegoers with these works, for, at the time, such songs were not always taken seriously by whites. Tamiris loved them and choreographically tried to reflect their moods of sorrow, aspiration, and faith.

Deeply interested in black culture, Tamiris appeared with the Bahama Negro Dancers in *Gris-Gris Ceremonial* at an outdoor concert at Lewisohn Stadium in 1933. The Bahamian women wore nothing but bands of transparent chiffon as brassieres. This display astonished the audience—but in entirely the wrong way. One critic, Joseph Arnold, snorted, "Nothing like this performance was ever seen outside burlesque."[6]

Delighting in iconoclasm, Tamiris performed *Dance of the City* in 1929 to the sound of a siren. Three resounding kettledrums boomed through *Revolutionary March,* in which Tamiris wore a flaglike costume. Performers in other works created their own music. The four dancers of *Triangle Dance* (1930) struck differently tuned triangles as they moved, and dancers beat their elbows on small drums carried in their hands in *Mourning Ceremonial* (1931).

Tamiris possessed an abundance of ideas, but her choreography occasionally had rough edges. As Gervase N. Butler admitted in *Dance Observer,* "Dancing is a gift for her, expression is something for which she has to strive."[7] Nevertheless, Tamiris relished hurling challenges at her audiences. Typically, in a program note of 1928 she commented, "Will people never rebel against artificialities, pseudo-romanticism and affected sophistication? The dance of today must have a dynamic tempo and be valid, precise, spontaneous, free, normal, natural and human."[8]

Martha Graham and Doris Humphrey were both dropouts from Denishawn. Graham was born in 1894 in Allegheny, Pennsylvania, a quiet suburb of Pittsburgh (later incorporated into that city) that was also the birthplace of two other remarkable American women: the painter Mary Cassatt and the experimental writer Gertrude Stein.

Dance lovers who share Graham's interest in symbolism surely make much of the fact that Allegheny, at the time, contained an arsenal, a penitentiary, a Presbyterian theological seminary, and an astronomical observatory.[9] Graham became a fighter. She freed herself from the prison of narrow-mindedness. She was fascinated by religion and ritual. And in her creative ambitions she metaphorically gazed toward the stars.

Her father was a doctor: an "alienist"—what we today would call a specialist in nervous disorders. Martha loved and was loved in return by Dr. George Greenfield Graham, who proved to be a kind, but strict parent with a keen eye. Once, when Martha was a little girl, he accused her of lying. How could he tell? Because, he explained, he could spot it from the way she moved. She never forgot that first lesson in psychology. For the rest of her life she proclaimed that movement never lies.

The Grahams, who prized straight posture and right thinking, were Presbyterians. But their household also included Lizzie, a former patient of Dr. Graham who, because she claimed he had saved her life, cooked and did household chores for the family. Lizzie, an Irish Catholic, took Martha to church with her and introduced her to a world, simultaneously spiritual and sensual, of candles, incense, and statues of saints.

When turn-of-the-century doctors did not know what else to prescribe for a perpetually ailing patient, they often recommended a "change of air." In 1908, the Graham family was ailing. Mrs. Graham was despondent over the loss of a son. Martha's sister Mary suffered from asthma attacks. Georgia, another sister (who also became a dancer), was not strong and had once been dangerously ill with scarlet fever. A "change of air" was in order. Dr. Graham moved his family to the sunny streets and Spanish-style houses of Santa Barbara, California.

Santa Barbara lifted the family's sprits. Martha thrived there. She was an editor of the Santa Barbara High School newspaper and captain of the girl's basketball team. When she graduated in 1913, the yearbook characterized her as "Capable, generous, willing to do— To the noblest standard is faithful and true." [10] But Martha was not quite sure just what she was "willing to do," although she was developing a hazy notion of what she wanted to do.

Just as a poster inspired Ruth St. Denis, so another poster inspired Martha Graham. One April day in 1911 she saw a poster of a woman in a bejeweled Oriental costume sitting on a small platform, her eyes closed in ecstasy. A photograph of Ruth St. Denis in *Radha*, it advertised forthcoming performances in Los Angeles. Martha vowed then and there that she would attend one, and by letting her do so Dr. Graham changed his daughter's life. [11]

Yet he would never have allowed Martha to be a dancer. Martha, both her parents assumed, would surely attend some prestigious women's college. Instead, she delayed the course of her higher education by going to the Cumnock School of Expression, a Los Angeles institution founded in 1894 which had a lower school, an upper school, and a junior college. Cumnock was, according to one of its brochures, devoted to "pursuits of learning and self-expression" and offered drama and dance classes as well as academic subjects. [12]

Dr. Graham died in 1914. Denishawn opened the next year. In 1916, Graham completed Cumnock's junior college program and enrolled at Denishawn. She was twenty-two. She looked forward to studying with her idol, St. Denis. But Miss Ruth was not particularly interested in her as a student. Rather, it was Ted Shawn who spotted her talents and, through rigorous training, turned her into a dancer.

At the Denishawn school, Graham developed a romantic attachment to Louis Horst, its musical director. The association of Graham and Horst lasted until 1948, Horst serving as her accompanist, composer, artistic mentor, and confidant.[13]

Denishawn increasingly dissatisfied her. She wished to do another kind of dancing—but what? She appeared in *The Greenwich Village Follies*, a sophisticated revue of 1923, and taught both in New York and at the Eastman School of Music in Rochester, New York. Yet revues and teaching failed to fulfill her. Then, on 18 April 1926, Martha Graham, assisted by a group of three women, offered her first program of choreography in New York. Less than a month later she turned thirty-two.

The early years of modern dance history are filled with an astonishing number of major dancers who, like Graham, began their careers late. Some—including Loïe Fuller, Maud Allan, Maggie Gripenberg, Gertrud Bodenwieser, and Mary Wigman—did not do so until they were about thirty, an age at which, today, no one would think of becoming a professional dancer. Fanatical ballet lovers occasionally seize upon these late starts as evidence that modern dance is somehow a lesser art, one appropriate only for luckless souls unfortunate enough to be barred from balletic careers.

Yet ballet dancers should never assume that they are automatically superior to other dancers. The little girl who dutifully performs exercises in the cloistered surroundings of some renowned ballet academy and then joins the ranks of an established company may be a wonderful dancing machine. But the narrowness of her training and experience can leave her permanently infantilized. In contrast, the modern dancers who started late did so because they felt compelled to dance. Their bodies, though untrained, must have been agile, and their wills were certainly strong. Indeed, in a real sense, they willed themselves into being dancers. Moreover, these dancers were adults determined to make modern dance an art form other adults could take seriously.

Graham attracted attention with her debut concert. Yet, as such titles as *Clair de Lune, Danse Languide, A Study in Lacquer*, and *Maid with the Flaxen Hair* suggest, her dances showed the influence of the decorative aspects of Denishawn style. Year by year, her flowing curves were strengthened into angularities and her range of subject matter widened. In 1928, Graham created *Immigrant: Steerage, Strike*. The laconic title of *Danse* (1929) in no way prepared audiences for its content. Graham wore a narrow tubular costume that deliberately limited her movements, and the choreography of this solo to the music of Arthur Honegger proceeded in abrupt percussive spasms. Graham performed the entire dance on a small platform; according to Martha Hill, a dance teacher who was one of her early students, Graham's determined stance made her look "as if she dared someone to come and move her feet." [14]

Later in 1929, she choreographed *Heretic*: to a Breton folksong played over and over, a lone woman (Graham) confronted a wall of human bodies that blocked her progress. Whenever the rebel tried to break through the opposition, the parts of the wall reassembled and the soloist fell to the ground. This stark kinetic drama may be Graham's first major work.

By 1930, Graham was sufficiently well known in dance circles that she was cast as the Chosen Maiden in the production of Stravinsky's *Le Sacre du Printemps* that Léonide Massine choreographed under the auspices of the League of Composers, which was performed in Philadelphia and New York City with the Philadelphia Orchestra, conducted by Leopold Stokowski. Massine, a choreographer for Diaghilev's Ballets Russes and one of the twentieth-century's greatest ballet choreographers, was then at the height of his fame, working with one of America's finest orchestras and a celebrated conductor. Graham, in contrast, was a promising newcomer—but one definitely worth watching.

She amazed audiences again in 1930 with *Lamentation*. Whereas most dancing, however unconventional, involves movement of the feet across the stage, this solo to the music of Zoltán Kodály was performed in a seated position on a bench. Encased in a tube of stretchable jersey, Graham twisted and thrust her body so that the jersey's constantly changing shapes suggested grief and anguish. *Lamentation* reminded Elizabeth Selden of "the shrouded dynamic figures of the German sculptor, Ernst Barlach," figures that "seem to be hanging or falling and insist on maintaining the oddest equilibrium." Clearly, as Selden so aptly put it, Graham was devoting herself to "difficult beauty." [15]

Doris Humphrey was born in 1895 in Oak Park, Illinois, a Chicago suburb. But she grew up in Chicago, where her parents managed a hotel that catered to a middle-class theatrical clientele. Business success always eluded her father, and her mother brought in extra money as a pianist and music teacher. The Humphreys sent Doris to Francis W. Parker's Chicago Institute, a school that reflected the educational reforms of the day and offered instruction in crafts, theatre, and music. Dance classes were taught by Mary Wood Hinman, an enlightened teacher who introduced her pupils to folk dance, ballroom dance, pantomime, and ballet. Doris also studied ballet with various teachers who passed through or settled in Chicago. Gradually, she began to teach.

In 1913, Mrs. Humphrey organized a little company consisting of Doris, another dancer, a bass-baritone, and an actress; like Ted Shawn and Norma Gould, they set out to entertain employees of the Santa Fe Railroad. Four years later, Doris went to study at Denishawn. Invited to stay, she both danced and taught for the organization and was part of the company on its tour of the Orient. When St. Denis began to experiment with music visualizations, Humphrey served as her assistant and choreographed music visualizations of her own.

Like Graham, Humphrey grew dissatisfied with Denishawn. She was one of the younger dancers who thought St. Denis and Shawn too easily compromised their ideals by working in the commercial theatre. At a Denishawn staff meeting in New York in 1928, Humphrey accused St. Denis of cheapening her choreographic effects when she performed in the *Ziegfeld Follies*. Humphrey's memoirs describe what followed:

> Miss Ruth burst into tears. Then she began to ramble almost incoherently about how she had always been respectable, while Isadora Duncan was running all over Europe having babies by different men, while she herself had always been a model of virtue. Also that the mysticism of the East had been her ideal and always would be, despite any deviations. Seeing her emotionally out of control, Shawn took up the defense and said to me:
>
> "Do you mean to say that Jesus Christ was any the less great because he addressed the common people?"
>
> "No," I answered, "but you're not Jesus Christ."
>
> "But I am," he said. "I am the Jesus Christ of the dance."
>
> This statement fell into a startled silence. There seemed to be no answer to it.[16]

Humphrey's answer was to leave Denishawn. Along with her went Pauline Lawrence, a musician and costume designer, and Charles

Weidman, a dancer and choreographer. Together, they formed the Humphrey-Weidman Company.

Three of Humphrey's dances of the late 1920s suggest her range. *Air for the G String,* choreographed in 1928, was a lyrical vision in which five women in floor-length shifts inspired by the paintings of Fra Angelico walked in serene patterns to music by Bach. *Water Study* (also 1928) evoked the movement of water in silence, without any illustrative musical accompaniment of rippling strings or stormy drums. Nevertheless, images of calm seas, swelling tides, and breaking waves were present in the choreography. *The Life of the Bee* (1929), which concerned the struggle in a hive between an old queen and a new, did have an accompaniment—an unusual one: people in the wings hummed on combs covered with tissue paper to suggest the buzzing of bees.

The Roaring Twenties roared out on an ominous note. The Wall Street stock market crashed in 1929. It was among the first in a gradually worsening series of economic calamities that occurred throughout the world, causing what came to be known as the Great Depression. This time of hardship saw the rise of militant right-wing and left-wing groups, and the dancers of the 1930s often found themselves involved with political as well as artistic struggles.

PART 3

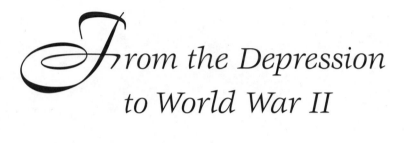

*From the Depression
to World War II*

$\mathscr{S}$TRUGGLES, DISPERSALS, AMALGAMATIONS

Dartington Hall • Margaret Barr • Louise Soelberg • Leslie Burrowes • Waldeen Falkenstein • Anna Sokolow • Uday Shankar • Ninette de Valois • Serge Lifar • Nini Theilade • Nina Verchinina • Léonide Massine • Jia Ruskaja • Kurt Jooss • Agnes de Mille

DURING THE 1930S, DESPITE THE WORSENING DEPRESSION, modern dance tried to put down roots in several nations. British audiences tended to be ardent ballet lovers. Nevertheless, British modern dance centers did exist. One was Dartington Hall, a progressive school and art colony founded in Devon by Dorothy Whitney Straight Elmhirst, the heiress to a trolley-car fortune, and her husband Leonard Elmhirst, an agronomist and social reformer. In addition to being a boarding school for children, Dartington Hall involved adults: artists, potters, furniture makers, and farmers, who gathered together in what they looked upon as a utopian community. To Dartington Hall came two dance teachers. The Seattle-born Louise Soelberg (the wife of Richard Elmhirst, Leonard's younger brother) had studied ballet with Adolph Bolm, eurhythmics with Dalcroze in Geneva, and modern dance with Elizabeth Duncan and Michio Ito; she had also taught at the Cornish School. Margaret Barr, born in India in 1904 of an English mother and an American dentist father, had studied drama in London and dance in America with Martha Graham and at the New York Denishawn.[1]

Barr organized a Dance-Drama Group at Dartington Hall in 1931 with Edmund Rubbra as staff composer and Alan Rawsthorne, another young composer, as her pianist. Barr's works featured strongly dramatic images rich in social or political implications.

Hebridean, one of Barr's most acclaimed pieces, depicted life in a fishing village. Set to traditional Hebridean music arranged by

Kennedy Fraser, it included a visually striking scene in which three women standing with their backs to the audience suggested the weaving of nets through the crossings and uncrossings of their arms. A jig followed. But work and play alike were interrupted by a disastrous storm.

In 1934, the Elmhirsts brought another and much better-known troupe to Dartington Hall: the Ballets Jooss, directed by the German choreographer Kurt Jooss. The school recommended an amalgamation of the companies of Barr and Jooss. Neither director liked that idea, and Barr moved her group to London, where it settled into a tiny studio-theatre in the shabby district near the King's Cross railway station. Because Barr now lacked the support an institution such as Dartington Hall could provide, her group had to struggle to survive.

Yet she continued to create. *Saturday Night* was a portrait of couples passing a beery evening in a pub. *The Three Sisters* showed how war affected a prostitute, a spinster, and a young woman. Barr's choreography derived from a heightening of natural gestures and emphasized group movement to such an extent that individual dancers were not even named in the printed programs.[2]

Barr remained in London until 1938, when financial problems forced her to disband her company. She moved to Australia, where she settled in Sydney and opened a school in a former church hall. She continued to choreograph until her death in 1991, and although she worked almost totally outside the Australian cultural establishment, she constantly sought to produce dances on Australian themes.[3]

Pupils of Central European teachers such as Wigman, Laban, and Bodenwieser also opened studios in England.[4] Among them was Leslie Burrowes, a student of Margaret Morris and Wigman who married the distinguished oboist Leon Goossens. The first English woman to receive a teaching certificate from the Wigman School in Dresden, Burrowes founded a London school in 1933 and for several years campaigned to make modern dance better appreciated in her native land.

In 1938, she and Louise Soelberg established the Dance Centre, a London organization designed to foster both the training of dancers and the mounting of productions. Unfortunately, the Dance Centre itself lacked a center. Burrowes and Soelberg could not find suitable space. Instead, they presented performances and lecture-demonstrations in their studios. But the necessity of maintaining separate

premises made it difficult for the Dance Centre to seem a truly unify-
ing force. Its activities were gradually curtailed. Then World War II,
with its restrictions and privations, put a temporary halt to the development of all British modern dance.

Mexico proved more receptive to modern dance, thanks in part to
the efforts of teachers and choreographers from the United States.
One was Waldeen Falkenstein, who was professionally known as
Waldeen and who had studied ballet with Theodore Kosloff and
modern dance with Michio Ito, with whose company she toured. A
poet as well as a choreographer, Waldeen announced in 1932 that she
hoped to create dances to poems by Emily Dickinson, Conrad Aiken,
and Wallace Stevens. During the mid-1930s, she successfully performed in Mexico City; deciding to remain there to teach and choreograph, she opened a school in 1940 and organized a company.[5]

Another young choreographer, Anna Sokolow, went to Mexico
City in 1939. Although New York remained her home, she returned
to Mexico several times. Soon Mexico developed its own choreographers, among them Guillermina Bravo and Josefina Lavalle, students
of Waldeen, and Ana Mérida, who had been in Sokolow's first Mexican group.[6]

Uday Shankar, the most internationally famous Indian dancer of
his day, was considered by European and American audiences to be
an exemplar of an ancient tradition. However, given his relationship
to that tradition, it is also possible to regard him as a modern dancer.
He did not simply preserve a dance form; he used it as the basis for
making radical experiments.

The son of a Hindu scholar (and older brother of the sitar player
Ravi Shankar), Uday Shankar, who was born in 1900, grew up in north
India.[7] As a child, he showed an interest in dance. But, in at least one
respect, Indians at the time resembled Americans and Europeans:
they did not consider dance a respectable career. Instead, Shankar
became an art student at London's Royal College of Art.

During the early 1920s, Anna Pavlova became fascinated by Indian
culture and desired to produce a ballet on an Indian theme. She was
introduced to Shankar in London, and they collaborated on *Radha
and Krishna*, which received its premiere in 1923. Shankar taught
Pavlova basic principles of Indian dance; she, in turn, taught the art
student showmanship.

Inspired to develop his own form of dance, Shankar was assisted by Simone Barbier, who came to him as an accompanist but who grew so enamored of Indian dance that she embarked upon a new career and became Shankar's dancing partner under the stage name of Simkie. She was as famous for her grace as he was for his vigor. In 1930, he founded a company that toured widely and was especially popular in America. Shankar, who died in 1977, continued to appear onstage into the early 1960s.

Shankar's creations were often inspired by mythology. But his technical vocabulary departed from Indian tradition. Desiring to present works that would be comprehensible outside India, he blended Indian dance with elements of Western dance and dispensed with many of the *mudras*, the complex symbolic hand gestures of Hindu dance.

In addition to mythological works, Shankar choreographed dances on contemporary themes, some of them showing an awareness of India's problems as a developing nation. *Labor and Machinery*—his Indian equivalent of a *ballet mécanique*—showed a struggle between humanity and machines from which humanity ultimately emerged triumphant.

Shankar's career suggests how troublesome it can be to apply labels to some forms of dance. To Westerners, Shankar seemed a traditionalist; to Indians, he may have been an iconoclast.

Even within a single culture, categorization many be difficult. Thus Western dance lovers may wonder where ballet leaves off and modern dance begins. During the 1930s, ballet choreographers sensitive to new developments in the arts occasionally incorporated elements of modern dance into their productions; certain modern choreographers, in turn, cast an inquisitive eye upon ballet and even wondered if it might be possible to unite the two forms.

Nevertheless, ballet and modern dancers often found themselves on opposite sides of debates. Ralph Taylor, an American critic, declared in 1935 that ballet offers nothing but "wish-fulfillment for the perpetually infantile, vicarious freedom for the old maid's suppression, release for the too-ready tears of the sentimental." Some modern dancers agreed. In the February 1938 issue of the *American Dancer* Helen Tamiris proclaimed, "Ballet is *passé*. I can almost hear its last breath."[8]

But in that same issue, Blanche Evan, an American modern dance teacher, sensed other ideas in the air. She wrote, "Whereas in the past the idea of compatibility between the two techniques of the ballet and the modern dance seemed preposterous, it now appears to be inevitable." Evan hoped that scientifically sound principles of both disciplines could be merged "to give the dancer a more varied, more brilliant and more meaningful technique than she has ever been able to possess in the whole history of professional dancing." Ballet, Evan argued, produces controlled footwork; modern dance stretches the back and promotes freedom in the spine. Whereas ballet fosters poise, endurance, lightness, and elevation, modern dance stresses the importance of nuances in movement qualities, dynamics, contrast, and climax.[9]

An interchange of techniques began to take place. In Gertrud Bodenwieser's *The Inconstant Prince*, the tale of a procrastinating prince asked to choose between two princesses, both princesses wore toeshoes. Ruth Page, a ballet dancer, toured as Harald Kreutzberg's partner. The early works of the British ballet choreographer Ninette de Valois contained both ballet and modern dance steps.

When Serge Lifar, the last choreographer to be encouraged by Diaghilev, became director of the Paris Opéra Ballet in 1929, he argued that "ballet must not borrow its rhythmical contour from music" and that ballet can exist independently of all musical accompaniment—ideas akin to those advanced by advocates of Absolute Dance.[10] Putting theory into practice, Lifar choreographed several works in silence, then noted down their choreographic rhythms and commissioned an obliging musician to orchestrate them. The most famous of these productions was *Icare* (1935). Retelling the Greek myth of Icarus's doomed attempt to fly, it was accompanied by the thundering rhythms of a percussion ensemble.

The soloists of the Ballets Russes companies of the 1930s occasionally ventured across the borderline into modern dance. One was Nini Theilade, a strikingly beautiful dancer who was born in Java.[11] Her father was a Danish journalist. Her Javanese mother taught eurhythmics and was Nini's first teacher. She was then sent to study ballet in Copenhagen and Paris. A child prodigy, Theilade began touring in 1929 at the age of fourteen in solos she created for herself. In 1932, she appeared in Max Reinhardt's production of *Everyman* at the Salzburg Festival, where she met and studied with Harald Kreutzberg.

Many of her dances emphasized her charm—for instance, *Impression from Tahiti* and *Danish Porcelain*, in which she portrayed a statue come to life. Others had more serious implications. For instance, as the goddess of the hunt in *Diana*, she succumbed to the hunting instinct and killed an innocent deer only to feel human—or godlike—remorse for having done so.

The Moscow-born Nina Verchinina was trained in Parisian ballet studios. But she also admired Isadora Duncan, and she studied with William Hinkle, a pupil of Laban. This exposure to modern dance taught her to project feeling through movement (as proponents of *Ausdruckstanz* sought to do), to let movement involve the entire body and not just the arms and legs (a principle insisted upon by Duncan), and to recognize the importance of what the Germans called *Spannung*. Verchinina even came to dislike pointe technique.[12]

Both Theilade and Verchinina were favored by Léonide Massine. Indeed, Verchinina declared Massine to be the only choreographer who fully understood her. An extraordinarily versatile and successful choreographer, Massine knew how to incorporate dances from various cultures and historical periods into ballet. During the 1930s, he choreographed for Colonel W. De Basil's Ballets Russes (of which Verchinina was a member) and Sergei Denham's Ballet Russe de Monte Carlo (with which Theilade danced). In such major ballets as *Les Présages*, *Choreartium*, and *St. Francis*, he infused ballet steps with the strength and fluidity of the torso associated with Central European modern dance.

Not all incursions of modern dance into ballet were greeted so favorably.

Jia Ruskaja was the stage name Eugenia Borisenko bestowed upon herself: it means "I the Russian"—and she had been born in Russia in 1902.[13] She settled in Italy and in 1932 introduced Orchestica, a form of modern dance she had developed, into the ballet school attached to La Scala, the Milanese opera house. Ruskaja (whose surname was also spelled Ruskaya and Ruskaia) believed that her method, which incorporated elements of Dalcroze and Duncan technique, promoted grace and suppleness, thereby preventing ballet dancers from becoming rigid.

The ballet students disagreed. They so resented her classes that in 1934 the school's directorate announced that henceforth students could have the choice of specializing in either Orchestica or classical ballet. Out of a student body of more than one hundred, only two people chose Orchestica. Ruskaja thereupon resigned.

Nevertheless, she had her revenge. Ruskaja came to dominate all Italian dance training. With support from the Fascist government, she opened a school in Rome in 1934 that survived every political change in the decades that followed. It emphasized ballet, but also offered modern dance—and, of course, Orchestica. Ruskaja's political supporters got a law passed in 1948 that named the school the National Academy of Dance; three years later, another law decreed that anyone wishing to teach dance in Italy had to possess a certificate from the academy. The dancers, choreographers, and teachers associated with La Scala and the Rome Opera protested vehemently against this. Opponents of Ruskaja also pointed out that men would, in effect, be forever barred from teaching dance, since her academy admitted only female students. Legal wrangling over the academy continued until 1966, when Ruskaja resigned as director; she died two years later, and in 1971 men were at last admitted to the school.

One of the most important attempts to amalgamate ballet with modern dance was that of Kurt Jooss. Born near Stuttgart, Germany, in 1901, Jooss first wished to be a singer, then studied drama, but without success. By chance, he discovered the work of Laban and became his student. In 1926–1927, he toured with Sigurd Leeder, another young dancer, in programs called *Two Male Dancers*. Also in 1927, Jooss was appointed dance director at the Folkwang, an art institute in Essen. There he built a strong dance school and company and gathered around him a loyal group of collaborators—among them Leeder, the designer Hein Heckroth, the composer Frederic ("Fritz") Cohen, and Aino Siimola, the dancer Jooss married in 1929.[14]

Reacting against the emotional excess of Expressionism at its worst, Jooss allied himself with the *Neue Sachlichkeit* (New Objectivity), an art movement that rejected extreme subjectivism in favor of a concern for structure and for the presentation of social issues; painters associated with it included Otto Dix and George Grosz. Jooss's love of clarity led him to investigate ballet; at the same time, he deplored the triviality to which ballet is so often susceptible.

Students at the Folkwang were offered modern dance, improvisation, composition, notation, music, anatomy, dance history, and analyses of the relationship of form to space. Technique classes included a modified form of ballet, but without pointe work or elaborate *batterie.*

Although Jooss's way of dancing may have been a hybrid, it proved a remarkably expressive one. Yet a few critics thought that Jooss did not go far enough in bringing ballet and modern dance together. Some even considered his disdain of pointe work esthetic puritanism. Jooss offered his own comments on his dancers' training: "I am often reproached that the style we teach is not clearly identifiable. But we are not teaching a specific style; what we are teaching is the dancer's craft. Style is a result of choreographic intention and choice."[15]

Jooss specialized in dramatic choreography that expressed ideas. He told stories that mattered about people who mattered. He could be capable of charm, as in *A Ball in Old Vienna.* Yet most of his choreography was sober. So were the stage productions of his company, which came to be known as the Ballets Jooss. Black curtains usually served as the only "scenery" and, for most of his company's tours, accompaniment was provided by two pianos, rather than an instrumental ensemble.

The Big City opened with a panoramic view of crowds passing through the streets of a metropolis, then focused upon the rueful story of a young working-class woman who deserts her working-class lover when she is seduced by a rich libertine. Acutely aware of political developments, Jooss made *Chronica* the story of a tyrant who, after establishing order with his dictatorship, rules despotically until, at last, he repents. Although the setting was fifteenth-century Italy, this work of 1939 could be viewed as a commentary on Hitler. But unlike Jooss's tyrant, Hitler never repented.

Jooss's greatest piece of social comment and very possibly his greatest work is *The Green Table.* It gave him instant acclaim when it triumphed over compositions by Rosalia Chladek, Trudi Schoop, Oskar Schlemmer, Gertrud Bodenwieser, and others to win first prize at the International Choreographers' Competition held in Paris in 1932.

A powerful denunciation of war, *The Green Table* was inspired by medieval paintings of the Dance of Death, in which a skeletal figure is shown leading people of all social classes to the grave. The work begins with diplomats arguing at an international conference, haranguing one another and pounding vociferously on a green-covered table. The music Cohen composed for this scene is a tango, a cheap cabaret tune suggesting that, for all their highflown rhetoric, these statesmen are treating life-and-death issues in a trivial manner.

When the opening shots of a war are fired, the diplomats vanish and are replaced by the ominous figure of Death. By deploying only a few dancers ingeniously in space, Jooss choreographically creates the illusion of armies marching to battle. Civilian families are torn apart. A profiteer makes money from the carnage. And Death comes to claim everyone. Yet he appears different in movement quality to each of his victims. To soldiers, he is an enemy. To a weary old woman, he is a comforter. To a young woman forced into prostitution, he is a seducer. To a captured guerrilla, he is judge and executioner. Shots again ring out—this time to signal a ceasefire. And the work closes with the hypocritical diplomats once again bickering around their conference table.

Revived by many companies since 1932, *The Green Table* has often seemed uncannily timely.

The ability of the Ballets Jooss to assimilate elements of ballet and modern dance techniques became apparent in 1941 when Agnes de Mille created *Drums Sound in Hackensack* for it. De Mille, an American choreographer born in 1909, was the granddaughter of the economist Henry George, the daughter of the playwright and producer William C. De Mille, and the niece of the film director Cecil B. De Mille. In terms of her training, she was a ballet dancer—but an unconventional one who took a keen interest in modern dance.

Whereas modern choreographers such as Georgi, Milloss, and Wallmann choreographed for ballet companies, it was—and still is—much rarer for a ballet choreographer to collaborate with a modern dance group. De Mille was invited to work with the Ballets Jooss after the company returned to New York from a South American tour. Its funds were low and Jooss himself was in England. Yet the group needed a premiere to enliven its scheduled New York season. After agreeing to choreograph for it, de Mille searched for a subject that would unite the European troupe with America. The result was a ballet about Indians and the New Amsterdam fur trade in which corrupt New Amsterdam burghers get Indians drunk while trading them whiskey for fur. Cohen based his score upon tunes in a collection of old Dutch folksongs.

Critics did not consider *Drums Sound in Hackensack* a major effort, a judgment with which de Mille concurs. Writing in the

American Dancer, Albertina Vitak praised the ballet's "vitality," yet confessed that it "falls a wee bit short at times in matters of subtlety."[16] What makes *Drums* significant, nonetheless, is that it is a sign of an ongoing artistic dialogue between ballet and modern dance. But after *Drums*, de Mille's work properly belongs to the history of ballet.

CATASTROPHE

The Nazis • Rudolf Bode • Jutta Klamt • Ruth Abramowitsch-Sorel • Jean Weidt • Kurt Jooss • Rudolf Laban • Mary Wigman • Gret Palucca • Harald Kreutzberg • Ernest Berk • Gertrud Kraus • Gertrud Bodenwieser • Valeska Gert

WHEN THE NAZIS GAINED POWER IN GERMANY IN 1933, every aspect of the country's social and cultural life was affected.[1] Adolf Hitler became chancellor on 30 January 1933. On 27 February of that year, the Reichstag (or Parliament) burned. No one has ever determined the cause. Yet the Nazis used this as a pretext to crush political opposition. Anti-Jewish riots became common; books were burned, and the National Socialist (Nazi) Party established one-party rule.

The Nazis soon formed the Reichskulturkammer and the Reichstheaterkammer, organizations under the supervision of Dr. Joseph Goebbels, the regime's propaganda minister, that oversaw all media and the arts. Included within these bodies was the Tanz-Bühne (Dance-Stage), which presented dance festivals under the direction of Rudolf Laban.

The Nazis announced they sought to purify dance of "non-Aryan degenerate" elements and to turn it into a "healthy" German art. They also desired a standardization of dance training and required all dance students to pass examinations—including examinations in ballet. As a result, ballet was now a required subject in virtually every German dance school, even in such a citadel of modern dance as the Wigman School in Dresden.

Reactions to the Nazi cultural decrees varied. Some choreographers, dancers, and teachers did not find it difficult to adjust to them. Among those who embraced the new policies were Rudolf Bode, the developer of a highly regarded gymnastics system,[2] and Jutta Klamt, a choreographer who combined dance with physical culture in her teaching and who believed that when dancers performed together they gained an awareness of a collective soul. In her *Sidelights*, a work of 1933, needy poor people struggled until, in an apotheosis, as Joseph Lewitan reported, the stage turned "all hues of brown" (the Nazi uniforms' color). Lewitan called this political symbolism "superficial, and . . . opportune." But Klamt remained unaffected by such chiding. Her husband Gustav, a Laban student, even changed his surname from Vischer (which could just conceivably be Jewish) to the more "Aryan" Fischer.[3]

Some German dancers realized they would have to flee the country. Jews and known leftists were totally unacceptable there, as were homosexuals. One of the first victims of the Nazis in dance was Ruth Abramowitsch-Sorel, a leading dancer of the Berlin Municipal Opera whose contract was not renewed, even though she had just won first prize in the Warsaw Dance Competition for a solo inspired by Salome; she migrated to Canada. Pola Nirenska, a Warsaw-born Wigman dancer, settled in England, moved to America in 1949, and began teaching in Washington, D.C., in 1951.[4] Jean Weidt was outside Germany when Hitler gained power. The militantly leftist dancer had the good sense not to return. After teaching in Moscow and Prague, he made Paris his home.[5]

The most famous group of émigrés was the Ballets Jooss. Refusing to renounce his Jewish colleagues, Jooss (who was not Jewish) fled Germany with his company in 1933. The next year, through the generosity of the Elmhirsts, they were able to establish their dance school at Dartington Hall. The troupe also toured internationally. One nation it visited was Chile, where three of its dancers—Rudi Pescht, Ernst Uthoff, and his wife, Lola Botka—remained to form a new company of their own, the National Ballet of Chile. At first, this group offered only works in the hybrid style of ballet and modern dance associated with Jooss. Gradually, however, purely classical technique began to be taught and classical ballets entered the repertoire. Ironically, the anti-Fascist Jooss was briefly kept in detention by British authorities in 1940 as a possibly "enemy alien"—apparently, simply because of the fact that he was German.[6]

Dancers who were neither committed Nazis nor on the Nazis' list of political enemies had a difficult choice to make. Should they leave Germany or stay? Many stayed. Given what is now known about the horrors of Nazi Germany, their decision continues to arouse bitter debate.

At the outset, Rudolf Laban was optimistic, declaring in 1935 that "the German dance had never before enjoyed such sympathetic and extensive support and help from the official authorities." The next year, he was even more affirmative: "We want to dedicate our means of expression and the articulation of our power to the service of the great tasks of our *Volk* [people]. With unswerving clarity, our *Führer* [Hitler] points the way." [7]

Yet Laban did not try to hide the fact that, at the time, he was in love with a Jewish woman.[8] The Nazis, at least for the moment, could look the other way at such impropriety: Laban was useful to them. The Berlin Dance Festival that he organized in 1934 featured many of the leaders of pre-Hitler German dance, among them Mary Wigman, Gret Palucca, Harald Kreutzberg, Yvonne Georgi, Dorothee Günther, Alexander von Swaine, and Lizzie Maudrik.[9]

Discussion of all German dance, however, was cloaked in highly nationalistic terminology. Thus the *Jahrbuch Deutsches Tanz 1937*, a yearbook of German dance, emphasized that Germany would tolerate only dance forms that were as German as possible in origin and nature.[10] But just what were those forms? Reviewing the 1934 festival, Lewitan had wondered "if what is surely an international art, can have purely national characteristics which are valuable; in other words, can anything be taken from the German dance and be proved exclusively German, and with what artistic and aesthetic significance?" [11] The idea still lingered that modern dance somehow transcended national boundaries.

An International Dance Festival was held in conjunction with the Berlin Olympic Games of 1936. The German participants included Wigman, Palucca, Kreutzberg, Günther, and Maja Lex. From abroad came, among other groups and soloists, the Zagreb Ballet, the Royal Flemish Opera Ballet, and a young Yugoslavian ballerina and choreographer, Mia Slavenska. But there were no representatives whatsoever from England, France, Sweden, the Soviet Union, and the United States. American modern dancers—Martha Graham prominent among them—generally supported a total boycott of the festivities.

Nevertheless, dance played an important part in the Olympics. The games opened on 1 August 1936 with *Olympic Youth*, a stadium event in several episodes. In "Children at Play," 2,500 boys and girls entered the arena and formed rings, after which they arranged themselves in the shape of the Olympic flag. Dorothee Günther devised tableaux for 3,500 girls in "Maidenly Grace," during which Gret Palucca danced a waltz. Harald Kreutzberg and Werner Stammer led groups of sword-bearing dancers in "Heroic Struggle and Death Lament"; then Mary Wigman and 80 women performed a ceremony of mourning. The finale was a massively scaled celebration to Beethoven's "Ode to Joy," with special effects provided by searchlights.[12]

Another monumental production had also been scheduled for the festival, Laban's *Von Tauwind und der Neuen Freude* (Spring Wind [or, in alternate translation, Warm Wind] and the New Joy), a work for a cast of a thousand dancers which depicted human spiritual endeavors, to music by Hans Klaus and texts drawn from Friedrich Nietzsche. But Goebbels, who attended the dress rehearsal, suspected that, for all his official rhetoric, Laban was not politically "safe" enough. The performance was canceled. Laban began to fall from favor, and attacks upon him grew. It was discovered that he had once belonged to the Freemasons, an organization prohibited by the Nazis. The smear campaign against him even included the accusation that this open and notorious womanizer was a homosexual.[13]

Laban, his health broken, escaped to England in 1938, where he found refuge at Dartington Hall with Kurt Jooss and Sigurd Leeder, who, despite the great theorist's ideologically soiled recent past, welcomed him as a master of modern dance.[14] A new life began for Laban. Around 1942, he started to analyze and notate workers' movements, and he was much in demand in England as an industrial consultant. Until his death in 1958, he taught, led workshops, and devised dance programs for British schools.

Other dancers did not break away from Germany. Kreutzberg toured abroad, yet always returned to Germany. Palucca and Wigman remained there. These dancers are said to have been essentially apolitical; now they found themselves caught up in a political maelstrom. Wigman's decision to stay in Germany particularly distressed her foreign admirers. This cultivated multilingual artist could have found work and honor anywhere. Why did she not leave?

Various speculations have been advanced. Perhaps Wigman had no real idea of what the Nazi regime might bring about. Perhaps she was a self-centered opportunist. Perhaps she thought that, simply because of her fame, she could help German dance retain its esthetic stature. And it has been suggested that she could not bear to leave her lover, who believed that cooperation between German industry and the Nazis might overcome the Depression.[15]

More than any other person's action or decision, Wigman's refusal to leave Germany helped destroy the reputation of German dance in America. After the war, people in many countries—including Germany itself—began to wonder, did *Ausdruckstanz* somehow culturally pave the way for the Nazis? Did it make it easier for them to triumph?

For all Germany's sponsorship of international festivals, there was a distinctly nationalistic streak in German dance (as, indeed, there was in the American dance of the time). Some of this was just local pride. Other aspects of this nationalism were more sinister. Several choreographers, including Wigman, were fond of theatrically invoking mighty powers. Outside the theatre, Hitler was a very mighty power and, with his goose-stepping multitudes in torchlight parades, made all of Germany one vast stage.

The Nazis must have found it particularly easy to seize upon Laban's idea of the movement choir. The sight of hundreds of people moving together in a common cause surely appealed to them—provided, of course, that the cause was their own. Yet Laban's ideas were not inherently Fascistic—nor were those of the other major exponents of *Ausdruckstanz*. In a nation wracked by discord, the ideal of communal solidarity could legitimately be advanced by democratic as well as totalitarian political parties. One of the most famous directors of movement choirs other than Laban was Martin Gleisner, a Socialist who left Germany in 1933.[16] The Nazis appropriated certain ideas which, as Emerson would have said, were "in the air" and then polluted them.

Unfortunately, too many German dancers did not appear to notice this until it was too late. Whatever the dancers thought of the Nazis and whatever the Nazis privately thought of them, German officials could point to such figures as Wigman, Palucca, and Kreutzberg as renowned artists who continued to work in the new regime. The Nazis used the dancers for their own propagandistic ends. Then they silenced them.

Dancers came under attack. Oskar Schlemmer's work was branded degenerate in 1937.[17] The Nazi Party leadership in Dresden drastically reduced funding for the school of Mary Wigman.[18] She moved to Leipzig to teach at the Academy of Performing Arts, thereby, as it turns out, missing the devastating bombing raids on Dresden in 1945.

The Nazis closed Palucca's school in 1939, and she was barred from teaching until the end of the war.[19] When Germany annexed Austria in 1938, Rosalia Chladek and her colleagues gave up activities at Hellerau-Laxenburg because they felt restricted; Chladek, however, became director of the Center for Dance Performance and Education at the University of Vienna in 1942, a post she continued to hold after the war until 1952, when she was named dance director of the Vienna Academy of Music and Performing Arts.[20]

Kreutzberg managed to arouse the wrath of Goebbels, who thereupon had him conscripted into the army. Sent to the Italian front, he surrendered to the Americans.[21]

Some of the choreographers forced to leave Germany and Austria found themselves cast in new roles as dance pioneers.

One was Ernest Berk, who, though born of an English family, was raised in Germany, where he studied modern dance, organized a company, and also presented duet evenings with his wife, Lotte.[22] In 1935, when the Berks were preparing a program, Nazi officials forbade Lotte to perform because she was not a pure Aryan. Berk gave the recital alone, after which some spectators cried out for his wife. She then rose from the audience and delivered a fiery anti-Nazi speech. The Berks were ordered to leave Germany within twenty-four hours.

Settling in London, they founded the Modern Dance Group in 1936. Ernest Berk thereby joined those valiant dancers who tried, often in vain, to persuade ballet-minded Britons that modern dance was worthy of attention. Berk's group led a precarious existence until it disbanded during World War II (although he continued to choreograph solos during the war). Yet it produced ambitious works, some of them featuring elaborate masks by Elise Passavan. Several compositions were on Asian themes, for Berk was interested in Oriental dance. *Tabu* (1938) was a Polynesian *Macbeth*, and *The Life of Buddha* (1939) had a scenario by the poet John Masefield.

Gertrud Kraus settled in Palestine in 1935, although she returned to perform in Europe until the outbreak of World War II. Through her work as a teacher in Palestine, she laid the foundation for contemporary Israeli dance. And she continued to choreograph.[23]

Just as Kraus brought modern dance to one remote corner of the world, so Gertrud Bodenwieser brought it to another.[24] After Germany's annexation of Austria, Bodenwieser and her husband left for Paris, where he found a job with French Radio. Bodenwieser continued with her company for a lengthy tour that began in South

America. But her husband, who was still in France at the time of the German Occupation, was sent to a concentration camp, where he died.

From South America, Bodenwieser traveled to New Zealand and then to Australia, settling in Sydney in 1939. Coming from the sophistication of Vienna, she initially found the raw energy of Australia intimidating. Gradually, however, she adjusted to her new surroundings. Like Margaret Barr, she founded a school and a company. But whereas Barr worked in relative isolation, Bodenwieser increasingly sought to bring modern dance to all Australia.

She began to choreograph on Australian themes—for instance, two versions of the famous Australian song *Waltzing Matilda* (1945 and again in 1954) and an *Aboriginal Spear Dance* (1956). Even more importantly, she took her company to remote corners of Australia and trained scores of teachers. It is through Bodenwieser, who died in 1959, that many Australians developed an interest in modern dance.

Some dancers who fled Hitler never quite adjusted to new countries. One who suffered from such uprooting was Valeska Gert. After having been banned from German stages in 1933, she went to London and from there to America, where she made her New York debut in 1936.

The mordant humor that Berliners relished was not always to American tastes. Reviewing a Los Angeles performance in 1940, the critic Dorathi Bock Pierre wrote, "Miss Gert's work is suffused with the overhanging morbid quality of doom which is peculiar in the European personality."[25] Gert failed to duplicate her European successes in the United States. Nevertheless, she did attract a following of young artists, actors, and writers.

During the 1940s, she ran the Beggar Bar, an informal nightclub in New York City's Greenwich Village that featured nightly entertainment, including performances by Gert. Tennessee Williams once worked there as a waiter and dishwasher. One of the hat-check attendants was Judith Malina, the actress who later co-founded the experimental Living Theatre with Julian Beck.[26] Gert may have been on the fringes of New York culture, but major talents knew of her and her satirical art. Who knows what rubbed off?

$\mathcal{M}$ODERN DANCE:
AN AMERICAN ART

Louis Horst • *Martha Graham* • *John Dewey* •
John Martin

WHEREAS EUROPE WAS THE CENTER OF MUCH MODERN dance experimentation in the 1920s, the 1930s established the United States as the home of modern dance at its most creative. German dance withered under the Nazis. Yet even if there had been no Nazi tyranny, America would still have become a formidable power in dance, for it rapidly developed its own distinguished choreographers.

In an ideal world, America and Germany might have remained friendly rivals, each country learning from and then trying to surpass the other's choreographic achievements. But, because of the Nazis, American apologists for modern dance took pains to distance themselves from Germany.

The first issue of *Dance Observer* appeared in February 1934. This new magazine, edited by Louis Horst, was militant in its advocacy of modern dance, and in that first issue Paul Love proclaimed German dance irrelevant to America. "The mysticism is Teutonic," he said, "and the muddlement likewise." That same year in *Dance Observer*, Martha Graham sought to distinguish between American and German dance: "There is a certain beat and a certain quality in the American dance that we do not find in the German dance, for instance. The movement of our country is a large one. It is centered. The gesture is in the air. It springs from the ground *up*, rather than from the ground *out*."[1]

A year later, Graham was even more fervently nationalistic: "To the American dancer I say: 'Know our country.'" She deplored the "common practice to seek instruction in lands alien to us, fettered as we are to things European." And she resoundingly announced, "Of things American the American dance must be made."[2] In little more than a decade, Graham, the champion of "things American," would be famous for dances based on Greek myths. Yet her rhetoric was typical of the 1930s.

Although modern dance often provoked bewilderment, Americans were growing increasingly aware of its existence. Joseph Arnold and Paul R. Milton assembled various critical responses to the art in "Modern Dance—Today and Tomorrow," a feature published in the *American Dancer* in March 1935. Sometimes modern dance inspired mockery. Thus Russell McLaughlin summed up a Detroit performance by Doris Humphrey and Charles Weidman by writing a parody of Gilbert and Sullivan:

> There is rhythm in [a] rhombus that is right,
> There is beauty in an elegant ellipse,
> There is pleasure watching bipeds
> Making parallelopipeds
> With their ankles and their elbows and their hips.

But Ralph Holmes of the *Detroit Evening Times*, another writer cited by Arnold and Milton, was less jolly in his censures. For him, Humphrey and Weidman constituted "a social symptom . . . for they have the power to distill dangerous ideas into more dangerous emotions. . . . The Humphreys and the Weidmans are very, very dangerous people; they make me shudder with fear."[3] In 1932, Nikolai Semenoff, a Russian-born ballet teacher with a studio in Cleveland, was so dismayed at the rise of modern dance and so appalled that the Cleveland Museum of Art had invited Humphrey to appear under its auspices that he committed suicide by jumping into Niagara Falls.[4]

To outsiders, modern dance must have seemed an austere nonconformist religion. Its practitioners usually wore plain costumes and stamped on the ground with their bare feet in ritualistic fervor. No wonder Louis Horst punningly referred to the early 1930s as "the revolting period of modern dance."[5] Moreover, modern dance was a religion divided into warring choreographic sects. The directors of modern dance groups demanded total loyalty. Shopping around to investigate other dance techniques was discouraged and to study ballet was to be guilty of heresy. (Many modern dancers sneaked off to ballet classes, nonetheless.) Like monks and nuns, modern dancers lived in poverty. Also like monks and nuns, they were visionaries who labored for more than material rewards.

Fiercely independent the moderns may have been. Nevertheless, they shared certain convictions. Virtually all believed that the torso is the source of the dance impulse and sought flexibility in torso movements. Likening the dancing body to a tree, Elizabeth Selden called the torso the strong trunk and the arms the tree's branches.[6] Unlike classical ballet dancers, the moderns did not try to disguise weight. Rather, acknowledging the existence of weight made subtle changes of energy possible, and lightness, when it did occur, became all the more significant.

So, too, the floor was something to dance on and return to, as well as to escape from. And the feet that stood on that floor were usually bare. Graham remarked that "putting shoes on is like wearing white gloves to keep you away from the dirty earth."[7] To those who objected that her dances lacked grace, Graham countered that "grace in dancers is not just a decorative thing. Grace is your relationship with the world, your attitude to the people with whom and for whom you are dancing, your relationship to the stage and the space around you—the beauty your freedom, your discipline, your concentration, and your complete awareness has brought you."[8]

In addition to creating dances, Americans theorized about them. Much of their speculation was influenced by the ideas of John Dewey, one of the leading philosophers of the time. Dewey stressed art as experience, even giving that title to the influential book on esthetics he published in 1934.

For Dewey, "science states meanings; art expresses them," and each art work is "a *new* object experienced as having its own unique meaning."[9] Artworks arise out of the experiences of their creators, but they are also, in themselves, fresh experiences for their perceivers. As Dewey put it, the artist "observes the scene with meanings and values brought to his perception by prior experiences. These are . . . remade, transformed, as his new, esthetic vision takes shape. . . . Creative vision modifies these materials. They take their place in an unprecedented object of a new experience." An artwork is "so formed that it can enter into the experience of others and enable them to have more intense and more fully rounded-out experiences of their own."[10]

Like all too many estheticians past and present, Dewey devoted no attention to dance. Nevertheless, his theory of art as experience must have excited modern dancers, who maintained that the creative idea always determines the specific choreographic form and who believed that, ideally, each new dance should have its own unique choreographic vocabulary.

Within the dance community, John Martin propounded a major esthetic theory.[11] Like Dewey, Martin proclaimed the importance of experience. For Martin, "Any movement, no matter how far removed from normal experience, still conveys an impression which is related to normal experience. There is a kinesthetic response in the body of the spectator which to some extent reproduces in him the experience of the dancer."[12]

Martin believed there are two basic types of theatrical dance: spectacular and expressional. In spectacular dance the emphasis is upon what the movement looks like, rather than upon what it "says." In expressional dance, the emphasis is entirely upon what the movement "says." Among the types of dancing Martin considers spectacular are tap, exhibition adagio, nightclub "fan" and "bubble" dancing—and classical ballet. The only type of dancing that fully qualifies as expressional is modern dance.

Dance lovers may find this categorization peculiar as well as intellectually provocative. To begin with, it could be argued that all movement is expressive of *something*—if nothing else, then of a performer's delight in physical agility. And since all dances are performed by three-dimensional beings moving in time and space, even the most dramatic or emotionally revealing piece of choreography must have some sort of visual appeal. Moreover, Martin's placing of ballet into the spectacular category and reserving the expressional category solely for modern dance suggests that he is promoting his personal prejudices under the guise of impartial theorizing.

Although Martin's categorizations reflect his time and taste, his theory of how dance communicates transcends the historical era in which it was formulated. Martin was convinced that all movements convey some sort of meaning. Choreographers arrange movements to produce reactions in their audiences. These movements are kinetic stimuli, and viewers respond to them with muscular sympathy. The responses need not be overt; usually, in fact, they are not. Nevertheless, a choreographer's organizing mind and a dancer's moving body transfer something to a spectator's receptive mind and body. Martin called this process of kinetic transfer metakinesis.

The movements that effect the transfer need not be obviously pantomimic or realistic. Rather, they create their effects through their degrees of tension and relaxation, strain and ease, weight and lightness. Often, a viewer can be unsure of a dance's literal meaning and still be moved by its power. As Pauline Koner has remarked, "The early modern dance dug way in. One was often unaware of its external design because one was so concerned with its inner meaning."[13] Metakinesis remains a concept worth discussing. If no one can say with absolute certainty how or why dances affect audiences, John Martin at least had an inkling of what is involved in the process of kinetic communication.

CROSSCURRENTS

*Louise Kloepper • Tina Flade • Erika Thimey •
Truda Kaschmann • Fé Alf • Kurt and Grace Cornell
Graff • Trudi Schoop • Hanya Holm • Yeichi Nimura •
Gluck-Sandor • Felicia Sorel • Pauline Koner • Esther
Junger • Lester Horton • Bella Lewitzky*

AMERICAN MODERN DANCERS MAY HAVE PROCLAIMED THE
Americanness of their art, yet they were exposed to varied influences.
During the 1930s—before as well as after the rise of Hitler—Central
European dancers settled in the United States. Americans also ven-
tured across the Atlantic to study with such artists as Wigman or
Chladek.[1]

In 1930, Louise Kloepper became the first American to graduate
from the Wigman School in Dresden; she taught for many years at
the University of Wisconsin in Madison. The next year, two other
Wigman students, Tina Flade and Erika Thimey, moved to the
United States. Truda Kaschmann, who had studied with Laban and
Wigman, began teaching in Hartford, Connecticut, in 1933. Fé Alf, a
Wigman pupil who migrated to New York in 1931, was respected as
both a teacher and a dancer.

Kurt and Grace Graff, who were husband and wife, made Chicago
their headquarters in the 1930s. It was also Mrs. Graff's hometown.
Previously known in American dance as Grace Cornell, she had studied ballet with Adolph Bolm, Chicago's pioneering and sometimes
experimental ballet master, and with Enrico Cecchetti in Italy. Then
she studied modern dance with Laban in Germany and introduced
his choreography to New York. As a member of Martha Graham's
company in 1931, she appeared in the premiere of *Primitive Mysteries.*
That year, she also danced in Edwin Strawbridge's *Le Pas d'Acier.*

In Berlin, she met and married Kurt Graff, a Laban pupil. They
came to the United States in 1932, began appearing regularly in

Chicago in 1933, and in 1935 opened the Little Concert House in that city's Hyde Park section, a district that includes the University of Chicago.[2] The Little Concert House served as a dance center, offering lectures and symposiums as well as performances.

The Graffs' company, the Graff Ballet, toured widely. Their use of "Ballet" paralleled that of Kurt Jooss, who called his troupe the Ballets Jooss. In both cases, "Ballet" referred to a form of contemporary theatrical dancing that incorporated, but was not limited to, elements of classical technique. The Graffs' varied repertoire included *Renaissance*, a commentary on the egotism of the Borgias, *Vintage—1912*, an impression of early American ragtime, and *Ode to the Living*, a symbolic account of how two women (one rich, the other poor) met death.

Albertina Vitak called a 1941 New York concert by the Graff Ballet "a distinctly pleasant experience." Its stars, she said, were "well trained, with vital personalities" and its ensemble was "a hand picked group of talented dancers." Other critics found the Graffs' works dated. For John Martin, a 1942 program was just "a very old-fashioned Tanzgruppe concert."[3] Nevertheless, the Graffs maintained a company into the early 1940s, continued to tour duet programs through the 1950s, and often taught at Jacob's Pillow.

Not all the European imports were solemn. Trudi Schoop, an impish comedienne, was born in Switzerland in 1903. After working as a cabaret entertainer, she organized her own Pantomime Ballet—employing the word "Ballet" in the same broad sense that Jooss and the Graffs did.

When she performed *Fridolin en Route* in the United States in 1935, she was often referred to as "the female Charlie Chaplin."[4] Wearing a black suit and a flat black hat like that of a country preacher, she played a man in *Fridolin*: a gentle bumbling innocent who, like Chaplin in his film roles, managed to triumph over obstacles. Schoop settled in Los Angeles, continued to tour until 1947, and then took up dance therapy as a new career.

The most influential German choreographer to move to America was Hanya Holm. She was born in Worms, Germany, and reference books occasionally list her year of birth as 1898, although in 1991 she declared herself to be ninety-eight.[5] Her father was a wine merchant, her mother an amateur scientist with an interest in the arts. They sent her to a convent school, but unlike some such institutions, which

can be stiflingly rigid, this one favored progressive educational theories and tried to give each student special attention. After developing
an interest in music, Holm was allowed to attend Hellerau. But in
1921 she saw Mary Wigman perform in Dresden and decided to study
at her school. She became a member of Wigman's company, a teaching assistant, and a choreographer.

She also became Hanya Holm. She had been born Johanna Eckert
and was, for a time, married to the artist Reinhard Martin Kunze.
But she found neither Eckert nor Kunze attractive as a stage name.
Instead, she chose Holm: it sounded right to her; it was also a name
related to ancient Nordic words that can mean holly, island, hill, and
the high seas.[6]

It was Sol Hurok, Wigman's shrewd American impresario, who
thought that a Wigman School in New York could be simultaneously
esthetically stimulating and financially profitable. Wigman was initially dubious; when she finally agreed to open such an establishment
in 1931, she placed Holm in charge of it. By 1932, Holm was already
planning to become an American citizen.[7]

Although Holm respected Wigman's basic pedagogical principles,
she modified Wigman's teaching methods to meet the special needs
of her new students, and she soon realized that some of the anguished
or cosmic themes to which German choreographers were drawn
were of little interest to Americans. After 1933, she also had to remind
Americans that the New York Wigman School had no connection
with the German government. She soon asked Wigman's permission
to change the name of the school; when it became the Hanya Holm
Studio in 1936, Holm announced, "A racial or political question has
never existed and shall never exist in my school. In my opinion, there
is no room for politics in art. I most emphatically refuse to identify
myself with any political creed which strangles the free development
of art, regardless of whether these political straitjackets are imported
from Europe or manufactured here."[8]

Holm's most ambitious choreographic achievement was *Trend*.
A complex piece of group choreography that required a cast of more
than thirty, *Trend* was first presented at the Bennington Festival of
1937. It received its New York premiere later that year at Mecca Temple,
the auditorium now known as the City Center. Her very seating arrangements at Mecca Temple were unusual. No one was placed in
the theatre's orchestra section. Instead, everyone sat in the balcony

and looked down on the action which occurred below on multi-leveled ramps designed by Arch Lauterer.

Trend, to music by Wallingford Riegger and Edgard Varèse, offered a symbolic vision of world conditions from World War I to the 1930s. It included scenes representing industrial regimentation, the self-indulgence of the leisured class, the desire for money, fanatical religion, and political despotism. An episode called "Cataclysm" developed into a kinetic crescendo of running and leaping. Nevertheless, after this evocation of social disintegration, *Trend* concluded with images of resurgence and assurance.

The monumentality of *Trend* made it akin to some of the German ensemble dances of the 1920s and 1930s. But unlike Wigman, who occasionally portrayed a charismatic leader in her group works, Holm took care not to cast herself as any sort of figure who could be interpreted as a supreme hero, social savior, or *Führer*. Rather, she stressed the interplay of individuals and groups.[9]

Several of Holm's works—serious and light alike—offered social commentary. The somber *Tragic Exodus* (1938) concerned political exile. *Metropolitan Daily* (1938) satirized a daily newspaper. Holm was also adept at creating "pure" dances—works that explored space and made audiences aware of the multitudinous movement qualities of which a dance might consist. She created *Dance of Introduction* (1938) as a way of presenting her dancers—and, possibly, the art of modern dance itself—to the audiences before which her company performed on tour. Looking back on it many years later, Walter Terry said that Holm seemed to be stating in the work that "these are my dancers, this is how we think and feel, and this is our home, the house of dance, and this is the way we move through this space which in the confines of the stage is our home. This is us."[10]

Holm's company was an attractive one. And she did not encourage its members to imitate her. Reviewing a Los Angeles performance by the Hanya Holm Group, Dorathi Bock Pierre observed that "Hanya Holm's movements are small, dainty, fussy, entirely European. If she had chosen ballet as her dance medium she would have been inevitably compared to Adeline Genée. Her group, however, have large, strong movements, peculiarly their own, and entirely American." Pierre thought that this peaceful coexistence of styles could have been brought about "only by a very great and unselfish soul."[11]

Later in her career, Holm became a successful choreographer of Broadway musicals, and she was especially influential as a teacher who both honored rational movement analysis and prized improvisation as a compositional tool. Among her pupils were Alwin Nikolais, Murray Louis, Valerie Bettis, and Glen Tetley.

Like his own teachers, Ruth St. Denis and Michio Ito, Yeichi Nimura infused Western modern dance with an aura of the Orient. Nimura was born in Suwa, Japan, in 1897 and, like Ito, came from a samurai family; his grandfather was a Shinto priest. An unruly young man, Nimura was sent to New York in 1918 to complete his education under the supervision of a relative who taught at Columbia University. Instead, he went his own way and became a dancer, studying ballet and Spanish dance, as well as modern dance with Ito and at Denishawn. With the American dancer Pauline Koner as his partner, he made his recital debut in 1930. Lisan Kay, another American dancer, soon became his partner and his wife, and they toured extensively in America and Europe.[12]

Nimura created dance on Oriental themes—among them, *Sword Ritual, Spear Episode,* and *Javanesque (Monkey God)*—as well as such a work as *Three Cosmic Poems,* in which allegorical figures of Man and Woman faced their destiny in a way that reminded the *Dancing Times* of modern German dance. The magazine's columnist, "The Sitter Out," commented, "It is difficult to say what of Mr. Nimura's dancing was pure Japanese and what was 'Western theatre.'" But that did not matter: "He obviously has a very finely developed sense of our theatre and is an exceedingly able mime. His dancing is virile and strong, and he possesses considerable elevation." One of Nimura's most unusual solos was *Wizard Cat,* in which he sprang into view, only to vanish and reappear. Lying on the floor, he arched his back and stretched, apparently hoping to be fondled. Then he unexpectedly bounded across the ground, turned in the air, and disappeared. The solo derived from a Japanese myth about the way in which human souls could be stolen and possessed by cats. The *Dancing Times* pronounced it "a startling interpretation."[13]

Nimura deliberately retired as a performer in 1940, when he was still at the height of his dancing powers. Until his death in 1979, he remained active as a teacher at New York's Ballet Arts School and choreographed for its students.

Several American choreographers defied simple categorization— among them, Gluck-Sandor. He was an independent-minded serious artist. At the same time, he was thoroughly at home in the commercial theatre, and at one time or another in his long career he staged dances for Chicago's Oriental Theatre, New York's Paramount Theatre, *Earl Carroll's Vanities*, nightclubs, and burlesque shows.

A New Yorker born sometime in the first decade of this century, Senia Gluck-Sandor dreamed of being a dancer as a young man. Instead, he worked as a stock clerk. He found himself fascinated by a woman in the next office, not simply because of her general charm, but because of her feet. One day he blurted out that her feet seemed to be made for dancing. "I know it," she said. "I do dance." And where? "The Neighborhood Playhouse," she replied.[14]

To the Neighborhood Playhouse he went. Gluck-Sandor, as he called himself professionally, also studied ballet with Michel Fokine and Spanish dance with Vincente Escudero, and he performed with the Metropolitan Opera Ballet. Like the Sakharoffs and the Graffs, Gluck-Sandor and his wife, Felicia Sorel, gave programs of solos and duets. They also headed a company. Throughout the 1930s (with some interruptions due to economic adversity), they tried to maintain their studio theatre, the Dance Center. Gluck-Sandor's productions were often ambitious. In 1932, he offered a danced version of *Salomé* (to music arranged from Strauss's opera) and his own versions of Stravinsky's *Petrouchka*, Manuel de Falla's *El Amor Brujo*, and Prokofiev's *Prodigal Son*.[15]

Petrouchka and *El Amor Brujo* were frequently revived. At various times during the 1937–1938 season, the leading role of Candelas in the latter was played by both Sorel and Klarna Pinska, a former Denishawn dancer; José Limón was cast as her lover. In *Petrouchka* on 2 April 1938, Gluck-Sandor danced the title role; Dorothy Barrett was the Ballerina doll, and Randolph Sawyer, a black dancer, was the Blackamoor. (Such interracial performances were rare at the time.) The Arlecchino in *Pierrot the Barber*, a commedia dell'arte work on the same bill, was Gerald Robins, who, as Jerome Robbins, would soon establish himself as one of America's greatest ballet and Broadway choreographers.

Robbins remembered his early days at the Dance Center, and he cast Gluck-Sandor as the Rabbi in *Fiddler on the Roof* in 1964. Gluck-Sandor, who died in 1978, was once again the Rabbi when the musical was revived in 1970.

The choreographer of the first production of *Petrouchka* in 1911 was the balletic reformer Michel Fokine. He opened a New York school in 1921 and modern dancers as well as ballet dancers studied with him, even though, despite his admiration of Isadora Duncan, he distrusted modern dance as an art form.

Among Fokine's students was Pauline Koner, who also studied Spanish dance with Angel Cansino and Dalcroze eurhythmics with the conductor Paul Boepple. Koner, who was born in New York in 1912, was the daughter of Russian Jews who had fled pogroms in their native land. Her father, a lawyer, devised a medical plan for the Workmen's Circle, a New York Jewish Socialist and benevolent organization, the first such plan in America. Although the Koners gradually grew more prosperous, they were not wealthy, and they were horrified to learn that Fokine charged $5 a lesson—an almost unheard-of sum at the time. Fortunately for their daughter, an arrangement was reached whereby Mr. Koner offered his legal services to Fokine in return for lessons for Pauline.

She later performed with Michio Ito and Yeichi Nimura. Yet, although she is now regarded as a prominent figure in modern dance, she is fond of pointing out that she never had a modern dance lesson in her life. Instead, she went her own way, becoming a dancing individualist in the most literal sense. During the 1930s, she was known primarily as a soloist. According to the critic Joseph Arnold, she possessed "grace, intelligence, a good stage presence, an attractive figure and an individuality that outlines all her compositions."[16]

Koner's solos of the 1930s tended to be of two kinds. Some derived from ethnic sources: for instance, *Spanish Impressions* and *Yemenite Prayer*. Others were examples of various types of modern dance: *Upheaval*, *Waltz Momentum*, *Cycle of the Masses*, *Bird of Prey*, and *Three Small Funeral Marches—For a Statesman, For a Canary, For a Rich Aunt*. Koner performed in the Soviet Union in 1934–1936 and on her return to America created dances that drew upon her Soviet experiences, among them *Free Day* (a lively solo based on the pattern of the Soviet work week, in which five days of work were followed by one free day) and *Lullaby to a Future Hero* (which evoked the strength and hopefulness of Russian women). Koner was responsive both to the American scene and to international events. Her programs of 1938 included *Summertime* (a jazz-influenced piece to music from George Gershwin's *Porgy and Bess*), *Song of the Slums*, *Tragic Response* (a commentary on the Spanish Civil War), and *Among the Ruins* (which depicted a Chinese civilian caught in a bombardment by Japanese warplanes).[17]

Esther Junger, another New York-born dancer noted for her solos, also stood, like Koner, apart from some of the modern dance factions of her time. Junger, whose father was a singer, was a sickly child and did not attend school until she was nine. Nevertheless, she became a physical education teacher and found herself increasingly interested in dance. She studied briefly at the New York Denishawn. But the teacher who exerted the greatest influence on her was Bird Larson, with whom she worked from 1925 to Larson's death in 1927. Junger made her debut as a solo dancer in 1930. Although she appeared with Gluck-Sandor's company the next year and also performed in revues, she devoted most of her choreographic energy to solos.

Her *Animal Ritual* (to percussion accompaniment) was inspired by animal movements. On many programs she paired *Wide-Open Plains*, a solo of spacious movements, with *Closed-In Cities*. Her *Inertia* showed a weary figure lethargically getting to its feet. A critic for the *New York World-Telegram* quipped that a substitute title for it could be *The Afternoon of a Yawn*.[18] Reviewing a concert in 1939, John Martin reminded readers of Junger's experience in musical theatre and suggested that two of her solos could easily be inserted into some sophisticated revue: *Torch Song*, to Gershwin's "The Man I Love," and *Bach Goes to Town*, to Alec Templeton's "swing" arrangements of Bach.

Discussing Junger's work in general, Martin said, "Her approach is characterized by the most complete directness. She is without pretense or affectation."[19]

Lester Horton was a choreographic individualist on the West Coast and did not bring his Los Angeles company to New York until shortly before his death in 1953. Born in 1906, Horton studied art and ballet and became involved in little theatre activities in his native Indianapolis. American Indian culture fascinated him, and in 1928 he was invited to California to stage a pageant based on Henry Wadsworth Longfellow's *Song of Hiawatha*. As a young Bohemian, Horton kept his hair long and bushy and favored Indian shirts and huaraches. He directed plays and pageants and worked with Michio Ito, then organized his own Lester Horton Dancers in 1932.[20]

Horton explored the black, Chinese, Japanese, and Mexican communities of Los Angeles and made friends in all of these districts. He staged dances on Mexican, Haitian, and American Indian themes. He also choreographed his own version of *Le Sacre du Printemps* in

1937. One dramatic subject that obsessed him all his life was the story of Salome. He created his first *Salome* in 1934; other versions followed in later years, one under the title *Face of Violence*. Under any title, *Salome* was forceful and macabre.

Also in 1934, Horton began his association with Bella Lewitzky, a strikingly dramatic performer who for the next fifteen years served as his choreographic guinea pig and leading lady. Together, they began to develop a systematized plan of teaching, laying the groundwork of what came to be known as "Horton technique."

Just as modern dancers often took work in the commercial theatre in order to earn money, so Horton's dancers appeared in stage shows and Hollywood films. Horton struggled to make ends meet. Yet he managed to survive and, by doing so, he demonstrated that New York did not have to be the only home for modern dance in America.

AMERICAN MODERNS

Ruth St. Denis • *Ted Shawn* • *The Men Dancers* •
Jacob's Pillow • *Martha Graham* • *Louis Horst* • *Doris
Humphrey* • *Charles Weidman* • *Helen Tamiris*

ONE AUTUMN DAY IN 1932, A GRIM-FACED TED SHAWN
drove to the New York Denishawn house accompanied by Barton
Mumaw, a young Denishawn dancer. There they met an equally
somber Ruth St. Denis and some other Denishawn dancers and staff
members who, like Mumaw, were bewildered and apprehensive.
Ruth and Ted had made a monumental decision.

Their marriage had disintegrated. Now, they thought, it was time
to end their professional partnership as well. Each wanted an independent career and accused the other of being an artistic burden.[1]

St. Denis and Shawn were at Denishawn House to divide up their
costumes: the jeweled belts and bracelets, the embroidered skirts and
feathered capes, the veils, wigs, and saris that had helped make Denishawn productions resplendent. But after the wardrobe trucks were
emptied, much of Denishawn still remained: stored at Denishawn
House was a vast collection of scenery for productions that would
surely never be staged again.

After consulting with St. Denis, Shawn announced to his startled
colleagues, "Miss Ruth and I have agreed that there is only one way
we can bear to bring Denishawn to an end—with fire—with a
cleansing fire that will free our spirits from material encumbrances
so we may each go on to achieve what we can, alone."[2] Outdoors, a
pyre was assembled onto which Shawn and the students threw stage
properties and backdrops representing everything from Babylonian
palaces to Indian pueblos. Shawn then doused the pile with kerosene
and set it ablaze.

A great era of dance had ended.

Yet St. Denis and Shawn never remained totally apart. They kept in touch throughout their lives: St. Denis died in 1968, Shawn in 1972. They took no legal action toward divorce and made several public reunions, including a Golden Wedding celebration in 1965.

The stately St. Denis, who reveled in her role as America's *grande dame* of dance, devoted herself largely to works on religious themes. Shawn had a new scheme: an all-male company. He acquired property in the Berkshire Hills of Massachusetts, a farm which before and during the Civil War had served as a station on the underground railroad: the network of havens established by opponents of slavery that sheltered southern slaves during their attempts to escape in the United States and Canada. A winding road in the neighborhood had been nicknamed Jacob's Ladder and a large boulder on the property led the entire farm to be called Jacob's Pillow.

Shawn's all-male company gave its first performance on 21 March 1933 in Boston.[3] That summer, the troupe made Jacob's Pillow its headquarters, thereby turning the old farm into an American Ascona, a dedicated community of young artists working under a creative leader.[4]

Shawn organized "tea-concerts" at the Pillow at which the men gave informal performances before an audience. These modest events were the forerunners of today's Jacob's Pillow Dance Festival. After the men's group disbanded in 1940, Mary Washington Ball organized a festival summer of performances and classes. The ballet stars Alicia Markova and Anton Dolin took over the festival in 1941, and Shawn was in charge from 1942 until his death in 1972. Other directors have succeeded him, but have maintained his basic policy of eclectic programming.

During the 1930s, Shawn created an all-male repertoire which, in effect, challenged the fraternity brothers who had assured him that men did not dance. The programs of Ted Shawn and His Men Dancers included music visualizations to Mozart's Symphony No. 40 and Bach inventions, Spanish and American folk works, and grandly scaled allegorical ensembles, many to original scores by Jess Meeker. *Labor Symphony* celebrated man's work in fields and forests, at sea, and in factories. *Olympiad* was a suite of sports dances. *O Libertad!* depicted scenes from New World history from the time of the Aztecs down to the California Gold Rush of 1849 and on to the Jazz Age and the Depression.

One allegorical work that attracted particular attention was *Kinetic Molpai*, a dance of 1935 with music by Meeker that took its title from the Molpê, a celebration of thanksgiving held on threshing floors in ancient Greece when the harvest was done.[5] A plotless kinetic psalm of resurrection, *Kinetic Molpai* concerned what its program note listed as themes of "Love, Strife, Death, and that which is beyond Death," and its choreography was based on falls, jumps, and opposing and parallel movements. Shawn created an expressive climactic image in which, after members of the ensemble fell to earth, their leader raised one man who then raised the next; each man, in turn, raised his neighbor until the whole group was on its feet.

Many skeptical dancegoers who came to scorn remained to cheer Shawn's men. But some critics found the Men Dancers' programs lacking in subtlety. Some dancegoers of a later time who have not seen a step of choreography by Shawn have sneered at what they fancy to be a corny "macho" brawniness about his productions. However, if Shawn wished to convince small-town—and culturally limited big-city—Americans of the legitimacy of male dancing, he had to show men engaged in activities to which no one at the time could take exception. Therefore he drew on themes of labor, sports, and heroic deeds. If men who dance onstage today can be tender as well as tough and vulnerable as well as vigorous, that is, in part, because Ted Shawn and His Men Dancers paved the way for them.

The choreography of some of Denishawn's rebels grew turbulent during the 1930s. Martha Graham, in particular, provoked controversy—to such a degree that her mother once asked in despair, "Why do people say such dreadful things about Martha? She was always such a sweet, old-fashioned girl."[6]

To some eyes, however, her choreography looked decidedly newfangled because of its angularity, broken patterns, abrupt changes, and asymmetrical groupings. Her choreographic tensions struck Elizabeth Selden as quintessentially urban:

She pictures in dance form the mind of the city dweller, at least to the degree in which New York is typical of him. That mind is always one trained chiefly indoors or in the skyscraper-dominated outdoors. It reflects a welter of associations gathered chiefly in libraries, in many art galleries, in the subway, in the concert hall, in the night café, in dimly lit streets, and in the glaring whiteness of square, sun-baked vertical walls. Martha Graham has translated its brittle, sharply-bitten vernacular into dance forms by the only method which is adequate to it: expressionism.[7]

Graham could have developed as she did only in a sophisticated urban milieu. Yet she—and her mentor, Louis Horst—also admired some sun-baked walls far from Manhattan: those of the Indian communities of the Southwest. Indian art, with its spare formal structures and geometric shapes, fascinated Graham and Horst, and the vast expanse of the southwestern landscape caused Graham to make choreographic contrasts between earth and air.

In 1931, the earth and air of the Southwest inspired her to choreograph a masterpiece: *Primitive Mysteries*, a three-part work derived from the rituals of Christianized American Indians. Each section of this dance for a somberly clad cast of women venerates the Virgin Mary, and its principal soloist (originally Graham herself) is a symbol of Mary. The work's three scenes concern the adoration of the Madonna, Mary's grief at the death of Jesus, and the joyousness of the Resurrection. All the episodes begin with solemn processionals and conclude with equally measured recessionals.

The choreography is angular throughout, and the dancers are often arranged in architecturally imposing, but asymmetrical, groupings; as a result, even moments of repose can seem charged with tension. Horst's music for flute, oboe, and piano is as austere as the choreography, and the tread of the dancers' feet often sounds as if it were an integral part of the score.

Like her choreography, Graham's teaching was notable for its nervous energy. She based her technique upon the drama inherent in a basic fact of life: breathing. Graham analyzed the way the act of breathing makes the torso contract in exhalation and expand in inhalation. Intensifying the dynamics of this natural process, she developed whiplash turns, fierce kicks, and sudden falls.

Possibly because her productions looked austere, the choreographically passionate Graham was sometimes accused of being excessively cerebral. Thus Joseph Arnold complained in the *American Dancer* that a Graham performance of 1933 was a "display of cold intellectualism, sexless and removed from living emotions."[8]

During a 1932 interview, Graham remarked, "Dancing is movement made divinely significant."[9] She loved such inspirational utterances. But those who disliked her could seize upon her oracular pronouncements as evidence that she headed some sort of choreographic cult.

Arnold had no use for her fervent admirers: "The Graham audiences . . . are largely composed of people who, in good Broadway patois, are termed 'phonies.' They go in for intellectual fads, are lavish in their praise and don't mean a word they say. The approval of Miss Graham by a typical Graham audience is therefore of no consequence." [10] It must be admitted that Graham, to some extent, cultivated the airs of a prophetess. With her dark hair and cavernous cheeks, she could look mysteriously wise or ineffably sad. And whereas Margaret Einert found her fascinating for being "very slender, ashen-faced, with straight raven hair and burning eyes," for Joseph Arnold she was merely "a very homely girl" with "a face like a death's head, white and bony." [11]

Graham persevered, gradually winning acclaim. In 1932, she was the first dancer to receive a Guggenheim Fellowship. Also that year, she and her group were invited to participate in the opening of a new 6,000-seat entertainment palace, the Radio City Music Hall. In 1936, when her anti-Nazi convictions caused her to reject an invitation to dance at the Berlin Olympics, she was sufficiently famous that her action came as a genuine rebuff to the Hitler regime. (Later in her life, she would adamantly refuse to perform in racially segregated South Africa.) By the end of the 1930s, Graham had achieved such eminence that she and her company danced *Tribute to Peace* (to G. F. Handel's "See, the Conquering Hero Comes," sung by the Westminster Choir) immediately after an address by President Franklin D. Roosevelt on the opening day of the New York World's Fair, 30 April 1939.[12]

Graham created a body of choreographic work so impressive that even her detractors had to take it seriously. Her productions of 1934 included two contrasting pieces. Whereas *American Provincials: Act of Piety, Act of Judgment* castigated Puritanism, *Celebration* was a buoyant dance based on jumping patterns.

Frontier (1935) was Graham's first collaboration with Isamu Noguchi, the sculptor who would regularly design productions for her through the mid-1960s. His décor for *Frontier* was simple: a short length of fence and a piece of rope that extended outward and upward from it in a V-shape. Yet, with that fence and that rope, Noguchi suggested the vastness of the Great Plains. So did the choreography. In this solo, Graham stood before the fence, leaned against it, and let an upraised leg rest on its top. All the while, she stared out across the prairie, wavering with momentary hesitation in awe of its grandeur, yet also boldly and confidently. *Frontier* paid tribute to the indomitable will of the pioneer woman.

Although never overtly propagandistic, Graham was keenly aware of political issues. *Chronicle* (1936) was a suite of episodes that commented on social tensions since World War I. One of its sections, "Steps in the Street," did so in an almost abstract manner, with contrapuntal patterns that conveyed a sense of unrest. *Deep Song* (1937) was a solo of grief inspired by the Spanish Civil War. *American Document* (1938) offered a panorama of scenes from American history that combined movement with a spoken text drawn from the writings of American authors and political thinkers. It was Graham's first dance in which the cast included a man: Erick Hawkins.

American Document was evidence that Graham's productions were growing more theatrically elaborate. During the 1940s, she would increasingly concern herself with plot and characterization.

Many of Graham's dances—among them, *Primitive Mysteries, Celebration, American Provincials,* and *Frontier*—had scores by Louis Horst. But Horst was important not simply because of his association with Graham. He was a theorist, an editor, and perhaps America's most influential teacher of dance composition.

Musically, he was a real "pro." Like Ted Shawn, Horst was a native of Kansas City, where he was born in 1884, the son of immigrant parents. But he was raised in San Francisco, where his father, a musician, had gone in search of work. He followed in his father's footsteps, becoming a pianist for vaudeville shows and silent movies, as well as for dance halls, mining camps, and gambling houses.

In 1909, he married Bessie ("Betty") Cunningham, a dancer who later appeared with Denishawn. Horst's own association with Denishawn began in 1915 when he accepted what he thought would be a temporary post as accompanist. Instead, he remained with the school and company for the next decade.

Horst eventually left to go off on his own. He studied musical composition in Vienna in 1925 and, while abroad, saw performances by European modern dancers. From 1926 to 1948, he was Graham's musical adviser and confidant, although he and Betty, who stayed in California, were never divorced.[13] Horst was devoted to Graham; convinced of her genius, he did everything to encourage her. Yet he was also on friendly terms with representatives of most of the dance world's factions. He composed thirty dance scores—eleven for Graham—and accompanied or conducted performances by such dancers as Doris Humphrey, Charles Weidman, Helen Tamiris, Harald Kreutzberg, Ruth Page, and Agnes de Mille. In 1934, he founded *Dance Observer* and remained its editor and one of its critics until his death in 1964, when it died with him.

A sternly worded unsigned editorial in the magazine's first issue (February 1934) introduced some of the issues *Dance Observer* would emphasize throughout its existence. The editorial deplored the lack of good dance writing in America, the notions that ballet is the highest form of dance and European culture is superior to American, and the way that concert bureaus and impresarios perpetuate the myth of American inferiority in the arts by consistently booking foreign attractions.[14]

A heavyset, patriarchal, jowly man with a massive head and bushy eyebrows, Horst was fond of cigars and dachshunds as well as music and dance. He was a commanding figure, and his sharp tongue could be cruel as well as witty. Although in no sense a conventionally handsome man, Horst exerted a strange power over young women, whom he loved to tease and terrify. He did both in his classes in dance composition, which he began teaching in 1928. "I know it hurts," he would say to students whose efforts he had just torn to shreds. "You didn't think it was going to be fun, did you?"[15]

Dismayed because so many dances he saw were amorphous in intention, subject matter, and movement content, Horst wished to provide novice choreographers with a solid compositional base that could help them find a theme and manipulate it effectively. Possibly because he was a musician, he turned to music history as he searched for structural models dancers might find useful. However, being a confirmed anti-Romantic, one period he passed over was the nineteenth century.

His two basic composition classes—which he called courses in the pre-classic and modern forms[16]— stressed the choreographic application of such devices of musical composition as repetition, inversion, amplification, and contraction, the specific musical forms of the "pre-classic age," and the art and music of the twentieth century.

Among musical forms, Horst considered *A-B-A* to be inherently satisfying, for it had a beginning, a middle, and an end. A theme (musical or choreographic) was introduced; a contrasting theme was added; and a resolution brought the work to a close. Horst extolled the *A-B-A* form so vociferously that wits sometimes joked that he taught "the ABC's of *A-B-A*." He also admired the theme and variations form, in which a theme is stated and then varied so that it constantly changes, yet at the same time preserves some of its essential nature.

Court dances from the fifteenth through the eighteenth centuries served as models in the course in "pre-classic forms." In some ways, that course was misleadingly named, for it did not concern itself with the authentic reconstruction of any old dances. Rather, Horst described them and then asked students to choreograph their own works based upon those dances' structures and moods, about which he had strong opinions. For him, a galliard had to suggest gaiety, a courant had to contain running steps, and a pavane had to convey a sense of pride or power.

Progressing to the course in "modern forms," students were introduced to such principles as asymmetry and dissonance. They examined the influence of primitive, archaic, and medieval art upon the twentieth century and analyzed such modern styles as Impressionism, Expressionism, jazz, Americana, and "cerebralism," a term which encompassed serial music and such types of abstraction as the geometric paintings of Piet Mondrian.

Horst's assignments were strict. They were also wildly arbitrary, for they were based upon his own esthetic likes and dislikes. As he grew older, he would be increasingly attacked for this. Yet he never regarded his exercises as foolproof formulas for compositional success. Rather, he hoped to sharpen dancers' wits and to encourage them to devote their minds as well as their feelings to the intricacies of dance making.

"Graceful dancing still abounds for those who are romantic," said Doris Humphrey in 1935. "But the modern dance is for those who have progressed toward and accepted a wider interpretation of contemporary life, one which includes both dark and light. It is for those who believe that art is a revelation of the meaning of life and not an escape from it."[17]

Humphrey was certainly capable of graceful dancing. With her keen blue eyes and glowing light auburn hair, she was an attractive woman who could seem deceptively fragile in appearance. She was also a quiet person, someone many of her colleagues found essentially introspective. In 1932, she married Charles Woodford, a seaman. It was a happy marriage, and the very fact that Woodford was occasionally away at sea for extended periods allowed Humphrey to have her own times of solitude.

Choreographically, however, Humphrey did not believe in navel-gazing. "The solo dancer is too much herself," she told an interviewer in 1931. "Her dancing is too much limited by size, by shape, by the color of hair and eyes. It is too characteristic and too limited to be the great dance of tomorrow. In the ensemble the audience receives only the true impressions of movement, design, accent." Although she choreographed fine solos, Humphrey specialized in group works, for she believed that group designs could make great themes clear and powerful. As she wrote in 1932, "Four abstract themes, all moving equally and harmoniously together like a fugue would convey the idea of democracy far better than one woman dressed in red, white and blue with stars in her hair." At its debut in 1928, the Humphrey-Weidman Company had sixteen dancers—a large number for a modern dance troupe of the time. Dancers were not always easy to find then. As Humphrey admitted, "I like groups of people so much better—but the people are not so good, so there we are." [18]

Humphrey was fascinated by designs in space. At the same time, she believed that movement without motivation was unthinkable. Therefore, the ways dancers interacted in space could suggest personal or social relationships and even be kinetic images of ideas or abstract concepts. Humphrey concerned herself with the ways in which human beings react to their environment. Yet her works were seldom literal depictions of any specific milieu. Like Graham in her own way, Humphrey sought to extract the essences of ideas or situations.

Just as Graham technique could be summed up in two words—contraction and release—so Humphrey was also associated with two terms: fall and recovery. She based her technique on the body's capacity to yield to or resist gravitational pulls. Humphrey believed that the drama of dance—and of life itself—derives from the multitudinous ways in which bodies manage to move between two motionless states: standing rigidly upright and lying flat (or even corpselike) on the ground. She might well have agreed with the seventeenth-century French philosopher Blaise Pascal, who said, "Our nature consists in movement; absolute rest is death." [19]

Humphrey's *Two Ecstatic Themes* (1931) consisted of a pair of related solos. "Circular Descent" was based on a slow, complex fall in which a woman yielded to a force that sought to press her downward. Then, in "Pointed Ascent," she rose from the floor with angular gestures. Yet both the downward and the upward progressions were interrupted by pulls in the opposite direction.

Humphrey's group works exemplified her movement concerns and philosophical principles even more strikingly. *The Shakers*, a dance of 1931 to traditional Shaker music, depicts members of a utopian Christian sect that idealized a simple celibate life free from carnal desires. Shaker religious services included singing, speaking in tongues, and a form of ecstatic dancing during which the worshipers appeared to be trying to shake their sins out of their bodies. Evoking such a service, Humphrey contrasts hops, shuffles, and downward motions of the hands in acknowledgment of the carnal earth with palms-up gestures symbolizing longing for God's grace. The way that separate groups of men and women draw near, as if magnetized, yet never touch suggests the sexual tensions that might develop in a celibate community. *The Shakers* remains one of Humphrey's most frequently revived compositions.

The monumentally scaled *New Dance Trilogy* (choreographed in 1935 and 1936 to music by Wallingford Riegger) examines forces of harmony and disintegration. Each part of the trilogy could be performed as a self-contained entity. Yet they were thematically linked—although in Humphrey's lifetime all three works were never performed on the same program because they were thought to be too strenuous for the dancers.[20] *Theatre Piece*, the first dance, was a satirical portrait of vain, superficial, and competitive people.

Humphrey looked at tormented personal relationships in *With My Red Fires*, a dramatic work in which a formidable matriarch thwarts her daughter's romantic desires. However, the way in which the tyrannical mother incited other people to pursue and punish the rebellious young lovers gave the piece social, as well as psychological, implications. Choreographed at a time when European dictators were, like domineering parents, squelching nonconformity, *With My Red Fires* was an attack on authoritarianism.

Having depicted social and personal troubles in *Theatre Piece* and *With My Red Fires*, Humphrey, who all her life refused to succumb to pessimism, offered a vision of harmonious order called, like the trilogy itself, *New Dance*. An abstract work, with no hint of historical period, geographical locale, or specific characters, the celebratory composition made its points solely through the implications of its patterning. A woman (Humphrey) led a women's dance; a man

(Weidman) headed a male ensemble. When the groups joined together, dancers came forward in solos, then returned to the group, the soloists never tyrannizing the members of the ensemble, the mass never totally swallowing up the individuals.

Humphrey admired Bach and used his music on several occasions. For a special Christmas Eve performance in 1934, she staged Bach's *Christmas Oratorio* with a cast that included the actress Lillian Gish as Mary and Weidman as the Angel of the Annunciation. In 1938, she created *Passacaglia in C Minor*, which choreographically followed the music's structure without being merely a music visualization. Humphrey called *Passacaglia* "an abstract composition with dramatic overtones. The persistently repeated figure in the minor mode suggested to the choreographer man's reiteration of faith in his ideals despite an imperfect world." [21] Thus *Passacaglia* was thematically related to *New Dance*: each was a statement of Humphrey's own faith in the possibility of human betterment.

Charles Weidman, Humphrey's partner, shared that faith. He was best known as a comic dancer and choreographer. Yet he could also be deadly serious. And some of his jokes could sting.

Weidman was born in Lincoln, Nebraska, in 1901. His father was a civil engineer and the city's fire chief; his mother had held the title of Champion Roller Skater of the Middle West. Weidman once thought of becoming an architect. But he was led into the theatre—by junk. While working at a junkyard, he was fascinated by the photos of such celebrated performers as Isadora Duncan, Ruth St. Denis, and Sarah Bernhardt that he found in the magazines that had been dumped there. He studied dance with a local teacher, Eleanor Frampton, who many years later would teach Humphrey-Weidman technique in Cleveland. When Weidman attended a performance by Denishawn, there before his eyes onstage were the architectural wonders of such places as Egypt and Greece—and there was dancing, as well.

Weidman went to Los Angeles to study at Denishawn and was soon taken into the company. Ted Shawn discovered something important about this young man: he was a superb mimic; even his bushy eyebrows could be expressive. Shawn created several solos for him that capitalized upon his mimetic talents—among them, *The Crapshooter*. Weidman also mimetically joined in a crap game in *Danse Américaine*, in which he portrayed a swaggering mill-town dude who, full of bravado, showed off, played baseball, flirted, and did some clog and soft-shoe steps. [22]

When Weidman and Doris Humphrey formed their own company, their choreographic styles complemented each other. Humphrey could be lofty; Weidman tended to be down-to-earth. Through his mastery of pantomime, he could indicate the presence of unseen people or things by the ways in which his eyes focused, his hands moved, or his head turned.

He staged dance versions of such literary works as Max Beerbohm's *The Happy Hypocrite* (1931) and Voltaire's *Candide* (1933). *American Saga* (1935) was based on tall tales about the legendary lumberjack Paul Bunyan. *Flickers* (1941) was a spoof of silent films in which the usually serious Humphrey delighted her admirers with her outrageous clowning as a vamp. Later in his career, Weidman choreographed works inspired by the writings and drawings of the humorist James Thurber: *Fables for Our Time* (1947), *The War between Men and Women* (1954), and *Is Sex Necessary?* (1960).

Two dances by Weidman painted portraits of his relatives. *On My Mother's Side* (1940) was a solo suite of pantomimes suggested by pictures in the Weidman family album. Wearing only a simple shirt and slacks, Weidman portrayed men and women alike, bringing them to life with the magic of his gestures. *And Daddy Was a Fireman* (1943) was a group work in which Weidman's father was seen courting a young woman and battling a rival in the fire department and the personification of Fire itself, both villains played, for symbolical reasons, by the same dancer.

Weidman also dared to venture beyond conventional representational mime. He called his own experimental form "kinetic pantomime." By this term, he sought to indicate that the gestures did not have to have a dramatic base and that they could develop according to their own movement logic, rather than by cause-and-effect psychological motivation. Thus his *Opus 51* (1938) was a kaleidoscopic collection of unrelated actions. Individual movement phrases might suggest a man taking a shower, a woman sweeping the floor, a nun telling her beads, and a man tugging at a fishing pole. But, like words in a nonsense poem, these activities were arranged not in sequences possessing specific meanings, but in a spirit of impish play.[23]

There was also a somber side to Weidman's choreography. In 1945, he created *A House Divided*, a work about Abraham Lincoln. Even some of his comic dances had serious implications. His *Atavisms* (1936), a suite of three dances, began with two comedies. *Bargain*

Counter showed a timid department-store employee overcome by a stampede of female shoppers. *Stock Exchange* satirically examined the dog-eat-dog world of high finance. But *Lynchtown*, the third dance, was a grim study in mass hysteria that depicted the way a lynching causes a whole community to be swept up in a paroxysm of hatred.

Each of the three dances can be performed as an independent item. Divorced from the other two, *Bargain Counter* can even resemble a choreographic *New Yorker* cartoon. But when *Bargain Counter* and *Stock Exchange* were originally presented along with *Lynchtown*, their merriment may not have seemed so innocent, for all three dances can be said to concern a reversion to primitive types of behavior.

The Humphrey-Weidman Company was unusual in several respects. It had two directors, each of whom was a choreographer, whereas other modern troupes were usually dominated by a single charismatic creative force. Denishawn had earlier shown that it was possible for a company to have more than one choreographer. But most choreographers after Denishawn had tended to work in isolation from their colleagues. Even today, American companies devoted to new works still favor productions by only one choreographer.

Humphrey-Weidman dances were also unconventional in appearance. The scenery for works often consisted of rearrangements of a set of boxes originally designed for the troupe by Erika Klein. Almost infinitely adaptable, these boxes could be stacked and shifted about to form a multitude of levels. As the years passed and the boxes grew older, complaints were occasionally voiced that Humphrey-Weidman stagings were starting to seem shabby. Nevertheless, the boxes were an ingenious solution to the problem of designing multipurpose units of scenery on a tight budget.

In contrast, Helen Tamiris was as flamboyant as ever. She used flowing movements in her *Walt Whitman Suite* (1934) to parallel the expansiveness of Whitman's poetry. *Toward the Light* (1934) was a struggle toward freedom. In one section of *Harvest 1935* (1935), a denunciation of war, members of the ensemble gathered in a formation that resembled a cannon and then discharged a dancer as a human cannonball; the grotesquerie of this sequence startled audiences.[24] *Adelante* (1939) showed the thoughts that passed through a soldier's mind just before his death before a firing squad during the Spanish Civil War. *Adelante* means "forward," and Tamiris brought her dance to an affirmative conclusion by heading a group that rushed across the stage to suggest the hopes of the people.

Along with Tamiris, many other militant choreographers of the 1930s raised a cry of "Forward!"

CHOREOGRAPHIC CONSCIENCES

Leftist dance · Workers' Dance League · New Dance Group · Black dance · Josephine Baker · Edna Guy · Hemsley Winfield · Asadata Dafora · Hampton Institute Creative Dance Group · Karamu · Eugene von Grona · Bernice Brown · Katherine Dunham · Helen Tamiris · Dance Repertory Theatre · WPA Federal Dance Project · Don Oscar Becque · Bennington · Martha Hill · Mary Josephine Shelly

NO SENSITIVE AMERICAN DANCER OF THE 1930S COULD have been unaware of political events and few dancers could have been indifferent to them. To step outside the studio door was to enter a world of unrest.

From overseas came the terrifying news of the rise of fascism. The Great Depression brought economic hardship to much of the world. Americans had to cope with unemployment, poverty, and racial discrimination. Various solutions were proposed. Franklin D. Roosevelt, who was elected president in 1932, promised America a "New Deal." Other idealists looked beyond the platforms of the Democratic and Republican parties toward Socialist visions of human equality. And, for some, the Soviet Union appeared to represent the hopes of the world's oppressed.

Politically minded dance productions expressed various liberal, democratic, Socialist, or explicitly Communist viewpoints. Some troupes were sponsored by labor unions: there was a Furriers Dance Group and a Needle Trades Workers Industrial Union Dance Group. Often, several political and artistic causes could be joined at a single mass gathering. Thus, for an interracial dance program held in New York in 1930, Edith Segal and Allison Burroughs choreographed a *Black and White Workers Solidarity Dance*; there was a speech by the Communist leader William Z. Foster and communal singing of *The Internationale*. Afterward, dance music was provided by Duke Ellington and His Orchestra.[1]

As the dance writer Jacqueline Maskey put it many years later, when the Workers' Dance League was founded in 1932, it "spread its wings (both Left) over a number of groups dedicated to social action."[2] From 1932 to 1936, the league (which changed its name to New Dance League in 1935) acted as a booking agency, organizing programs for left-wing dance groups and soloists. Its members included ensembles with such names as the Red Dance Group, American Revolutionary Dance Group, Rebel Dance Group, and Nature Friends Dance Group. Most were ephemeral.

But one organization survived for decades: the New Dance Group, which was founded in 1932 and took as its slogan, "The dance is a weapon in the class struggle."[3] The New Dance Group sought to bring dance performances to working-class people; it was also a school, offering modern dance and ballet classes at the lowest possible tuition.

Inevitably, opponents of the Workers' Dance League accused all its members of being Communists. Nadia Chilkovsky, one of the organization's leaders, refuted these charges in 1934. She called the league nonsectarian and claimed that of its 800 members only 20 were avowed Communists. Just as inevitably, some dancegoers branded league productions as "propaganda." Chilkovsky responded:

> We ask, what is not propaganda? And, furthermore, what dances in what eras have not been propaganda dances? . . .
>
> Each dance expresses a social point of view, either that of the ruling class or that of the potential power that has not yet gained control. . . . Either you act to maintain the status-quo or you militate against it for revolutionary change. No artist can be passive today.[4]

Although all art may be propaganda of some sort, all propaganda is not necessarily art. The worst of the socially conscious dances were stridently propagandistic. Reviewing a program sponsored by the Workers' Dance League in 1934, Paul Love sighed, "One comes away from the recital with the feeling of having seen excited, obstreperous children." Love pointed out a weakness shared by many politically minded artistic groups past and present: they preach to the converted. The league's purpose, he suggested, "should be, not the repetition of old stories to its own class, but the dissemination of those stories to the very classes it snubs: the bourgeoisie and the 'aristocrats.'. . . The Workers' Dance League at present sways nobody but its own coterie."[5]

Yet, even if their works were crude at times, socially conscious dancers were nevertheless bold enough to take stands on major issues. From their groups came at least four choreographers who would be important for decades to come: Anna Sokolow, Jane Dudley, Sophie Maslow, and William Bales.

The 1930s also saw the rise of black dance companies.[6] All had to battle intellectual incomprehension as well as outright prejudice. Whereas modern dancers theoretically upheld total creative freedom, some of these same dancers believed that blacks should perform only works "appropriate" to them—a point of view that implied that blacks themselves were not capable of determining what was "appropriate."

Several myths about black dancers had to be refuted. Eunice Brown summarizes some of the problems:

> Everyone expects the Negro to have perfect rhythm and to be able to dance without training. All Negroes do not have perfect rhythm and no dancer, whatever the color of his skin, can dance without training. . . . By convention, the Negro is expected to be an entertainer, especially in the field of dance, and most people do not expect the Negro to be serious about anything. The Negro dancer faces another danger, and it is a grave one. He is often singled out as a good dancer and made much of regardless of whether or not he is a good dancer. Often-times people discard their artistic standards in their effort to "accept" the Negro.[7]

As Brown noted, white audiences had little trouble accepting African-American dancers as entertainers. Among the stars of the period was Josephine Baker, who was born in St. Louis in 1906. After appearing in revues, she went to Paris in 1925 and soon became a star of the French music halls. Famous for her theatrical ebullience, Baker in 1927 tried to describe her personal style:

> I turn my shoulder like the wheel of a machine in flesh. I play billiards with my eyes. I stick out my lips when it pleases me. I walk on my heels or on all fours according to my fancy. I tell who I am with my hands and arms. I row and swim in the air; I leap and perspire. Et voilà.[8]

But Baker, though certainly idiosyncratic, devoted herself to musical theatre, rather than to ballet or modern dance, and, significantly,

France (especially Paris) remained the center of her activities until her death in 1975. Just as Loïe Fuller, Isadora Duncan, and Maud Allan considered themselves to be better understood in Europe than in America, so Baker and certain other black performers felt more at home in France than in the United States.

Yet black modern dancers did persevere in America. On 29 April 1931, Edna Guy, Hemsley Winfield, and their New Negro Art Dance Group offered what was billed as the "First Negro Dance Recital in America."[9] Winfield, an actor who turned to modern dance, developed a style that combined German Expressionist and African-American influences. He performed at the Metropolitan Opera House in 1933 when he choreographed and appeared as the Witch Doctor in the Metropolitan Opera's production of Louis Gruenberg's opera *The Emperor Jones*, which starred Lawrence Tibbett. Unfortunately, Winfield died of pneumonia in 1934, when he was only twenty-seven.

Edna Guy continued to perform, occasionally surprising critics in the process. Thus, after a concert by her company in 1934, Ralph Taylor wrote, "Contrary to expectations, Miss Guy has none of the loose-jointed flippancy usually associated with the Negro dancer. Instead, her movements are characterized by a general compactness, which at times becomes . . . confining."[10]

Asadata Dafora (who sometimes used Horton as his surname) attracted attention in 1934 with *Kykunkor (The Witch Doctor)*, which he termed a "native African opera" based on folklore from Sierra Leone, where he was born in 1890.[11] Originally trained as an opera singer, Dafora blended acting, singing, dancing, ritual, and chanting. The production showed young women in a "maiden village" (a place used for the instruction of prospective brides) visited by a young man from another tribe. After he chooses a bride, a jealous rival has a witch cast a spell on him. He falls dead, only to be restored by a witch doctor who strangles the witch. In *Kykunkor* and subsequent productions, Dafora (who died in 1965) made stories or depictions of African life the basis for works that sought to reveal some of the spiritual aspects of African culture.

Several black dance companies were founded outside New York. Virginia's Hampton Institute Creative Dance Group made its first appearance off-campus as a concert attraction in Richmond, Virginia, in 1935, presenting works by Bernice M. Smothers and Charles H. Williams. The company's varied programming was inspired by that of Ted Shawn, who staged a suite for it called *Labor Rhythms*.[12]

That same year, the Karamu Dance Group, organized by Margaret Witt, became a major component of the Performing Arts Division of Karamu House, a community center founded in Cleveland by Russell and Rowena Jelliffe in 1915. Interracial in faculty and student body, Karamu did much to bring the area's dancers together.

During the late 1930s and early 1940s, there was also cooperation between black and white dancers in Minneapolis. Bernice Brown, a Minnesota dancer who had studied physical education at Mankato State College, came to teach dance at a Minneapolis settlement house in 1937. Two years later, she began to collaborate with Gertrude Lippincott and Ruth Hatfield, directors of the city's Modern Dance Center, an organization designed to promote dance in the Midwest. Black dancers started to appear in racially mixed productions of the center, and until her untimely death in 1942, Brown choreographed pieces bearing such titles as *Negro Lament, Statement for Peace, Street Cries, Chain Gang Songs, Boogie-Woogie,* and *Then I Saw the Congo* to a reading of Vachel Lindsay's poem *The Congo.*[13]

In New York, Eugene von Grona, stirred by a desire to provide black dancers with training and employment opportunities, organized the American Negro Ballet in 1937. The eclectic choreography of this idealistic white dancer included an *Air* to Bach, a version of Stravinsky's *Firebird Suite,* and *Southern Episode,* which contrasted village and city life. The poet James Weldon Johnson praised von Grona for "defying the traditions that would limit the Negro's art to native or instinctive art."[14]

The most celebrated black dancer to emerge during the 1930s was Katherine Dunham, who was born in 1912 in Glen Ellyn, Illinois.[15] Her French-Canadian mother died when Katherine was young. Her father, a descendant of slaves from Madagascar, then married a schoolteacher from Iowa and moved his family to Joliet, Illinois, where he ran a dry-cleaning establishment.

Katherine attended Joliet Junior College and the University of Chicago, as did her brother Albert, who formed a drama company with which she acted. Katherine was an anthropology student who wrote a master's thesis on Haitian dance. But she was also a dancer, who studied ballet with such Chicago teachers as Ludmilla Speranzeva, Ruth Page, and Mark Turbyfill, a poet and dancer with whom she founded a short-lived Ballet Nègre in 1930. Speranzeva helped Dunham establish the Chicago Negro School of Ballet in 1934, an institution that taught ballet, Spanish, and modern dance and sponsored a Negro Dance Group. Also in 1934, Dunham appeared in *La Guiablesse*, a ballet based on Martinique folklore that Page choreographed for the Chicago Opera Ballet.

In 1935–1936, two Julius Rosenwald Foundation fellowships enabled Dunham to study dance in Haiti, Jamaica, Martinique, and Trinidad. Over the years, she grew ever more closely associated with Haitian culture and even became a priestess of Haiti's Voudoun religion.

In 1937, she took her Negro Dance Group to New York. The next year, she married the Chicago artist and stage designer John Pratt. New York became her headquarters in 1939, when she worked with Labor Stage Inc. and choreographed *Pins and Needles*, a satirical revue produced by the International Ladies' Garment Workers Union. George Balanchine cast her in a leading dance role in *Cabin in the Sky*, the Broadway musical with a black cast that he both directed and choreographed in 1940.

Dunham continued to choreograph, drawing upon African, African-American, and Caribbean sources. She eventually developed a form of revue that delighted audiences around the world. However, in the late 1930s she had only begun to explore the wealth of theatrical material that she thought was inherent in black culture. She declared in a 1938 interview that it was her aim both "to take *our* dance out of the burlesque—to make of it a more dignified art" and "to develop a technique that will be as important to the white man as to the Negro." [16]

She was proud of black culture. Yet she wished to share it with everyone; in that 1938 interview she stated that she saw nothing inherently objectionable in a white dancer performing to spirituals:

> I think she [a white dancer] should [dance a spiritual] if it is within her background and emotional understanding. For instance, I am a Negro, but I was reared in the North, and in white schools with white associates. Naturally, I heard spirituals, but until I was fully grown I probably heard them much less than a white girl in the South. Why then should I dance them and she not? [17]

What should African Americans dance about? That question was often asked. And certain well-meaning white dancegoers may have unwittingly contributed to prejudice by claiming that black dancers should confine themselves to specifically black subject matter. All such theories of exclusivity were countered by George Beiswanger, a (white) critic and esthetician:

The theory that the Negro should do—and no one else—his own special kind of dancing, that which has sprung out of the doings and sufferings, the pleasures and joys, the protests and passions of his past, is a last refuge of race prejudice. We permit ourselves the notion because it seems to pay the Negro so fine a compliment. But what kind of compliment is it which carries the implication, tacitly embraced if not openly stated, that to the Negro all other realms of dance are racially closed? . . . it is necessary and high time to assert with conviction and vehemence that the Negro has just as much right to the entire heritage of human dance as anyone else. . . . We shall have set ourselves completely straight on this matter on that day when a Negro ballerina takes centre stage at the Met.[18]

Although modern dance prized distinctively individual styles and most modern companies were headed by a single choreographer, dancers sensed that a proliferation of troupes might splinter the dance field, making it harder than ever to attract audiences and gain financial support.

Some people wondered, why not pool resources? Helen Tamiris led an important attempt to gather the choreographic clans. She founded the Dance Repertory Theatre—which was not, as its name might imply, a single dance group but an administrative "umbrella" assisting several groups. In 1930, the Dance Repertory Theatre sponsored a January season by the companies of Tamiris, Martha Graham, Doris Humphrey, and Charles Weidman; the same companies, plus Agnes de Mille and her partner Warren Leonard, shared another season in February 1931. Unfortunately, that was the end of the Dance Repertory Theatre.

Theoretically, the idea of a single administrative staff scheduling, coordinating, and publicizing performances was a good one. But the dancers involved with Tamiris's project remained suspicious of one another and tempers flared. As John Martin put it, "everybody stepped pretty generally on everybody else's toes."[19] Nevertheless, Tamiris never gave up trying to bring dancers together.

One attempt to do so occurred under the auspices of the United States government itself. Alarmed by the unemployment caused by the Depression, Congress established the Works Progress Administration (WPA) to provide job opportunities for people on relief. Actors, directors, stage designers, and dancers were assisted by the

WPA's Federal Theatre Project, formed in 1935 under the direction of Hallie Flanagan.[20]

The Federal Theatre staged productions across the country. Although most of them were plays and musicals, there were also dance events. In Chicago, the Federal Theatre offered modern dance works by Katherine Dunham, Berta Ochsner, and Kurt and Grace Graff. But the Chicago Federal Theatre's most enduring contribution to American dance was a comic ballet: *Frankie and Johnny*, a choreographic adaptation of a salty old ballad about infidelity that was choreographed in 1938 by Bentley Stone and Ruth Page to a score by Jerome Moross and remains in the repertoires of several American companies.

Unfortunately, the Federal Theatre's New York dance activities were troubled. The Dance Project, a special division of the Federal Theatre, was established in December 1936 under the direction of the choreographer Don Oscar Becque, who headed an executive committee consisting of Doris Humphrey, Charles Weidman, Helen Tamiris, Gluck-Sandor, and Felicia Sorel. The budget allowed for the employment of 185 dancers; the group that was assembled included ballet and modern dancers, and it was Becque's task to keep everyone productively busy.

Becque, who was part Choctaw Indian, was born in Oklahoma and had studied ballet before becoming interested in modern dance.[21] He began giving New York performances in 1928. Like other modern dancers of the time, he was fascinated by works without accompaniment, and his creations bore such titles as *Movement Studies: Slow, Fast, Stately, Dance without Beginning or End, Plastic Tensions*, and *Simultaneous Designs*. An unsigned review in the *New York Times* said of a 1929 concert that Becque's "physical technique is not in any sense fluent and his sense of composition is frankly chaotic."[22]

Nevertheless, although not a major choreographer, Becque played an active part in the modern dance scene; because he was not allied with any single faction, it was possible to hope that he might be able to pacify dance's warring factions. Hallie Flanagan highmindedly declared, "Since we did not think Federal Theatre should sponsor any one school of acting, we had a number of choreographers, each with a group."[23] But those choreographers and groups could not get along, and the Dance Project was plagued by petty squabbling and bureaucratic red tape. Few of its planned productions made it to the stage. In October 1936, an unsigned editorial in *Dance Observer* complained that the project's Federal Dance Theatre had produced only three works: Weidman's *Candide*, Tamiris's *Salut au Monde*, and Becque's *Young Tramps* (which Flanagan praised as a portrait of "disinherited youth on the roads of America").[24]

Worse yet, Becque was accused of being an incompetent administrator. According to *Dance Observer*, at a meeting of angry dancers in 1936, "Gluck-Sandor said he had worked with everybody in the theatre from Stanislavski to Minsky, but never with anyone who knew less about theatre, less about choreography than Mr. Becque."[25] Petitions were signed calling for his removal. Becque resigned as director, yet remained with the Dance Project until 6 February 1937, when he severed all connections with it.[26]

Becque was replaced as dance director by Lincoln Kirstein, the erudite critic, polemicist, dance historian, and champion of ballet who had brought George Balanchine to America in 1934. Kirstein's tenure was brief. Faced with what must have seemed a horde of dancers with disparate backgrounds, he came up with the idea of a vast pageant tracing the history of dance. Assigning roles, he told Tamiris, "And I think you're the one to dance Isadora Duncan." Instead of being flattered, she replied, "And who will dance Tamiris?" Kirstein resigned shortly thereafter.[27]

No replacement for him was named. WPA dance events in New York were officially administered by Stephen Karnot of the New York Theatre Project. However, it was Tamiris, working without a title, who managed to hold the Dance Project together.[28] For it, she created *How Long Brethren?* to black protest songs, and *Adelante*, her dance about the Spanish Civil War. In 1939, partly in response to complaints that too many Federal Theatre productions extolled left-wing causes, Congress abolished the project; all activities of the WPA ceased in 1943.

A far more influential bringing-together of dancers occurred at the summer Bennington Festivals at Bennington College in Vermont.[29] Bennington, a women's college in the Green Mountains, had opened in 1932, its curriculum stressing learning by doing, a diversity of educational programs, and, most importantly, the arts. When, at its founding, Martha Graham was asked to recommend a dance teacher, she suggested Martha Hill. It was an inspired choice.

Born in East Palestine, Ohio, in 1900, Hill graduated from the Kellogg School of Physical Education in Battle Creek, Michigan, in 1920.

She taught ballet and Swedish gymnastics there until 1923, when she became director of dance at Kansas State Teachers College in Hays. She held that post until 1926—the year she visited New York and saw Graham's debut concert, an event that changed her life. Overwhelmed by Graham, Hill studied with her. At the same time, she continued her academic dance education, eventually receiving a B.S. from Columbia University in 1929 and an M.A. from New York University in 1941. Inexhaustibly energetic, Hill danced with the Graham company (1930–1931) and taught at the University of Oregon (1927–1929), Columbia University Teachers College (1929–1930), and, beginning in 1930, New York University. Even after she joined the Bennington faculty, she retained her ties with NYU, regularly spending two days a week in Vermont and the rest of her time in New York until 1951, when she gave up both Bennington and NYU to head the newly formed dance department at the Juilliard School in New York.

The Bennington Festival was Hill's idea and, with the blessing of Robert Devore Leigh, Bennington's president, she co-directed it with Mary Josephine Shelly, a former administrator and physical education teacher at Columbia University Teachers College's experimental New College. The first summer session of the Bennington School of the Dance in 1934 offered classes taught by Martha Graham, Doris Humphrey, Charles Weidman, and Hanya Holm. Performances began to be presented in 1935, and the Bennington Festival continued until wartime austerity and gasoline rationing forced it out of existence in 1942. In 1939, in recognition of its national importance, the Bennington summer dance program temporarily moved to Mills College in Oakland, California.

The idyllic Vermont mountain setting made Bennington something of an American Ascona. But unlike its Swiss counterpart—or Ted Shawn's Jacob's Pillow of the 1930s—Bennington was not dominated by a single guru. Rather, its students were exposed to the works, techniques, and ideas of its four resident choreographers, each of whom returned annually to the campus. Although a modern dance center, in 1936 Bennington presented the debut performances of Ballet Caravan, a company directed by Lincoln Kirstein that featured new American ballet choreography. Among the important modern works that received their premieres at Bennington were Graham's *American Document* (1938), *El Penitente* (1940), *Letter to the World* (1940), and *Punch and the Judy* (1941); Humphrey's *New Dance* (1953), *With My Red Fires* (1936), and *Passacaglia in C Minor*

(1938); Weidman's *Opus 51* (1938); and Holm's *Trend* (1937). The festivals also gave choreographic opportunities to such younger talents as José Limón, Eleanor King, Esther Junger, Erick Hawkins, Jean Erdman, Jane Dudley, Sophie Maslow, William Bales, and Anna Sokolow.

Despite this variety, Bennington had its critics. Joseph Arnold Kaye (who also wrote as Joseph Arnold) accused Bennington in 1935 of ponderous intellectualism. Calling it "an enterprise that should be encouraged," he praised "the thoroughness, the extreme thoughtfulness of almost everything that goes on in the classes of the Bennington School of the Dance." Nevertheless, he added that "it is this thoroughness, this thoughtfulness, this elaborate extensiveness, which proves a disagreeable element of the school." [30]

As an example of Bennington's pedantry, Kaye singled out a prospectus in which Martha Hill claimed that she would teach "techniques and technical progressions based upon a fundamental analysis of movement for the dance. The material derives from a formulation of the principles, forces and factors present in all movement of the human body, and from a consideration of the content and significant form to be discovered in the medium of movement." Reflecting upon this, Kaye sighed: "There is no heart in what they do. Only a mental searching." [31] But what delighted students was Bennington's combination of intellectual seriousness and creative excitement. The school lived up to the statement of intention its founders had published in the *Bennington College Bulletin* of February 1934:

> The modern dance, in common with the other arts of this period, is a diversified rather than a single style. At the same time it possesses certain identifying characteristics which are common to all of its significant forms. To the most advantageous plan of study is, therefore, one which reflects this diversification and, by affording comparisons, aims to reveal the essentials of modernism in the dance. [32]

Bennington prided itself on its diversity. Looking back, however, it now seems evident that it promoted only certain kinds of diversity. Its key choreographers and teachers remained Graham, Humphrey, Weidman, and Holm. No other choreographers were given such prominence, not even as special guests—a fact that has irked the admirers of Tamiris, who, for reasons that remain shadowy, was never invited to participate in Bennington activities. There were no examples of European modern dance—Holm was considered to be growing increasingly American in outlook. Bennington also ignored unclassifiable dance forms—for instance, the eclecticism of Pauline Koner or the dramatic character sketches associated with Agnes de Mille and Angna Enters.

Pessimists can see in Bennington the beginning of a modern dance orthodoxy and the formation of an establishment that would rule American modern dance through World War II and during the postwar period, both in New York and, in later years, at Bennington's successor, the American Dance Festival in New London, Connecticut. But all forebodings about Bennington are offset by its genuine accomplishments. Bennington produced works and trained dancers. It also trained teachers—especially, college dance teachers from across America who returned home each summer with lofty ideals, practical pedagogical methods, and, often, a desire to sponsor campus dance performances by touring companies on what came to be known as the "gymnasium circuit."

By the outbreak of World War II, America had become the supreme power in the modern dance world. Yet America was not a haven for all dancers. After the Japanese bombed Pearl Harbor in 1941, people of Japanese descent were moved into detention centers. The discriminatory racism of this policy—no comparably extreme measures were taken with people of German or Italian descent—so deeply embittered Michio Ito that he decided to return to Japan. After the war, he became active in Japanese theatrical activities and remained so until his death in 1962. But he never made any further contributions to American dance.[33]

PART 4

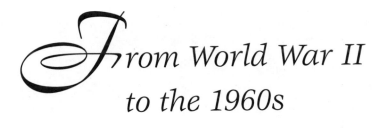

From World War II
to the 1960s

AMERICAN VICTORIES

The 92nd St. Y • Dance Notation Bureau • Jacob's Pillow • Colorado College • American Dance Festival • Martha Graham • Doris Humphrey • Charles Weidman • José Limón • Anna Sokolow • Jane Dudley • Sophie Maslow • William Bales • Valerie Bettis • Helen Tamiris • Hanya Holm • Lester Horton • Daniel Nagrin • Lotte Goslar • Katherine Dunham • Pearl Primus • Talley Beatty • Donald McKayle • Carmen de Lavallade • Janet Collins

WORLD WAR II AFFECTED ALL AREAS OF AMERICAN LIFE, including the dance community. Many male dancers were drafted. Ruth St. Denis aided the war effort by working as a riveter; Maud Allan became a draftsperson for an aircraft company.

During and just after the war, America experienced one of its periodic "dance booms." Perhaps the liveliness of the art made it an antidote to despair. In any case, ballet gained new popularity. Modern dance, although less familiar to the general public, also thrived. Indeed, it acquired increased stability. It was now an art with an honorable past as well as an eventful present—an art with its own traditions and stable institutions.

New York City's Young Men's and Young Women's Hebrew Association inaugurated its dance program in 1937. Under the supervision of William Kolodney, director of the institution's Educational Department, the 92nd St. Y—as it was known to several generations of theatregoers—became a major center for performances by young and established modern dancers.

The Dance Notation Bureau was founded in New York City in 1940 by three dancers: Ann Hutchinson (who later married the dance historian Ivor Guest), Helen Priest Rogers, and Eve Gentry. It remains the world's most important center for research into notation.

Among the flourishing summer dance centers were Jacob's Pillow and the annual summer dance workshop at Colorado College in Colorado Springs, which Hanya Holm established in 1941. There she and her faculty taught classes and presented new works. After the war, the traditions of the Bennington Festival were continued when Martha Hill established the American Dance Festival on the New London campus of Connecticut College in 1948. Ruth Bloomer, Hill's co-director in New London, had been a student at the first Bennington session. Jeanette Schlottmann, who became festival director in 1959, had studied with Martha Graham and Louis Horst. When Schlottman left the festival in 1963, she was succeeded by Theodora Wiesner, who had studied with Margaret H'Doubler and had attended all but two of the Bennington sessions. The festival was evidence of the way in which each new generation of modern dancers was linked to older choreographers and teachers.

Martha Graham's creativity continued unabated. From the 1940s onward she modified her choreographic style several times, occasionally to the bewilderment of some of her previous admirers.

In general, Graham's productions grew increasingly elaborate in their theatrical trappings. Her collaborations with Isamu Noguchi continued. More men were added to her company. And she developed an interest in narrative. Amid the gloom of World War II, she offered *Appalachian Spring* (1944), a joyous dance to a score by Aaron Copland that celebrates the building of a new home for a young pioneer married couple. Graham also created several purely lyrical pieces, notably *Diversion of Angels* (1948), a tribute to the joys and sorrows of young love.

But she attracted most attention for her dance-dramas on mythological, literary, and historical themes. Her plots—especially those based on mythology—reflected the widespread interest in psychoanalysis that was common in the 1940s and 1950s, a time when many analysts regarded mythological characters as universal psychological archetypes.

Often Graham's dramatic works concern a woman at a crucial point in her life, and the stage action may go both backward and forward in time as she remembers her past while preparing for her future. Other figures in Graham's dramatic dances may be both characters in the story and symbolic embodiments of the heroine's thoughts and feelings. And always the heroines are passionate women of the sort that Graham liked to call "doom-eager." To convey their passions and predicaments, Graham emphasized turbulent movements, including wrenchings, shudderings, and a variety of falls.

Letter to the World (1940) is a commentary on the poetry and life of Emily Dickinson, who is portrayed by two characters. One, who only dances, symbolizes those aspects of Dickinson that the world saw; the other, who both moves and speaks lines from Dickinson's poetry, represents her private self. Both aspects of Dickinson are confronted by a formidable antagonist, a character called the Ancestress, who represents New England's Puritan tradition.

Cave of the Heart (1946) retells the Greek myth of Medea, suggesting Medea's venomous jealousy through violent lurches, thrustings, and off-balance turns. Whereas most of Graham's dramatic dances, including *Cave of the Heart, Letter to the World,* and *Deaths and Entrances* (a 1943 piece inspired by the Brontë sisters), depict familiar literary or historical figures, she occasionally invented mythological scenarios entirely her own, as she did in the introspective *Dark Meadow* (1946), in which the characters include a woman who appears to be venturing forth on a journey, an earth mother, and a summoning, erotically forceful man.

Symbolism always mattered more than literally realistic dramatic action in Graham's mythological creations. *Night Journey* (1947), based on the story of Oedipus and Jocasta, begins shortly before Jocasta's suicide, which was prompted by the discovery that she had unwittingly married her own son. The action proceeds backward in time as she relives her troubled past. The rope she eventually uses as a noose serves at various points as an umbilical cord and a web binding husband and wife tragically together.

Graham occasionally altered myths to suit her own purposes. *Errand into the Maze* (1947) was adapted from the myth of Theseus and Ariadne. But whereas in the myth a man goes into a labyrinth to confront a monster known as the Minotaur, in the dance it is a woman who embarks upon a perilous mission and the male monster she confronts is not simply a wild beast, but a personification of her own fears. As Noguchi summarized the work, "The theme, based on the story of the Minotaur, is the extremity we must all face: ourselves." Graham once offered a personal interpretation of one detail of Noguchi's setting by likening its sculptural doorway to the pelvic bones "from which the child I never had comes forth, but the only child that comes forth is myself." [1]

Graham often spoke as if she felt herself possessed by destiny. So it is no wonder that her heroines were women moved by great powers outside themselves or buried deep within their psyches. Thus in *Seraphic Dialogue* (1955), Joan of Arc, who believed herself guided by saints, looks back upon her earthly life and views herself as Maid, as Warrior, and as Martyr, each aspect of her life portrayed by a different dancer. Then the beatified Joan achieves eternal glory.

Graham's most ambitious mythological achievement is the evening-long *Clytemnestra* (1958). This, too, is a retrospective piece in which the action proceeds in psychologically significant flashbacks, rather than in chronological order. Clytemnestra, the queen who killed her husband for having sacrificed one of their children to the goddess Artemis, and who in turn is killed by her surviving children, is forced by the gods of the afterworld to ponder and relive her bloody past until she is finally able to come to terms with it. The tumultuous choreography dwells obsessively on themes of love, lust, guilt, and retribution.

In 1959, Graham was invited by the New York City Ballet to create a new work to the music of Anton Webern in collaboration with George Balanchine. Eventually, each choreographer produced an independent, self-sufficient piece, and both were performed together under the title of *Episodes*. Balanchine contributed an abstraction, Graham a dance-drama about Mary Stuart. *Episodes* attracted considerable attention as vociferous factions of dancegoers argued over which was the better approach to choreography: the abstract or the dramatic.

Tired of coping with the vagaries of New York commercial managements, the Humphrey-Weidman Company in 1940 opened a small playhouse, the Studio Theatre. There the company could present its own productions, and it also rented the space to other groups.

One of Doris Humphrey's major works of the 1940s was *Inquest* (1944), inspired by a British newspaper report of 1865 that told of a man who had died of starvation while trying to keep his family alive by repairing worn-out shoes. Humphrey's dance, to music by Norman Lloyd, began with the sound of footfalls in the street. Dancers representing the poor entered. A report of the case was read, the narrator serving in turn as judge, jury, and the voice of the people, as the story of the workman's death was told in pantomimic movement. Then pantomime gave way to expressive dance as the man, his wife, and their child joined their neighbors in an anguished ensemble. George Beiswanger likened *Inquest* to the writings of Maxim Gorki and Lev Tolstoy and to Vincent Van Gogh's paintings of Belgian coalminers. It reminded him that "truth is not always beauty, despite the authority of Keats; but where truth is, there can be art."[2]

Humphrey never performed again after *Inquest*, for she grew increasingly crippled with arthritis. Nevertheless, she continued to choreograph. She planned each new dance carefully in her mind and transmitted her ideas to dancers, both by giving them detailed instructions and by inspiring them with such images as "feel the rise and fall of a wave in your own breath" or "get up from the floor as if you were a seedling reaching for the light."[3]

Out of such compositional methods came several important dances, among them *Day on Earth* (1947) and *Ruins and Visions* (1953). The former is an allegorical depiction of relationships involving a man, the two women he loves at different points in his life, and the daughter he has by one of them. *Ruins and Visions* is a study of the ways in which people attempt to ignore reality. Beginning with a scene in which a doting mother tries to shield her son from the outside world, it continues by showing people avoiding agitated crowds in the street; at last, the shock of war and death bursts upon everyone. Nevertheless, *Ruins and Visions* concludes with a contrapuntal ensemble implying that the characters have at long last learned to cope with reality. Such a finale was typical of Humphrey. As many of her colleagues have recalled, despite her own disabilities and her awareness of social injustice, Humphrey refused to give up or give in.

However, her illness was a contributing factor in the disbanding of the Humphrey-Weidman Company; the Studio Theatre closed its doors in 1944 and she and Weidman went their separate choreographic ways. Although Weidman continued to choreograph, he also had to overcome alcoholism. But, by the time of his death in 1975, he was once again an active and highly respected figure on the New York dance scene, teaching, reviving old works, and occasionally creating new ones.

Humphrey became an especially successful teacher of dance composition. Indeed, her only serious rival in the field at the time was Louis Horst. Before her death in 1958, she completed her book *The Art of Making Dances*, which remains a standard text on dance composition. She also served as a choreographic adviser to Pauline Koner and José Limón, a former member of the Humphrey-Weidman Company who founded his own troupe in 1946.

José Limón danced like a god—and, sometimes, like a demon or a madman. His very appearance was awesome. With his olive skin, high forehead and cheekbones, receding black hair, and piercing black eyes, he resembled a monumental sculptural figure.

The eldest of eleven children, Limón was born in Mexico and was proud of his Mexican heritage. However, he grew up in the United States—mostly in the Los Angeles area—to which his father, a music teacher, had moved in 1908 (the year of the dancer's birth) to escape political unrest.[4] Limón studied music and art and, after determining to become a painter, came to New York in 1929, but a performance that year by Harald Kreutzberg and Yvonne Georgi converted him to dance. A friend who had known Charles Weidman in high school suggested that he study at the Humphrey-Weidman Studio—a sensible recommendation, for, unlike the all-female troupes of Graham and Tamiris, the Humphrey-Weidman organization had welcomed men at its outset. Limón was soon taken into the company: though inexperienced, he was obviously talented.

Limón performed with Humphrey-Weidman at the Bennington festivals and, along with Anna Sokolow and Esther Junger, received a Bennington choreographic fellowship in 1937. A desire to strike out on his own led him to California, where he formed a dancing partnership with May O'Donnell. In 1941, he married Pauline Lawrence, who persuaded him to return to New York. He served with the Army in World War II, then formed his own company with Doris Humphrey as artistic adviser. She created fine roles for him in *Day on Earth* and *Ruins and Visions.* But he was especially imposing in her *Lament for Ignacio Sánchez Mejías* (1946), inspired by a poem by Federico García Lorca on the death of a bullfighter.

Limón began to choreograph dances in which the movements were often based upon the heightening of dramatically meaningful gestures. Two works of 1949 attracted widespread attention. *La Malinche* was a terse piece in the style of a folk-play staged in a Mexican village square; it told the story of an Indian woman who allows herself to be seduced and exploited by the explorer and conqueror Hernando Cortez. Feeling remorse over her betrayal of her people, she joins them in an insurrection against the conquistadors. *La Malinche* summed up many of the conflicts of Mexican history.

The Moor's Pavane is not only Limón's most popular creation, but also perhaps the best-known work in all modern dance and one that has been staged by many groups, including such ballet companies as American Ballet Theatre, the Joffrey Ballet, and the Royal Danish Ballet. A retelling of *Othello*, it uses only four characters from Shakespeare's tragedy, who, to music of Henry Purcell, dance out their passions within the confines of a Renaissance court dance. But unruly emotions break through the formal constraints, and the work gains its power through its tensions between decorum and violence.

Limón assembled a troupe of striking individuals who nevertheless interacted harmoniously like members of a fine chamber-music ensemble. Pauline Koner appeared for many years with Limón on what she has termed a "permanent guest artist basis," and prominent among the male soloists was Lucas Hoving, a Dutch-born dancer and choreographer who had studied with Yvonne Georgi and had danced with the Ballets Jooss.

Limón could be both ferocious and exalted in his dancing and choreography. Typically, he once proclaimed, "Dancers are part soldier, part gladiator, part matador. They possess the dignified courage of the first, the brute daring of the second, the finesse of the last."[5]

Just as Limón gained experience with the Humphrey-Weidman Company, then broke away to choreograph on his own, so other dancers followed a similar pattern of serving what was, in effect, an apprenticeship with an established master before asserting their independence.

Out of the Graham company came Anna Sokolow. Her surname means "falcon" in Russian, and, as choreographer and teacher, she has often been as fierce as that bird.[6] A notoriously demanding disciplinarian, she once explained her harshness in the studio by telling some students, "I don't dislike you, that's not why I'm hard on you. But I love dance more than I love you."[7]

When Anna Sokolow's niece once asked her why the Sokolow family left Russia, she replied, "Why does any Jew leave Russia?"[8] For Jewish people at the turn of the century, Russia was a land of poverty and pogroms. Anna was born of immigrant parents in Hartford, Connecticut, in 1907. Three years later, the family moved to New York City. Anna's father suffered from Parkinson's disease, which increasingly debilitated him and forced him to spend much of his time in a hospital. Her mother worked as a sewing-machine operator in the garment industry and was active in trade-union activities and the Socialist Party.

The Sokolows lived in poverty on the Lower East Side. But, like many Jewish immigrants, they prized education and culture. Anna studied dance at a settlement house with Emily Hewitt, a pupil of Bird Larson. She continued her studies at the Neighborhood Playhouse; and in 1928, when it opened an uptown school specifically designed for the training of professionals, Anna studied there with Louis Horst, Martha Graham, Michio Ito, and Benjamin Zemach. She became Horst's assistant in his composition classes and in 1930 joined Graham's company, remaining for eight years.

Even while she was with Graham, Sokolow had her own small group, the Dance Unit, and gained a reputation as a choreographer with a strong social conscience. One of her most successful early solos was *Case History No. —*, which showed a calamitous progression from poverty and unemployment to futility and crime. *Excerpt from a War Poem* was a scathing indictment of a Fascist poem by F. T. Marinetti that claimed "war is beautiful" because "it realizes the long dreamed of metallization of the human body" and "creates the spiral smoke of burning villages."[9]

The Mexican painter Carlos Mérida saw Sokolow's choreography during a New York visit and made arrangements for her to perform in Mexico City in 1939. A misinformed publicist billed her as a Russian ballerina, yet she achieved considerable artistic success and accepted an invitation to remain in Mexico, establishing a government-sponsored dance company, La Paloma Azul (The Blue Dove) in 1940. Although the group disbanded for lack of financial support, it stirred up interest in modern dance.

Sokolow attained her real choreographic stature in the 1950s and 1960s. Another Mexican invitation inaugurated this new period of creativity. In 1953, Guillermo Keys, a young choreographer, invited Sokolow to create a work for a season of modern dance in Mexico City. The result was *Lyric Suite*, to Alban Berg's composition of the same title, a plotless dance in which Sokolow responded not only to the music, but also to the titles Berg gave the sections of his score: for instance, "Andante amoroso," "Allegro misterioso," and "Presto delirando."

Next, in 1955, came *Rooms*, a portrait of lonely people in a big city, set to a jazz score by Kenyon Hopkins. Very much an urban choreographer, Sokolow has said, "I like to look into windows to catch glimpses of unfinished lives. Then I ask: 'What is there, and why.'" [10] She decided to employ chairs as theatrical symbols of rooms, each dancer on a chair thereby becoming someone alone in a room and leading a life of unfulfilled desire or quiet desperation.

Not all of Sokolow's works were bleak. *Poem* (1956), for instance, was a lyrical piece to the music of Scriabin. Yet it aroused controversy when it was presented in Mexico City. Some members of the audience pronounced it pornographic because of its passionate embraces and an all-male section that could be interpreted as a depiction of homosexual love.

Although Sokolow was admired for her seriousness, dancegoers were occasionally annoyed by certain of her choreographic mannerisms. In several works, dancers marched to the footlights and gave the audience an inquisitorial look that gained the nickname of the "Sokolow stare." Sokolow also loved having one dancer after another repeat despairing phrases in canon. Of course, Sokolow's pessimism was often disquieting. Nevertheless, Clive Barnes, after seeing a somber work called *Deserts* in 1967, said that "her recognition of pain, the force and value she gives to pain, to me seems valuable in a callous world. Miss Sokolow cares—if only to the extent of pointing out that the world is bleeding. I find hope in such pessimism." [11]

Jane Dudley, Sophie Maslow, and William Bales gave their first joint concert in 1942. Performing through the mid-1950s both as a trio and as the heads of their own large company, they featured dances inspired by social issues, contemporary American life, and folklore. They hoped all of their productions would possess broad appeal. As Maslow explained, "We're popular, if by 'popular' you mean 'of the people.' But this is the Age of the Common Man and it is the common people who are the backbone and the strength and hope of our civilization and our culture. We as artists, and above all, as thinking people, are touched by problems of our fellow men because they are our problems." [12] The Dudley-Maslow-Bales repertoire contained pieces as various as Dudley's *Short Story*, a study in frustration, and such examples of Americana as Bales's *To a Green Mountain Boy* and Dudley's *Dust Bowl Ballads* and *Folksay*. The latter included songs by Woody Guthrie and recited poetic excerpts from Carl Sandburg's *The People, Yes*. George Beiswanger said of the trio, "They make one like dancing very much." [13]

Valerie Bettis danced in Hanya Holm's company before making her solo debut in 1941. She became especially famous for *The Desperate*

Heart, a solo about solitude and troubled memories inspired by a poem by John Malcolm Brinnin. Like Helen Tamiris, Bettis was theatrically glamorous and was at home in musicals and films as well as on the concert stage. When she choreographed *Virginia Sampler* for the Ballet Russe de Monte Carlo in 1947 she became the first American modern dancer to create a work for a ballet company. The second was Merce Cunningham, who, later that same year, choreographed *The Seasons* for Ballet Society, the forerunner of the New York City Ballet.

Bettis was not the only modern dancer who found Broadway congenial. Between 1943 and 1957, Tamiris choreographed eighteen musical comedies, including *Up in Central Park, Annie Get Your Gun, Inside U.S.A.* (in which Bettis was a featured dancer), and *Plain and Fancy*. Perhaps it was only to be expected that the flamboyant Tamiris would flourish on Broadway. But Hanya Holm—who to some dancegoers epitomized high seriousness—fared equally well in the theatre, creating dances for such hits as *Kiss Me, Kate, My Fair Lady*, and *Camelot*.

Until his death in 1953, Lester Horton remained active in Los Angeles. His later works included further revisions of *Salome*, as well as *The Beloved*, a savage portrait of a stern, religiously bigoted husband who kills his wife when he suspects her of infidelity. Horton welcomed dancers of all races into his company and, a generous man, offered a multitude of scholarships. Among the dancers who worked with him in the years before his death were Alvin Ailey, Carmen de Lavallade, Joyce Trisler, and James Truitte.

Daniel Nagrin, Tamiris's husband, studied with Graham, Holm, and Sokolow, as well as at several ballet studios. He became known for such dramatically terse solos as *Strange Hero*, a commentary on the way people glorify gangsters, and *Indeterminate Figure*, a study of an indecisive man incapable of changing the world around him.

Lotte Goslar perpetuated modern dance's mimetic tradition. A Dresden-born pupil of Gret Palucca and deeply influenced by Valeska Gert, Goslar performed in Berlin cabarets until 1933, when her anti-Fascist sentiments caused her to leave Germany. She settled in America, at first in Los Angeles and later in the New York area, and in 1954 formed her Pantomime Circus, a troupe offering her theatrical blendings of dance, mime, and comedy. Goslar shares Gert's fascination with human quirks and oddities. But unlike Gert's works, her comedies and satires are usually gentle rather than acerbic.

Child Prodigy is a portrait of an infant wonder who, in rebellion against being constantly trotted out to perform, bites her teacher's finger. *Life of a Flower* shows a flower responding to such vicissitudes as stinging bees, drenching rains, and glaring sunlight. In *Grandma Always Danced*, Goslar begins as an infant and theatrically progresses through life as a bride, a mother, and an old woman. As the title suggests, she always manages to dance. The solo ends with Grandma as an angel in heaven still kicking up her heels.

Katherine Dunham once declared, "I am not a dancer, I am not an ethnologist. I am an evangelist." [14] She was right. She brought her message of dance to America and then to the world. Her company toured Mexico in 1947 and the next year visited London, where it was rapturously received. From 1950 to 1960, it was an international success. [15]

Dunham presented her dancers in revues with such titles as *Tropical Revue* (1943), *Carib Song* (1945), *Bal Nègre* (1946), and *Caribbean Rhapsody* (1947). Each was a well-paced show based upon African, African-American, and Caribbean sources, and she said that in her productions she sought not to reproduce customs and ceremonies literally but to convey their essential meaning. [16]

Like Dunham, Pearl Primus was a trained anthropologist. Born in Trinidad in 1917, she moved to the United States with her family when she was two. She studied at the New Dance Group and was a major in biology and premedical studies at Hunter College, from which she graduated in 1940; she also did graduate work in anthropology at New York University. She gave her first solo recital in 1943 at the 92nd St. Y and made her first appearance with a company there a year later. In addition, she performed as a dance soloist at a popular nightclub, Café Society Downtown.

Her interest in the development of black culture led her to do choreographic research in America and abroad. During 1944, she visited seventy black churches and picked cotton with sharecroppers to gain firsthand knowledge of southern life. On a visit to the West Indies in 1953 she met Percival Borde, the dancer she married a year later. Foundation grants enabled her to make several trips to Africa, on one of which she was adopted by the citizens of Nigeria and renamed Omowale ("child returned home"). [17]

Primus's dances reflected those travels. *Dark Rhythm* was based on dances from Sierre Leone, the Belgian Congo, Nigeria, and Liberia.

Strange Fruit showed a black southern woman's reaction to a lynching. *Hard Time Blues* was a protest against sharecropping. Inspired by a poem by Langston Hughes, *The Negro Speaks of Rivers* sought to parallel the poem's liquid verbal rhythms with comparable liquid choreographic rhythms.

Such major black choreographers as Dunham and Primus inspired other dancers. Talley Beatty, a former Dunham dancer, embarked upon his choreographic career in 1947. His important works included *The Road of the Pheobe Snow* (1959), a study of life on the "wrong" side of the railroad tracks; *Come and Get the Beauty of It Hot* (1960), a suite from which two sections, "Toccata" and "Congo Tango Palace," are often excerpted and presented as independent items; and *The Stack-Up* (1983), which is set in an inner-city neighborhood.

A performance by Dunham made Donald McKayle decide to dance. He studied at the New Dance Group and made his professional debut in 1948 in a program of works by Sophie Maslow and Jean Erdman. Among his most often revived creations are *Games* (1951), in which the games played by city children reveal their longings and fears, *Rainbow 'Round My Shoulder* (1959), a portrait of men on a southern chain gang, and *District Storyville* (1962), an evocation of the early days of jazz in New Orleans.

Although the successes of Dunham, Primus, Beatty, and McKayle were signs that black choreographers were winning recognition, black dancers still had to struggle against misconceptions as well as outright prejudice. Two cousins—Carmen de Lavallade and Janet Collins—studied in Los Angeles with Lester Horton. De Lavallade had a distinguished career as a modern dancer and, once she achieved renown, made guest appearances with ballet companies. Collins was strongly attracted to ballet from the outset. But no ballet companies at the time were willing to risk hiring a black dancer, until in 1951 she was finally appointed a principal dancer of the Metropolitan Opera Ballet, with which she performed until 1954.

Collins occasionally puzzled critics fond of putting dancers into categories. At her choreographic debut in 1949, she danced everything from spirituals to a Mozart rondo. John Martin, who admired her, called her technical base balletic and her choreographic personality modern, feeling obliged to note (using the terminology of the time) that although Collins was a Negro, she was not a "Negro dancer." [18]

The notion that African Americans should devote themselves only to certain types of dances persisted in some quarters. After a performance in 1944, Lois Balcom of *Dance Observer* overheard an otherwise admiring voice say of Pearl Primus, "Of course she'll never become a great modern dancer because she can't get away from her race." That remark prompted Balcom to retort that anyone voicing such an opinion was misinformed not only about the abilities of black dancers but also about the nature of modern dance itself. Then Balcom, like so many of its champions past and present, affirmed that modern dance could never be encompassed within any single system, style, or technique.[19]

$\mathcal{E}$XPLORERS AND DISSENTERS

Abstract Expressionism • May O'Donnell • Jean Erdman • Mattie Haim • Merle Marsicano • Midi Garth • Eleanor King • Katherine Litz • Sybil Shearer • Erick Hawkins • Alwin Nikolais • Murray Louis • Phyllis Lamhut • Merce Cunningham • Chance Dance • Paul Taylor

AFTER WORLD WAR II, MANY AMERICAN THEATREGOERS almost inevitably associated modern dance with large-scale, dramatically based works, especially those of Martha Graham and José Limón. Both choreographers were major forces; both were much imitated. Nevertheless, some American choreographers resisted or systematically rejected mythic, symbolic, or literary source materials, preferring instead dances that were plotless rather than narrative and emotionally evocative rather than thematically explicit.

It could be argued that these choreographers were upholding one of the great traditions of modern dance. After all, such artists as Isadora Duncan, Gret Palucca, and Mary Wigman had rarely told specific stories in movement. Nor, in their early pieces, did Graham and Doris Humphrey.

Some of the newer choreographers were responding to important changes in the fine arts during the 1940s and 1950s. The Abstract Expressionist painters—among them, Jackson Pollock, Robert Motherwell, and Willem de Kooning—were surprising the art world with canvases which, though nonfigurative, seemed rich in emotional turbulence. These artists, who favored strong, bold brushstrokes, were often called "action painters" because their canvases could be regarded as records of the sheer act of painting.

A similar concern for art as process developed in literature. Many writers began to reject tight formalisms. Charles Olson, an influential poet of the period, declared (in the capital letters he sometimes used when he made pronouncements) that "FORM IS NEVER

MORE THAN AN EXTENSION OF CONTENT" (a phrase he borrowed from one he found in a letter from another poet, Robert Creeley) and that "ONE PERCEPTION MUST IMMEDIATELY AND DIRECTLY LEAD TO A FURTHER PERCEPTION."[1]

Within the modern dance field the argument began to be voiced that reliance upon dramatic subject matter was proving stultifying. Works derived from stories, poems, plays, or myths were denounced as excessively "literary." And it was undeniable that the choreography of the less gifted imitators of Graham and Limón was often ponderous.

As early as 1944, Edwin Denby called attention to some of the faults that could vitiate dramatic choreography. Reviewing Doris Humphrey's *Inquest*, he praised it for its moral fervor, yet noted a disquieting difference in works of its kind

> between getting the ideas and following the dances. One grasps the moral implications quickly and agrees with them. But the full rhetorical exposition of these ideas in dance form takes a good deal longer. The result is that one's response is complete before the dance is finished. . . .
>
> Intellectually speaking, an interesting dance is a continuous discovery. The ideas it presents do not precede it, they are found after one has perceived the movement.

Denby believed that the most satisfying sort of dance "creates its own novel meaning as it goes along."[2]

Louis Horst used to warn students, "Don't lean on a dramatic idea. The dance will become a pantomime and the dancer merely a deaf and dumb actor."[3] Choreographers who avoided "leaning" on drama assumed several esthetic stances as they sought to stand on their own feet.

May O'Donnell was particularly concerned with figures in space. A Californian born in Sacramento, where she studied ballet, she took modern dance classes after moving to San Francisco. Among her teachers was Estelle Reed, who was familiar with Wigman technique. She also studied in New York with Hanya Holm. But it was Martha Graham who particularly impressed her. She joined the Graham company in 1932, remaining with it for eight years and returning to it on several occasions as a guest artist. After leaving Graham, she and her husband, the composer Ray Green, returned to San Francisco, where O'Donnell founded a studio in association with another

Graham alumna, Gertrude Shurr. Later, they opened a studio in New York.

In such earlier compositions as *Of Pioneer Women* and *So Proudly We Hail*, O'Donnell explored Americana themes. But the work with which she caused something of a stir was the plotless *Suspension*, a dance to music by Green that received its premiere in San Francisco in 1943. At a time when much modern dance was passionately hot, *Suspension* was cool, clear, and unhurried.

Discussing a New York performance in 1945, Robert Sabin said, "By establishing different focuses of balance, and working out variations of movement with them as a center, Miss O'Donnell succeeded in breaking down the visual space and visual planes of the stage. The spectator felt that the dancers were moving through space as if it were a sustaining and distorting fluid, like water."[4] Such an abstraction might not have seemed unusual to audiences familiar with the German choreographers who had been influenced by the Bauhaus, but to Americans of the 1940s it looked distinctly novel.

The Honolulu-born Jean Erdman danced with Graham from 1938 to 1943 and, like O'Donnell, often returned to the Graham company as a guest artist. Erdman's husband was Joseph Campbell, one of our century's foremost authorities on mythology. Yet, although Erdman did treat mythological subjects, she did not create stormy dance-dramas as Graham did, and her works tended to be impressionistically evocative.

Doris Hering called Erdman's *Daughters of the Lonesome Isle* (1954) "a strangely compelling atmosphere piece. Both the movement and the music [by John Cage] gave the impression of floating through a sort of nebulous other-world, the non-objective, non-representational world that has preoccupied so many artists, but rarely with the success achieved by Miss Erdman."[5]

Mattie Haim, who danced with Graham from 1931 to 1934, allowed her mystical inclinations to develop a dance style remarkable for its long periods of stillness. Calling Haim's dancing "a personal, seemingly religious rite," Hering observed, "Miss Haim's concept of dance seems to center about absence of movement, rather than its presence. . . . The effect is trance-like and totally abstract." Analyzing *Five Cantos in Silence* in 1946, Hering wrote, "As the movement progressed one could perceive no real relationship between arms and body and body and legs. The three units seemed disembodied—one from the other—not in the formal decorative sense associated with ballet, but almost in a floating unreal sense."[6]

Merle Marsicano, who was born in Philadelphia and settled in New York, studied ballet and Spanish dance, as well as modern dance with Martha Graham and Louis Horst. After her marriage to the painter Nicholas Marsicano in 1949, she became acquainted with such Abstract Expressionist artists as Jackson Pollock and Franz Kline and such experimental composers as John Cage and Morton Feldman. She gave her first full-evening dance concert in 1954 and developed a spare, delicate style that emphasized movements of the utmost limpidity.

As she told the dance writer William Como, "I began by making the simplest movements, lifting an arm so slowly that it seemed to take eons of time to rise." Among the dances that developed out of these investigations was *Figure of Memory* (1954), in which she sought to give "an impression of dragged-back time." Summarizing her career, she told Como, "Over the years I've tried to exclude all those extravagances that are outside of the bodily music in which I wish to present myself. Dance itself is *more* than I need to say. And more than anyone should need to say—or see."[7]

Midi Garth was another miniaturist. Garth, who studied composition with Horst and technique at the Graham school and the New Dance Group, specialized in wispy, impressionistic, and reticent sketches. Typically, *Prelude to Flight* (1959) concerned not flight itself, but a preparation for it. As Don McDonagh noted, Garth's dances "did not 'shout' but instead 'whispered' their significance."[8]

Eleanor King joined the Humphrey-Weidman Company at its inception and remained with it until 1935. She later worked throughout America and the Far East and taught for many years at the University of Arkansas.

Although she choreographed in several styles, she was best known for her evocative small-scale mood studies. With its low bending toward the ground and gazes skyward, *Song of Earth* (1935) paid tribute to heroic effort. *Mother of Tears* (1935) was built upon pulled-in gestures of grieving. *Northwest Spirit Dance* (1945) vividly depicted an American Indian woman possessed by a spirit who causes her to shake, stamp, and jump ecstatically. It was one of several works that revealed King's interest in Native American culture. In some ways, her pieces derived from the desire shared by many early modern dancers to give outward form to inner feeling; in that sense, they were traditional. Yet as modern dance became more extravagantly theatrical, they seemed novel for their very economy of means.

Katherine Litz, who performed with the Humphrey-Weidman Company for seven years beginning in 1936, was a delicately comic and sometimes faintly melancholic portraitist who achieved her effects with a few deft choreographic strokes. For instance, in *The Fall of a Leaf* (1959), a movable band on her costume increasingly restricted her range of movement and the solo became a symbolic commentary on aging. Lillian Moore wrote of Litz, "Everything she does from the consciously naive *Story of Love from Fear to Flight,* with its fluttery hands and maidenly tremors, to the wry and sardonic *Fall of the [sic] Leaf* has about it an air of dilapidated gentility."[9]

Sybil Shearer quickly gained a reputation for choreographic unpredictability. That, perhaps, was only to be expected, for she was inspired to become a modern dancer by reading a statement in John Martin's book *The Modern Dance*: "Modern dance is a point of view rather than a technique."[10]

Although Toronto-born, Shearer grew up in Nyack, New York, and on Long Island. She showed talent as a painter and her father, a businessman, hoped she would become a commercial artist. But after graduating as an English major from Skidmore College, she decided to become a dancer. Shearer may have agreed with Martin that modern dance is "a point of view," but she took care to develop a technique which, despite her comparatively late start, was a formidable one. Margaret Lloyd commented: "She can do anything with her body. She can liquefy it to the point of dissolution, or coil it taut as a steel spring, only to let it go in lashes of energy. She can practically turn herself inside out with convulsive movements, or flow with the placidity of a sunlit stream."[11] Ballet did not appeal to her esthetically. Nevertheless, she became a balletic virtuoso and, later in her life, gave her company classes that incorporated elements of the Cecchetti method of ballet training. She sampled the modern idioms at Bennington, finding the Humphrey-Weidman approach most congenial to her. After performing with the Humphrey-Weidman Company, she made her New York solo debut in 1941.

She was hailed from the start. But instead of developing her career in New York City, she turned her back on its theatrical rat race and moved to the Chicago area, eventually settling in the suburban community of Northbrook.

Theatrically, Shearer was often eccentric. Her concert appearances, though eagerly awaited, were infrequent. She presented full-evening programs without intermissions and disdained curtain calls.

At times, she paid little attention to the niceties of stage makeup and grooming. And although her productions were always imaginatively lighted by Helen Morrison, her devoted artistic collaborator, her costumes could be fantastic in one piece and disconcertingly drab in the next.

Shearer freely mixed lyrical movements with realistic pantomime. Some of her dances were sketches of foolish or pitiful people. Others resembled fairy tales of her own invention. Still others were reflections of a very personal nature mysticism.

Typically, a 1946 concert included such items as *In the Field* (a sacred fertility rite), *In a Vacuum* (a tragi-comic study in neurotic movement), *O, Lost!* (in which the dancer fumbled toward the light), *Is It Night?* (a response to the recent dropping of the atomic bomb on Hiroshima), and *Let the Heavens Open That the Earth May Shine* (a choreographic hymn of praise). Like Rosalia Chladek, Shearer created cycles of loosely related solos or group works. Her *Once upon a Time* (1951) consisted of portraits of fanciful creatures who might have stepped from fairy tales or myths. Shearer gave each a name: thus Medigma was a witch; Yanchi moved with a delicate Oriental sinuosity; Relluckus was a graceless ragged hag; Ziff fluttered aimlessly; and Inigra radiated confidence. Reviews of *Once upon a Time* reflect the extremes of opinion that Shearer's productions elicited. Martin, ordinarily one of her strongest admirers, could only sputter, "Just how fey can you be?" But Walter Terry thought the cycle would appeal "to those who will adventure with her, believe in her dreams and in their own, accept what she does whether they fully understand or not." [12]

Shearer invented proverbs to serve as the titles for the sections of another suite, *Fables and Proverbs* (1970). "Without wings the way is steep" was a struggle to climb and reach out. In "All is not gold but almost," a strange creature hopped from one pool of light to another in an alchemical attempt to transform brass into gold. Other sections bore such titles as "The sunbeam will outlast us all" and "The message is in the mind." It is not surprising that this free-spirited dancer once called her choreography "reality for those who understand it so, and a fantasy for those who regard it so." [13]

Four innovators proved unusually influential as teachers, company directors, and choreographers: Erick Hawkins, Alwin Nikolais, Murray Louis, and Merce Cunningham.

Hawkins, who was born in Trinidad, Colorado, in 1909, studied Greek at Harvard, and his love of both the open spaces of the West and classical learning influenced his choreography. Almost by chance, he attended performances by Yvonne Georgi and Harald Kreutzberg that awakened a passion for dancing in him. He studied with Kreutzberg and at the School of American Ballet, joined Lincoln Kirstein and George Balanchine's American Ballet in 1935, and in 1937 choreographed *Show Piece* for Ballet Caravan, the troupe Kirstein founded to develop new American choreographers.

During Ballet Caravan's residency at Bennington, Hawkins first encountered Martha Graham. Impressed by her work, he started to find ballet technically and esthetically rigid. In 1938, he became the Graham company's first male dancer, remaining with it until 1951. Graham and Hawkins were married in 1948; two years later, they separated, and they were divorced in 1954.

Hawkins's early dances reflected many of that period's choreographic preoccupations. He made excursions into Americana—lightheartedly in *Yankee Bluebritches* (1940), with dramatic seriousness in *John Brown* (1945)—and turned to Greek mythology in *The Strangler* (1948), a retelling of the story of Oedipus and the Sphinx.

But just as he had rejected ballet, Hawkins grew dissatisfied with much of the modern dance he saw during the 1940s and 1950s. Believing that dance teachers were placing inordinate emphasis upon tension and strain and that the preoccupation of many choreographers with tormented heroes and heroines had made modern dance neurotic, he increasingly sought to create images of beauty in his own compositions. A firm believer in collaborations, he often worked with Ralph Dorazio, a sculptor, and his second wife, Lucia Dlugoszewski, a composer whose scores are notable for their delicate timbres.

Dorazio and Dlugoszewski participated in the making of *Here and Now with Watchers* (1957), a dance for two people that is the first major example of the refined style Hawkins prized. Like Sybil Shearer, Hawkins delighted in verbal fantasies, and the sections of *Here and Now with Watchers* bear such titles as "Inside Wonder of Whales (says my body of things)" and "Like Darling (shouts my body and shows itself transparent)." The choreography was born out of Hawkins's conviction that "the important essence of all dancing is *movement* quality, and its excellence, or lack of excellence," and the program note included the statement, "I would like to show the miracle of two people, the perfection of the one beside the perfection of the other and the poetry of the space between them." [14]

Hawkins's *8 Clear Places* (1960) concerned such things as stars, trees, rain, snow, and squash. But instead of having dancers literally attempt to be plants, weather conditions, or heavenly bodies, Hawkins tried to express the essential state of being of, say, a squash or a rainbow. The equally evocative *Geography of Noon* (1964) derived from his observations of butterflies.

Hawkins also honored human work and play. *Cantilever* (1966) was a tribute to the beauty of bridges, and *Classic Kite Tails* (1972) translated the darting of kites into dancing.

Alwin Nikolais has been called choreography's Wizard of Oz. Nikolais himself said he was a choreographic polygamist because he sought "a polygamy of motion, shape, color, and sound." [15] Whatever one called him, he was a creator of a multimedia form that made dazzling use of theatrical illusion.

Nikolais (1912–1993) was born in Southington, Connecticut, and as a young man worked as a puppeteer and as a pianist for silent films. A performance by Mary Wigman made him want to study with one of her disciples—but not primarily to learn dance. Rather, he was intrigued by her use of percussion instruments. He found a Wigman-trained teacher, Truda Kaschmann, in Hartford. His love of dance soon equaled his love of music, and he studied at the Bennington summer schools, where he was particularly impressed by Hanya Holm's teaching. After military service in World War II, he became her assistant.

In 1948, he joined the staff of the Henry Street Settlement Playhouse—the former Neighborhood Playhouse—and it remained his base until the late 1960s, when he found larger quarters necessary. He turned the tiny Henry Street Playhouse into a magician's box of marvels. Playing theatrical conjuring tricks, he not only choreographed his productions, but also designed scenery, costumes, and lighting and composed their electronic scores.

Nikolais transformed the appearance of dancers by encasing them in fantastic constructions or by attaching sculptural shapes to their bodies. He also flooded dancers with changing light patterns so as to blur distinctions between illusion and reality and make it difficult for spectators to determine which shapes before them were real and which were shadows or slide projections. Nikolais's use of technology made him an artistic heir of Loïe Fuller and Oskar Schlemmer.

Masks, Props and Mobiles (1953), Nikolais's first major multimedia effort, has a much-praised episode in which dancers encased in bags stretch themselves into odd shapes as they move. The shape of dancing bodies in *Kaleidoscope* (1962) was altered with the aid of discs, poles, paddles, hoops, straps, and capes. Nikolais subtitled *Imago* (1963) "The City Curious," and its inhabitants included scurrying robotlike figures, men with fantastically long arms who are hooked together as if in a giant chain, and men and women who move between lines of elastic tape stretched from one side of the stage to the other. At various points in *Sanctum* (1964), dancers had to swing from a trapeze, manipulate silver poles, and struggle to escape from enclosures that kept changing size.

Some of Nikolais's productions can be enjoyed simply as abstract studies in motion. Others possess thematic implications: the way a tower explodes after dancers have struggled to erect it in *Tower* (1965) brings to mind the biblical story of the Tower of Babel, and with the aid of slide projections Nikolais makes dancers resemble water plants and creatures in *Pond* (1982).

Echoing complaints once brought against Schlemmer, Nikolais's detractors contended that he dehumanized dancers. But George Beiswanger defended Nikolais's choreographic approach by pointing out that Nikolais "wants things to move, to be seen, and to be heard, and he wants the resulting aliveness of things to be apparent even when the things are dancers. Hence the props dance and the dancers prop (not that they do not dance as well). Now one may take this in two ways, as dehumanizing the dancer or as animizing the thing. I am inclined, perhaps perversely, to the latter view."[16] It can also be argued that, by uniting dancers with scenic effects, Nikolais choreographically expressed ecological concerns and that the harmonious or contentious encounters between dancers and objects are parables of ways in which people interact with their environment in the real world.

However one interprets them, Nikolais's productions are almost always entertaining. He not only resembles the Wizard of Oz, he is also akin to the Wizard's creator, L. Frank Baum, that lover of peculiar animated gadgets. Nikolais himself once admitted, "I am a compulsive creator—if you gave me a schnauzer, two Armenian chastity belts and a 19th-century dish pan—I would attempt to create something with them."[17]

In addition to training dancers, the Nikolais studio has encouraged choreographers—among them Murray Louis and Phyllis Lamhut. Each has performed with the Nikolais company as well as in each other's works.

Louis, who was born in 1926, began his dance studies with Anna Halprin in San Francisco after military service during World War II. Back in his native New York, he became Nikolais's artistic associate in 1949 and has headed his own successful company, which on several occasions merged with that of Nikolais.

A remarkable virtuoso, Louis can isolate parts of his body and make his limbs move in various, even seemingly contradictory, ways, as if each had a will of its own. His less successful choreography can sometimes appear unduly twitchy. But when he is at his creative best, his dancing and that of his company can be precise and expertly timed, especially to comic effect.

Among his most acclaimed comic pieces are *Junk Dances* (1964), a portrait of a husband and wife (Louis and Lamhut) surviving marital vicissitudes in what can be interpreted either as a literal junkyard or a theatrical metaphor for an emotional trashpile, and *Hoopla* (1973), a tribute to circus acts. His works also extend from the somber all-male *Calligraph for Martyrs* (1961) to the lyrical *Porcelain Dialogues* (1974).

Lamhut, who was born on Manhattan's Lower East Side in 1933, received her early dance training at the Henry Street Settlement; although she has studied elsewhere, she has remained closely associated with Nikolais and Louis, as well as with the Hanya Holm Studio. She first attracted attention as a deft comedienne, then expanded her scope to create large-scale ensembles with some of the fervor of the German *Ausdruckstanz*.

Merce Cunningham's innovations have been especially controversial and influential. Born in Centralia, Washington, in 1919, he began to study dance locally at the age of twelve. Intending to become an actor, he enrolled at the Cornish School in Seattle, where he was encouraged to dance by Bonnie Bird, a former member of the Graham company who was on the Cornish faculty. There he also met John Cage, a young experimental composer. Together, Cunningham and Cage developed unconventional ideas of dance composition.

Committed to a dance career, Cunningham attended Bennington's 1939 session at Mills College in Oakland, California, where he attracted the attention of Martha Graham. After moving to New York, he danced with her company, 1939–1945, and presented his first New York choreography in 1942 in a concert he shared with Jean Erdman and Nina Fonaroff. He also toured as a dance soloist in musical programs by Cage. After 1945, he devoted himself full-time to his own choreography, with Cage serving as his artistic adviser.

Cunningham could be dramatically forceful as a performer, both in the Graham repertory and in his own early pieces. In 1945, Robert Sabin of *Dance Observer* called *Experiences* "the most gripping thing" Cunningham had done and found that it "marks a new advance in dramatic realization. Its ferocity and body dynamics, its 'freezes' (in which the movement is suddenly arrested with tremendous effect) are not only exciting as examples of virtuosity but they show a spirit of creative experimentation which promises well for the future." In that same review, Sabin noted that Cunningham was blessed with a sense of humor and found his *Mysterious Adventure* "deliciously impish in flavor." [18]

Cunningham continued to receive praise for his dramatic presence and whimsical comedy. But he put these qualities to unconventional use. Even at the beginning of his career, he stood apart from many of his choreographic colleagues. Reviewing a 1944 concert, Sabin presciently observed that the event was unusual for its "pure, unadulterated dancing. . . . He is a classicist (if one may venture to use that dangerous word) in the sense that he absolutely believes in dance as an independent medium of expression with its own laws and objectives." [19]

Printed programs for Cunningham's concerts often included this credo: "Dancing has a continuity of its own that need not be dependent upon either the rise and fall of sound, or the pitch and cry of words. Its force of feeling lies in the physical image, fleeting or static. It can and does evoke all sorts of individual responses in the single spectator." [20] Cunningham's dances were plotless. Nevertheless, they were perceived as having their own special choreographic personalities and atmospheres, possibly because the specific kinds of movements he favored in each prompted similar reactions in the audiences that beheld them. Thus, no one ever called Cunningham's harsh *Winterbranch* sweet or his lyrical *Summerspace* savage.

Cunningham often commissioned new music, and his designers over the years included such eminent artists as Robert Rauschenberg, Jasper Johns, Frank Stella, and Andy Warhol. Yet he made no attempt to have dance phrases coincide with musical phrases and the décor for his dances never literally illustrated anything in them. In 1959, when he choreographed *Septet* to an existing score—Erik Satie's "Trois Morceaux en Forme de Poire"—some audiences were startled by Cunningham's treatment of the music—as, for instance, in moments when dancers stood perfectly still to loud chords that might have inspired other choreographers to devise passages of frantic activity. Cunningham has said, "It is hard for many people to accept that dancing has nothing in common with music other than the element of time and the division of time."[21] In his productions, dancing, music, and stage design do not provide one another with mutual support; rather, they coexist.

Cunningham came to believe that any space can be danced in and that any point in space can be of interest. For him, stage space was an empty field. He therefore ignored traditional theories of stage direction that maintain that stage center is "strong," whereas movements at the sides of the stage may be "weak."

Just as any point in space can be significant, so, for Cunningham, any movement, however fancy or ordinary, can serve as a dance movement. This theory paralleled John Cage's belief that any sound can be used in a piece of music. Concertgoers found many of the sounds in Cage's early works beguiling, for he explored the possibilities of what he called the prepared piano: a piano with objects carefully placed upon its strings so as to alter their customary timbres. Cage's prepared pianos reminded audiences of unconventionally tuned harpsichords or Balinese gamelans. But as Cage continued his experiments, he alienated some listeners with electronic scores that were found loud, harsh, and grating. The music he composed for Cunningham's *Aeon* outraged dancegoers at its premiere at the American Dance Festival in 1961. It "ran its fingernails over our eardrums," Doris Hering complained, and Louis Horst dismissed it as "shattering and ear-splitting noise." A scientist in the audience even announced, "The sound level in that auditorium is dangerous for human ears."[22]

Whatever sounds may have accompanied them, Cunningham's choreographic phrases were so lucid that his style was sometimes compared with ballet. Nevertheless, despite what could be called his "classical" tendencies, his choreography was often controversial. His theories regarding chance and indeterminacy helped make it so. These words bewilder some dancegoers, who regard them as synonyms for improvisation. But Cunningham's choreography is not improvised; his dancers do not invent their steps as they go along. Indeed, if he had not publicly announced that he employed chance in making some works, spectators might not even suspect that he had done so.

Cunningham first employed chance in 1951 when he choreographed *Sixteen Dances for Soloist and Company of Three*, a work inspired by the Indian theatre's nine traditional categories of human emotions. Unable to decide which emotion should follow which onstage, Cunningham threw a coin to determine the order; but once that order was established, it remained unaltered. For *Suite by Chance* (1953), he prepared elaborate charts of possible movements, then selected the specific ones to be employed by tossing coins. If he had not said that he had done so, few (if any) spectators could have guessed it.

In contrast, effects of indeterminacy can be visible in the theatre—provided one sees more than a single performance of a given dance. In indeterminate compositions, the choreographer or the dancers can alter the order of sequences or omit some of them at each performance. But, once again, they do not have the freedom to improvise. Although Cunningham devised thirteen brief dances for his suite *Dime a Dance* (1953), only eight of them were ever presented on any night. The cast members of *Field Dances* (1963) were assigned a specific number of things to do, but were left free to do them at whatever speed they chose, as often as they wished, and in any order.

Cunningham's fascination with chance and indeterminacy had historical precedents, for the Dadaists and Surrealists had made use of chance. Like them, Cunningham believes that most people too easily become creatures of habit. Through chance, however, artists can discover images or patterns that their purely rational minds might not have invented. Chance also allows creators to ignore or transcend conventional cause-and-effect logic. Chance leaves room for surprise.

One never knows quite what to expect of Paul Taylor. His choreography keeps slipping unpredictably from style to style and theme to theme.

His father was a physicist; his mother managed a dining room in a Washington, D.C., hotel, and they divorced when he was young. Taylor, who was born in 1930, was attracted to both art and athletics. As a student at the University of Syracuse, he was asked to serve as a partner in a program by the campus modern dance club. That so whetted his interest in dance that he finally summoned the courage to tell his athletic coach that he wished to become a professional dancer. The coach proved more sympathetic to dance than Ted Shawn's fraternity brothers had been. "Kiddo," he said, "you sound like you've gone bonkers, but I guess there's no stopping you."[23]

Taylor studied dance at Juilliard and performed with the companies of Cunningham and Graham. When Graham and George Balanchine collaborated on *Episodes* in 1958, Balanchine created a solo especially for Taylor. In the mid-1950s, Taylor began offering his own programs. Much of his early choreography was whimsical or eccentric. Typically, *Three Epitaphs* (a 1960 revision of a 1956 piece called *Four Epitaphs*) depicted bizarre creatures totally encased in black costumes designed by Robert Rauschenberg who slouched and loped to recordings of old New Orleans funeral music in a manner that was simultaneously funny, grotesque, and endearing.

A 1957 concert by Taylor left one distinguished dance critic totally speechless. The entire program was based on walking and running steps and simple, but significant, changes of position. In *Epic*, Taylor, neatly attired in a business suit, slowly moved and paused and resumed his steps to recorded time signals. *Duet*, for Taylor and Toby Glanternik, involved held positions: Taylor remained standing and Glanternik remained sitting throughout the piece—and that was the entire dance. The uncompromising simplicity of these works so befuddled Louis Horst that his review for *Dance Observer* consisted of nothing but a blank space with his initials at the bottom of it.

Although Taylor reveled in absurdity, he soon demonstrated that his choreographic personality was split in several ways. His *Aureole* (1962) surprised dancegoers not with its oddity, but with its lyricism, and this dance to the music of Handel became one of Taylor's most popular creations. Its serene joy has even struck some audiences as balletic. However, its resemblance to ballet is superficial, and when Taylor stages *Aureole* for ballet companies, he finds that members of these troupes often find it difficult, for the choreography abounds with "unclassical" swings of the arms and jutting hips; moreover, whereas many ballets require their dancers to take lightness for granted, the dancers in *Aureole* are made to appear weighted bodies which achieve lightness.

Because of its sheer diversity, Taylor's work has come to epitomize the pluralism of modern dance since the 1960s. Taylor himself ignores all restrictive compositional theories. For him, as he put it, "There are no rules, just decisions." [24]

American modern dance increasingly branched out in many directions. As early as 1946, when she saw concerts by Anna Sokolow and Merce Cunningham on the same day, Doris Hering felt impelled to compare them because, she said,

> they typify opposite poles of approach in the contemporary dance. Anna Sokolow is a realist. She is socially conscious. . . . So absorbed does she become in the social and socializing aspects of her art that detail is sometimes neglected for over-all effect; and form is neglected for content.

As for Cunningham, his

> dance language is for the initiated few who are as interested in contemplating Mr. Cunningham's navel as he is himself. The effect tends to be over-intellectual and a little precious.
> But there are compensations in going along with Mr. Cunningham. He is a dancer to the core. There isn't a crude or clumsy bone in his supple body. His phrasing and sense of form approach perfection. [25]

More than a decade later, the gulf between dramatically oriented and abstract dance had widened so far that Walter Terry in 1961 thought it necessary to distinguish between an old guard and a new guard:

> In general, the old guard looks upon modern dance as a way of communicating the inner passions, the psychological responses, the hidden dreams of man's heart and mind. The avant garde, in general, explores the formal relationships of bodies as they move through, or pause in, space and as they are guided (or not guided) by fixed or unfixed rhythms, sounds and colors.

Yet, given dance's ability to communicate, even as it may also visually and kinetically please or excite, many works of inner passion also possess outward structural beauty, and studies of formal relationships can often be rich in emotional nuance. As the Hollywood writer and film producer Jon Boorstin has said of theoretically divergent esthetic approaches in his own field, "These two concerns, creating a credible flow of time and creating a story, aren't as different as they might seem." [26]

$\mathcal{J}$CONOCLASTS

Assemblage • Happenings • Anna Halprin • Simone Forti • Susanne K. Langer • James Waring • Robert and Judith Dunn • Judson Dance Theatre • Ruth Emerson • Elaine Summers • Steve Paxton • Yvonne Rainer • Fred Herko • Lucinda Childs

RADICAL CHANGES OCCURRED IN AMERICAN MODERN DANCE in the late 1950s and early 1960s, some of which had parallels in the art world. During the 1950s, Claes Oldenburg, Jasper Johns, Robert Rauschenberg, and other artists developed an interest in what has come to be known as Assemblage. They constructed works, many of which looked deliberately scruffy, out of such objects as discarded clothing, lumber, machine parts, cardboard, paper wrappers, toothbrushes, and razor blades. The art writer Roni Feinstein has declared that "more than any movement in the past, Assemblage gave artists the license to make works of art from any materials whatsoever." What most people might regard as junk could turn up in Assemblage as art. As Oldenburg wrote in 1961, "I am for an art that embroils itself with the everyday crap & still comes out on top." [1]

Various styles of representational painting began to challenge the primacy of Abstract Expressionism. The most iconoclastic of these was Pop Art, which derived its imagery from such ordinary, even banal, sources as movies, comic books, and advertising displays. Pop artists—including Oldenburg, Andy Warhol, Roy Lichtenstein, James Rosenquist, and Tom Wesselmann—looked upon American consumer society in a deadpan manner and simultaneously celebrated and satirized aspects of it.

Merce Cunningham theorized that any movement could serve as a dance movement. But, for the most part, the movements in his works, however strangely they may have been arranged, could be related to traditional dance steps. Other creators took Cunningham's theories to extreme conclusions in dances and movement-oriented theatre pieces derived from decidedly unconventional sources. Among these new forms were the productions known as Happenings.

Cultural historians often trace the origin of Happenings to a performance in 1952 at Black Mountain College, an experimental college near Asheville, North Carolina, founded in 1933. Black Mountain emphasized the arts and attracted several dancers and dance musicians. Fritz Cohen, Kurt Jooss's musical director, taught there from 1942 to 1944, as did his wife, the Jooss dancer Elsa Kahl. But the most influential figures in the college's dance community were Merce Cunningham and John Cage, who were in residence there in the summers of 1948, 1952, and 1953.

Black Mountain encouraged collaborations between its resident artists. In 1948, it presented Erik Satie's play with music, *Le Piège de Méduse*, in a staging by the theatre directors Helen Livingston and Arthur Penn, with choreography by Cunningham, who also portrayed a mechanical monkey. Cage was the pianist. Willem and Elaine de Kooning designed the scenery, and the important role of the Baron was played by the architect and visionary social thinker Buckminster Fuller.[2]

Whereas this production could be described as a theatrical collaboration in the Diaghilev tradition, John Cage's *Theatre Piece No. 1*, in 1952, was a collaboration of a very different kind. Diaghilev's choreographers, artists, and composers pooled their creative resources to work toward a common goal; in contrast, *Theatre Piece No. 1* was a collection of separate but overlapping events. Cage assigned each participant a time slot; what was done during that time was entirely the performer's choice.

The action took place in the college dining hall within and outside a circle of chairs on which the audience sat. Memories differ as to what actually occurred, although it is widely agreed that Cage climbed a ladder and read something. But what? Some recall it was an essay on the mystical theologian Meister Eckhart; others say it was a lecture on Zen; still others claim it was an excerpt from the Bill of Rights or the Declaration of Independence. The poets M. C. Richards and Charles Olson read at various times from other ladders. Cunningham danced among and around the chairs. He was joined by a stray dog which had wandered in from outside and fitted in with the proceedings as easily as any of the humans did. Robert Rauschenberg played scratchy records on a wind-up phonograph, David Tudor played a prepared piano and a small radio, and movies and slides were projected on the walls and ceiling (or, according to some reports, on slanting surfaces that had been installed for the occasion).[3]

Theatre Piece No. 1, though seen by few people, became an artistic legend. As interest in collage, "Junk" sculpture, and Pop Art grew, its open-ended, cheerfully anarchic form appealed to artists who began to devise their own Happenings. These later performances attracted the attention of the media; gradually, in popular parlance, the term "Happening" became virtually synonymous with "Free-for-all," and many people who never saw them assume that Happenings were totally formless gatherings at which things "just happened" without any structure or purpose. But the works staged in the late 1950s and early 1960s by such artists as Allan Kaprow, Robert Whitman, Jim Dine, Red Grooms, and Claes Oldenburg were not like that at all.

These Happenings were mixed-media productions in which the action proceeded not according to a single narrative line, but according to intuition or free association. They tended to be nonverbal, and they often made use of movement, although it was seldom conventional dance movement. Many Happenings were presented in nontheatrical spaces, some of them big enough to allow several episodes to be performed simultaneously or to permit spectators to wander from activities in one area to totally different events elsewhere.[4]

The first work to be specifically termed a Happening was Kaprow's *16 Happenings in 6 Parts*, staged in a New York art gallery in 1959. The space was divided into three rooms and spectators seated in each of them were given instructions about how and when to move to the next room. The things they saw included people performing such simple (but precisely timed) movements as bending, pacing, and touching the left hand to the right arm; other people arranged blocks, bounced a ball, struck and extinguished matches, squeezed orange juice, and played the ukulele, flute, and banjo.

Some Happenings were whimsical. In Grooms's *The Burning Building* (1959), which reminded some people of children's toys come alive, a cardboard building sported "flames" of red painted canvas and men dressed as firemen carried cardboard axes, burst into Irish jigs, and ate a paper turkey. For Oldenburg's *Injun*, presented in Dallas in 1962, an entire house was decorated to serve as the setting. It thereby became something of a haunted house. One room was as crammed with newspapers and refuse as the hideaway of an eccentric recluse. A woman in another room divided her time between gazing wistfully out a window, kicking a ball across the floor, and vanishing into a closet. A woman stationed in the kitchen covered the lower part of her face with masking tape, sprayed black paint on the walls, and washed her feet in a bucket. The tub in the house's bathroom was filled with mud.

Dancers devised equally striking experiments. Prominent among these innovators was the San Francisco choreographer Anna Halprin (also known as Ann Halprin). Born in Winnetka, Illinois, in 1920, Halprin received thorough grounding in many of the established modern dance techniques. She was a graduate of the University of Wisconsin, where she was deeply influenced by Margaret H'Doubler, and she performed on Broadway in 1944 in *Sing Out, Sweet Land*, a folk musical choreographed by Doris Humphrey. She and her husband, the landscape architect Lawrence Halprin, moved to San Francisco in 1945, and she formed a company there with Welland Lathrop, a respected teacher and choreographer who had once served as a teaching assistant to Louis Horst and in 1941 had briefly performed with the Graham company.

Halprin was first known for strongly dramatic dances, one of the most successful of them being *The Prophetess*, a solo which depicted the biblical prophetess Deborah leading her people into battle. Although living outside New York, she became sufficiently well known that in 1955 she was invited to participate in a two-week festival of modern dance presented in New York by ANTA (American National Theatre and Academy). Whereas the invitation excited her, the festival dismayed her because many of the dances she saw struck her as formula-ridden. "Something inside me started going dead," she later recalled. "I felt depressed, discouraged, distrustful, and I knew my career as a modern dancer had just died."[5]

The Halprins lived in Kentfield, a suburb of San Francisco on the slopes of Mount Tamalpais. Their five-acre wooded property included both an indoor studio and an outdoor platform theatre known as the "dance deck." Returning from New York, Halprin severed her association with Lathrop, founded her own Dancer's Workshop, and began to experiment on the deck. As she put it, "I wanted to explore in a particular way, breaking down any preconceived notions I had about what dance was, or what movement was, or what composition was." Emerson might have said that she was trying to establish an original relationship with nature. In particular, Halprin said, "We began to explore systems that would knock out cause and effect. . . . I wanted to find out things that I'd never thought of, that would never come out of my personal response."[6]

Although Halprin made improvisation her principal tool in this process of discovery, she never let it be simply a gush of activity. Instead, she favored structured improvisations in which dancers had to invent new movements within prescribed limits. For instance, they could be asked to do anything they wished, provided that they always moved forward. Or they could be required to perform a fixed number of gestures—of any kind—while they crossed the stage.

Halprin's workshop attracted artists, composers, and writers as well as such intellectually inquisitive dancers as Yvonne Rainer, Simone Forti, Meredith Monk, Trisha Brown, and Kei Takei, all of whom became important choreographers. Even dancers who had never seen or worked with her somehow knew about her in the late 1950s and early 1960s.

Her productions were often compelling, and she knew how to employ objects in striking choreographic ways. *The Five-Legged Stool*, a two-act production of 1962 with music by Morton Subotnick, was based almost entirely upon tasks. The dancers always had choreographic chores to do—for instance, they were required to pour water, throw objects into the air, and change clothes—and they always had to do them in the same way; yet they could do them in any order. Several sequences evoked emotional states, notably one in which Halprin methodically delivered forty wine bottles, one after the other, to an ominous and apparently disembodied hand that dangled down from above the stage; the relentless pacing made these activities seem images of compulsive behavior. Near the end of the piece, two dancers kept colliding and crashing to the floor to discordant taped sounds; at the same time, performers stationed in the audience sang the hymn "A Mighty Fortress Is Our God." But, after this chaotic activity, the production concluded peacefully when a snowstorm of feathers fell silently upon the stage.

Asked to produce a work for La Fenice, the Venice opera house, during the Venice Biennale of 1963, Halprin studied the historic theatre and decided that its stage looked like a fireplace in a living room; she feared her company of six would be visually insignificant within its confines. Therefore, for her *Esposizione*, which had music by Luciano Berio, she suspended an enormous cargo net across the proscenium, on which the dancers clambered. Their movements derived from the task of shifting loads of bulky material, Halprin burdening them with automobile tires, gunnysacks, bundles of rags, rolled-up newspapers, and hassocks filled with tennis balls.

Halprin took her company to New York in 1969 in *Parades and Changes*, to music by Subotnick. During the course of the evening-long piece, Halprin danced to a one-man band while a goat looked on and people raced up the aisles of the Hunter College Playhouse and descended on rope ladders from the balcony; they later performed a rollicking, stomping dance on a set of resonant wooden platforms. As its title suggested, *Parades and Changes* was a kaleidoscope of shifting theatrical moods. The sequence that caused the most comment—delighting some viewers with its sculptural beauty and offending others with its nudity—was one in which the dancers, after slowly walking through the auditorium and onto the stage, stood in a line directly facing the audience. They then took off all their clothes, wrapped themselves in brown paper, and rolled into the orchestra pit.

Halprin's career took a new, and for some commentators a controversial, turn in the late 1960s, when she began to stage communal rituals designed to promote personal growth and social harmony. By continuing to work in this field she, in effect, went from devoting herself to dance as a theatrical art to dance as a form of therapy or consciousness raising.

Halprin inspired dancers to make their own experiments. Simone Forti (who was also known as Simone Morris and Simone Whitman) studied with Halprin in the 1950s and moved to New York in 1959. Like Halprin, she was fascinated by objects, as she revealed in three compositions of 1961. *Slant Board* consisted of movements on a steep wooden ramp. Groups of people clustered tightly together in *Huddle*. Then individuals left the huddle to climb slowly over it, using the other performers' bodies as supports and, in effect, treating the group of dancers as an architectural object. In *Platforms*, a man and a woman got under two platforms, whistled, and eventually came back into view—and that was all that happened.

The action in Forti's dances was clear and unambiguous. Her movements could be viewed as images of effort, yet they were never symbolic. At a time when such choreographers as Graham, Humphrey, and Limón prized heroic gestures, Forti was resolutely mundane. Her detractors accused her of banality, but, for her admirers, Forti celebrated the ordinary human gesture.

The pedestrian movements and manipulations of objects in the dances of Halprin, Forti, and other similarly minded choreographers

could be interpreted as a refutation—conscious or unconscious—
of certain aspects of a theory of dance that was influential at the time
and that remains important. Susanne K. Langer, who taught philosophy at Connecticut College and who regularly attended the American Dance Festival there, was one of the few estheticians of her day to
take dance as seriously as such arts as painting and music.

Langer insisted that dance exists apart from all other arts, that it is
"neither plastic art nor music, nor a presentation of story, but a play
of Powers made visible." For Langer, these powers, or forces, are of a
special kind: they are what she terms virtual powers. From a philosophically rigorous standpoint, all forces that cannot be scientifically
measured are illusory: they are virtual, rather than actual. Yet, if they
are not measurable, they do exist, and we can perceive them, just as
we can perceive such other intangibles as rainbows or reflections in a
mirror.[7]

The concept of virtual powers led Langer to state:

> The primary illusion of dance is a virtual realm of Power—not actu-
> ally, physically exerted power, but appearances of influence and agency
> created by virtual gesture.
>
> In watching a collective dance—say, an artistically successful bal-
> let—one does not see *people running around*; one sees the dance draw-
> ing this way, drawn that way, gathering here, spreading there, fleeing,
> resting, rising and so forth; and all the motion seems to spring from
> powers beyond the performers.

As a result, "the dance creates an image of nameless and even bodi-
less Powers" and "both space and time, as perceptible factors, dis-
appear almost entirely in the dance illusion."[8]

Langer's concept of the dance illusion as an interplay of forces implies both that dance is a crafted thing, not an outpouring of pure
self-expression, and that the experiences that dance presents are
fictive: Martha Graham did not necessarily have to be personally sad
every time she offered *Lamentation*, and the performers in even so
resolutely a non-narrative and antisymbolic piece as Forti's *Huddle*
clustered together for esthetic reasons and not because they were
football players or homeless refugees.

Yet in a curious way Langer's theory of virtual powers threatens to
dematerialize dance, which is, after all, an art of very real solid bodies. Halprin, Forti, and other choreographers sympathetic to them
wanted the body and its exertions to be fully apparent. That is one

reason for their use of tasklike movements and objects. If spectators at one of their dances told them that, above all, they were conscious of *people running around,* they might well have taken that as a compliment, possibly to Langer's surprise.

If the theatrical plainness of Forti could be viewed as evidence that some choreographers were impatient with heroic gestures, so could another, but much more extravagant, style, associated with James Waring and some of his students and company members. Waring was an eclectic who could mix ballet, modern dance, and vaudeville dancing in works which were, by turns, flamboyant, whimsical, nostalgic, and unabashedly sentimental.

Waring's classes were balletically based, and, before his sudden death in 1975, he had staged productions for the Manhattan Festival Ballet, a small New York classical company, and Netherlands Dance Theatre, which required its members to be proficient in both ballet and modern dance. Yet he was generally regarded as a modern dance choreographer.

Waring was born in 1922 in Oakland, California, where he received his first dance lessons from Raoul Pausé, a local teacher who taught ballet and *plastique,* a freely flowing style of movement prized early in the century by Michel Fokine in his attempts to make Russian ballet less stiff. After army service in World War II, Waring studied in San Francisco with Halprin and Lathrop and at the San Francisco Ballet School. He later recalled, "I was the only person I knew of at the time in San Francisco who was studying ballet and modern with equal seriousness. I did not find them contradictory."[9] He moved to New York in 1947.

Waring's output was almost bewilderingly varied. Yet there were themes and styles to which he often returned. Thus *Mazurkas for Pavlova* (1967) was one of many fond tributes to vanished eras of ballet history. Several works, from *The Wanderers* (1951) to *Arena* and *Winter Circus* (both 1968), concerned acrobats, clowns, freaks, or strolling players.

Waring called some of his more freewheeling plotless pieces "celebrations" or "jubilees." The cast of *At the Hallelujah Gardens* (1963) included a live goose, and there were never less than two different things going on simultaneously. An even busier production was *Double Concerto* (1964), in which the stage situation was significantly altered every ten seconds; the resultant flicker of activity strained spectators' perceptions as well as the performers' muscles. Waring also created florid dramatic dances, among them *The Phantom of the Opera* (1967), a mimetic retelling of that classic horror story which, though wildly exaggerated, was still fundamentally serious.

Waring could wander freely from style to style because of his philosophy of art:

> Art can be anything you point your finger at and say, "This is art." Art involves selecting and naming. An artist is free to select anything and call it art. But, of course, you and I are also free to accept or reject it as art.
>
> Dance is whatever you claim it to be. I am free to point to any movement and say, "This is dance." [10]

Many of Waring's dances proved ephemeral. But his views—including his reluctance to fix rigid distinctions between "high" and "low" art—were influential. And his wide range of interests made it only natural that he would be a friend and teacher of some of the iconoclastic choreographers who participated in the first concert of what has come to be known as the Judson Dance Theatre.

The first Judson concert was an outgrowth of a composition workshop led by Robert Dunn, a musician married to Judith Dunn, a dancer and choreographer who had performed with Merce Cunningham's company. Many young dancers of the time wished to band together in an informal workshop that would encourage a freer discussion of the choreographic process than was possible in what they considered to be the increasingly rigid classes of such an authority as Louis Horst.

Dunn, who taught composition intermittently from 1960 to 1965, had studied with John Cage, who impressed him with the notion that anything is possible in art. Dunn's assignments emphasized chance procedures and game plans as choreographic strategies. Unlike the dictatorial Horst, who made his word law, Dunn permitted everyone in the workshop to comment, often at length, on the dances presented there. A lively exchange of ideas resulted.

By 1962, workshop members had created a body of pieces they felt could be shown to an audience. Therefore they sought a space in which to present them. Two sympathetic pastors offered them the Judson Memorial Church, a congregation affiliated with both the

Baptist Church and the United Church of Christ. Designed by Stanford White in Romanesque Revival style in 1892, the church had long been active in the life of Greenwich Village. Howard Moody and Al Carmines, its ministers during the heyday of the Judson Dance Theatre, were known for their devotion to social issues and for their love of the theatrical arts—even though Carmines's grandmother had once warned him, "A praying knee and a dancing foot never grew on the same leg."[11]

The first dance program at Judson, on 6 June 1962, was a three-hour marathon that attracted 300 spectators, all of whom, despite temperatures of more than 90 degrees Fahrenheit, crowded into a space without air conditioning. The press release for the event said that compositions shown would be based on "indeterminacy, rules specifying situations, improvisations, spontaneous determination, and various other means."[12] Among the participants were Bill Davis, Judith Dunn, Robert Dunn, Ruth Emerson, Richard Goldberg, David Gordon, Deborah Hay, Fred Herko, Gretchen MacLane, John Herbert McDowell, Steve Paxton, Rudy Perez, Yvonne Rainer, Carol Scothorn, Elaine Summers, and Jennifer Tipton.

Several works can be cited as exemplifying the evening's spirit. Despite its title, Ruth Emerson's *Narrative* told no story; instead, it was based on walking patterns and changing relationships in space. The choreography for Elaine Summers's *Instant Chance* was structured by the use of Styrofoam blocks with numbers on their sides. When the blocks were thrown into the air, the numbers that came up when they fell determined which of several prepared movement sequences came next. Steve Paxton's *Transit* was a solo in which he made use of many types of movement, among them balletic steps, what dancers call "marked" movements (movements performed in rehearsal without the full energy they would have in performance), and pedestrian activities; some phrases were repeated in several different ways.

For Fred Herko's *Once or Twice a Week I Put on Sneakers to Go Uptown*, Remy Charlip, who was both an artist and a dancer, designed a multicolored robe and a cap with strings of beads and shells that hung down over Herko's forehead. The choreography for this solo, which Herko performed barefoot, consisted of swaying and shuffling steps likened by some observers to those of the Suzie-Q, a social dance. Herko's colleague Steve Paxton was not the only person who found all this "very campy and self-conscious."[13] But its presence on the program indicated that the Judson choreographers were willing to countenance bizarre humor.

That Judson concert outraged many people. But Allen Hughes, who that year had succeeded John Martin as dance critic of the *New York Times*, was bold enough to write, "The chances are . . . that their [the Judson choreographers'] experiments will influence dance development in this country somehow."[14] He was right.

Dance concerts were offered at Judson throughout the 1960s and on into the 1970s. The original Judson choreographers were joined by such adventurous choreographers as James Waring, Meredith Monk, Kenneth King, Phoebe Neville, and Twyla Tharp. In time, however, this loosely knit group dispersed and, sooner or later, the dancers went their separate ways.

In the years following the first Judson programs, choreographers, both at Judson and in other performance spaces, continued to explore ways of putting movements together. Some favored improvisation and chance procedures. Others created theatrical collages. The process of composition was often prized higher than perfection of dance technique; to deglamorize the body and emphasize physicality itself, dancers began to wear jeans, T-shirts, sweat suits, and coveralls, rather than conventional stage attire. A few dancers appeared in the nude.

Lucinda Childs created two "ordinary," yet startling, dances in 1964. *Carnation* involved the manipulation of objects: a plastic bag, a sheet, socks, sponges, hair curlers, and a colander. The choreography called attention to the capacities of those objects to be light, heavy, rigid, or flexible. But the solo was also filled with quirky humor. At one point, Childs, who was seated at a table, put the colander on her head, attached the curlers to the colander, and stuck the sponges into her mouth. After removing the curlers and the colander, she dumped them into the bag, into which she also stuck one of her feet.

Street Dance, prepared for one of Robert Dunn's composition workshops, took place in a studio. After turning on a tape recorder, Childs and another dancer got into the building's freight elevator and vanished from sight. Suddenly, a taped voice announced, "Go to the window." Those who did beheld Childs standing in a doorway outside. Then she and the other dancer crossed the street and disappeared, only to return to the studio in the elevator. The work may sound almost banal in its ordinariness. Yet people who saw it found it mysteriously beautiful.[15]

Its audacity was typical of a period in which, as Yvonne Rainer has said, choreographers had "a daredevil willingness to 'try anything.'"[16]

ℱERTILE GROUND, BARREN SOIL

Ruth Abramowitsch-Sorel • Elizabeth Leese • Les Automatistes • Contemporary Choreographers of Toronto • Le Groupe de la Place Royale • Rachel Browne • Contemporary Dancers of Winnipeg • Renate Schottelius • Ana Itelman • Guillermina Bravo • Anna Sokolow • Inbal • Batsheva • Berto Pasuka • Françoise and Dominique Dupuy • Jerome Andrews • Karin Waehner • Jacqueline Robinson • Birgit Åkesson • Birgit Cullberg • Kurt Jooss • Jean Weidt • Gret Palucca • Mary Wigman • Dore Hoyer

A DISPERSAL OF DANCERS PROMOTED THE DEVELOPMENT of modern dance in several countries during and after World War II.

Fleeing the Nazis, Ruth Abramowitsch-Sorel settled in Montreal, Canada, in 1944, founding both a school and a company. Her works initially attracted attention for their psychological portraiture and social commentary. *Mea Culpa* was a study of a sinner's return to grace. *La Gaspésienne* treated a French-Canadian theme: the difficulties faced by a young woman from the rural Gaspé peninsula when she moves to the city. In the 1950s, critics began to call Abramowitsch-Sorel's works dated, and she eventually returned to Europe and settled in Warsaw, where she died in 1974. Despite the fluctuations of her critical reputation, she helped introduce Canadians to modern dance.[1]

So did Elizabeth Leese, a Danish-born former member of Trudi Schoop's company, who taught in Toronto at the school of Boris Volkoff, a prominent ballet teacher, and then opened her own studio in Montreal in 1945. Leese had studied with Kurt Jooss and, like him, was interested in the blending of ballet and modern dance techniques. One of her most ambitious efforts in making such a crossover was *The Lady from the Sea*, a choreographic adaptation of Henrik Ibsen's play which Leese's group first showed at a Canadian ballet festival in 1952 and which was later performed by the National Ballet of Canada.

Although Montreal society, and French Canada in general, can be straitlaced, Montreal artists have often been iconoclastic. McGill University, Canada's oldest university and an important intellectual force in English-speaking Montreal, had offered modern dance classes as early as 1929.

In 1948, a group of artists called Les Automatistes created a stir by issuing a manifesto calling for the end of French-Canadian stuffiness. One of the Automatistes was Françoise Sullivan, who had studied both dance and anthropology in New York. Her choreography combined an interest in ritual with a Surrealist love of spontaneity and trust in the power of the unconscious. She created two dances about the seasons in 1948: *L'Eté* and *Danse de la Neige*. The latter was performed in February in a park, a nontheatrical site that was considered extremely unorthodox at the time. Sullivan then gave up dancing for sculpture for several decades, returning to choreography in 1977.

The international influences upon Canadian dance were especially evident in 1960 when a group called Contemporary Choreographers of Toronto held a modern dance festival. The participants included Ruth Tutti Lau, a German dancer; Nancy Lima Dent, a Canadian dancer who had studied in New York with Humphrey and Holm; Bianca Rogge, a Latvian dancer who had studied at the Wigman School in Berlin; and Yone Kvietys, a Lithuanian dancer influenced by Wigman and Laban who in 1954 had founded the Montreal Modern Dance Company with Biroute Nagys, a German dancer, and Alexander MacDougall, a Montreal dancer who had performed with Leese and with the Ballets Jooss in England.

In 1962, the composer Pierre Mercure organized a Modern Music Week in Montreal. The event featured such composers as Karlheinz Stockhausen, Iannis Xenakis, and John Cage, and several choreographers, among them Merce Cunningham and Alwin Nikolais, as well as Jeanne Renaud and Françoise Riopelle, both of whom had been associated with the Automatistes. Renaud and Riopelle were encouraged to continue working together by Vincent Warren and Peter Boneham, two members of Les Grands Ballets Canadiens of Montreal who were interested in experimental choreography. Renaud and Boneham founded Le Groupe de la Place Royale in Montreal in 1966 and that year their organization became the first modern dance troupe to receive a grant from the Canada Council.

Modern dance also sprang up on the Canadian prairie. Winnipeg, a geographically isolated but often culturally enterprising city, was the home of Canada's oldest ballet company, the Royal Winnipeg Ballet, founded in 1938 by two English dancers, Gweneth Lloyd and Betty Farrally. The Contemporary Dancers came into being there in 1964 through the determination of Rachel Browne, a Philadelphia-born member of the Royal Winnipeg Ballet who had become drawn to modern dance. Over the years, the Contemporary Dancers and other Canadian troupes have offered works by both Canadian and foreign choreographers.

Other nations in the Western Hemisphere also benefited from diverse influences. Argentine audiences, dance students, and teachers responded favorably to visits by American dancers,[2] among them Pauline Koner and Miriam Winslow, the Japanese dancer Mitsumi Kuni, and such representatives of European dance as Dore Hoyer, Margarethe Wallmann, Harald Kreutzberg, the Sakharoffs, and the Ballets Jooss. Among the important figures in Argentine dance is Renate Schottelius, a German dancer who had studied with Wigman and danced with Jooss. She came as a refugee to Buenos Aires, started performing there in 1945, and founded a company in 1955. The previous year, Ana Itelman, an Argentine dancer, had established her own company. Itelman has also choreographed for musical theatre productions and the ballet company attached to the Teatro San Martín.

With the opening of the Academia de la Danza Mexicana in Mexico City in 1947, Mexico gained a nationally subsidized modern dance school.[3] But the progress of this academy and Mexican dance in general has often been slowed by factionalism within the dance community. When the José Limón company performed at the Palacio de Bellas Artes in 1950, Limón was asked to remain in Mexico and reorganize the program of dance training at the National Academy. He declined a permanent appointment, but returned a year later to teach and choreograph.

Guillermina Bravo founded the Ballet Nacional de México in 1948. In 1977, she went to Africa to study witchcraft, which she calls "a science the world over."[4] The visit reflected a long-standing interest in the subject, for in 1962 she had choreographed *Danzas de Hecheirfa* (*Witchcraft Dances*), based on ancient Mexican ceremonials. A concern for Mexican history and traditions is reflected in many of her works, including *Juego del Pelata* (*Ball Game*), inspired by a sacred Mexican Indian sport that concluded with the ritual sacrifice of one of the players.

Israeli dance after World War II was deeply affected by the choreography and teaching of Anna Sokolow. When the American Fund for Israel Institutions invited Jerome Robbins in 1953 to survey the nation's dance resources, he was particularly impressed by the Inbal Dance Theatre, which, under Sara Levi-Tanai's direction, preserved the music and dance of the Yemenite Jews. Her choreography for Inbal (which means "tongue of the bell" in Hebrew) combined traditional and contemporary steps. Robbins admired its theatrical vitality. However, he thought Inbal suffered from a lack of high production standards. When other commitments prevented him from assisting the troupe, he suggested that Sokolow should go to Israel.

She trained the dancers in ballet and modern techniques, increased their professional discipline, and helped make Inbal's programs effective. When Inbal made its American debut in 1957, it was immediately successful. Sokolow kept returning to Israel and in 1963 founded her own short-lived group, the Lyric Theatre.

That year, the Baroness Bethsabee de Rothschild, the daughter of a financier and philanthropist, announced the formation of Batsheva, a modern-dance repertoire company. A supporter of Martha Graham (who gave Batsheva her blessing), the baroness offered dancers good salaries and working conditions.[5] The company offered works by many choreographers, yet never managed to keep an artistic director for an extended period. In 1967, the baroness organized another company, Bat-Dor.

Ballet dominated postwar British dance, although a few modern dancers, including Ernest Berk, continued to work on the fringe of the scene.

A black company which enjoyed a brief success was Les Ballets Nègres, which made its debut in 1946 under the direction of Berto Pasuka, a choreographer born in Jamaica of an Indian mother and an African father, who had come to Britain early in World War II.[6] His troupe prompted new debates on old issues: What is a ballet? Can a work be called a ballet if it is not choreographed in the classical idiom? Pasuka obviously was willing to follow the precedent of Kurt Jooss in his use of the term "ballet."

Pasuka's lively *Market Day* depicted a Jamaican market. Other productions were serious in tone. *They Came* examined Western influences upon African culture. In *De Prophet*, a Jamaican religious leader finds he can work miracles. But when he grows overconfident and fails in an attempt to fly to heaven, he is jailed as a lunatic. The London critic Arthur H. Franks called *De Prophet* a forceful work, yet noted that "in his attempts at symbolism . . . Pasuka does not achieve such a great success." He added, "No doubt he will eventually carry his researches into deeper waters."[7] But economic hardships prevented Les Ballets Nègres from continuing.

Across the Channel, postwar French modern dance also remained marginal.[8] Yet some intrepid dancers persisted.

After Jean Weidt returned to Germany in 1949, his company was reorganized as Les Ballets Modernes de Paris by a married couple, Françoise and Dominique Dupuy, both of whom had studied and performed with Weidt. Françoise (b. 1925) had also studied with a Dalcroze teacher and had been a member of the Lyon Opéra Ballet; Dominique (b. 1930) had studied ballet with Olga Preobrajenska and Nicholas Zvereff. In addition to leading a company, the Dupuys gave duet programs.

They were tireless promoters of modern dance, and their productions included the collaboratively choreographed *Cants de Catalunya* (to Catalan songs, 1956), Dominique's *La Femme et Son Ombre* (1968), and Françoise's *Antigone* (1968). In 1962, the Dupuys organized the Festival des Baux-de-Provence, France's first dance festival.

Among other choreographers who helped keep French modern dance alive were Jerome Andrews, an American-born pupil of Graham, Humphrey, Holm, and Horst, and Jacqueline Robinson. Born in 1922 of an English father and a French mother, Robinson was a pupil of Wigman, who in 1957 opened L'Atelier de la Danse, a Parisian dance center which continues to serve as a school, a performance space, and a forum for lectures and discussions. Robinson also became a historian of French modern dance.

The most important figures in Scandinavian modern dance since Maggie Gripenberg were two Swedish choreographers born in 1908, Birgit Åkesson and Birgit Cullberg. Both were products of distinguished modern dance schools. Both later worked with ballet companies, and Cullberg became known primarily as a ballet choreographer.

Åkesson, however, in addition to her balletic accomplishments, was a highly regarded modern dance soloist.

Åkesson received a diploma from the Wigman School in Dresden in 1931. She made her debut as a soloist in 1934 with programs in Paris and Stockholm. From the outset, it was clear that, although trained in *Ausdruckstanz*, she could not be easily classified. Unlike the Expressionists, she disdained strain, grimacing, and anguish, adopting a restraint and economy of gesture that led her to be called Post-Expressionist. She trained herself to move parts of her body independently, so that she seemed to dance in counterpoint with herself. This illusion of bodily fragmentation led some critics to compare her solos to Cubist paintings.

Åkesson's curious choreographic aloofness made P. W. Manchester begin a review with a paragraph of only three words: "Birgit Åkesson is." Manchester went on to explain: "She is not attempting to solve the world's problems; she is not even making a statement. Her work is not emotional; it is as impersonal as a tree ... the movements are not symbols—they do not mean anything—they simply are."[9]

For Fernau Hall, *Soir Bleu*, a solo in silence, "seemed like a sculpture in movement, rather than dancing in the ordinary sense of the word," and in *Movement*, another silent solo, "the images seemed to grow and develop in an organic way according to their own laws, like plants photographed by stop-motion cameras." Selma Jeanne Cohen commented on the pictorial and sculptural aspects of Åkesson's solos:

> Eschewing flow, emotional continuity, and conventional dramatic development, her dances are constituted primarily of a sequence of poses, many of them extremely interesting as visual design. She has little concern with moving through space. ... For the most part, her work is static and pictorial rather than dramatic.[10]

The slow pace of many of Åkesson's works bothered American audiences when she performed in New York in 1949 and 1955 and at the American Dance Festival in 1956. George Beiswanger acknowledged that her solos "crawl and writhe like a slug or an upended caterpillar, hardly moving at all." But, he found, "if one lets the movement have its way, it generates a compelling, almost hypnotic beauty."[11]

Working totally apart from American influences, Åkesson in Stockholm, like Merce Cunningham in New York, came to regard the theatrical arts as independent entities. Some of her dances were unaccompanied. Others were to music by Bach, Antonio Vivaldi, and

Béla Bartók or to commissioned scores by the prominent Swedish composer Karl-Birger Blomdahl. Yet she made no attempt to match choreographic and musical phrases.

An extreme example of her tendency to separate the arts is *Eye: Sleep in Dream*, a twenty-minute solo of 1953 filled with contrapuntal movements. It used music by Blomdahl and a poem, inspired by watching the first rehearsals of the work, by Erik Lindegren. But dancing, music, and poetry never were simultaneous. First, a voice was heard reading the poem. Then Åkesson began to move in silence. And the music was played only in the blackouts between the danced sequences.

For a decade beginning in 1957, Åkesson choreographed works for the Royal Swedish Ballet, several of which—*Sisyphus, The Minotaur, Icarus*, and *Nausikaa*—were inspired by mythological themes. She also provided the choreography for *Aniara*, Blomdahl's science-fiction opera of 1959 about a spaceship carrying the remnants of humanity after earth's final nuclear disaster.

Åkesson stopped performing in 1965. A few years later, she gave up choreography to devote herself to scholarly studies in African and Asian dance. But in 1989 she returned to choreography by creating *Autumn Leaves* and *Shades*, two related solos, both unaccompanied, which were performed on Swedish television by Chiang Ching, a Chinese-born modern dancer.

Birgit Cullberg, whose father was a banker, first saw dance at the age of ten when she attended a recital by someone who, she later realized, performed in the style of Isadora Duncan.[12] The program piqued her curiosity. Yet her family did not encourage her to dance. Instead, she went to an art school and then to the University of Stockholm, where she studied the history of literature and wrote a thesis on flower symbolism in Romantic poetry. She also saw performances by Mary Wigman, Harald Kreutzberg, and the Ballets Jooss and studied modern dance with teachers in Stockholm. Finally, in the mid-1930s, she took the decisive step of going to England and enrolling in the Jooss-Leeder School at Dartington Hall, remaining there until the outbreak of war in 1939.

Back in Sweden, Cullberg offered concerts, both as a soloist and as the leader of a small group. Realizing that her late start left her technically limited, she also undertook an intensive study of ballet. Cullberg married the actor Anders Ek in 1942 and they became parents of three children, all of whom pursued theatrical careers: Niklas Ek became a dancer with the Royal Swedish ballet, Mats Ek is a choreographer, and his twin sister Malin Ek is an actress. Family duties caused Cullberg to be creatively inactive for several years, although she wrote dance criticism for *Dagens Nyheter*, a prominent Stockholm newspaper. In 1946, she and Ivo Cramér, another choreographer, organized their own Svenska Dansteatern.

When Cullberg received a grant in 1949 that enabled her to observe new developments in postwar European dance, she was so excited by her travels that she plunged into choreographic activity. The result, in 1950, was *Miss Julie*, a balletic adaptation of August Strindberg's play about a neurotic aristocratic woman's infatuation with a manservant. The work was soon taken into the repertoire of the Royal Swedish Ballet, and it has been revived by many European and American ballet companies.

Since then, Cullberg has created new works and revived old ones for such organizations as the New York City Ballet, American Ballet Theatre, and the Royal Danish Ballet. In 1967, assistance from the Swedish government enabled her to found the Cullberg Ballet, which offers productions by herself, Mats Ek, and other choreographers. Cullberg has also been active as a choreographer for television.

Cullberg began as a modern dancer. But all her mature works can be performed only by ballet dancers. Like Jooss, she sought a fusion of techniques, noting that "the free dance, especially that of the Jooss and Graham schools, has worked out a system for training . . . dynamic power, a system which the ballet—with its striving for pure lightness—lacked." [13]

Many of her ballets are based on literature or mythology—for instance, *Medea, Odysseus, Romeo and Juliet, The Lady from the Sea* (after Ibsen), and *Moon Reindeer* (after a Lapp legend). The French-born ballerina Violette Verdy has analyzed Cullberg's style:

> The movements in her choreography are not that original; they are not there to show their own inventiveness, to be admired for themselves. The steps are deceptively simple; they take their color from the subject. . . . This is danced drama. It seems mentally constructed, like a screen scenario, and then filled with dance. Her choreography is a reflection of her thought, not a song by itself. [14]

When World War II ended, many sensitive Germans felt that their modern dance still remained under the shadow of the Nazis. No one could demonstrate that *Ausdruckstanz* and fascism were necessarily linked. Nevertheless, it was ballet, rather than modern dance, that flourished in postwar Germany.

Inevitably, Communist East Germany was influenced by Soviet ballet. In West Germany, ballet was considered artistically liberating. Even though the Nazis had tried to introduce more ballet into dance school curriculums, ballet was still regarded as an art that knew no boundaries, and by encouraging their ballet companies Germans felt themselves once again part of the international artistic community.

Moreover, German ballet could be daring, as well as traditionally classical. The most scandalous German dance production after the war was a ballet: *Abraxas*, a retelling of the Faust story to a score by Werner Egk in which the devil was a woman. Its first production, choreographed by Marcel Luipart and presented at the Bavarian State Opera in Munich in 1948, was considered so religiously and sexually shocking that it was withdrawn from the stage as a result of protests. Soon afterward, there were new productions of *Abraxas* by other choreographers throughout Germany: scandal is always good at the box office.

Ballet companies flourished in Stuttgart, Düsseldorf, Leipzig, Dresden, Hamburg, West and East Berlin, and other cities. Yvonne Georgi returned to the Hanover Opera as ballet mistress in 1954 and remained active there until her death in 1975. She was now essentially a ballet choreographer, creating works—including a highly regarded version of Stravinsky's *Agon*—in Hanover and as a guest choreographer for other troupes.

Kurt Jooss came back to Germany in 1954 to head the dance department at the Folkwang School in Essen, continuing in that post until 1968, after which he worked as a freelance choreographer until his death in 1979. He developed an admirable dance program in Essen. Yet German ballet companies achieved such prominence that some observers from other countries feared Jooss had paddled himself into an artistic backwater, and little was heard about his activities. However, in the last years of his life he was once again in demand, staging revivals of *The Green Table* and, occasionally, a few other works for ballet as well as modern dance companies everywhere.

Jean Weidt may have been a radical, yet when he settled in East Germany in 1949, after feeling that his activities in Paris had been undervalued, he encountered old-fashioned bureaucratic stodginess in the supposed "People's Democracy." Nevertheless, working in Schwerin, Karl-Marx-Stadt, and East Berlin, he never lost his faith in politically committed dance. But his efforts were always over-shadowed by the East German ballet companies.

They also overshadowed those of Gret Palucca, who reopened her Dresden school. It attracted pupils from around the world until her death in 1993, and she soon became more important as a teacher than as a choreographer.

America never really appreciated the humor of Valeska Gert. When she returned to West Berlin and opened a new cabaret in 1947, she found that her bitter topical satires were not to the liking of the post-war German audience either.[15] In 1950, she moved to the North Sea island of Sylt, where she ran another cabaret. She acted occasionally in movies and played the old medium in Federico Fellini's *Juliet of the Spirits*.

Mary Wigman moved to West Berlin in 1949 and founded a school which, like her old one in Dresden, had an international student body. She also taught summer courses in Switzerland. In 1957, Wigman choreographed an acclaimed production of *Le Sacre du Printemps*; it was her last major dance piece.

Although treated with respect, Wigman somehow remained on the margin of postwar German dance, whereas before the war she had been at its center. Hellmut Gottschild, a student who later moved to Philadelphia, found her "an admirable, wonderful woman." Yet, he confessed, "I had trouble with her language." She spoke loftily, whereas, said Gottschild, "My generation was more skeptical, and that sort of talk sounded a little dusty to us . . . we sometimes felt ourselves at the end of an era"[16]—a feeling that was intensified when, reversing what had been a more usual state of affairs, ballet students started calling the moderns old-fashioned.

Wigman viewed the passage of time philosophically, though she was plagued with poor eyesight and wracked with coughing fits—the toll of decades of chain smoking. Late in her life she wrote: "I would not wish to have missed anything that life took from me and gave me. Even the mistakes I have made I cannot regret. Because life always presents its bill in the end. And one has to pay it in full. No, I am not afraid of death. Is he not the most faithful companion of old age and his hour the last act of purification one has to go through?"[17]

Wigman died in Berlin in 1973.

The only new German modern dancer to be praised as a major artist in the years immediately following World War II was Dore Hoyer, and she was not totally "new." Hoyer, born in 1911, had studied with Palucca, 1929–1930, had danced with Wigman's company, 1933–1936, and had begun to offer choreographic programs before the war. But she made her major contributions to German dance after the war when she moved from East Germany to the West because her style was incompatible with the Socialist Realism favored by the Communist East German authorities. Cast as the Chosen One in Wigman's 1957 production of *Le Sacre du Printemps*, she gave a performance that the critic Paul Moor described as "vital, raw, almost violent."[18] By that time, she had already attracted critical attention with her own choreography.

"Technically she surpasses every German classical dancer," wrote Horst Koegler, one of that country's leading music and dance critics.[19] But she never displayed her technical strengths for their own sake, and her choreography tended to be austere. She specialized in solos, both to existing music and to scores composed for her by her musical adviser, Dimitri Wiatowitsch. Hoyer rarely concerned herself with choreographic narratives or psychological conflicts. Rather, her dances revealed emotional essences.

The Great Song, a cycle of five solos, began and ended with "Dance of the Divine Possession," in which she revolved on her own axis while also traveling across the stage in circles, her skirt swaying like a bell as she moved. When Hoyer performed this at the American Dance Festival in 1957, Doris Hering thought she could have been "cleansing and purifying the dancing ground."[20]

This love of spinning, which Hoyer shared with Wigman, was also apparent in her *Revolving Dance*, to Ravel's *Bolero*—not in its lush orchestral version, but in a spare piano arrangement that emphasized its rhythmic structure. As Ravel's basic melody was heard again and again, Hoyer turned ceaselessly, never moving from the spot and indicating each fresh entry of the musical theme with a gesture of her hands. Although Ravel based his composition on a Spanish dance form, the choreography contained no references to Spain. Instead, it was often compared to the revolving of dervishes, whirlpools, and the earth itself.[21]

Hoyer toured and taught in South America as well as in Germany during the 1950s and 1960s. Yet she increasingly felt that her achievements were unrecognized, especially in her native land. In late December of 1967, she committed suicide.

If only she had lived a few years more! No one could have predicted it in the ballet-dominated 1960s, but Germany was about to witness a rebirth of modern dance, and some of its exponents came to regard Dore Hoyer as a prophet. Hoyer was a lonely woman, lost in an alien dance world.

PART 5

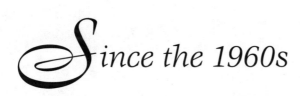

Since the 1960s

$\mathcal{S}$TABILITY AND CHANGE

José Limón • Martha Graham • American Dance Festival • Jacob's Pillow • Alvin Ailey • Katherine Dunham • Paul Taylor • Merce Cunningham • Judson Dance Theater • Postmodern dance • Deborah Hay • Yvonne Rainer • Trisha Brown • Lucinda Childs • Laura Dean • Dana Reitz • Gus Solomons, Jr. • Steve Paxton • Contact improvisation • Pilobolus • Molissa Fenley • Senta Driver • John Butler • Glen Tetley • Lar Lubovitch • Twyla Tharp • Mark Morris • David Gordon • Kenneth King • Robert Wilson • Meredith Monk • Phoebe Neville • Eiko and Koma • Kei Takei • Bill T. Jones • Arnie Zane • Garth Fagan

WHEN JOSÉ LIMÓN DIED IN 1972, IT WAS WIDELY ASSUMED that his company would die with him. Instead, his dancers vowed to keep their troupe together; under the direction of first Ruth Currier, and later Carla Maxwell, it continued to present not only its Limón and Doris Humphrey repertoire, but also works of other choreographers. So, too, the Graham company survived the death of Martha Graham.

The decision of such groups to go on dancing is proof that modern dance is capable of stability. The Jacob's Pillow Dance Festival (which presents modern dance among many dance forms) is flourishing, as is the modern dance–oriented American Dance Festival. Under the guidance of Charles L. Reinhart, who became its director in 1969, the festival steadily expanded its programs until it outgrew Connecticut College. In 1978, it moved to new quarters on the campus of Duke University in Durham, North Carolina.

There are other success stories in American modern dance. For instance, the Alvin Ailey American Dance Theater, which was founded in 1958, is one of the world's most popular troupes. By 1991, it had performed for an estimated 15,000,000 people in 48 states and 45 countries.[1] Ailey, who was born in 1931, studied with Lester Horton in Los Angeles and Martha Graham, Hanya Holm, and Charles

Weidman in New York. His best-known work is *Revelations* (1960), a stirring tribute to the black religious tradition. His range extended from the jazz-inspired *Blues Suite* to the lyricism of *The Lark Ascending*, and he choreographically championed the music of Duke Ellington.

His group was never only a showcase for his own efforts. From its inception, it has emphasized a broad repertoire. Many of its productions deal with black American history and culture. Yet the multiracial organization refuses to limit itself to any specific style or subject matter. In addition to reviving works by such established choreographers as Horton, Ted Shawn, Anna Sokolow, May O'Donnell, Katherine Dunham, Pearl Primus, Donald McKayle, and Talley Beatty, it has presented dances by such younger talents as Donald Byrd, Ulysses Dove, and Bill T. Jones. After Ailey's death in 1989, his policies were continued under the artistic direction of Judith Jamison, a former leading dancer of the company.

Katherine Dunham founded a clinic in Haiti in 1961 and, later, an arts center in East St. Louis, Illinois, an economically depressed slum community. Teaching dance to everyone—from militant young people to small children and the elderly—she sought, as she put it, "to socialize the young and old through 'culturization,' to make the individual aware of himself and his environment, to create a desire to be alive." [2]

Until she died in 1991 at the age of ninety-six, Martha Graham remained a charismatic force. She declared in 1989 that "the energy of the world is available to all of us. It moves the planets and makes everything work. We can all use it. Only we become frightened or frustrated or too tired to use it. I use it." She did indeed. And when she allied herself with cosmic powers, she could be awesome, even fearsome. Agnes de Mille recalls, "When she was done with an idea or a person, she cast that idea or person off, shedding a skin as snakes do, dropping habits, customs, loyal associations—yes, even friends. To some this appears phoenixlike; to others, reptilian. And, naturally, the rejects were not happy." [3]

Graham, who ended her performing career in 1969, was ill, personally troubled, and heavily dependent upon alcohol in the late 1960s. After her retirement as a dancer, she totally withdrew from her company. But when she returned to it in 1972, she had been creatively reborn. Many of her later works—including *Mendicants of*

Evening (1973) and *Acts of Light* (1981)—were lyrical pieces that showed off the physical beauty and technical dexterity of her dancers. Yet she never lost her love of myth and ritual, and she choreographed her own forceful version of *Le Sacre du Printemps* in 1984.

Some of the rebels of the 1950s and 1960s—for instance, Paul Taylor, Merce Cunningham, Alwin Nikolais, Murray Louis, and Erick Hawkins—began to find themselves revered as established masters.

Of all the American modern choreographers since Graham, it is Taylor who has developed the most diverse repertoire for his company. He tries to make each new work have a form, a style, and what could be called a movement palette uniquely its own.

Many of his most popular creations—among them, *Airs* (1978) and *Arden Court* (1981)—are genial. Pleasant to behold, they can at the same time be stimulating to think about because of the compositional principles on which they are built. Thus *Arden Court* is undeniably lyrical. But Taylor achieves lyricism not by emphasizing graceful steps for women, as some choreographers might do, but by stressing the male dancers in the cast. Taylor makes the men move with great speed, but the overall effect is idyllic, rather than purely athletic.

Taylor is a moralist as well as an entertainer. In serious and humorous works alike, he grapples with the problem of how to achieve a golden mean in life, and he deplores extreme behavior of any kind, be it puritanical or licentious. In *Big Bertha* (1971), members of a seemingly ordinary family are driven to violence and sexual depravity by an alluring, yet menacing, automaton. The apparently elegant people of *Cloven Kingdom* (1976) shed their fine manners and behave like beasts. *Le Sacre du Printemps (The Rehearsal)*—Taylor's disquieting interpretation of Stravinsky—is simultaneously a detective story about gangsters and a kidnapped baby and a peek into the backstage life of a dance company rehearsing a detective-story ballet. Because Taylor deliberately fails to supply motivation for many of the startling events in his *Sacre*, this work of 1980 can be viewed as a choreographic depiction of life at its most irrational and inexplicable.

Taylor remains fascinated by the ambiguities of movement. *Esplanade* (1975) is made up of nothing but such ordinary actions as walking, running, sliding, falling, and jumping. But these commonplace steps are taken to virtuoso extremes: only trained dancers can walk and run with such ease and abandon. In *Polaris* (1976), Taylor offers the same dance twice with no choreographic changes whatso-ever. Yet each presentation of this basic dance has different lighting designs and is performed by a different cast to different music by Donald York—and the effect each time is totally dissimilar. Taylor knows how to please the eye and how to test his audience's powers of perception.

So does Merce Cunningham, who continued to choreograph dances in various moods, as well as intellectually provocative ninety-minute pieces he called Events. Each consisted of sections of existing works or of new dances still in rehearsal. But instead of presenting these excerpts as independent separable items, they were so com-bined and rearranged as to form a wholly new artistic entity and were performed to different musical scores than the ones that ordi-narily served as their accompaniment.

For some dancegoers, Events constituted a virtual dismantling of Cunningham's repertoire and a blurring of differences between one dance and another. But Events could be defended as evidence of Cunningham's abiding interest in the unpredictability of life and a recognition of the fact that everything in the universe is in a state of perpetual flux.

No New York choreographers of the 1960s aroused more passion-ate outbursts of praise and blame than those who either worked with or were influenced by the Judson Dance Theatre. A term came into use that continues to be employed: "postmodern dance." Such a thing existed, many observers felt. But just what was it?

When Yvonne Rainer and some of the other early Judson dancers started calling themselves postmodern, they were speaking primarily in a chronological sense: they considered themselves choreographers who had come after a certain sort of dance that was dominant at that time. They rejected both the dramatic dances associated with Gra-ham and Limón and the technically polished abstractions of Cun-ningham and Hawkins. Nevertheless, it was possible to wonder if, beyond a desire to break with the recent past, these newer choreo-graphers shared a sufficient number of abiding interests to make a simple definition of postmodern dance possible.

One of the first critics who attempted to define postmodern dance was Michael Kirby. What inspired him to do so was a program pre-sented by Deborah Hay in 1967 that included a seventeen-minute dance called *Group One*. During the course of it, a film was shown of twenty-two people repeatedly trying to wedge themselves in a triangular formation in the corner of a room. The live action involved choreography for eight people carrying poles which they occasionally lowered and brought together with a clacking sound and for five other people who entered, formed lines and circles, dispersed, and reentered. All the movements were simple and required no virtuosity.

On the basis of *Group One* and similar works he had seen, Kirby argued that "an *objectification* of dance" had occurred and that whereas traditional dance depends upon empathy and invites spectators to "read themselves into" a performance by means of muscular sympathy, this new form of dance totally dispensed with empathetic appeals. In a lecture published in 1978 he said, "I propose that traditional dance, such as ballet, is highly empathetic, whereas postmodern dance is not empathetic . . . dances that involve effort are more empathetic than those that do not."[4]

Kirby's statements take into account the spareness that was a characteristic of many of the innovative dances of the 1960s. Nevertheless, it is risky to build a theory on the presence or absence of empathy, for the only absolute way of determining whether any dance has an empathetic appeal would be to monitor the response of each spectator who beholds it. For Kirby, *Group One* did not rely on empathy. Yet, conceivably, other dancegoers might have "read themselves into" the lowering and clashing of the poles and the ways the performers kept joining together and breaking apart.

When Sally Banes published *Terpsichore in Sneakers* in 1980, she singled out for special attention as postmodernists Simone Forti, Yvonne Rainer, Steve Paxton, Trisha Brown, David Gordon, Deborah Hay, Lucinda Childs, Meredith Monk, Kenneth King, Douglas Dunn, and the dancers (among them, Rainer, Paxton, Brown, Gordon, and Dunn) who formed the improvisationally based collective the Grand Union. Few critics would exclude any of them from a list of postmodern dancers. Yet it is extremely difficult to define what they had in common, other than a desire to create works that differed from the period's choreographic norms. Several (especially Forti, Rainer, Paxton, and Brown) favored ordinary movements performed in real (rather than dramatically fictive) time. Prizing the physicality of the body apart from the stylizations of any dance class, they sometimes made games, sports, work movements, and pedestrian activities the sources of their choreography; they also had little interest in overt theatricality. On the other hand, Monk and King were highly theatrical almost from the start of their careers, and Brown has become increasingly so.

To complicate matters further, the term "postmodern," as Banes points out,[5] tends to mean different things when applied to different art forms. Postmodern painting and architecture are often playful and eccentric and filled with references (sometimes ironic, sometimes nostalgic) to art styles of the past. In this sense, such choreographers as James Waring, Twyla Tharp, and, possibly, Monk could be called postmodern, whereas the bluntness and rigor of Forti, Rainer, and Brown make their creations akin to what in art is known as conceptualism and minimalism.

Nevertheless, it was felt in the 1960s that something new had happened in dance and postmodern was what it was called. "Postmodern" can now be seen as one of those terms which (like absolute dance, *Ausdruckstanz*, or modern dance itself) initially seems precise but which, the more one ponders it, becomes increasingly fuzzy in its implications. Yet it is not valueless, for, again like those other terms, it serves as a sign that some sort of new choreographic development has occurred.

The leaders of the 1960s modern dance establishment were certainly aware that something new was going on. Many members of the older generation disliked it. Thus Louis Horst thundered, "These kids take toilet-flushing for music and structureless immobility for dancing. To rebel, to be way out is fine. But they don't know how far they can go and still be with us!"[6] The supporters of postmodernism, of course, experienced no such esthetic difficulties.

Yvonne Rainer, who was born in San Francisco in 1934, was active in that city's little theater groups. It was only after she moved to New York in 1956 that she developed a serious interest in dance, studying dance with Edith Stephen (a teacher and choreographer who stressed improvisation) and at the Graham and Cunningham schools, as well as at several ballet studios. She returned briefly to the Bay Area in 1960 to study with Anna Halprin.

Rainer's choreography was often rough-hewn. Some of her early pieces were emotionally fraught, as well. She had a screaming fit in *Three Seascapes* (1962) and in other works she barked, wailed, and squeaked. She grew less self-consciously bizarre as she became fascinated with game structures, pedestrian movements, and task activities. She also began to affirm the sheer physicality of people and objects: the fact that things *were* was enough for her and, in addition to stripping her dances of plot and characterization (as many abstractionists had already done), she discarded development, tension, and climax.

Yet Rainer remained fascinated by the body as an intricate physical instrument capable of performing many kinds of actions. Her *Terrain* (1963) contained both sequences involving walking, running, crawling, waddling, and jostling and a classical adagio sequence she had learned in a class taught by the Danish-born ballerina Nina Stroganova. In *We Shall Run* (1963) twelve performers jogged for seven minutes to the "Tuba Mirum" movement of the Berlioz *Requiem*. The steps may have been simple. Yet the constant changes of floor patterns made the choreography hard to remember. Some members of the audience refused to countenance this as dance. But Allen Hughes countered in the *New York Times*, "If it isn't dance, what is it?" Another critic, Jill Johnston of the *Village Voice*, called *We Shall Run* a work about "the heroism of the ordinary. No plots or pretensions. People running. Hooray for people."[7]

In 1966, Rainer created the first version of *Trio A*, a piece that became part of a longer composition called *The Mind Is a Muscle* and was later incorporated into Rainer's *Rose Fractions* and *Connecticut Composite*. But its movements could also be performed by a solo dancer or a whole group of people. The four-and-a-half-minute work became one of the most celebrated examples of Judson choreography.

Trio A was filled with torso twists, arm swings, foot tappings, low skips, and backward kicks and lunges. All these steps were performed without pause or stress in a continuous flow of movement that neither built to a climax nor dwindled away, and at no time did the choreography require the performer (or performers) to gaze directly at the audience. Moreover, when more than one person danced *Trio A* (and the steps for everyone in the cast were exactly the same), the choreography never demanded that everyone be in perfect unison; therefore, because bodies of different sizes may take slightly more or less time to do certain steps, the dancers kept slipping in and out of synchronization.

Trio A was difficult. Yet it was presented without ostentation and made no attempt to amaze an audience. It was a dance of physical dexterity that avoided emphasizing personal vanity. It was an honest tribute to human physicality.

An esthetically puritan streak in Rainer made her declare in a manifesto, "NO to spectacle no to virtuosity no to transformation and magic and make-believe." But her iconoclasm did not lead to nihilism. As she said in a lecture,

> I am beginning to think that there is not really such a thing as cause and effect. The fact that one thing apparently follows another out of necessity, destiny, history . . . is a comforting belief. In the absence of belief, the possibilities of the world become inexhaustible. . . . I was born in a cage, I grew up in a cage, I continue to live in a cage—but god-damn it—it doesn't matter—because all things are possible, and it can be spring again.[8]

After 1973, Rainer gave up choreography to devote herself to filmmaking.

Like Rainer, Trisha Brown is fascinated by structures. The particular kinds she favors have often been whimsical or fantastic, and she once described herself as a bricklayer with a sense of humor.

Brown, who was born in 1936, studied modern dance at Mills College and at the American Dance Festival at Connecticut College; she was exposed to more experimental approaches to choreography by working with Anna Halprin. Her own choreography grew increasingly unconventional and occasionally caused Louis Horst to explode when she presented examples of it in his composition classes. Brown managed to absorb all the influences to which she had been exposed; looking back on her sometimes tumultuous encounters with Horst, she was able to say, "and yet I liked him very much. I really did."[9]

Beginning in the late 1960s, Brown began to devise what she calls Equipment Pieces, works in which, by means of ropes, pulleys, harnesses, and mountain-climbing gear, dancers were able to walk on walls or on the sides of buildings. In *Roof Piece* (1971), she stationed dancers on rooftops across a twelve-block area of Lower Manhattan. They transmitted semaphorelike gestures to one another in a relay fashion, the gestures proceeding in a downtown direction for fifteen minutes, then uptown for the next fifteen. The outdoor setting made *Roof Piece* intensely physical; but because no single spectator on the ground could see all the performers on all the roofs at the same time, this was also a cerebral, conceptual dance.

At about the same time that Brown produced *Roof Piece*, she started offering what she termed Accumulations. In an Accumulation, a movement is presented and repeated, then a second is added, both are repeated, a third is added, all three are repeated, then a fourth is added—and so on in a structure comparable to that of the song "The Twelve Days of Christmas." Accumulations could last from just under five minutes to almost an hour.

Some of Brown's early works were performed by casts of both dancers and nondancers. Over the years, however, her steps grew increasingly intricate until only highly skilled dancers could attempt them. Her productions also became more scenically elaborate.

Brown developed what could be called a slippery style: her choreographic patterns take shape onstage, only to be almost instantly erased. This mutability of imagery can be compared with the blurred shapes in many of the paintings of Robert Rauschenberg, an artist who has collaborated with Brown on several occasions. Slides by Rauschenberg of such ordinary things as pliers, light bulbs, ferns, clouds, clocks, and railroad cars passed one after another in an orderly fashion across four screens in *Glacial Decoy* (1979). But the actions of the dancers created an effect of blurring as people rushed onstage, only to be pulled back into the wings as if by some offstage magnetic force.

Laurie Anderson's score for *Set and Reset* (1983) included repetitions of the phrase "Long time no see," and the production challenged the audience to see clearly. Films—blurred images of what looked like people, animals, and machine parts—were projected on suspended geometrical shapes designed by Rauschenberg. Beneath these hanging objects, dancers assembled in groupings akin to knots and whorls. Spectators were left free to look as they pleased at the films or the dancers or to try to assimilate both.

Lucinda Childs's works also grew increasingly complex. During the 1970s, she developed an interest in patterning. The specific actions she devised were often as ordinary as walking and skipping, but these activities were varied by means of constant changes of direction.

For *Dance* (1979), to a commissioned score by Philip Glass, the artist Sol LeWitt designed geometric backdrops that complemented the geometric qualities of the choreography. The production included film sequences that showed larger-than-life images of the dancers performing the work. Audiences were thereby able to compare the dance on film with the real dancers on stage.

Available Light (1983), to a score by John Adams, was dominated by a platform designed by the architect Frank Gehry. On top of it, two dancers kept performing the basic steps from which the work was made; on the stage below them, ensembles wove these steps together. This division of the cast permitted Childs to present the same types of movement material both as individual steps and as a whole fabric of motion.

Several choreographers since the 1970s have shared a concern for patterning. Geometrical formations dominate many of the works of Laura Dean, who studied at the School of American Ballet and at the Cunningham and Graham studios and who was once a member of Paul Taylor's company. Dean's dances are filled with deliberately repetitive sequences and also with passages which, though they initially seem further repetitions of previously used material, are subtle modifications of it.

She is best known for the spinning movements which have virtually become her choreographic trademarks. Although Dean is aware that spinning occurs in various cultural and religious traditions, she insists that she gives it no specific spiritual significance; rather, spinning is movement she finds esthetically satisfying. The harmonious interactions of people in Dean's creations have led some critics to compare them with folk dancing, and in 1993 Dean choreographed *Light* for Aman World Music and Dance, a Los Angeles company that specializes in folk dances from around the world. Nevertheless, she says, "I have never taken a folk dance lesson. . . . It is simply the kind of dancing I like to do." [10]

Dean has collaborated on occasion with the composer Steve Reich. But for such works as *Dance* (1976), *Music* (1979), *Tympani* (1980), *Night* (1980), and *Magnetic* (1986), she has composed her own music in order to achieve a complete fusion of sights and sounds. She has also choreographed for such classical companies as the Joffrey Ballet, the New York City Ballet, and the Ohio Ballet.

Dana Reitz and Gus Solomons, Jr., also share a fondness for intricate patterns, but their dances are otherwise dissimilar. Reitz's works are based on improvisations, from which she devises dances that look as delicate as calligraphic drawings. Solomons, a former architecture student at the Massachusetts Institute of Technology, studied dance in Boston with Jan Veen, who acquainted him with Laban's theories. Laban's image of a dancer as the center of an imaginary cube of space appealed to Solomon's architectural sense, and he has built dances from complex structural principles.

The Canadian critic Max Wyman has written, "In the late 1960s the body became . . . the place where you found yourself, where you became centred; and the art form of the body attracted new chic. As the body became liberated, the imaginative response—the assertion of the human spirit—became bolder."[11]

Health—the well-being of body, mind, and spirit—has been an urgent issue for the general public since the 1960s. People from all walks of life have jogged daily through the street or have enrolled in physical fitness classes.

Several choreographers have sought ways of using the physical art of dance to promote personal or social growth and harmony. Anna Halprin has created communal rituals, as has Deborah Hay. Working with people with no dance training, Hay began to choreograph celebratory circle dances. Each lasted about an hour and drew upon such sources as meditation, breath patterns, ritual movements, folk dancing, and Tai Chi Chuan (a traditional Chinese exercise system that emphasizes letting go and yielding to the flow of nature). Because Hay refuses to allow anyone to watch her events without participating in them, it can be argued that these ceremonies (like those of Halprin) can no longer be considered theatrical performances.

Critics have likewise argued over whether contact improvisation is a theatrical art. Contact improvisation is a form developed in the early 1970s by Steve Paxton, a former Cunningham dancer and a principal figure in the early Judson Dance Theatre.

In the past, improvisation had been taught in America by many teachers, among them Hanya Holm (who, in turn, had been a student in Mary Wigman's improvisation classes in Germany), Alwin Nikolais and Murray Louis (both pupils of Holm), and such otherwise disparate choreographers as Anna Halprin and Daniel Nagrin. For the most part, these choreographers used improvisation as a tool to discover new movements; once they had done so, that material was then incorporated into a dance. In contact improvisation, however, the improvisatory process is itself the dance.

Contact improvisation in its most basic form involves two people who, in effect, have a dialogue in motion. They relate to each other, lean against each other, roll and slide on the floor, and climb over each other, communicating by sensing each other's presence and through a constant give-and-take of weight and energy.

Contact devotees claim that contact sessions can be as visually fascinating in their own way as ballet or conventional modern dance. Other dancegoers have doubts. In any case, nothing prevents improvisers from taking movement sequences that have pleased them in contact sessions and incorporating them into the choreography of their next theatrical dance.

Surely few dancers of the 1960s had ever heard of J. E. Crawford Flitch. But his remarks of 1910, quoted earlier in a discussion of Isadora Duncan, could also apply to the efforts of a newer choreographic generation. Like Isadora, many post-Judson choreographers believed the art of dance had grown infirm. The remedy they prescribed was the one Flitch believed the Duncanites recommended: a return to nature. Some of the 1960s choreographers did so by favoring ordinary, unadorned movements; others created communal rituals.

Yet, in every era, dancers and audiences alike never seem content with simplicity alone. Just as earlier modern dancers eventually became dissatisfied with Duncan's Hellenism, so many later choreographers of simple steps and patterns found that, as they continued to work, their creations grew increasingly intricate. Virtuosity is often, and justifiably, decried when it becomes an end in itself. Nevertheless, virtuosic skill does help make dancing exciting to watch.

Some choreographers who wished to develop dancers' technical abilities had to face the problem of finding a source for new virtuosic steps. Their own esthetic predilections often ruled out ballet or the established modern dance techniques. Instead, they turned to sports, athletics, acrobatics, and gymnastics. Such activities were obviously spectacular; at the same time, they could not be considered over-refined or artificial.

The most internationally popular American troupe to emerge from gymnastics is Pilobolus. This was the brainchild of some Dartmouth College students who had never had dance lessons before they enrolled in a class taught at Dartmouth by Alison Chase. Three of them—Jonathan Wolken, Robb (later known as Moses) Pendleton, and Steve Johnson—choreographed a dance called *Pilobolus* for Chase. And, in 1971, Pilobolus (which is a kind of fungus) became the name of a troupe founded by Wolken, Pendleton, Robby Barnett, and Lee Harris. Brainy as well as athletic, these young men combined gymnastic movements with clever ideas. When they performed at a college dance festival, they attracted the attention of Murray Louis, who helped arrange New York performances for them at the headquarters of the Nikolais and Louis companies.

The fact that the Pilobolus repertoire was collaboratively choreographed reflected the egalitarian spirit of the time. In works by Pilobolus, bodies often cling precariously to one another, yet no one topples. The physical closeness of these male bodies was regarded as remarkable and the group's productions were sometimes considered examples of male bonding.[12] Before the advent of Pilobolus, the sight of such constant contact might have disconcerted audiences. But the respect for physicality and the shedding of what came to be regarded as repressive notions about the body which were fostered by the counterculture of the 1960s made Pilobolus not only acceptable, but likable. Women were eventually added to the company, new male dancers joined it, and its founders increasingly devoted themselves to choreography, rather than performing. Pilobolus members also founded little groups of their own: Momix, ISO, Crowsnest.

Molissa Fenley is another choreographer interested in athletics. Although she studied dance at Mills College, she was also involved with running and weightlifting there and came to prefer athletic exercises to dancers' warmups. Fenley created grueling works—especially solos for herself—that required great endurance. One of the most ambitious is *State of Darkness*, a solo version of Stravinsky's *Le Sacre du Printemps*, in which Fenley resembles not the sacrificial victim usually associated with this piece, but a female warrior.

However, even as gymnastically inclined choreographers were emphasizing hearty athletic movements, there were dancers who were refining their techniques. To gain fluency and versatility, they regularly attended ballet as well as modern dance classes. As a result, these dancers moved brilliantly. Yet some observers charged they moved much too balletically[13]; they pointed out that although ballet training develops speed, line, and brilliance, it pays little attention to such matters as weight, gravity, contractions, and twisting, spiraling, asymmetrical, and off-balance movements.

One dancer's alarm over the balleticization of modern dance influenced much of her choreography. Senta Driver, a former member of the Paul Taylor company, began to stress effort and gradations of energy in productions for her troupe, which she called Harry. She made dancers' feet thump as well as go pitter-patter across the floor.

Exploring ways in which people can carry one another, she not only had men carry women (as they traditionally do in dance), but also made women carry men. The unisex partnering which is now common in American dance had at least one of its sources in Driver's partnering experiments of the mid-1970s and early 1980s. She also incorporated passages of shoeless pointe work into her dances.

Some choreographers relished the opportunity to cross back and forth between ballet and modern dance. Driver herself choreographed for the Pennsylvania Ballet and the eclectic North Carolina Dance Theater. Other choreographers, including Lar Lubovitch, Glen Tetley, and John Butler, found it congenial to create technically demanding pieces for a variety of companies. Tetley, who danced with American Ballet Theater and the Joffrey Ballet as well as with Graham, has been particularly successful in Europe. He first called attention to himself as a choreographer in 1962 with *Pierrot Lunaire*, in which commedia dell'arte figures revealed their Expressionist torments on a construction that resembled a playground jungle gym. He went on to create *Voluntaries* (1973), a rhapsodic work in the repertoires of several ballet companies, and his own versions of such ballets as *Daphnis and Chloe* and *Le Sacre du Printemps*.

Another successful crossover choreographer is Twyla Tharp, a former member of Paul Taylor's company who, in addition to directing her own troupe, has choreographed for ballet companies, films, Broadway, and the ice-skater John Curry. Tharp, who was born in 1942, has become both versatile and popular.

Yet at the start of her career she was considered formidably austere. Although her dances have continued to be structurally intricate, her early ones were unaccompanied; until the beginning of the 1970s, her dancers tended to be severe, even slightly truculent, in stage presence. But over the years she has let her dancers relax and has choreographed to music ranging from Haydn to jazz.

Re-Moves (1966) and *After "Suite"* (1969) are typical of her earlier efforts. Attesting to Tharp's love of structural ingenuity was the fact that one section of *Re-Moves* was the same as the work's opening sequence, except that all its steps were danced backward. *After "Suite"* (inspired by a work by Merce Cunningham called *Suite for Five*) took place in three adjacent squares of space. As each section was completed, it was repeated in another square but as a variant of itself by means of repatterning and shifts of focus; at the same time, new material was introduced in the first square.

Tharp began to attract the general public with *Medley* in the summer of 1969. Despite its formal complexity, *Medley* was not intimidating. It received its premiere on a Connecticut College lawn during the American Dance Festival and was repeated later that summer in New York's Central Park. *Medley* is particularly remembered for its magical ending: a long adagio for dancers spaced across the lawn, all of whom moved so slowly that it was almost impossible to tell if they were moving at all. As dusk fell, the performers appeared to fade into the darkness.

After *Medley*, Tharp turned overtly theatrical. Her choreography continued to emphasize sudden changes, lunges, and dartings, as well as abrupt shifts from sharply emphatic steps to shrugs and slouches. But her productions' trappings became more elaborate and beguiling. Tharp's love of jazz was reflected in *Eight Jelly Rolls* (1971), to the music of Jelly Roll Morton, and *The Bix Pieces* (also 1971), for which the accompaniment included both recordings by Bix Beiderbecke and excerpts from Haydn, as if to suggest that jazz and Haydn shared a comparable rhythmic suppleness. *Deuce Coupe* (1973), one of Tharp's creations for the Joffrey Ballet, was set to songs by the Beach Boys.

Tharp has occasionally ventured into choreography with dramatic implications. For instance, *The Catherine Wheel* (1981) showed the decay of family, social, and political life, and in 1993 she created *Demeter and Persephone* for the Martha Graham Dance Company, thereby becoming the first choreographer to work with that group who had no previous ties with it.

Like Tharp, Mark Morris can be gleefully eclectic. A former dancer with Laura Dean and Lar Lubovitch, Morris, who was born in 1956, burst upon the choreographic scene in the early 1980s, creating dances to a wide variety of musical accompaniments. In 1982, his compositions included such items as *Songs that Tell a Story*, to southern gospel songs, and *New Love Song Waltzes*, an impetuous ensemble to the music of Brahms, and 1984 brought forth *Gloria* (Vivaldi), a depiction of people striving for, and attaining, divine grace. Working on a grand scale, he choreographed *L'Allegro, il Penseroso ed il Moderato* (1988), an evocation of the character types referred to in this secular oratorio by Handel to a text by Milton, and *Dido and Aeneas* (1989), a danced interpretation of Purcell's opera in which he cast himself both as the tragic heroine and as the malicious sorceress who brings about her downfall.

Morris has also choreographed for ballet companies. And he served, 1988–1991, as dance director at the Théâtre de la Monnaie, the Brussels opera house that had previously been the home of Maurice Béjart's controversial ballet company.

Whereas some choreographers associated with or influenced by the Judson Dance Theatre concerned themselves with structural patterns, others sought to create what could be called a theatre of images. And their images were often haunting, whimsical, bizarre, or terrifying.

This sort of dance-theatre had many sources. Happenings and Pop Art may have influenced some early examples of it. David Gordon's *Random Breakfast* of 1963 seems very much a product of its time. Gordon studied both with such a freewheeling choreographer as James Waring and with such pillars of the modern dance establishment as Graham and Horst, and he became a comic and occasionally impish choreographer.

Random Breakfast, which was performed in a Washington, D.C., roller skating rink and later at the Judson Church, satirized several art and entertainment styles. Gordon himself did a Spanish dance wearing a strapless evening gown that left some of the hair on his chest fully visible. His wife, Valda Setterfield, was featured in a parody of Pop Art and Happenings in which, dressed as a nun, she leaped up and down on bedsprings and shoved a cream pie in her own face. In still another episode, Gordon simply smiled and looked shy for four minutes to Judy Garland's recording of "Somewhere over the Rainbow."

Kenneth King tends to view the world as a scientific or metaphysical puzzle. He has danced to texts filled with elaborate word games and references to both science and science fiction. At times, he invented a host of characters that served as alter-egos for himself; these figures included a Russian dancer, a transvestite spy, Isadora Duncan's son, the philosopher Friedrich Nietzsche, and the eccentric custodian of something called the Transhimalayan Society for Interplanetary Research. But he has also eschewed such eccentric characterization to emphasize abstract choreographic phrases which seem to change with the speed of thought.

Phoebe Neville, in contrast, specializes in brief dances which are often hauntingly enigmatic in content, but gesturally clear and precise. Neville calls Helen Tamiris and Daniel Nagrin her most inspiring teachers; however, in her concern to give objective expression to inner experience, she follows in the tradition of Mary Wigman. One of her most striking compositions is *Cartouche*. When the curtain rises, a woman is seen sprawled on the floor and a man is standing on her back, making oratorical gestures. Then the woman topples this tyrant. But instead of looking triumphant, as might be expected after her act of rebellion, she turns despairing as if realizing that all power can corrupt.

Robert Wilson and Meredith Monk are associated with grandly scaled productions. Wilson's creations—including the pictorially rich *The Life and Times of Sigmund Freud* (1969) and *The Life and Times of Joseph Stalin* (1973)—often unfold in hypnotic slow motion.

Stalin, which lasted twelve hours—from 7 P.M. to 7 the next morning—presented fantastic images of some of the people and forces that shaped the twentieth century, and the cast of 125 included performers dressed as historical figures, a chorus line of black "mammies," and another chorus line of ostriches.

In addition to devising original productions, Wilson has staged operas and plays. One of the most celebrated of these efforts was the musical spectacle *Einstein on the Beach*, to music by Philip Glass. Andrew de Groat choreographed the premiere of the four-and-a-half-hour work in 1976; Lucinda Childs was the choreographer of its 1984 revival. *Einstein* abounded with images of space, time, light, energy, and power, and Wilson distorted the audience's sense of time by contrasting slow-motion episodes with whirling dance ensembles.

Meredith Monk has become a one-woman theatre: a choreographer who composes the scores for and stage-directs her own productions. Her multimedia works frequently defy categorization; she herself once referred to them as "mixed pickles." [14]

Monk, who was born in 1943, sang before she talked, could read music before she read words, and began dancing at the age of three. She studied Dalcroze eurhythmics and ballet and was a dance major at Sarah Lawrence College, where one of her instructors (and one of the greatest influences on her career) was Bessie Schönberg, an inspiring teacher of dance composition.

Monk's productions resemble theatrical mosaics, for they are built from small fragments of activities. As these units interlock, their significance gradually intensifies.

Several of her most elaborate spectacles were conceived for specific and often nontheatrical sites. The three-evening *Juice* (1969) proceeded on a diminishing scale. The first evening's events were staged on the great spiral ramp that Frank Lloyd Wright designed for New York's Guggenheim Museum. The second installment was in a small proscenium theater; the third in a loft. There were no live performers whatsoever in that final presentation. Instead, the audience at the loft saw videotapes of the work's cast and an exhibition of the props used in the other two sections. In contrast, the three-part *Vessel* (1971) gradually expanded in scale. A fantasy inspired, in part, by the story of Joan of Arc, *Vessel* began in Monk's own small loft apartment. The next part was in an Off-Off-Broadway theatre. And the conclusion took place in a parking lot, which became a public square in which Joan was burned in the light of a welder's torch.

Education of the Girlchild (1973), an allegorical account of the course of life, concluded with a structurally unusual solo in which an apparently ancient woman became increasingly agile as she danced down a strip of cloth. The effect was that of seeing life in reverse from old age to infancy.

Quarry (1976) concerned the fantasies of a sick child. But it soon became clear that the society in which she lived was also sick and that members of her family were subject to persecution, just as the Jews were under Hitler. Monk called *Juice* a "theater cantata," *Vessel* an "opera epic," and *Girlchild* simply an "opera." She has also composed totally musical works. And the Houston Grand Opera commissioned *Atlas* from her in 1991. This three-act opera about a woman explorer treated life as a journey or adventure—a theme dear to Monk. All the stage action was carefully choreographed, and the vocal text contained few actual words. Instead, the vocalists sang sounds that were intended to express their characters' emotions, while the story was told through their movements and personal interrelationships. *Atlas* was an opera by a composer who was also obviously a choreographer.

Eiko and Koma, a Japanese-born couple who settled in America, concern themselves with the workings of the forces of nature in their collaboratively choreographed pieces. Although they studied dance in Japan, they encountered the greatest influence upon their development only after they had gone to Europe in 1972 to study and perform. When they expressed curiosity about Wigman's teaching methods, acquaintances referred them to Manja Chmiel, who had studied both with Wigman and at the Dorothee Günther School and who had settled in Hanover. A demanding and charismatic teacher, Chmiel encouraged the Japanese dancers to develop their own distinctive style, and they made their American debut in 1976.

Eiko and Koma create dreamlike productions in slow motion. Although their dances may seem like visions, their subject matter derives from the real world. In *Fur Seal* the two dancers wore glistening black costumes that suggested sealskin and, snorting and grunting, performed ungainly movements, dragging themselves across the floor and clumsily embracing as if mating. Yet, despite their fondness for themes drawn from nature, these dancers seldom attempt literal imitations of anything in the natural world. The way they slowly stretched outward in *Tree* may have suggested the unhurried growth of trees. But the movements did not duplicate the shapes of any actual tree.

Eiko and Koma also ponder human effort. They kept laboring up and toppling down a sand dune in *Beam*. In *Thirst*, they portrayed two beings forced to endure extreme deprivation. And in *Elegy* they struggled in water, which could have symbolized both the source of life and a pool of tears at the apocalyptic end of history.

Kei Takei, another Japanese-born choreographer, is also preoccupied with struggle. Her teachers include Anna Sokolow—when Sokolow was a guest teacher in Japan and after Takei came to New York in 1967—and Anna Halprin. Since the late 1960s, Takei has been choreographing an apparently endless cycle of dances called *Light*, each section of which depicts labor, hardships, and the bearing of burdens.

Choreography concerned with social issues has continued to be produced as America has faced such matters as racism, economic inequality, homelessness, feminism, equal rights for gays, and AIDS.

Arnie Zane, co-founder with Bill T. Jones of the Bill T. Jones/ Arnie Zane Dance Company, died of AIDS in 1988, but Jones has retained the name of his artistic collaborator and longtime companion in the name of his troupe. Jones has choreographically concerned himself with the AIDS crisis in several ways. *D-Man in the Waters* is a tribute to Damian Acquavella, another dancer who died of AIDS. Far from being a lugubrious elegy, this is an exuberant dance to the Mendelssohn "Octet," and the way the cast appears to plunge and swim through space suggests the heroic efforts of people who, though troubled by misfortune, nonetheless try to stay afloat in life. In *Red*

Room (a solo which can be danced by either a man or a woman) the small steps of which the choreography is made seem attempts to keep moving despite adversity.

Garth Fagan Dance is the outgrowth of Bottom of the Bucket, But . . . , a company Fagan founded in Rochester, New York, in 1970. The group's original name is an indication of the indomitability Fagan prizes. His works often look choreographically gnarled; but, like trees, they are sturdy.

Among Fagan's ambitious productions is *Griot New York* (1991), a full-evening work with music by Wynton Marsalis and décor by the sculptor Martin Puryear, which presents a panorama of African-American experiences. Fusing such disparate idioms as ballet, Afro-Caribbean, Hispanic, jazz, and ballroom dance, it attests to the pluralism of American modern dance at the end of the twentieth century.

CONTEMPORARY BRITISH DANCE

Margaret Morris • Ballet Rambert • Christopher Bruce • Robin Howard • London Contemporary Dance Theatre and School • Robert Cohan • Moving Being • Richard Alston • Strider • Mary Fulkerson • Second Stride • Siobhan Davies • New Dance • X6 • Robert North • Ian Spink • Rosemary Butcher • Michael Clark • DV8 • Lea Anderson • Dance Umbrella

SOMETIMES THINGS HAPPEN AND NO ONE CAN QUITE explain why. Advocates of modern dance made repeated attempts to introduce that art to Great Britain, with little lasting effect. A fresh campaign to bring modern dance to ballet-loving Britain was launched in the 1960s. This time, something happened; in only a few years, Great Britain was one of the leaders of the modern dance world.

When he was asked, in conversation, why this remarkable change took place, Robin Howard—who did much to bring it about—simply shrugged and replied, "The time just seemed to be right for it." [1]

Yet the late 1950s and early 1960s did not initially appear to be ushering in a new era of British dance. After settling in England, Rudolf Laban attracted a coterie who regarded him as a pedagogical patriarch until his death in 1958. But few of the dancers and teachers he influenced had much influence outside certain British schools.

After World War II, Ernest Berk and his students founded the Dance Theatre Commune, which continued until 1978. Yet many London dance lovers considered its activities of marginal importance. The productions of Lilian Harmel and Hilde Holger, two Viennese-trained modern dancers, were regarded in a similar fashion, although both maintained studios for many years. Harmel, who was born in England, studied Dalcroze eurythmics and ballet in Vienna, and established a London school in 1946. Holger, a pupil of Gertrud Bodenwieser, left her native Austria after the Nazis seized power there. She founded a school in Bombay, India, in 1939 and after the war moved to England, where she opened a studio in 1951.

Margaret Morris became involved with a bold, but short-lived venture in Scotland. In 1960, she founded a full-scale company which she called the Scottish National Ballet, a choice of name which horrified some partisans of classical ballet and modern dance alike. The programs of Morris's new company featured both traditional Scottish songs and dances and contemporary pieces by Morris and other choreographers. Among the premieres was *Gods in the Gorbals*, choreographed by Morris and Bruce McClure, which showed ancient Celtic gods coming to the Gorbals, a notorious Glasgow slum.

The Scottish National Ballet, which remained almost entirely unknown outside Scotland, did not survive beyond 1961. Modern dance still seemed to be a suspicious foreign artistic interloper. John Ashford, who became director of the Place Theatre in London in 1986, is not the only Briton to confess, "We are very xenophobic on this island."[2]

Yet outside influences did seep into the British dance scene. Dance companies from abroad regularly visited Britain before and after World War II. Although most of them were balletic, they served as reminders of how varied dance can be. American modern dancers also visited Britain. Martha Graham's company made its London debut in 1954. Although it stimulated a small and articulate band of critics and dancegoers, it mystified other people and its performances were sparsely attended. But when Graham returned in 1963, she received a considerably more favorable reception, and the houses were nearly all sold out. The companies of Merce Cunningham, Paul Taylor, and Alvin Ailey also visited Britain in the early 1960s.

And suddenly, unexpectedly, modern dance became a thriving British art.

In 1966, Ballet Rambert completely transformed itself. Ballet Rambert was the creation of Marie Rambert (1888–1982), a Polish-born dancer and teacher who began her career as an enthusiast for "free" dance. She idolized Duncan and studied with Dalcroze.

It was Rambert's knowledge of eurhythmics that brought her into the ballet world. She was hired by Serge Diaghilev in 1913 to help the choreographer Vaslav Nijinsky analyze Stravinsky's complex score for *Le Sacre du Printemps*. Working with Diaghilev's Ballets Russes, she developed a new respect for ballet as an art (and, she later confessed, fell secretly in love with Nijinsky). After settling in London and marrying the playwright Ashley Dukes, she established her own ballet school in 1920. Its students gave occasional performances throughout the 1920s; in 1931, when her husband opened a tiny play-house called the Mercury Theater, the Rambert troupe began to perform on a regular basis.

Rambert may have been a convert to ballet, but she never lost the modern dancer's faith in individual creativity, and she nurtured and guided a remarkable number of gifted choreographers, among them Frederick Ashton, Antony Tudor, Andrée Howard, Frank Staff, and Walter Gore. Inevitably, however, her discoveries would desert the Mercury for companies that performed on larger stages and were headed by less volatile directors (for Rambert was as celebrated for her fits of temperament as she was for her taste and intellect). But she never gave up in her search for fresh talent.

Eventually, her company outgrew the Mercury, and from the 1940s onward it danced in many theatres. Premieres continued to be emphasized, but the company also staged fine versions of such nineteenth-century classics as *Giselle, La Sylphide*, and *Don Quixote.*

Therefore it came as a surprise in 1966 when Rambert and Norman Morrice, her latest choreographic protégé, announced that Ballet Rambert was to be reorganized as a contemporary company and that its members would be required to be proficient in modern dance. A precedent existed for this sort of ensemble: Netherlands Dance Theater, which had been established in the Hague in 1959 by the American choreographer Benjamin Harkarvy and for which the Dutch choreographer Hans van Manen created many works. Both Harkarvy and van Manen were ballet-trained yet interested in modern dance, and the hybrid company they developed exerted a tremendous influence throughout Europe.

Netherlands Dance Theatre stressed new productions, a policy that has been continued by Jiri Kylian, its director since 1975. In its early years, there were creations by such modern dance choreographers as John Butler, Glen Tetley, and Anna Sokolow, all of whom made contributions to the new Rambert repertoire, as did Morrice who, though classically trained, had studied at the Graham school during a stay in New York, 1961–1962. Morrice left Rambert in 1974 to do freelance choreography; he directed the Royal Ballet from 1977 to 1986. He was succeeded as director of Rambert by John Chesworth (1974–1980) and Robert North (1981–1986).

With the transformation of her company, Rambert in effect retired, serving as an artistic inspiration to her troupe, but leaving its day-to-day running to others. The new Ballet Rambert soon developed a choreographer of its own: Christopher Bruce, who joined the company in 1963, became one of its principal dancers, and remained with it during its esthetic metamorphosis. In order to emphasize its commitment to contemporary choreography, Ballet Rambert changed its name to Rambert Dance Company in 1987.

The other major contributions to British modern dance in the 1960s were made by Robin Howard, a man blessed with visionary idealism and sound practical sense. The great-grandson of the Canadian railway magnate Lord Strathcona, the grandson of Prime Minister Stanley Baldwin, and the son of a member of Parliament, Howard was educated at Cambridge and studied law, although he never practiced. He served as a lieutenant in the Scots Guards during World War II and lost both his legs in battle. After the war he became a successful hotel owner and restaurateur. Yet, though he was a convivial man, he was not content merely to provide people with good food and fine wine. Howard had a mission—and he remained devoted to it until his death in 1989 at the age of sixty-five.

The horrors of war made him responsive to the causes of world peace and social justice. And he discovered dance. Indeed, he once confessed that he was drawn to dance "partly because it was a total contrast to warfare."[3] Ballet first attracted him. Yet, although he continued to admire it, he did not find it totally satisfying.

Then came Martha Graham's sparsely attended and financially ill-fated London season of 1954. Looking back on it, Howard wryly commented, "Legend has it that there were only thirty-five people in the stalls on the second night, and I am one of the five thousand people who claim to have been among those thirty-five. I was in fact there." Indeed he was. Graham astonished him and, he said, his reaction was "shock, and then marvel and wonder."[4]

Howard became a lover of modern dance: of Graham's choreography, in particular, but also that of other choreographers. By the 1960s, he was sufficiently devoted to the art as to vow to do something to further it. He sponsored Graham's London engagement in 1963 and provided funds enabling British dancers to study in New York at the Graham School and American modern dancers to teach in England.

In 1966, the same year as the Rambert transformation, Howard established the London School of Contemporary Dance. A year later, the London Contemporary Dance Theatre gave its first performances, and in 1969 Howard supervised the remodeling of an old drill hall into an arts center containing studios and a theatre which was named the Place. By 1970, Howard's school had 63 full-time students; the enrollment in the mid-1970s rose to about 120.⁵ Jane Dudley was appointed senior teacher in 1969, and Nina Fonaroff, another former Graham dancer, was also on the faculty. Understandably enough, given Howard's background, the London Contemporary school and company were rooted in Graham technique; yet Howard exposed students to a variety of other influences. Those students came from many backgrounds. Some had received ballet training. Others were theatre students or students from art schools, which, in the late 1960s and early 1970s, were centers of cultural ferment in Britain.

Indeed, Geoff Moore, one of Britain's unclassifiable choreographic talents of the day, had no formal training as a dancer and was entirely the product of art schools. In 1968, the Welsh-born Moore founded Moving Being, a multimedia group that specialized in theatrical collages involving movement, films, slides, music, and spoken words. His productions often juxtaposed images. A television set was seen playing inside a huge mouth in *Accumulator* (1969); two men and a woman, all wearing white hospital gowns, slowly changed positions in *Trio* (1969) to the reading of texts about sleep, dreams, and memory; as they moved, the woman sometimes seemed a real person involved in some emotional relationship to the men, whereas at other times she could have been a figment of their imaginations. *Signs* (1971) brought together dancers representing Alice in Wonderland, Hamlet, Ophelia, and the French theatrical theorist Antonin Artaud—all of them people (fictional or real) who experienced identity crises. Moving Being was in residence at the Place, 1969–1972, after which it moved to Cardiff, Wales.

The London Contemporary Dance Theatre's first director and one of its principal choreographers was the former Graham dancer Robert Cohan. As a soldier in England during World War II, the American-born Cohan had attended a Sadler's Wells ballet performance of Robert Helpmann's *Miracle in the Gorbals* and had been deeply affected by this balletic depiction of Christ's return to the Glasgow slums.

Like Howard, Cohan was branded by his wartime experiences, especially by his memories of the way in which Allied soldiers trying to prevent the Germans from reaching Paris would hurry ahead without stopping to take prisoners. Instead, they would promise the Germans safe treatment if they would come out of hiding; when the

Germans did so, they would be lined up behind a building and shot.[6] Cohan certainly knew what Howard meant when he called dance a contrast to warfare.

As director of LCDT, as the troupe was often known for short, Cohan brought approximately 200 works to the stage, making that company the most choreographically productive group in the history of British dance.[7] Despite his affinities to Graham, only two of these works were by her: *El Penitente* and *Diversion of Angels*. The repertoire was eclectic from the outset.

Of Cohan's own compositions, *Cell* (1969) received praise as a tense study of people trapped in either a real prison or a prison of the mind. *Stages* (1971) depicted a journey of self-confrontation and discovery. *Class* (1975) celebrated a dancer's daily training. *Stabat Mater* (1975) choreographically reflected the emotions of the Virgin Mary.

In some ways, the growth of the London Contemporary school and company contradicted the way modern dance had developed elsewhere in the world. Whereas most modern troupes devoted themselves to a single choreographer, London Contemporary Dance Theatre was always choreographically eclectic—as was Ballet Rambert both before and after its transformation. And whereas many modern dance choreographers have begun with a vision and then have devised a technique to express it, Robin Howard attempted to stimulate British dancers by importing techniques—notably, Graham technique, but others as well—in the hope that exposure to unfamiliar ways of moving would inspire choreographers with new ideas.

Modern dance purists might have charged that Howard was reversing the proper order of things: ideas, they would argue, should precede steps, otherwise modern dance could become as codified as classical ballet. Indeed, as early as the mid-1970s, some young dancers felt that London Contemporary had already become "establishment." But the school was trying to cope with the problem—a chronic one in modern dance—of trying to give students a sound technical foundation while at the same time allowing them to remain open to unconventional ways of performing and choreographing.

London Contemporary certainly succeeded in producing capable dancers and developing a well-organized curriculum. In the 1980s, it helped make modern dance accepted on the college level in Britain, establishing a B.A. Degree Course in cooperation with the University of Kent, which produced its first dance graduates in 1985.

London Contemporary and Ballet Rambert also developed choreographers. This surely must have pleased Robin Howard, Norman Morrice, and Marie Rambert, for opponents of their efforts could easily have accused them of foisting a foreign art upon the British public. British modern dance may have had its roots in a Graham-based technique, but it flowered in its own way.

Christopher Bruce, who has choreographed for other companies as well as Ballet Rambert, was one of the first—and remains one of the most successful—British choreographers to blur conventional distinctions between ballet and modern dance. Bruce, who was born in 1945, has remarked, "I suppose I'm a mongrel; but mongrels often make the most interesting dogs."[8]

As a dancer, Bruce was praised for his dramatic presence, and his choreographic works are also often strongly dramatic, even when they do not tell an actual story. He is also drawn to social and political themes. *There Was a Time* (1973) used the Trojan War to criticize all power struggles. *Cruel Garden* (1977), created in collaboration with the mime Lindsay Kemp, combined dance, mime, and song in an exploration of the life and writings of Federico García Lorca, the great Spanish poet who was executed by Fascist forces during the Spanish Civil War. The hallucinatory *Ghost Dances* (1981) condemned political repression in South America. And by combining Anglo-Irish and American folksongs in *Sergeant Early's Dream* (1984), Bruce suggested both nostalgia for an old world and hope for a new.

Richard Alston (b. 1948) was the first choreographer to emerge from the London Contemporary organization, and he rapidly established himself as a major figure in British dance. His rise to prominence was welcomed by Robin Howard, even though Alston favored ways of moving unlike those emphasized at London Contemporary. Howard has said that it was not until Alston came upon the scene that he felt confirmed in his belief that Great Britain could produce its own important modern dance choreographers.[9]

Like many of his contemporaries in British modern dance, Alston came from a background in the visual arts, having studied theatre design at the Croydon Art College. A growing interest in dance led him to the Rambert Ballet School; in 1967, he became one of the first students to enroll at the London School of Contemporary Dance. He soon developed an interest in choreography, making his choreographic debut in 1968 with *Transit*.

From the start of his career, Alston stood out among his classmates at London Contemporary. Alston absorbed the school's Graham-based technique, yet did not find it totally congenial: physically, because his long thin body found Graham contractions difficult; temperamentally, because he preferred cooler choreography than Graham's turbulent dance-dramas. Instead, he was attracted to the grace and lucidity of Merce Cunningham's technique. The influence of Cunningham upon Alston was apparent in several early works, among them *Nowhere Slowly* (1970), a piece which existed in various versions; it could be danced to several different scores and its sections could be performed in any order.

After choreographing for the London Contemporary Dance Theatre, Alston directed his own company, Strider, from 1972 to 1975. The first independent group to spring from the London Contemporary framework, Strider was Alston's creation, yet also served as a showcase for other choreographers. It emphasized Cunningham rather than Graham technique, as well as an approach to body alignment known as release technique, which had been developed by Mary Fulkerson, an American dancer and choreographer who had joined the dance faculty at Dartington Hall and who also served as a teacher for Strider.

Alston studied in America, 1975–1977. Back in London, he began to work with Ballet Rambert in 1979 and was named resident choreographer in 1980. Two years later, he formed another company, Second Stride, with Siobhan Davies and Ian Spink. In 1986, he was appointed artistic director of Ballet Rambert (renamed Rambert Dance Company in 1987), a post he held until 1992.

Although Alston's choreography has been varied, it can be said that he has had an abiding interest in pure dance. He himself has stated that he wishes to create "dances about dancing." [10]

Some of his early works, however, reveled in "impurity." *Combines*, a fifty-minute piece of 1972 that was created in collaboration with the performance artist and film-maker Sally Potter, offered mixtures of sounds and sights. The accompaniment ranged from Bach, Mozart, and Schubert to "Georgia on My Mind" and "Stormy Weather." Films and slides were projected on several screens. And the choreography included both pedestrian movements and complex dance steps.

Alston soon preferred esthetic harmony to such theatrical jumbles. His *Rainbow Bandit* (a 1977 revision of a work of 1974) could be described as a gradual attainment of clarity. It began with a deliberately chaotic section filled with conflicting strands of activity, but these were eventually sorted out in the piece's last section.

As he developed, Alston increasingly turned to music, rather than dramatic situations, as a source of inspiration, developing a style that stressed ease, efficiency, and the avoidance of strain—qualities that made several of his pieces seem quasi-balletic. His choreography is rhythmically precise and the movements he favors have been called cool and sometimes even asexual.[11]

In 1981, he choreographed a successful version of Stravinsky's *Le Sacre du Printemps*. Yet Alston has admitted that he finds narrative troublesome, saying, "I will *not* waste good music on telling stories."[12] Usually, Alston allows movement qualities to establish moods or suggest emotions. *Apollo Distraught* (1982) emphasizes tensions between Apollonian (contained) and Dionysian (explosive) movements. There is also an affectionate allusion to ballet history in a sequence in which a female soloist dances an adagio with three men, a reversal of the central situation in *Apollo*, George Balanchine's masterpiece of 1928, in which a male god dances with three Muses.

Alston consciously pares narration away from his choreography. For *Night Moves* (1981), to the music of Mozart, Alston supplied his designer, the painter Howard Hodgkin, with a scenario concerning Mozart and people the composer knew so that Hodgkin could gain a sense of the work's overall style. But although the actual dance appears to show the confrontations of guests at a party, the narrative is underplayed.

Alston's lucidity suggests the influence of ballet and Cunningham. But he also admires Twyla Tharp and shares her interest in popular culture. His *Java* (1983, revised 1985) looks back on the 1940s and 1950s and is set to recordings by the black pop group the Ink Spots; *Strong Language* (1987) contains references to disco dancing; and his version of Gershwin's *Rhapsody in Blue* (1988) honors Fred Astaire and exhibition ballroom dancing.

One of Alston's classmates at the London School of Contemporary Dance was another former art student who developed into an important choreographer: Siobhan Davies. Like Alston, Davies, who was born in 1950, entered the school during its first year. Before that, she had studied at the Hammersmith College of Art and Building, and while enrolled at London Contemporary she continued part-time at the St. Martin's School of Art. As a dancer, she is essentially a product of London Contemporary and remained closely identified with it as a performer and choreographer until the 1980s, when a desire to create more works than London Contemporary's schedule and budget permitted prompted her to work with other groups, including Rambert, Second Stride, and her own Siobhan Davies Dance Company, which she founded in 1988.

Alston cast her in many of his productions and her choreography, like his, has sometimes been called cool and understated. Nevertheless, she has gone her own way. She made her choreographic debut in 1972 with *Relay*, a piece for London Contemporary Dance Theatre that derived from such sports activities as running, hurdling, boxing, and wrestling. Since then, she has choreographed both "pure" dance works and dances that emphasize emotional situations and dramatic developments.

Among her mood pieces are *The Calm* (1974), which contrasts peacefulness and agitation, with peace at last prevailing, and *New Galileo* (1984), in which the stage space is constantly redefined by changing lighting patterns. The austere *Step at a Time* (1976) emphasized the flexibility and ease of the upper body; the movement was so devoid of what the critics Mary Clarke and Clement Crisp referred to as emotional "clutter" that they called the choreography "white."[13]

When she uses dramatic material, Davies does so with restraint, presenting, repeating, and varying key movements, sometimes in a contrapuntal manner that makes her characters seem to be engaged in kinetic conversations.[14] *Something to Tell* (1980), inspired by Davies's reading of Anton Chekhov's stories and plays, expressed the feelings of a lonely woman. *Silent Partners* (1984) was a series of duets showing a man and a woman passing through a series of relationships. What they learned from each was evident in the way that movement ideas from one duet would be brought into the duet that followed it. Whereas some choreographers exploring such a theme would choose an emotionally passionate score as accompaniment, Davies, typically restrained, had all her duets danced in silence except for the last, for which there was music by Orlando Gough.

The School for Lovers Danced (1985) was an adaptation of Mozart's *Così fan tutte*, to some of the music from that opera. It is Davies's most literal dramatic creation. But in *Wyoming* (1988) she once again favored emotional implications rather than explicit statements, and the choreography was her response to the vastness of America's Great Plains.

By the mid-1970s, modern dance groups were starting to proliferate in Britain, causing such a major funding body as the Arts Council Dance Theatre Sub-Committee to wonder how—or even whether—it ought to support them. In 1976, the critic Peter Williams voiced his opposition to such funding: "Let us, for the present at any rate, forget about 'experiments' and 'experimental projects' in connection with dance . . . everything has been done before." [15]

Such a view, of course, did not please the dancers engaged in such "projects"; more than ever, there appeared to be a wide gap between the dance establishment (into which some of the most iconoclastic dancers would put Rambert and London Contemporary) and a rebellious younger generation. To let the world—and one another—know what they were up to, some of the rebels in 1977 established a magazine, *New Dance*, which, until its demise in 1988, offered its own lively and opinionated comments on the dance scene.

Soon the compositions of some of the younger choreographers began to be referred to as New Dance. The practice thereby gave the dance world yet another term which, like *Ausdruckstanz* or postmodern dance, was significant without also being easily definable. Yet the existence of the term "New Dance" was a sign that British modern dance was not confined to Rambert or London Contemporary, and the fact that its advocates preferred it to postmodern dance, which was associated with the United States, indicated that British dance lovers no longer thought it necessary to look abroad for esthetic inspiration.

The magazine *New Dance* was founded by the X6 Collective (Emilyn Claid, Maedée Duprès, Fergus Early, Jacky Lansley, and Mary Prestidge), a group of dancers of varying backgrounds. Their headquarters was the top floor of an old warehouse in London's Docklands district where, from 1976 to 1980, they offered classes, workshops, and performances by themselves and by choreographers outside the collective. The late 1970s saw growing political disillusionment in Great Britain, and X6 interpreted social issues from a radical viewpoint. Working in harmony as a collective, these dancers sought ways of presenting political ideas in art and of gaining control over their lives and over a society which they considered repressive.

Claid, Lansley, and Prestidge questioned stereotypical images of women in dance in their *Bleeding Fairies* (1977). Early choreographed several pieces exploring the emotional relationships of men. He also put his Royal Ballet training to use in *Naples* (1978), a tribute to August Bournonville's great nineteenth-century ballet *Napoli*, but with a twentieth-century setting. He and Lansley reinterpreted another classic in their *I, Giselle* (1980), a feminist retelling of the familiar scenario in which Count Albrecht, rather than Giselle, goes mad and dies. Claid danced *Making a Baby* (1979) when she was seven months pregnant and intended the work to be a sharing of her personal experiences with her audience.

Other choreographers also rose to prominence in Britain. Although American-born, Robert North was largely British trained (at both the Royal Ballet School and London Contemporary). He developed into a versatile choreographer, working with Rambert and London Contemporary as well as with several ballet companies. His *Troy Game*, a spoof of machismo and muscle-building created for London Contemporary in 1974, became an international hit, finding its way into the repertories of such companies as Dance Theater of Harlem and the Royal Ballet.

Ian Spink had been a member of the Australian Ballet and the contemporary-based Dance Company of New South Wales and had already begun to choreograph when he left his native Australia to participate in the International Course for Choreographers and Composers, which Robert Cohan directed at the University of Surrey in 1977. He has lived in the United Kingdom since then. With Richard Alston and Siobhan Davies, Spink founded Second Stride in 1982 and became its sole director in 1988. He has absorbed all sorts of choreographic influences—including those of Alston, Merce Cunningham, and Pina Bausch—and has devised his own form of imagistic dance-theatre.

Spink is fond of long complex passages of movement. He has compared the steps in his *Canta* (1981) to big wallpaper patterns, and Steve Goff, one of his dancers, says that Spink creates "something of a movement continuum within which the phrasing is always twisting and turning, renewing and discovering itself, and giving an impression of limitless breath." [16] But Spink also likes to disrupt his patterning with quirky dramatic or humorous touches and sudden shifts of tone, and his productions are theatrical collages that often involve elaborate scenic designs, costumes, and props.

During the course of *26 Solos* (1978), three elegantly dressed women kept entering and departing, and their dancing was punctuated by bizarre details: one acquired a moustache, another brushed her teeth, the third put drops in her eyes. Spink is fascinated by the absurdities and irrationality of ordinary life. *Dead Flight* (1980) evoked the claustrophobia and tensions of passengers on an airplane. Episodes in *Further and Further into Night* (1984) were inspired by *Notorious*, Alfred Hitchcock's suspense film about the daughter of a Nazi sympathizer who falls in love with an FBI agent. *Bösendorfer Walzer* (1986) combined references to the plot of Michel Fokine's fairy-tale ballet *The Firebird* with incidents involving such prominent Surrealists or Dadaists as Tristan Tzara, Salvador Dali, Frida Kahlo, and René Magritte. *Weighing the Heart* (1987) was filled with layers of mystical imagery; Spink's sources included the Apocryphal story of Tobias and the Angel, the *Egyptian Book of the Dead*, the libretto of Mozart's *Magic Flute*, and the lives of such religious figures as John the Baptist, Mary Magdalen, Mohammed, and Simone Weil.

In contrast to such theatrical extravagance, Rosemary Butcher, who has studied in England and America, has always been something of a minimalist. Butcher, who founded her company in 1975, emphasizes spare arm and upper-body movements and geometrical floor patterns. Yet she has also come to realize that dancers are more than objects in space and that they can suggest relationships as well as create kinetic designs. Thus, her *Touch the Earth* (1987) was not a totally hermetic abstraction, but an evocation of ways in which members of a community claim, measure, and settle on their territory.

Several younger British choreographers have delighted in being anarchical, irreverent, and provocative. Michael Clark, though a disciplined choreographer of technically demanding dances, likes to fill his productions with candid sexual references, cross-dressing, and nudity, and their accompaniment is often ear-splitting rock music. In Lloyd Newson's choreography for a company called DV8, dancers take great physical risks, throwing themselves at one another and against the floor and walls to express shifting emotional relationships that may involve sexual stereotyping, states of loneliness, and the struggles of people to assert themselves or to relate to others. Lea Anderson choreographs for two groups: the all-female Cholmondeleys (pronounced Chumlies) and the all-male Featherstonehaughs (pronounced Fanshaws); the names of both derive from old English family names which are now considered funny because of the discrepancy between the way they are written and the way they are pronounced. Anderson specializes in sharp, succinct, and often comic dances that have the impact of pop songs, and her troupes have performed in cabarets as well as in theatres.

Kim Brandstrup, a Danish dancer and choreographer who was trained at the London School of Contemporary Dance, now directs Arc Dance Company. He is known for his works on literary and dramatic themes, among them idiosyncratic freestyle treatments of *Peer Gynt* and *Hamlet* (in a piece called *Antic*) and *Crime Fictions*, which evokes both Hollywood *film noir* thrillers and the mystery novels of Raymond Chandler. Matthew Bourne's company, Adventures in Motion Pictures, has attracted attention with Bourne's unconventional treatments of ballet classics, including a *Nutcracker* in which the traditionally festive family party is set in a dreary Dickensian orphanage and an all-male *Swan Lake* in which the swans are fierce bare-chested men. Bourne's purpose in such revisions is not simply satirical but an attempt to uncover unfamiliar layers of meanings and emotions in familiar tales.

The range of British modern dance and its relationships to modern dance elsewhere in the world have been emphasized by a number of festivals, perhaps the most important of them being London's annual Dance Umbrella, which was founded in 1978 in an attempt to bring together a significant cross-section of British and foreign choreography. Like most such ventures, it is controversial: conservative balletomanes find it bewildering, young rebels pronounce it hidebound, and xenophobic dancegoers have occasionally resented the importation of companies from abroad (especially from America). Also, given the multiplicity of its attractions, it is inevitable that its productions will include failures as well as triumphs. Nevertheless, Dance Umbrella simultaneously affirms the validity of British modern dance and provides international standards against which local efforts can be measured.

In a curious way, the success of modern dance in Great Britain is indicated by the kinds of difficulties that began to plague its established companies in the late 1980s and early 1990s. Both Rambert and London Contemporary were faced with the task of renewing their creative vitality. Robert Cohan retired as director of London Contemporary in 1989; neither Dan Wagoner, who succeeded him, nor Nancy Duncan, Wagoner's successor, found ways to blaze new trails for it, and the company disbanded. Christopher Bruce, who followed

Richard Alston as director of Rambert in 1992, also had to find ways of preserving that company's tradition of innovation.

The problems of these British troupes are similar to those with which the Graham, Limón, and Ailey companies have had to deal in America. How should a company continue? *Why* should a company even attempt to do so? American groups did not have to answer such questions for several decades. But contemporary British dance was only slightly more than twenty years old in 1989.

British modern dance not only grew, it grew quickly, producing an important body of achievements. No one would be worrying about its renewal if there had not first been growth.

$\mathscr{A}$ LEAGUE OF DANCING NATIONS

Maurice Béjart • Ballet Théâtre Contemporain • Carolyn Carlson • Le Théâtre du Silence • GRCOP • Jean-Claude Gallotta • Maguy Marin • Anne Teresa de Keersmaeker • Raatiko • Jorma Uotinen • Reijo Kela • Tanztheater • Johann Kresnik • Pina Bausch • Reinhild Hoffmann • Susanne Linke • Butoh • Tatsumi Hijikata • Min Tanaka • Dai Rakuda Kan • Sankai Juko • Ushio Amagatsu • Akaji Maro • Kazuo Ohno • Yan Mei-qi • Hu Jia-lu • Toronto Dance Theater • Daniel Williams Grossman • Robert Desrosiers • Anna Wyman • Paul-André Fortier • Edouard Lock • Ginette Laurin • Margie Gillis • Jean-Pierre Perreault • Marie Chouinard • Linda Rabin • Australian Dance Theater • Meryl Tankard • Douglas Wright • Sydney Dance Company • Graeme Murphy

FOLLOWING ITS ESTABLISHMENT AT CONNECTICUT COLLEGE in 1948, the American Dance Festival occasionally offered performances by foreign artists. But since the early 1980s, the festival in its new home in Durham, North Carolina, and under Charles L. Reinhart's direction, has regularly scheduled groups from Europe, Asia, and Latin America. The festival calls itself American. But that designation has come to indicate a desire to present not only American choreography, but also works by foreign choreographers which American audiences might otherwise miss. There now exists what amounts to a league of modern dance nations.

Touring American modern dancers have done much to arouse curiosity about the art abroad. Yet they have not conquered and colonized the world, forcing all other dance communities to imitate American models. Rather, their example has inspired new choreographers to undertake their own voyages of creative discovery.

That point was made bluntly clear in 1990 when a Belgian promoter of dance announced that he did not feel obliged to import

American attractions because he thought that American dance no longer had much to offer.[1] American dance enthusiasts might regard that remark as an example of local boosterism or even xenophobia. Nevertheless, though it may have been intemperate, it did serve as a reminder that modern dance is not exclusively an American art.

Just as in Britain, modern dance eventually flourished in ballet-loving France.

One iconoclastic French ballet choreographer was even regarded by his admirers as an innovator whose achievements were akin to those of the great modern dancers. Maurice Béjart, who was born in Marseille in 1927 (some sources say 1924), received fine classical training and since the late 1950s has attracted international attention as a choreographer for his companies based first in Brussels, Belgium, and later in Lausanne, Switzerland. Béjart experimented with electronic music, staged erotic versions of *Bolero* and *Le Sacre du Printemps*, choreographed a *Firebird* in which the protagonist was not a bird but a guerrilla partisan, and used Berlioz's *Romeo and Juliet* to preach a message of "make love, not war." For many ballet-goers—especially among the young—on the Continent, Béjart was a modernist who reinvigorated traditional classicism.

French audiences also saw modern dance groups, including those of Martha Graham, Merce Cunningham, and Alwin Nikolais. Possibly because his multimedia spectacles appealed to their love of décor, the French especially admired Nikolais; in 1978, he was asked to direct the Centre de Danse Contemporain, a modern dance center in Angers which he headed until 1981.

Angers, at the time, was already involved with dance. During the 1960s, the French sought to decentralize culture, so that the arts would flourish in cities other than Paris. One company that formed a part of this scheme was Ballet-Théâtre Contemporain, organized in Amiens in 1968 with the backing of the Ministry of Culture and with Jean-Albert Cartier as director. It moved to Angers in 1972 and disbanded in 1978. Its repertoire choices were deliberately eclectic; like Ballet Rambert and Netherlands Dance Theater, it produced works by modern as well as classical choreographers.

One of Nikolais's principal dancers also helped stimulate French interest in modern dance. Carolyn Carlson, who was born in Oakland, California, in 1943, performed with the Nikolais troupe from 1964 to 1971, after which she settled in Europe. Her dancing and choreography so impressed the management of the Paris Opéra that in 1975 that august institution appointed her *danseuse étoile chorégraphique* (a title invented expressly for her) and she headed her own group within the Opéra organization. For the first time since the Dalcroze period of the 1920s, modern dance had managed to gain a toehold at the Opéra. In 1980, she left Paris to head a new group at La Fenice, the Venice opera house, remaining there until 1984, after which she pursued an independent choreographic career, including several years as director of the Cullberg Ballet in Stockholm.

Yet modern dance remained at the Paris Opéra. Carlson's successor there came from Le Théâtre du Silence, which, contrary to what its name led some unwary audiences to expect, was not a mime troupe, but a modern dance company organized in La Rochelle in 1971 by Brigitte Lefèvre and Jacques Garnier, two classically trained French dancers who had developed a passion for modern dance. Le Théâtre du Silence produced works by many choreographers ranging from Béjart to such Americans as Merce Cunningham and Lar Lubovitch.

In 1980, Garnier was hired to replace Carlson at the Opéra. There he organized GRCOP (Groupe de Recherche Chorégraphique de l'Opéra de Paris), a modern dance group which nevertheless drew its personnel from the ranks of the Paris Opéra Ballet. Until Garnier's unexpected death at the age of forty-eight in 1989, when the company disbanded, GRCOP offered a varied repertoire and its choreographers included Carolyn Carlson, the French modern dancer Maguy Marin, the German choreographer Susanne Linke, and such Americans as Paul Taylor and David Gordon.

By the late 1980s, France had become the home of many modern dance troupes. Their choreographic styles differed considerably. Nevertheless, foreign critics who observed them sometimes claimed to find a creative tension in these French works between dance as an abstract art and dance as a conveyor of drama. When several French choreographers were featured at the American Dance Festival in 1983, one of them, Caroline Marcadé, told Jim Wise of the *Durham Morning Herald* that, unlike much currently fashionable American abstract dance, French dance was "pure emotion." However, when Anna Kisselgoff, of the *New York Times*, remarked during a panel discussion that French dance was deeply involved with what she referred to as the Human Condition, some of the visiting choreographers angrily insisted that they were primarily concerned with movement problems.[2]

Several French choreographers came to be known for large-scale productions. Thus, among the works by Jean-Claude Gallotta, who directs the Grenoble-based Groupe Emile Dubois, is the five-hour *L'Hommage à Yves P.* In "Les Survivants" (The Survivors), a section of this piece, the dancers appear to be surviving the strains of daily life as they dart back and forth, wait in lines, scratch themselves, and squabble. Hordes of children at one point suddenly emerge from a trapdoor and, after frisking merrily, duel with the adults. Gallotta says his desire is to "create the waking dream. Sometimes they are nightmares."[3]

Maguy Marin, France's most internationally famous modern dance choreographer, studied in the dance department of the Toulouse Conservatory and at Mudra, Béjart's school in Brussels. She danced with Béjart's company, Carolyn Carlson, and the Strasbourg Opera Ballet and has choreographed for her own company as well as for the Paris Opéra Ballet and the Lyon Opéra Ballet.

Marin revealed her ability to create bizarre characterizations in *May B* (1982), a tribute to Samuel Beckett filled with woebegone figures who could have stepped from that author's plays and novels. *Eh, Qu'est-ce que ça m'fait à moi!?* (*Hey, What's All This to Me*), produced in 1989, the bicentennial of the French Revolution, took a cynical view of political posturing by showing authority figures sending innocents off to war and former revolutionaries aging into senile fogies in a nursing home.

Marin's *Cinderella*, created for the Lyon Opéra Ballet in 1985, may be the most unusual treatment Prokofiev's fairy-tale ballet has ever received. All its characters were dolls, the setting was a dollhouse, and the way the familiar Cinderella story was enacted by these dolls reflected the way children at play often invest their toys with their own hopes and fears.

Like Marin, the Belgian choreographer Anne Teresa de Keersmaeker studied at Mudra. She choreographed her first work in 1980, studied dance at New York University, 1980–1981, and returned to Belgium, founding a company called Rosas in 1983. In 1991, she became dance director at the Théâtre de la Monnaie, the Brussels opera house which has long been a strong supporter of dance. Previous dance directors there have included Maurice Béjart and Mark Morris.

Keersmaeker choreographically unites what might superficially seem to be two irreconcilable artistic tendencies: minimalism and

Expressionism. Structurally, her works often consist of phrases which are incessantly repeated and embellished.

Nevertheless, in such works as *Rosas Danst Rosas* (1983) and *Elena's Aria* (1984), the gathering force and intensity of the movements create kinetic images of tension, pain, shame, and anguish. And the emotional power of *Elena's Aria* is intensified through the use of a film showing buildings being demolished and a taped collage that includes opera recordings, a speech by Fidel Castro, and quotations dealing with betrayed love.

Since the 1970s, Finnish modern dance has become increasingly important.

Raatiko, a company in Vantaa, Finland's fifth largest city, was founded in 1972 by Marjo Kuusela and Maria Wolska. Its dancers are known for their strongly dramatic stage presence, and the repertoire emphasizes pieces inspired by real life and social issues, as well as choreographic adaptations of works by Finnish writers and such foreign novels as John Steinbeck's *The Pearl* and Fyodor Dostoevsky's *The Idiot*.

Jorma Uotinen, Finland's leading contemporary choreographer, has been able to move back and forth between ballet and modern dance. The two major influences on him are the ballet teacher Serge Golovine and Carolyn Carlson, with whose Paris Opéra company he once danced. He had also studied at the school of the Finnish National Ballet and performed with that company.

Yet his choreography for himself and his company, the City Theater Dance Group, has been in a modern dance vein. The critic Rebecca Libermann has remarked, "To watch Uotinen dance is like watching a volcano. He is intense, deliberate in every gesture and movement, controlled, vibrant and eruptive." As a choreographer, he employs many kinds of movement, as well as, on occasion, speech, and his productions can be extravagant or grotesque. According to Libermann, Uotinen "calls everything that happens on stage a 'vision.'"[4]

"We should see everything for the first time," says Uotinen, "because actually we are always seeing things for the first time."[5] Uotinen wrote this in the program note for *Death and the Maiden*, a 45-minute dance about loss and despair to Schubert's "Death and the Maiden Quartet," in which a man has visions of a woman who obsesses him. Eroticism is also one of the themes of *Powder of Darkness*, a work inspired by eighteenth-century decorum with scenery depicting mirrors and gardens. The deliberately slow-paced choreography shows erotic power games hidden behind what the critic Auli Räsänen calls "powdered façades,"[6] and the work's three characters entangle themselves in two heterosexual relationships and one homosexual affair, each character at various times serving as oppressor and oppressed. Uotinen can also choreograph on a grand scale, and one of his most successful creations is *Kalevala*, a mythological spectacle based on a Finnish epic.

In 1991, Uotinen was appointed assistant to Doris Laine, the artistic director of the Finnish National Ballet, and he succeeded her in that post when she retired the next year. Taking over the company, he announced that he planned a repertoire that would include both classical works (as in the past) and new contemporary productions.[7]

Reijo Kela became a maverick of Finnish dance. Although he has said that he has been influenced by Merce Cunningham,[8] he has surely been more inspired by Cunningham's questing spirit than by a desire to work within the specific framework of Cunningham's technique and esthetics.

Kela, then largely unknown outside Finland, created a sensation with *Everyman*, offered on a workshop program at the American Dance Festival in 1987. He placed spectators inside cagelike constructions, stared at them intently while dancing explosive passages of movement, then dismantled the cages and out of them built a Viking ship on which he seemed to sail off into the unknown.

In Finland, Kela is known for site-specific works. *A Dance for You* could only be performed for an audience of one. Kela placed ten chairs—each of a different design—in a room and had viewers enter one person at a time. The solo he then danced depended on the chair that person chose to sit in, each chair being associated with a different piece of choreography. For *City Man*, he constructed (with the permission of municipal authorities) a little house in downtown Helsinki and allowed passersby to watch him through an enormous Plexiglass window. He remained on view for an entire week, dancing alone and with other performers and going about such ordinary activities as eating and sleeping.

Thanks to a German dance form known as *Tanztheater*, Germany has once again become a major force in world modern dance. *Tanztheater* (which means "dance theater") is hard to define. As its name implies, it is essentially dramatic. Yet when it tells stories it usually does so neither in a straightforward fashion nor in the chronologically skewed manner of some of Martha Graham's works. Rather, *Tanztheater* productions tend to be collages of incidents pertaining to some overall theme. The choreography itself may be a collage of actions ranging from conventional dance steps to ordinary everyday activities, and there may be speech as well as music. Settings are often elaborate, but in a gritty or somber, rather than a fanciful, manner. *Tanztheater* choreographers often depict conflicts and power struggles, both between individuals and between social classes. And their productions tend to be dark in tone, although their grimness can be alleviated by sardonic humor.

It is not surprising that *Tanztheater* developed in Germany, where after the war spiritually troubled artists, philosophers, and political commentators began to discuss how much they had compromised themselves during the Nazi regime. In response to the cultural tragedy of the recent past and the moral uncertainties of the present, a new Expressionist style began to develop in German art. The influential artist and theoretician Joseph Beuys urged artists to deal with the contradictions of society, history, and culture, and a manifesto drawn up in 1961 by two other artists, Georg Baselitz and Eugene Schöndeck, called for the development of a painting style that acknowledged the power of the irrational.[9]

Tanztheater was one choreographic response to calls of this kind. It also affirmed the artistic validity of *Ausdruckstanz*, yet used that dance form's expressive force in new ways. *Tanztheater* was an art for a country in which, as the German critic Nobert Servos put it, "dance has lost its innocence."[10]

Like many artistic movements, *Tanztheater* was not the creation of a single person. Rather, it emerged as the result of like-minded artists in several German cities. However, Johann (also known as Hans) Kresnik very early developed a personal choreographic style that resembled what came to be known as *Tanztheater*. Kresnik now claims, "I invented dance theater before anyone else had thought of it."[11]

Born in Bleiburg, Austria, in 1939, Kresnik was ballet trained and danced with ballet companies in Graz, Austria, and Cologne, Germany. But by the late 1960s he felt that he never wanted to take another traditional ballet step again. He had also begun to choreograph. Since then, he has headed companies in Bremen and Heidelberg and has often collaborated with the composer Walter Haupt.

Kresnik is interested in the effect of social conditioning on individuals and has brooded over German history, wondering how and why a nation of composers, poets, and thinkers could have started two world wars and perpetrated the Holocaust. These concerns have inspired many of his productions; his earlier works also reflected his revulsion against the war in Vietnam. Kresnik's productions have often been grotesque, violent, and, for some audiences, unpleasantly graphic in their details. *Sylvia Plath* (1985) depicted in a hallucinatory fashion scenes from the life of an American poet who committed suicide in 1963 and presented her as the victim of a rotten society. Her opponents included her husband and father, and Plath at last became a puppet of society. *Murderer Woyzeck* (1987) was suggested by both the 1836 play by Georg Büchner and the 1925 opera by Alban Berg about a downtrodden soldier who eventually murders his wife. In Kresnik's version, performers spit at one another and Woyzeck is forced to drink from a spittoon. *Macbeth* (1987) used the plot of Shakespeare's tragedy to demonstrate that all power corrupts and that bloodshed leads only to more bloodshed. These themes were startlingly illustrated in scenes in which the stage was filled with bathtubs into which bodies were lowered and by the way a death figure kept tipping buckets—and, finally, whole bathtubs—of blood and entrails into the orchestra pit.

Kresnik has been chided for what the critic Horst Koegler calls "provocative sledgehammer and bulldozer antiaesthetics." But Kresnik himself contends, "I want to bring about change not through force, but through persuasion."[12]

Several exponents of *Tanztheater* studied at the Folkwang School in Essen. Among those former students is Pina Bausch, whose name has become virtually synonymous with *Tanztheater*. The daughter of a restaurant owner, Bausch, who was born in 1940, began her studies at the Folkwang in 1955, when it was still under the direction of Kurt Jooss. Among her other instructors there was Lucas Hoving, the ex-Jooss dancer who had joined José Limón's company and who returned on occasion to Essen as a guest teacher. Bausch received a scholarship in 1961 to attend the Juilliard School in New York, where her teachers included Limón and Louis Horst in modern dance and Antony Tudor, Alfredo Corvino, and Margaret Craske in ballet. Upon her return to Germany, Bausch danced with the Folkwang Ballet, 1962–1968, and began to choreograph for it. She was once again in the United States in 1971, appearing at the American Dance Festival in Hoving's *Zip Code*, for which she choreographed her own solo. In 1973, she was invited to become dance director in Wuppertal, which had a tradition of supporting dance. As director of the Wuppertal Dance Theater, she has made the name of that small industrial city internationally famous.

Bausch first won praise in Wuppertal for her versions of two Gluck operas, *Iphigenia in Tauris* (1974) and *Orpheus and Eurydice* (1975). She made these works danced operas, giving the singing characters choreographic alter-egos whose movements expressed those characters' feelings.

Later in 1975, Bausch created a well-received *Sacre du Printemps*, conceiving Stravinsky's ballet as a violent sacrificial ritual performed on a stage covered with earth. As the dancers moved, the dirt churned up by their actions stuck to their costumes and was smeared on their bodies. The sheer physicality of these characters and their environment was therefore unmistakable. Since *Sacre*, Bausch has repeatedly strewn stages with various kinds of material to make sure that audiences never forget that dancers—indeed, all people—are part of a physical world that can be nasty as well as beautiful.

A man did indeed play an operatic tape in *Bluebeard Listening to a Tape Recording of Béla Bartók's Opera, "Bluebeard's Castle."* He constantly stopped and restarted the recording, compulsively repeating passages. He listened to this music in a setting that depicted a shabby house with a floor covered with dead leaves that may have symbolized crumbling emotions and a dead marriage. That man tormented a woman; she, in turn, fought with him. The stage filled with an ensemble of tormenting and tormented lovers who often moved in a deliberately ungainly manner.

With *Bluebeard*, as this piece of 1977 is usually called for short, Bausch articulated many of the themes that were to preoccupy her for the next two decades: sexual warfare, lust for power, loneliness, frustration, dread. She soon discarded both overtly mythological references (Iphigenia, Orpheus) and direct parallels to familiar stories (Bluebeard). Instead, she favored scenes from daily life and encouraged her dancers to discuss in rehearsals relevant episodes from their own lives or those of their friends and relatives. Speaking of her choreographic process, she has said that she always begins by asking dancers questions. In one instance, she recalled, "I might have asked them about Christmas. I always ask about Christmas—well not always, but fairly often. Each time it's a different question. This time everybody in the company described Christmas dinner, the things they normally eat. Yesterday I asked if anyone had ever been so frightened they'd messed their pants and when was the first time they'd felt they were a man or woman." [13]

Out of such probings little dance sequences develop which in the finished production sometimes follow one another like scenes in a revue and at other times are juxtaposed like images in a cinematic montage. The performers often speak as well as move, and Bausch has frequently had them descend from the stage and wander through the aisles of the theatre so that spectators may realize that theatrical reality is a microcosm of all reality, including that of the audience.

Kontakthof (1978) showed lonely people meeting in some shabby ballroom or community center. The way they kept preening revealed their tendency to treat their bodies as subjects on display (and, possibly, also to be bought and sold).

An enormous hippopotamus (actually, a construction guided by people inside it) waddled about in *Arien* (1979), for which Bausch flooded the stage with water, through which the dancers had to splash. The water variously became both a symbol of the life force and an obstacle that bedraggled the performers as they contended with it.

Turf covered the stage in *1980* (named after the year of its composition). Its multitude of scenes emphasized childhood memories, social rituals, and the process of growing old; in addition to dancing, the members of Bausch's multinational company talked about themselves and their backgrounds. Whereas *1980* was comic in a bittersweet manner, *Carnations* (1983) was harsh. The stage was a field of hundreds of flowers. But they were guarded by ominous watchdogs; as they moved through them, the dancers trampled the flowers underfoot, an action that could be interpreted as a kinetic metaphor for a loss of innocence.

Bausch has attracted critical acclaim and vituperation around the world. Her supporters tend to praise her for developing a new form of Expressionist and dramatic (if not necessarily narrative) dance. However, one German admirer takes another view: according to Norbert Servos, "By simultaneously repelling literary constraints and concretizing the abstraction of dance, the Wuppertal Dance Theater made dance—perhaps for the first time in its history—aware of itself, emancipated it to its own modes." [14] Such words might surprise or even amuse students of dance history, for, over the years, comparable claims have been made for *Ausdruckstanz*, Absolute Dance,

George Balanchine's abstractions, and Merce Cunningham's treatment of the elements of a dance production as independent entities. Nevertheless, Servos's remarks are a salutary reminder that, despite their spoken texts and scenic effects, Bausch's productions create their impact primarily through movement. For Bausch, *Tanztheater* is indeed dance, as well as theatre.

Reinhild Hoffmann (b. 1943), another prominent exponent of *Tanztheater*, came to dance late, enrolling at the Folkwang School when she was twenty-one. She credits the teaching of Jooss and the theories of Laban as major influences upon her career. Hoffmann began to choreograph in 1975 and has headed companies in Bremen and Bochum. Like Bausch, she is concerned with power struggles, social conventions, and the freedoms and restrictions of individual behavior within accepted social patterns. Also like Bausch, her group works often consist of scenes arranged in a collagelike manner. However, unlike Bausch, she does not have her dancers talk.

Describing her choreographic process, she said:

> I love watching. Sitting in a restaurant, when I see someone at the next table, a story begins. Details of where a person comes from and where he's headed for are woven about him, and I think the imagination would not develop so far if the person were to rise and address me. What is mute fascinates me. That's why I've never really used speech on stage. . . . Speech would take away the mystery surrounding a person.[15]

Hoffmann has created solos for herself over the years and has performed solo programs. In many of these solos, objects take on symbolic functions. As Hoffmann slides from a sofa onto the floor and toward the audience in *Solo with Sofa*, it soon grows evident that her dress and the sofa cover are all part of one enormous piece of cloth. She battles with this entangling material, but it resists her and seems to triumph over her, pulling her back to the sofa, which is, in effect, part of herself, something that ties her down. In *Stones*, Hoffmann collects stones and puts them in slings attached to her body; gradually, they so weight her that she has to drag herself forward. She carries two yard-long boards on her back in *Boards*; they make her body imposing to behold, yet limit her mobility.

Hoffmann has also staged large-scale *Tanztheater* productions. *Weed Garden* (1981) examined relationships between members of a family. In one scene, a son kills his domineering mother, then puts on her gown and gloves and takes her place beside his father, dominating him just as she did. *Erwartung/Pierrot Lunaire* (1982) was set to two Expressionist vocal works by Arnold Schoenberg. Hoffmann had an opera singer portray the heroine in *Erwartung*, which shows a woman searching for her lover in a forest and finding him dead. But Hoffmann also surrounded her with dancers representing the fancies of her anguished imagination. She matched Schoenberg's bizarre fantasies in *Pierrot Lunaire* with equally strange choreographic episodes, including one in which a pregnant transvestite gives birth to yards of cloth which cover the stage.

Callas (1984) is not a straightforward biography of the singer Maria Callas, but a phantasmagoric set of images of her career that show the professional problems she had to face and the artistic insensitivity of affluent Philistines. Although inspired by fairy-tale motifs, *Machandel* (1987) is no sweet fantasy. Rather, it serves as a reminder that many of the Grimms' tales are grim indeed, and Hoffmann has choreographed scenes involving lurking dangers, abandonment, abduction, and parental cruelty. *Machandel* emphasizes the fear as well as the wonder, and the terror as well as the magic, of fairy tales.

Susanne Linke (b. 1944) is yet another important choreographer to have emerged from the Folkwang. She also has ties to the Wigman tradition. Because she contracted meningitis as a small child, she was unable to speak until she was six. Movement fascinated her, and she studied gymnastics. Then, in 1964, she entered the Wigman School in Berlin, remaining there until 1967. Linke calls Mary Wigman "by far the strongest person I ever met in my life. . . . With her, everything you did had to have a spiritual basis." Linke was too young to have seen Wigman dance and knew her only as teacher and mentor. But she did see Dore Hoyer perform, and Hoyer's concerts profoundly impressed her: "My solo dance evenings—that's Dore Hoyer's influence." [16]

Linke came to Essen in 1967 to study at the Folkwang. She was a member of its performing group, the Folkwang Tanzstudio, becoming its co-director, with Reinhild Hoffmann, in 1975 and its sole director in 1977. She has choreographed for various companies and has presented solo programs in Europe and North and South America.

Among her group works is *Ruhr-Ort* (1991), a large-scale production that depicts life in a grimy steel works in the German industrial area of which Essen is a part. Linke's laborers are seen doing actual work movements, hammering away on a steel plate and hauling aluminum bars. They are also shown in the washroom and at ease on a cigarette break.

Linke is best known internationally for her solos. *Schritte Verfolgen* (*Retracing Stages of Development*, 1986), her own autobiography in movement, shows a stumbling child trying to overcome a handicap and eventually finding freedom through dance. In her evenings of various short solos, she, like other *Tanztheater* choreographers, is concerned with the struggles between one's self and one's surroundings. *Bath Tubbing* is a portrait of a woman dominated by an object: a bathtub which she scrubs compulsively. She also balances on its edge, slides in and out of it, lifts and tilts it, and gets trapped under it. This woman is obsessed by the tub. Yet, though she cleanses it, she never allows herself to be cleansed by it.

Analyzing her choreography, Linke says each of her solos is

> a battle to stay upright, not to fall, although I fall all the time . . . I only realized later that my solos always involve water. Water gives me a feeling of security, that I am being buoyed up, that I don't need to stand. And don't quite sink. But I must also be active to stay afloat. . . .
>
> Death is really the thing that fascinates me most. Death is always an element in my pieces, although not really obviously, because people don't want to see such things.[17]

Several of Linke's solos combine death and water images. In *Transfiguration*, to the last movement of Schubert's "Death and the Maiden Quartet," Linke appears to be drowning in currents of water, and in *Flood*, after laboriously unrolling a bolt of fabric, she lets it ripple and then plunges into it.

Linke has also revived some of Dore Hoyer's solos. She thereby calls attention to the relationships between *Tanztheater* and *Ausdruckstanz*.

The power of the best examples of *Tanztheater* is undeniable. Yet even some of that dance form's admirers are occasionally disturbed by its peculiar obsessions. Although *Tanztheater* choreographers claim they are basing their productions upon human experience, it can be argued that they regularly ignore whole areas of experience.

Tanztheater offers many images of power struggles, family tensions, sexual rivalries, and social repression. But little attention is paid to maternal love, conjugal affection, loyal friendships, religious devotion unaccompanied by fanaticism, selfless ethical or political idealism, and sensual pleasure devoid of debauchery.

Several factors may account for this. As dramatists from Aeschylus to Samuel Beckett have known, the theatrical depiction of human misery can inspire profound musings about the meaning of existence. The *Tanztheater* choreographers follow in this tradition. Moreover, German choreographers are acutely aware that the achievements of great dance artists before them were corrupted by the Nazis and that some of those dancers and choreographers were willing to collaborate with the forces of fascism. The *Ausdruckstanz* choreographers sometimes created symbolic visions of destiny, power, and momentous struggles, and the Nazis were quick to interpret them according to their own ideology.

Tanztheater choreographers are also concerned with power: not, however, on a lofty symbolic plane, but in the gritty reality of everyday life. *Tanztheater* can therefore act as an ongoing act of social criticism that will not let Germans—or anyone else tempted by power—forget bitter truths. As Susanne Linke has remarked, "The German people are torn. They're a focal point of wars, too full of conflict. We are a grand people, but so full of ambivalence. Where there's a lot of light, there's a lot of shadow." [18]

It is surely significant that another grotesque form of dance developed in another great nation defeated in World War II: Japan. That Butoh, as this form is known, is often hallucinatory and violent may also be attributed to the fact that, in addition to being attacked with conventional weapons, the Japanese cities of Hiroshima and Nagasaki were destroyed in atomic bomb raids and the survivors of those bombings were exposed to nuclear radiation. Butoh is a response to a post-Hiroshima world.

But it is not the only form of Japanese modern dance. Thanks to pupils of Mary Wigman, including Takaya Eguchi, German modern dance was known to some extent in Japan before the war. With the coming of peace, American modern dancers taught in Japan. One of the results was what could be called a cosmopolitan style. Speaking of many Japanese modern dancers of the 1980s, the critic Miyabi Ichikawa declared that "their work is the result of global modernization. Tokyo, New York, Paris—all the metropolitan cities—have more in common with each other than with rural areas in their own countries.... Also, remember that originality is not an important aspect of our culture, as it is in America." [19]

Butoh certainly cannot fit that description. Whatever else it may or may not be, Butoh is undeniably "original." Butoh is often translated as "dark soul" dance, and its productions have been called living nightmares. Tatsumi Hijikata, one of the founders of Butoh, referred to his style as Ankoku Butoh, by which he meant "black" or "dark dance," in the sense that this type of dance emphasized taboo topics that could not ordinarily be mentioned in polite society.[20] The Butoh choreographers were inspired both by the destructive forces of the modern world and by the demons of their own folklore and traditions. These choreographers were deliberately rebellious and often had their dancers stick out their tongues at the audience, a subversive act in etiquette-conscious Japan. So, too, the convulsive quality of Butoh movements, even in productions that concerned rebirth as well as destruction, could be viewed as a rejection of the refined concepts of beauty associated with traditional Japanese art.

In 1959, Tatsumi Hijikata devised a choreographic version of Yukio Mishima's homoerotic novel *Forbidden Colors* which included a scene in which a male dancer had sex with a chicken squeezed between his thighs before yielding to the amorous advances of Hijikata. For his *Rose Dance* of 1965, Hijikata painted his back to look as if the skin had been peeled aside to reveal the organs underneath. Hijikata's *Rhapsody in Futashimaya* began with a child playing on the floor and moving freely, but he was then transformed into a rigid doll. The accompaniment was "The Swan," the same piece by Camille Saint-Saëns to which Fokine choreographed *The Dying Swan*. In a sense, both choreographers were concerned with death: Fokine with physical death, Hijikata with the death of the spirit caused by rigid social codes.

Still another choreographer, Min Tanaka, traveled the length of Japan in 1977, dancing every day, naked and usually outdoors, in an effort to feel the differences in the ground beneath his feet. He called this composition—part dance, part penitential ritual—*Hyperdance*.[21]

Two Butoh companies which have traveled widely outside Japan are Dai Rakuda Kan, founded in 1972 by Akaji Maro, and Sankai Juku, founded in 1975 by Ushio Amagatsu, a former member of Maro's group.

Dai Rakuda Kan startled audiences at the 1982 American Dance Festival with *Sea-Dappled Horse*, which, for the dance writer Annalyn Swan, appeared to take place in "some primordial bog" populated by, among other creatures, "a filthy and autistic samurai," a chorus line of women "dressed in long formal gowns, whose mouths open in silent screams and whose eyes stare wildly," and an assortment of writhing men and women clad in nothing but G-strings.[22]

Among Amagatsu's best-known productions for Sankai Juku are *Kinkan Shonen* (1978), a phantasmagoria that combines myths with memories of growing up in Japan, and *Jomon Sho* (1982), an evocation of prehistory that begins when four dancers, looking like seed pods or cocoons, are lowered head downward toward the stage with ropes attached to their ankles. Sankai Juku has become famous for this sequence; the troupe has occasionally performed it outdoors, with the dancers lowered from the tops of buildings—on one occasion in 1985 with fatal consequences to one of the dancers.

Not all Butoh choreographers are preoccupied with theatrical violence. Kazuo Ohno (b. 1906) is revered as one of the elder statesmen of Japanese dance. Ohno has stated that "the world of Butoh must be that of the mother's womb."[23] He was inspired to study dance when he saw a performance by the great Spanish dancer La Argentina in 1928; he was later profoundly influenced by Kreutzberg.

He paid tribute to La Argentina in 1977 when he choreographed *Admiring Argentina*, a ninety-minute solo in which he wore feminine apparel, thereby finding a contemporary use for the old Japanese theatrical convention of female impersonation. The elderly Ohno performed wisps of passionate and coquettish Spanish dance, yet never looked incongruous doing so. Rather, it was as if he were a medium at a séance summoning up a great artistic spirit from the past.

Modern dance companies have been established in other Asian countries, including the People's Republic of China.[24] That nation's cultural expression is controlled by the government, which at various times has been unsympathetic to foreign influences. Yet in 1986 Yan Mei-qi, principal of the Guangdong Academy of Dance in Guangzhou (the former Canton), was able to visit the American Dance Festival in North Carolina and ask Charles Reinhart, the festival's director, for assistance in establishing a modern dance department at her school. The students who graduated in 1990 formed the nucleus of China's first modern dance company, which made its debut on 28 July 1990.

Other choreographers also showed interest in modern dance. In 1988, Hu Jia-lu, resident choreographer of the First Ensemble of the Shanghai Dance Drama Theater, presented a program of works choreographed in the modern idiom; a year later, he studied at the Graham School in New York. Among Hu's creations are *A Country Track*, a love story which shows the influence of Western pop dance forms; *Soliloquy*, a symbolic drama in which a patient and a surgeon exchange places; and *Rope Waves*, a depiction of a family conflict in which a ball, representing a child, is tossed back and forth by quarrelsome parents and then sent into the audience.

Modern dance continues to flourish in Canada. David Earle, Patricia Beatty, and Peter Randazzo, three choreographers influenced by Martha Graham, established the Toronto Dance Theater in 1968. The company was forced to struggle for financial security and audience comprehension. Yet it managed to persist. Since the 1980s, it has presented the works of Christopher House, whose compositional energy and clarity quickly established him as one of Canada's finest young choreographers. House became artistic director in 1994.

Other choreographers associated with Toronto include Daniel Williams Grossman and Robert Desrosiers. Grossman, a San Francisco-born former member of Paul Taylor's company, established his own Canadian troupe in 1978, and his dances range from witty and athletic pieces to social and political commentaries. Desrosiers, a former member of the National Ballet of Canada (to which he has returned as a choreographer), favors extravagant, almost Surrealist, stage effects.

Anna Wyman, an important choreographer on Canada's West Coast, founded her Anna Wyman Dance Theater in Vancouver in 1971. An Austrian-born dancer originally trained in ballet and later influenced by Laban's theories, Wyman came to specialize in productions that made elaborate use of props, films, and lasers.

Montreal has continued to be a vital center of dance activity. Its choreographers have questioned the values of traditional Quebec society, while at the same time proclaiming a Québécois identity. Both Paul-André Fortier and Edouard Lock have created forceful works about sexual power struggles. Lock, in particular, is associated with frenzied and physically risky dances to loud pop music. Ginette Laurin creates gravity-defying choreography, and her troupe is appropriately called O Vertigo Danse. Margie Gillis is known for emotionally charged solos, Jean-Pierre Perreault for somber ritualistic dances. A love of ritual is also apparent in the dreamlike creations of Marie Chouinard. In contrast, Linda Rabin's compositions have tended to be structured, severe, and abstract.[25]

Modern dance continues to develop in Australia and New Zealand. Australian Dance Theater was founded in Adelaide in 1965 by Elizabeth Cameron Dalman, a jazz and modern dance teacher who had studied in Essen at the Folkwang and with Leslie White, a ballet teacher who was a former member of the Royal Ballet. In its first seasons, the company was eclectic, presenting classical, jazz, and modern works. The group has been reorganized several times since then and has become basically modern-dance oriented.

Several Australian and New Zealand dancers who have worked abroad have returned to choreograph in their native lands—for instance, Meryl Tankard, an Australian-born former member of Pina Bausch's troupe, and Douglas Wright, a New Zealand dancer who performed with Paul Taylor.

Australia's Sydney Dance Company has attracted considerable international attention. The present organization is an outgrowth of the Dance Company of New South Wales, founded in 1965 by Suzanne Musitz, at that time a soloist with the Australian Ballet. At first it devoted itself to giving demonstrations in schools, but after 1971 it also offered programs for adults. In 1975, Musitz was succeeded by Jaap Flier, a former member of Netherlands Dance Theater; under the direction of Flier and his wife, the dancer and teacher Willy de la Bye (who had previously served as a director of Australian Dance Theater in one of its periods of reorganization), works by John Butler, Anna Sokolow, and Glen Tetley were brought into the repertoire. The Fliers returned to Europe in 1976.

They were succeeded by Graeme Murphy, a young Australian dancer and choreographer who had performed with the Australian Ballet; Janet Vernon, another former member of the Australian Ballet, was named assistant director. The group was renamed Sydney Dance Company in 1979 and made its New York debut in 1981. Like such groups as Netherlands Dance Theater and the Rambert company, the Sydney troupe expects its dancers to be acquainted with both classical and modern techniques.

It offers works by several choreographers. However, Murphy's choreography provides it with its own distinct artistic personality. Its dancers are as good-looking as film stars or fashion models, its productions are always well designed, and Murphy delights in audacious theatrical touches.

His *Poppy* (1981) is a phantasmagoric depiction of Jean Cocteau's life and focuses upon his opium addiction. In Murphy's modern-dress interpretation of Ravel's *Daphnis and Chloë* (1980) Cupid rolls in on a skateboard and the pirates are members of a motorcycle gang. *Some Rooms* (1983) features scenes in which a man moves through rooms including a bedroom, a bathroom, a locker room, and a library. *After Venice* (1984) is loosely based on *Death in Venice,* Thomas Mann's novella about an aging writer's ultimately fatal obsession with a young boy. However, in the dance version the youth looks considerably more worldly and sexually omnivorous than Mann's character, so that it becomes possible to speculate that the writer became infected with AIDS as a result of his infatuation.

Modern dance has taken root throughout the world, and it is impossible to predict where it will flower next. It has shown signs of growth in areas as remote from one another as Asia, South America, and Eastern Europe and Russia, especially now that those formerly Communist nations have abandoned the politically based esthetic that formerly prevailed as orthodoxy.

The varied manifestations of modern dance draw upon the history and traditions of the countries in which it flourishes, but choreographers are also open to foreign influences. Modern dance has allied itself on occasion with other dance forms, including ballet. Yet it repeatedly and proudly proclaims its independence everywhere.

CONCLUSION:
THE UNDEFINABLE
REDEFINING ART

MODERN DANCE THRIVES, AND IT KEEPS GROWING AND changing. It has always been much too varied to fit into any single narrow definition. Indeed, its capacity to change and redefine itself is a sign of its creative health. Speaking of significant manifestations of all twentieth-century arts, Sheldon Cheney noted in 1934 that "our whole temper, as Moderns, impels us to resist the ideas of setness, limitation, and finality."[1] Scores of dancers today would still agree with him.

Modern dance's most bitter opponents distrust such openness, and the view that modern dance lacks a tradition and is somehow so amorphous and free-form as to be chaotic persists in some circles, especially among diehard balletomanes. Yet modern dancers did not spring from nowhere. A few modern dancers, especially in the earlier days of the art, could be considered largely self-taught. Most others, however, have pedagogical pedigrees.

Indeed, it is possible to draw up sturdy esthetic family trees. Duncanism may have been technically limited. Nevertheless, just as Anna Pavlova inspired ballet dancers, Isadora inspired modern dancers, and her "Isadorables" grew up to become teachers and to preserve her repertoire. Raymond Duncan directly influenced Margaret Morris, Valeria Dienes, and Akarova. Dalcroze or his eurhythmic theories helped form Maggie Gripenberg, Mary Wigman, Michio Ito, Yvonne Georgi, Rosalia Chladek, and Meredith Monk. From the Wigman School came Vera Skoronel, Harald Kreutzberg, Gret Palucca,

Yvonne Georgi, and Hanya Holm, to mention a few prominent names. Martha Graham, Doris Humphrey, and Charles Weidman studied at Denishawn. The Graham School has had an incalculable effect upon several generations of American dancers, as well as upon dance in Israel, Great Britain, and beyond. The London Contemporary Dance School has done much important work of its own to shape the course of British dance. Considerable influence has also been exerted by the New York schools of Merce Cunningham and Erick Hawkins (both former Graham dancers) and Alwin Nikolais (a pupil of Holm).

Even some of modern dance's most idiosyncratic figures did not arise out of thin air. Merle Marsicano and Mattie Haim studied with Graham; Midi Garth with Graham, with Louis Horst, and at the New Dance Group. Sybil Shearer danced with the Humphrey-Weidman Company. Anna Halprin, who also worked with Humphrey, was a product of Margaret H'Doubler's dance department at the University of Wisconsin. Pina Bausch came from the Folkwang.

Many modern dancers have been trained in other arts—and even in purely scholarly fields (notably Valeria Dienes, who held a degree in philosophy, and Katherine Dunham and Pearl Primus, who studied anthropology). Gus Solomons, Jr., was once an architecture student. Merce Cunningham and Yvonne Rainer worked in theatre. Kurt Jooss studied theatre and music. Other musically trained choreographers include Maud Allan, Michio Ito, Gertrud Kraus, Yvonne Georgi, and Asadata Dafora. Several choreographers have composed their own scores: among them, in recent years, Alwin Nikolais, Meredith Monk, and Laura Dean. A remarkable number of modern dancers were once art students: to name only a few, Rudolf Laban, Oskar Schlemmer, Harald Kreutzberg, Alexandre Sakharoff, Angna Enters, Uday Shankar, José Limón, Paul Taylor, Richard Alston, and Siobhan Davies.

The moderns have always emphasized that their dance is an adult art for adult audiences (not that children cannot enjoy much of it, as well). But so is ballet at its best. And Diaghilev's Ballets Russes is one of the most important experimental companies in the entire history of dance. Why, then, did the moderns—many of whom had studied ballet, and many of whom continue to study ballet—not remain with that form? A glib answer is that some of those dancers started ballet training too late to succeed in a ballet company or had bodies that did not conform to companies' physical ideals, but that is not enough.

The moderns became modern dancers out of inner necessity. The most creative ones still do. The fact that, over the decades, such dancers as Isadora Duncan, Ruth St. Denis, Margaret Morris, Ruby Ginner, the Wiesenthal Sisters, Martha Graham, Doris Humphrey, Erick Hawkins, and Paul Taylor investigated ballet, only to reject it, surely says something both about their inquisitive, questing spirit and about the limitations of ballet (at least, the ballet they knew). If dancers of such diverse styles and temperaments found ballet unsatisfactory, then, it can be argued, there must have been a problem with ballet. So too, of course, the fact that such modern dance choreographers as Yvonne Georgi, Birgit Cullberg, Aurel Milloss, and Glen Tetley devoted much of their later careers to ballet companies serves as a reminder that choreographic tastes are complex and capable of change and that ballet is not necessarily a closed system.

As far back as 1902, Genevieve Stebbins commented on the necessity of balancing technique and expression:

> When before the public in the pulpit, on the platform, or the stage, forget all rules, or rather make no effort to recall them. Your motto there should be "heart work, not headwork."
>
> "Then why study art's rules and formulae?" I hear you ask.
>
> Because much of your practice will cling to you, without conscious thought; because nature rarely showers all her gifts on one head. Inspiration may be yours without bodily power to express; or you may be virtuosos without the still small voice within.[2]

From time to time, words—for instance, *Ausdruckstanz*, Absolute Dance, and *Tanztheater*—have attempted to describe some of the dialects in which that "still small voice" can speak. Yet such terms are only provisional. Even such a recently coined term as "postmodern dance" is not as helpful as it promised to be, for debates continue to arise over its meaning.

However, if postmodern implies a critique of, or an alternative to, a dance form regarded as "modern," then, it can be argued, all manifestations of modern dance and its offshoots have provided that throughout modern dance history, from the time when Martha Graham, Doris Humphrey, and Helen Tamiris disdained the decorative choreography of Duncan and Denishawn to the rebellion of the Judson dancers against both dramatic dance and excessively polished technique.

Choreographic contemporaries as well as successive generations often serve as artistic counterweights to one another. In the late 1920s and early 1930s, one could contrast the austere Graham to the flamboyant Tamiris; in Germany, other contrasts could be made between the emotionally strong, but seldom literally dramatic Mary Wigman, the vigorous abstractions of Gret Palucca, and the specifically dramatic character sketches of Valeska Gert. In more recent years, Paul Taylor's eclecticism has been balanced by Merce Cunningham's unwavering fidelity to one form of abstraction; and the haunting and mysterious dramas of Eiko and Koma and Meredith Monk are countered by the brilliant patterning of Lucinda Childs and Laura Dean. Modern dance bears witness to what dogmatic art critics and historians often overlook: the fact that "the works of art created in any given period seldom fall into the conventional categories of art history."[3]

The works of each gifted choreographer, in effect, constitute a model of what dance can be. All of these models enrich the culture of the time, yet all prove inadequate and are eventually superseded by new models or by invigorating renovations of older ones. As John Martin put it in 1930, "It is in the very nature of the arts that the ultimate can never be realized."[4]

Throughout his writing career, Martin insisted that modern dance was not so much a technique as a point of view. Modern dance certainly continues to encourage individual viewpoints and offers many types of choreographic models. Conceivably, one reason why ballet in the late twentieth century has often seemed lacking in choreographic excitement is a lack of a variety of models to be accepted or rejected by newer choreographers; thus American ballet is dominated by the example of George Balanchine, who, though a masterful choreographer, was also only human and therefore imperfect.

Just as modern dance emphasizes a multitude of choreographic viewpoints, so, too, it has developed several systems of training, including those associated with such seminal figures as Wigman, Jooss, Graham, Humphrey, Weidman, Holm, Nikolais, Hawkins, and Cunningham. Contrary to what might be feared, this abundance of training methods rarely confuses dancers, and students frequently study several techniques. Technical pluralism and choreographic diversity call attention to the manifold and, by implication, still unexploited possibilities of dance as an art. Moreover, some of these techniques—for instance, those of Graham and Cunningham—are so highly developed that their advocates can claim, without undue exaggeration, that modern dance has attained in less than a century a level of technical complexity comparable to that which it took ballet several centuries to achieve.

Yet modern dancers have, in general, tended to view technical expertise as a means to expression, rather than as an end in itself. When, as happened in the 1960s, some younger choreographers thought that certain styles and techniques had become too set and too ornate, those older ways of moving were rejected, and the rebels sought out first principles on which to build anew. At worst, such cycles of rejection and reconstruction can leave modern dance susceptible to faddism. Fortunately, at the same time, the most talented modern dancers have been acutely aware of their art's genuine challenges. The painter Robert Henri once noted that what each artist eventually leaves behind is "so much for others to use as stones to step on or stones to avoid."[5] The modern dancers continue to bequeath newer generations both stepping-stones toward fresh achievements and memorials to outdated causes.

For all their determined individualism and their occasionally ferocious rivalries, they have done so in a remarkably cordial manner. Ever since American teachers imported Delsartian ideas from Europe and such Americans as Loïe Fuller, Isadora Duncan, Maud Allan, and Ruth St. Denis found fame in Europe, modern dancers have crossed political, as well as artistic, boundaries with ease. National styles do arise in modern dance. Nevertheless, the art has tended to be internationalist in outlook. When its development has been stunted, the causes are not so much esthetic crises as political catastrophes like the outbreak of World War I or the rise of Hitlerism— all of which fostered an excessive and unhealthy nationalism.

The protean qualities of modern dance make it an enemy of all dogmas. It may therefore be an art needed in the kind of world free of despotic absolutes that the Czechoslovak playwright and statesman Václav Havel envisions when he writes:

> Things must once more be given a chance to present themselves as they are, to be perceived in their individuality. We must see the pluralism of the world, and not bind it by seeking common denominators or reducing everything to a single common equation.
>
> We must try harder to understand than to explain. The way forward is not in the mere construction of universal systemic solutions, to be

applied to reality from the outside; it is also in the seeking to get to the heart of reality through personal experience. Such an approach promotes an atmosphere of tolerant solidarity and unity in diversity based on mutual respect, genuine pluralism and parallelism. In a word, human uniqueness, human action and the human spirit must be rehabilitated.[6]

Modern dance has always been an art built on uniqueness, particularity, and personal experience. Its history is a reminder that all arts can change their courses and that people can change their minds and their visions.

NOTES

INDELIBLE EPHEMERAL

1. Taylor quotation from Selma Jeanne Cohen, ed., *The Modern Dance*, p. 101; Dupuy quotation from Jacqueline Robinson, *L'Aventure de la Danse Moderne en France (1920–1970)*, p. 11.
2. Cohen, *The Modern Dance*, p. 21.
3. Barnes quotation from Anne Livet, ed., *Contemporary Dance*, p. 28; Paul Taylor, *Private Domain*, p. 40.
4. Lists of names and commentary on them can be found in Elizabeth Selden, *Elements of the Free Dance*, p. 3; and Valerie Preston-Dunlop and Susanne Lahusen, eds., *Schrifttanz*, p. 2.
5. Ernst Schur, *Der Moderne Tanz*, p. 3; Sachetto program in Dance Collection of New York Public Library for the Performing Arts.
6. J. E. Crawford Flitch, *Modern Dancing and Dancers*, p. 9; Caroline Caffin and Charles H. Caffin, *Dancing and Dancers of Today*, p. 3.

SETTING THE STAGE

1. Emerson quotation from *Selections from Ralph Waldo Emerson*, ed. Stephen E. Whicher (Boston: Houghton Mifflin Company, 1960), p. 350.
2. The quotation from William Merritt Chase and the basic information about world's fairs come from caption material for "Paris 1889," an exhibition at the New-York Historical Society, 5 September–15 November 1990; Isadora Duncan quotation from Irma Duncan and Allan Ross Macdougall, *Isadora Duncan's Russian Days*, p. 7.
3. Further information about physical education can be found in Ann Barzel, "European Dance Teachers in the United States," *Dance Index* 3:4–6 (April–June 1944): 72; Valerie Preston-Dunlop and Susanne Lahusen, eds., *Schrifttanz*, pp. 47–48; Richard Kraus and Sarah Alberti Chapman, *History of the Dance in Art and Education*, pp. 108–120; Nancy Lee Chalfa Ruyter, *Reformers and Visionaries*, pp. 90–103.

4. Genevieve Stebbins, *Delsarte System of Expression*, p. 485; the condition of women is also discussed by Elizabeth Kendall in *Where She Danced* (see especially pp. 3–9, 18–19).

5. Ruyter comments on the theatrical scene in *Reformers and Visionaries*, pp. 8–10.

O PIONEERS!

1. Information about Fuller's dances can be found in Sally R. Sommer, "Loïe Fuller's Art of Music and Light," *Dance Chronicle* 4:4 (1981): 389–401; "The Sitter Out," *Dancing Times* (May 1921): 640; "The Sitter Out," *Dancing Times* (March 1923): 600; Fuller's autobiography is *Fifteen Years of a Dancer's Life*.

2. The Baum quotations are taken from the 1979 reprint of *The Road to Oz* (New York: Ballantine Books), pp. 48, 159.

3. Skirt dancing is discussed in J. E. Crawford Flitch, *Modern Dancing and Dancers*, pp. 71–79; Artur Michel, "Kate Vaughan, or the Poetry of the Skirt Dance," *Dance Magazine* (January 1945): 12–13, 29–32, and "Skirt Dancing," *Dancing Times* (December 1916): 76–77.

4. "Loïe Fuller, World Famous Dancer Answers Last Curtain Call," *American Dancer* (February 1928): 10.

5. Basic information about Delsarte can be found in Ted Shawn, *Every Little Movement*; Genevieve Stebbins, *Delsarte System of Expression*; Minna Curtiss, *Bizet and His World*.

6. Shawn, *Every Little Movement*, p. 22.

7. Stebbins, *Delsarte System of Expression*, p. 383.

8. Shawn, *Every Little Movement*, p. 28.

9. Stebbins, *Delsarte System of Expression*, p. 257.

10. Stebbins, *Delsarte System of Expression*, p. 392.

ISADORA DUNCAN, HELLENISM, AND BEAUTY

1. Isadora Duncan, *My Life*, pp. 15–16.

2. Nancy Lee Chalfa Ruyter discusses Duncan's training in *Reformers and Visionaries*, pp. 34–35, as does Victor Seroff in *The Real Isadora*, pp. 22, 26.

3. Duncan, *My Life*, p. 34.

4. Duncan, *My Life*, pp. 49, 52.

5. Edward Gordon Craig, *The Theatre—Advancing*, pp. 233–234.

6. Robert Henri, *The Art Spirit*, p. 34.

7. A detailed study of Duncan's programming is found in June Layson, "Isadora Duncan—A Preliminary Analysis of Her Work," *Dance Research* 1:1 (Spring 1983): 39–49.

8. This point is discussed by Elizabeth Selden in *Elements of the Free Dance*, pp. 90–93.

9. Duncan's Hellenism is discussed by Ruyter in *Reformers and Visionaries*, pp. 37–38.

10. Whitman's poem can be found in standard editions of *Leaves of Grass*.

11. Duncan, *My Life*, p. 72.

12. Layson, "Isadora Duncan," pp. 43–44.

13. Layson, "Isadora Duncan," p. 44.

14. Paul Magriel includes Carl van Vechten's description of the *Marseillaise* solo

and *Marche Slave* in the Duncan section of *Nijinsky, Pavlova, Duncan*, pp. 30 – 31 (the volume's three sections, originally published separately, have separate pagination).

15. Titterton quotation from J. E. Crawford Flitch, *Modern Dancing and Dancers*, p. 110.
16. Duncan, *My Life*, p. 56.
17. Jacqueline Robinson, *L'Aventure de la Danse Moderne en France*, pp. 59 – 60.
18. Donald Spoto, *Madcap*, p. 26.
19. John D. Cook, "Raymond Duncan," *Opera and Concert* (April 1948): 23.
20. Oscar Wolfe, "Raymond Duncan the Executive," *Dance Magazine* (February 1930): 50; Cook, "Raymond Duncan," p. 24; Robinson, *L'Aventure*, pp. 56 – 59.
21. Program file, New York Public Library Dance Collection.
22. Obituary, *New York Times*, 17 August 1966.
23. Flitch, *Modern Dancing and Dancers*, pp. 103 – 104.
24. Flitch, *Modern Dancing and Dancers*, pp. 119 – 120.
25. Leonhard M. Fiedler and Martin Lang, *Grete Wiesenthal*, pp. 181 – 182.
26. Caroline Caffin and Charles H. Caffin, *Dancing and Dancers of Today*, p. 254.
27. Morris's autobiography is *My Life in Movement*.
28. P. J. S. Richardson, "The New School of Dancing: Miss Margaret Morris and Her New Technique," *Dancing Times* (May 1917): 246.
29. Morris, *My Life in Movement*, p. 22.
30. "Round the Classes," *Dancing Times* (January 1914): 250.
31. "Paris," *Dancing Times* (May 1913): 515.
32. Basic information about Ginner can be found in Ruby Ginner, "The Revival of the Greek Dance," *Dancing Times* (October 1935): 39 – 41, 44; and M. C., "Obituary: Ruby Ginner," *Dancing Times* (May 1978): 464.
33. "More Displays," *Dancing Times* (June 1917): 287 – 289.
34. Ruby Ginner, "Greek Dancing," *Dancing Times* (January 1921): 329.
35. Information about Paul Swan can be found in the Dance Collection program file and his obituary, *New York Times*, 2 February 1972; see also Walter Terry, *Ted Shawn*, p. 62.
36. Surveys of Allan's career include Felix Cherniavsky, "Maud Allan," *Dance Chronicle*, four installments, 6:1 (1983): 1– 36, 6:3 (1983): 189 – 227, 7:2 (1984): 119 –158, and 8:1– 2 (1985): 1– 50; and Lacy McDearmon, "Maud Allan: The Public Record," *Dance Chronicle*, 2:2 (1978): 85 –105; her own vague autobiography is *My Life and Dancing*. See also Felix Cherniavsky, *The Salome Dancer*.
37. Allan, *My Life and Dancing*, p. 73.
38. Allan, *My Life and Dancing*, pp. 63 – 65.
39. Cherniavsky, "Maud Allan" (I), p. 29.
40. Flitch, *Modern Dancing and Dancers*, p. 117.
41. Flitch, *Modern Dancing and Dancers*, p. 115.
42. Discussions of "Salomania" can be found in Cherniavsky, "Maud Allan" (II), pp. 192, 216 – 217; Deborah Jowitt, *Time and the Dancing Image*, p. 110; Elizabeth Kendall, *Where She Danced*, pp. 74 –76; and Sally R. Sommer, "Loïe Fuller's Art of Music and Light," *Dance Chronicle*, 4:4 (1981): 395.
43. Program file, Dance Collection.
44. Caffin and Caffin, *Dancing and Dancers of Today*, p. 217.

45. Caffin and Caffin, *Dancing and Dancers of Today*, p. 217.

46. Caffin and Caffin, *Dancing and Dancers of Today*, pp. 225–226.

47. Rita Sacchetto, "Symphonic Dance of the Future," *Musical America*, 12 February 1910, p. 2.

RUTH ST. DENIS AND THE EXOTIC

1. Nancy Lee Chalfa Ruyter compares them in *Reformers and Visionaries*, p. 57; useful biographies of St. Denis include Suzanne Shelton, *Divine Dancer*, and Walter Terry, *Miss Ruth*; St. Denis's autobiography is *An Unfinished Life*.

2. Shelton, *Divine Dancer*, p. 6.

3. St. Denis, *An Unfinished Life*, p. 4.

4. Terry, *Miss Ruth*, p. 15.

5. Shelton, *Divine Dancer*, p. 22.

6. Terry, *Miss Ruth*, p. 20.

7. St. Denis's propriety is discussed by Shelton in *Divine Dancer*, p. 23; and Terry in *Miss Ruth*, pp. 30–31.

8. Terry, *Miss Ruth*, p. 37. The poster story is the one told by St. Denis herself in *An Unfinished Life*, pp. 51–52; Shelton (*Divine Dancer*, p. 46) offers a slightly different version in which St. Denis spies the poster in the window of, rather than inside, the drugstore, but she gives no explanation for her variant and immediately follows it with a quotation from *An Unfinished Life*.

9. Shelton, *Divine Dancer*, p. 54.

10. Terry, *Miss Ruth*, pp. 2–3.

11. Quotation translated by Christena L. Schlundt in "Into the Mystic with Miss Ruth," *Dance Perspectives* 46 (Summer 1971): 21.

12. Mark E. Perugini, "Sketches of the Dance and Ballet," *Dancing Times* (November 1912): 76.

13. Schlundt discusses this philosophical tradition in "Into the Mystic with Miss Ruth," pp. 44–45.

14. Information about M'Ahesa can be found in Hans Brandenburg, *Der Moderne Tanz*, pp. 41–44; Karl Ettlinger, "Sent M'Ahesa," *Tanzdrama* 14 (n.d.): 32–34; Kineton Parkes, "Dancing the Emotions: The Art of Sent M'Ahesa," *Dancing Times* (November 1925): 141–143.

15. T. S., "Berlin," *Dancing Times* (May 1927): 163; Ettlinger, "Sent M'Ahesa," pp. 32–34.

16. Information about Magdeleine can be found in J. E. Crawford Flitch, *Modern Dancing and Dancers*, pp. 117–118; and Henry Marx, "Madeleine: Two Reviews," *Drama Review* 22:2 (June 1978): 27–31.

17. Villany's press coverage is reported in *Adorée Villany, Phryné Moderne devant l'Aréopage* (*Sunday Chronicle* review is quoted on p. 48); see also "Paris," *Dancing Times* (March 1913): 391–393; Denby's reminiscence comes from Edwin Denby, *Dance Writings*, p. 17, but no specific date is given for the concert.

DANCING INTO THE FUTURE

1. Information about Dr. Reisner can be found in Walter Terry, *Ted Shawn*, pp. 25–27, 30–31 (where a typographical error renders his name as Riesner); and Rebecca Read Shanor, *The City That Never Was*, pp. 58–64.

2. Ralph Taylor, "Ted Shawn," *Dance Observer* (January 1935): 3.

3. Terry, *Shawn*, p. 11.

4. Deborah Jowitt, *Time and the Dancing Image*, p. 142.

5. Information about Gould can be found in Naima Prevots, *Dancing in the Sun*.

6. Prevots, *Dancing in the Sun*, p. 26.

7. Nancy Lee Chalfa Ruyter, *Reformers and Visionaries*, p. 66.

8. Terry, *Ted Shawn*, pp. 60, 62; and Ted Shawn, *One Thousand and One Night Stands*, p. 26.

9. Walter Terry, *Miss Ruth*, p. 102.

10. Terry, *Ted Shawn*, p. 67.

11. Information about Colby can be found in Ruyter, *Reformers and Visionaries*, pp. 111–115; and Mildred Spiesman, "The Natural Dance Program," *Dance Magazine* (June 1951): 16, 42–45.

12. Marcia B. Siegel, *Days on Earth*, p. 6.

13. Irwin Spector, *Rhythm and Life*, p. 14.

14. Shona Dunlop MacTavish, *An Ecstasy of Purpose*, p. 13.

15. Elsa Findlay, "Lessons with Monsieur Jaques," *Dance Magazine* (August 1965): 41; and Spector, *Rhythm and Life*, p. 70.

16. H. P., "Eurhythmics," *Dancing Times* (May 1926): 189.

17. Susie Lee, "Our Educational Pages," *Dancing Times* (April 1923): 771.

18. Information about these exercises can be found in H.P., "Eurhythmics," pp. 189–191; Lee, "Our Educational Pages," p. 771; Ruyter, *Reformers and Visionaries*, pp. 131–133; "Dancing in the Dark," *Dancing Times* (July 1938): 393; "The Eurhythmics of Jacques [*sic*]-Dalcroze," *Dancing Times* (December 1914): 86–88.

19. Selma Landen Odom, "Wigman at Hellerau," *Ballet Review* 14:2 (Summer 1986): 44.

20. Prevots, *Dancing in the Sun*, p. 180.

21. Ruyter, *Reformers and Visionaries*, p. 133.

22. Valerie Preston-Dunlop and Susanne Lahusen, eds., *Schrifttanz*, p. ix.

23. Further information on eurythmy can be found in Robb Creese, "Anthroposophical Performance," *Drama Review* 22:2 (June 1978): 45–74; and Marjorie Raffé, Cecil Harwood, and Marguerite Lundgren, *Eurythmy and the Impulse of Dance*.

24. Rudolf Laban, *A Life for Dance*, p. 85.

NEW TIMES, NEW ARTS

1. Elizabeth Selden, *The Dancer's Quest*, p. 14.

2. Mary Wigman, "The Central European School of Dance," *Dancing Times* (December 1928): 324.

3. Valerie Preston-Dunlop and Susanne Lahusen, eds., *Schrifttanz*, p. 50.

4. Commentaries on dance and Expressionism include Dianne S. Howe, "The Notion of Mysticism in the Philosophy and Choreography of Mary Wigman 1914–1931," *Dance Research Journal* 19:1 (Summer 1987): 19; Preston-Dunlop and Lahusen, *Schrifttanz*, pp. 2–3.

5. Information about the Dancers' Congresses can be found in Rudolf Laban, *A Life for Dance*, p. 185; Giora Manor, *The Life and Dance of Gertrud Kraus*, pp. 13–18; Preston-Dunlop and Lahusen, *Schrifttanz*, p. 33.

6. Wigman, "The Central European School of Dance," p. 324.

7. Basic information about Laban includes John Foster, *The Influence of Rudolf Laban*; John Hodgson and Valerie Preston-Dunlop, *Rudolf Laban*; Samuel Thornton, *Laban's Theory of Movement*; Laban's autobiography is *A Life for Dance*.

8. Thornton, *Laban's Theory of Movement*, pp. 4–5.

9. Foster, *The Influence of Rudolf Laban*, p. 20.

10. Laban describes these dances in *A Life for Dance: The Deluded*, pp. 95–96; *Gaukelei*, pp. 96–98; *Fool's Mirror*, pp. 3–6.

11. Cornell's program is announced in John Martin, "The Dance," *New York Times*, 17 January 1932; Martin's review appeared in the *New York Times*, 20 January 1932.

12. Thornton, *Laban's Theory of Movement*, pp. 42, 43; Irma Otte-Betz, "The Work of Rudolf von Laban," *Dance Observer* (December 1938): 147; Vera Maletic, "Wigman and Laban: The Interplay of Theory and Practice," *Ballet Review* 14:3 (Fall 1986): 92; Selden, *The Dancer's Quest*, p. 113.

13. Naima Prevots, "Zurich Dada and Dance: Formative Ferment," *Dance Research Journal* 17:1 (Spring–Summer 1985): 5.

14. "Berlin," *Dancing Times* (March 1930): 697.

15. Information about movement choirs can be found in Horst Koegler, "In the Shadow of the Swastika: Dance in Germany, 1927–1936," *Dance Perspectives* 57 (Spring 1974): 4; Laban, *A Life for Dance*, p. 155; Maletic, "Wigman and Laban," pp. 92–93.

Form, feeling, pattern, passion

1. John Martin, *Introduction to the Dance*, p. 230.

2. Basic information on Wigman in English can be found in Mary Wigman, *The Language of Dance* and *The Mary Wigman Book*; and Hedwig Müller, "At the Start of a New Era," *Ballett International* 6:12 (December 1983): 6–13; Müller is also Wigman's German biographer.

3. Wigman, *Language of Dance*, p. 8.

4. The English versions of Wigman's titles are taken from the chronology in *The Language of Dance*, pp. 113–118.

5. Wigman, *Language of Dance*, p. 41.

6. Wigman, *Mary Wigman Book*, p. 138.

7. J. Lewitan, "The Month in Germany," *Dancing Times* (February 1933): 582.

8. Ruth Seinfel, "Congo Drum Booms Rhythm for Miss Wigman's Dances," *New York Times*, 19 January 1931.

9. Wigman, *Mary Wigman Book*, p. 97.

10. Wigman, *Mary Wigman Book*, p. 161.

11. *New York Times*, obituary, 20 September 1973.

12. Martin, *Introduction to the Dance*, p. 235.

13. Virginia Stewart and Merle Armitage, *The Modern Dance*, pp. 100–101.

14. Ruth Page, "Kreutzberg as I Remember Him," *Dance Magazine* (August 1968): 40.

15. Ralph Taylor, "Harald Kreutzberg," *Dance Observer* (April 1935): 40.

16. Doris Hering, "Harald Kreutzberg," *Dance Magazine* (April 1953): 65.

17. Walter Terry, *New York Herald Tribune*, 11 November 1947.

18. J. Lewitan, "The Month in Berlin," *Dancing Times* (April 1932): 20.

19. Etta Linick, "Dance Concerts in Berlin," *American Dancer* (May 1932): 18–19.

20. Hedwig Müller, "Exceeding All Bounds," *Ballett International* 6:3 (March 1983): 24.

21. Müller, "Exceeding All Bounds," p. 22.

22. Hildenbrandt quotation from Müller, "Exceeding All Bounds," p. 22; Gert quotation from Valerie Preston-Dunlop and Susanne Lahusen, eds., *Schrifttanz*, p. 13; "Berlin," *Dancing Times* (December 1929): 281.

23. Grant Code, "Valeska Gert," *Dance Observer* (December 1940): 148; *Vossische Zeitung* quotation translated in advertising flyer for 1940 concerts at the Cherry Lane Theatre, New York City.

24. Müller, "Exceeding All Bounds," p. 25.

25. Müller, "Dance between Ecstasy and Death," *Ballett International* 7:12 (December 1984): 40.

26. Müller, "Exceeding All Bounds," p. 22.

27. "Notes from Central Europe," *Dancing Times* (March 1927): 745.

28. Wigman, *The Mary Wigman Book*, p. 145.

29. J. Lewitan, "The Month in Germany," *Dancing Times* (May 1932): 130–131.

30. J. Lewitan, "The Month in Germany," *Dancing Times* (January 1933): 439.

31. Werner Schuftan, *Manuel de Danse*, p. 60.

32. Rudolf Arnheim, "Visiting Palucca," *Dance Scope* 13:1 (Fall 1978): 6.

33. Wigman, *The Mary Wigman Book*, p. 62.

34. Arnheim, "Visiting Palucca," p. 8.

35. "Berlin," *Dancing Times* (April 1928): 31; Lewitan, "The Month in Germany," *Dancing Times* (January 1933): 439; Linick, "Dance Concerts in Berlin," p. 18.

36. Gret Palucca, "Letter to the Editors," *Dance Observer* (April 1934): 33.

37. Linick, "Dance Concerts in Berlin," p. 18.

38. Arnheim, "Visiting Palucca," p. 9.

39. Arnheim, "Visiting Palucca," pp. 8–9.

40. "Berlin," *Dancing Times* (January 1929): 539.

41. Program note for reconstructions of Schlemmer dances presented by the Kitchen at the Ethnic Folk Art Center, New York City, 30 October–7 November 1982.

42. Descriptions of these dances based on reconstructions presented in New York City by the Kitchen at the Ethnic Folk Art Center, 30 October–7 November 1982, and at the Solomon R. Guggenheim Museum, 19–22 January 1984.

43. Susanne Lahusen, "Oskar Schlemmer: Mechanical Ballets?" *Dance Research* 4:2 (Autumn 1986): 67.

44. J. S., "Dancing in Berlin," *Dancing Times* (November 1926): 163.

45. Lahusen, "Oskar Schlemmer," p. 67.

46. Quoted in program for reconstructions of Schlemmer dances at the Solomon R. Guggenheim Museum, New York City, 19–22 January 1984.

47. Elizabeth Selden, *The Dancer's Quest*, p. 102.

48. Elizabeth Selden, *Elements of the Free Dance*, p. 145.

49. Andreas Liess, *Carl Orff*, p. 17.

50. Selden, *The Dancer's Quest*, p. 104.

51. Various writers show different preferences in their use of these terms, although the essential meanings remain the same. John Martin uses *Anspannung* and *Abspannung* in *The Modern Dance*, p. 32; Preston-Dunlop and Lahusen favor *Spannung* and *Entspannung* in *Schrifttanz*; and Selden refers to *Spannung* and *Abspannung* in *The Dancers' Quest*, pp. 160–162.

FAMILY TREES AND HARDY GROWTHS

1. Natalia Roslavleva, "Prechistenka 20: The Isadora Duncan School in Moscow," *Dance Perspectives* 64 (Winter 1975): 11.
2. Roslavleva, "Prechistenka 20," p. 32.
3. Victor Seroff, *The Real Isadora*, pp. 306–308.
4. Seroff, *The Real Isadora*, pp. 311, 344.
5. Seroff, *The Real Isadora*, pp. 328–329.
6. Seroff, *The Real Isadora*, p. 432.
7. Information about Valeria Dienes drawn from Gedeon P. Dienes, "Memories of Dr. Valeria Dienes," in *Proceedings of the Tenth Annual Conference, Society of Dance History Scholars*, pp. 145–146; "Looking Back," *Hungarian Dance News* 1 (1987): 32; and letters to author from Gedeon P. Dienes.
8. Information about Gripenberg from Saga Ambegaokar, "Maggie Gripenberg (1881–1976)," in *Proceedings of the Tenth Annual Conference, Society of Dance History Scholars*, and "Maggie Gripenberg" (master's thesis, University of California, Riverside, 1985).
9. Information about Atkinson from Mary Clarke and Clement Crisp, *London Contemporary Dance Theatre*, p. 10; "Dance Study Supplement Part One— Contemporary Dance," *Dancing Times* (October 1989): iii; John Foster, *The Influence of Rudolph Laban*, p. 78.
10. Atkinson's theories summarized from Madge Atkinson, "Natural Movement," *Dancing Times* (October 1937): 17–20, and "Blending Nature and Art in 'Natural' Dancing," *Ball Room* (December 1926): 27–28.
11. All information on Akarova comes from Anne Van Loo, ed., *Akarova*.
12. Irwin Spector, *Rhythm and Life*, p. 210.
13. The most complete study of Ito's career is Helen Caldwell, *Michio Ito*; useful summaries include Caldwell's "Michio Ito: An American Pioneer," *Dance Magazine* (May 1977): 89–90; and Naima Prevots, *Dancing in the Sun*, pp. 176–190.
14. Pauline Koner, *Solitary Song*, p. 24.
15. Koner, *Solitary Song*, pp. 26–27.
16. Elizabeth Selden, *The Dancer's Quest*, p. 84.
17. Caldwell describes Ito's dances throughout *Michio Ito*; other discussions include Koner, *Solitary Song*, pp. 28–30; and Anna Kisselgoff, "Dance: Michio Ito Salute," *New York Times*, 4 October 1979.
18. Conversation with the author.
19. John Martin, *New York Times*, 25 September 1932.
20. From a program at New York City's 92nd St. YM-YWHA, 27 November 1950.
21. John Martin, *New York Times*, 25 September 1932.
22. Paris Opéra information from Ivor Guest, *Le Ballet de L'Opéra de Paris*,

pp. 158–160; Spector, *Rhythm and Life*, p. 261; Stéphane Wolff, *L'Opéra au Palais Garnier (1875–1962)*, pp. 274, 281.

23. Basic information about the Sakharoffs can be found in Emile Vuillermoz, *Clotilde et Alexandre Sakharoff*; also Jacqueline Robinson, *L'Aventure de la Danse Moderne en France (1920–1970)*, pp. 72–76.

24. Robinson, *L'Aventure de la Danse Moderne en France (1920–1970)*, p. 76. Information about the Sakharoffs' choreography from "The Sakharoffs," *Dancing Times* (April 1922): 593–594; "Paris Notes," *Dancing Times* (June 1922): 775–777.

25. Nadja, "Close-ups about Paris," *American Dancer* (July 1932): 24.

26. Edouard Szamba, "Our Paris Letter," *Dancing Times* (July 1938): 408.

27. Vuillermoz, *Clotilde et Alexandre Sakharoff*, pp. 10, 73.

28. Information about Saint-Point from Günter Berghaus, "Dance and the Futurist Woman," *Dance Research* 11:2 (Autumn 1993): 27–42; Leslie Satin, "Valentine de Saint-Point," *Dance Research Journal* 22:1 (Spring 1990): 1–12; and letter to author from Nancy Moore.

29. Satin, "Valentine de Saint-Point," p. 3.

30. Satin, "Valentine de Saint-Point," pp. 7–8; *New York Times*, 4 April 1917.

31. Basic information about Bodenwieser can be found in Shona Dunlop MacTavish, *An Ecstasy of Purpose*.

32. "The Sitter Out," *Dancing Times* (June 1929): 215, and (July 1929): 320–322.

33. Information about Bodenwieser technique from MacTavish, *An Ecstasy of Purpose*, p. 16, and conversations with Keith Bain.

34. Further discussion of this issue can be found in Deborah Jowitt, *Time and the Dancing Image*, p. 175, and Giora Manor, *The Life and Dance of Gertrud Kraus*, pp. 29–30.

35. Information about Tordis can be found in Manor, *The Life and Dance of Gertrud Kraus*; Judith Brin Ingber also talks about her in "The Gamin Speaks: Conversations with Gertrud Kraus," *Dance Magazine* (March 1976): 45–50.

36. Manor, *The Life and Dance of Gertrud Kraus*, pp. 6–8.

37. Information on Weidt can be found in Horst Koegler, "In the Shadow of the Swastika," *Dance Perspectives* 57 (Spring 1974): 11; Susan A. Manning, "Reviews," *Dance Research Journal* 18:2 (Winter 1986–1987): 70–73; and Robinson, *L'Aventure de la Danse Moderne en France (1920–1970)*, p. 121.

38. Manning, "Reviews," p. 72.

39. Robinson, *L'Aventure de la Danse Moderne en France (1920–1970)*, pp. 70–71.

40. Information about Gurdjieff taken from Mel Gordon, "Gurdjieff's Movement Demonstrations: The Theatre of the Miraculous," *Drama Review* 22:2 (June 1978): 33–44; and X. Theodore Barber, "Four Interpretations of Mevlevi Dervish Dance: 1920–1929," *Dance Chronicle* 9:3 (1986): 335.

41. Lincoln Kirstein, *Nijinsky Dancing*, p. 14.

42. Brendan Gill, *Many Masks*, pp. 291–301, 419–420.

43. Fernau Hall, *An Anatomy of Ballet*, p. 123.

44. Comments on *Tanzgymnastik* taken from John Martin, *Introduction to the Dance*, pp. 233–234; Mary Wigman, *The Mary Wigman Book*, pp. 52–53; conversation with Josephine Schwarz.

45. Arnold L. Haskell, "The Central European Dance Viewed by a 'Balletomane,'" *Dancing Times* (September 1930): 546–547.

46. References to these figures can be found throughout Valerie Preston-Dunlop and Susanne Lahusen, eds., *Schrifttanz*; see also J. V. K., "Berlin," *Dancing Times* (January 1930): 478–479.

47. Milloss's career is chronicled by Patrizia Veroli in her series for *Dance Chronicle* (see bibliography); material for this biographical sketch is also taken from a conversation with Milloss.

48. Mary F. Watkins, "Public Again Hails Dancing of Kreutzberg," *New York Herald Tribune*, 21 January 1929.

49. Koegler, "In the Shadow of the Swastika," p. 11.

DENISHAWN

1. Ernestine Stodelle, *Deep Song*, p. 23 (Stodelle also describes the school, pp. 22–26).

2. Jane Sherman, *The Drama of Denishawn Dance*, p. 16; and Jane Sherman and Barton Mumaw, p. 94.

3. Ruth St. Denis, *An Unfinished Life*, p. 259.

4. St. Denis, *An Unfinished Life*, p. 172; and Stodelle, *Deep Song*, p. 27.

5. Walter Terry, *Ted Shawn*, p. 10.

6. Descriptions can be found in Sherman, *Drama of Denishawn Dance*.

7. Stephanie Jordan discusses music visualizations in "Ted Shawn's Music Visualizations," *Dance Chronicle* 7:1 (1984): 33–49.

8. Sherman, *Drama of Denishawn Dance*, p. 8.

9. Marcia B. Siegel, *Days on Earth*, p. 60.

10. Ted Shawn, *One Thousand and One Night Stands*, p. 34.

11. Sherman, *Drama of Denishawn Dance*, p. 5.

AMERICAN FERMENT

1. Margaret Einert, "Exit Romanticism," *Dancing Times* (July 1929): 325.

2. Ruth Eleanor Howard, "An Interview with Ruth St. Denis," *American Dancer* (February 1929): 12.

3. Mary Wigman, *The Mary Wigman Book*, p. 132.

4. John Martin, *Introduction to the Dance*, p. 237.

5. Discussions of European influences on American dance include Susan A. Manning, "The Americanization of Wigman"; Deborah Jowitt, *Time and the Dancing Image*, pp. 167–168; and Naima Prevots, "Zurich Dada and Dance," *Dance Research Journal* 17:1 (Spring–Summer 1985): 3–8.

6. "Four Recitals Given by Dancers," *New York Times*, 22 April 1929; Margaret Einert, "What New York Is Doing," *Dancing Times* (September 1928): 593, and "Some New York Impressions, 1929," *Dancing Times* (September 1929): 525; Manning, "The Americanization of Wigman," p. 2.

7. Information on Zemach from Prevots, *Dancing in the Sun*, pp. 197–216; Elizabeth Selden, *The Dancer's Quest*, pp. 84–85.

8. Information on Wiener from Grant Code, "Hans Wiener," *Dance Observer* (March 1941): 46.

9. Einert, "Some New York Impressions, 1929," p. 525, and "Exit Romanticism," p. 325.

10. Ralph Taylor, "Edwin Strawbridge," *Dance Observer* (May 1935): 1, 55; see also Pauline Koner, *Solitary Song*, pp. 49–51.

11. Stacey Prickett, "From Workers' Dance to New Dance," *Dance Research* 7:1 (Spring 1989): 51.

12. M. E. Smith, "Behind the Broadway Footlight," *American Dancer* (June 1928): 29; Richard L. Stokes, *Evening World*, 30 April 1928.

13. Gervase N. Butler, "Jacques Cartier," *Dance Observer* (March 1935): 1, 32.

14. Ginnine Cocuzza, "Angna Enters," *Drama Review*, 24:4 (T88) (December 1980): 93–102; Betty Carne, "About Angna Enters," *American Dancer* (July 1931): 14.

15. Anne Sprague MacDonald, "The Neighborhood Playhouse," *Dance Observer* (December 1938): 144–145; "A Tribute to Irene Lewisohn," *Dance Observer* (May 1944): 55–56.

16. Information on Larson from Robert D. Moulton, "Bird Larson, the Legend," *Dance Observer* (April 1959): 53–54; and Mildred Spiesman, "The Bird Larson School of Natural Rhythmic Expression," *Dance Magazine* (September 1951): 22, 35–36.

17. "The Call Board," *American Dancer* (July 1936): 32; "Dancers Barefoot in Church," *New York Mail* (4 April 1921); Margery Rex, "N.Y. Rector Would Restore Dance to Old Place in Religious Ritual," *New York Evening Journal*, 6 April 1921.

18. William Norman Guthrie, *The Relation of the Dance to Religion*, pp. 17, 34–35.

19. H'Doubler is discussed by Nancy Lee Chalfa Ruyter in *Reformers and Visionaries*, pp. 117–123; see also "Margaret H'Doubler," *Dance Magazine* (April 1966): 33, 72.

20. Cornish's autobiography is *Miss Aunt Nellie*.

21. Nellie C. Cornish, *Miss Aunt Nellie*, p. 269.

22. Lucile Marsh, "Critiquing the Critics," *American Dancer* (January 1934): 10.

23. Jennifer Dunning, "Rediscovering a Pioneer Dance Critic," *New York Times*, 5 March 1987.

Rebels

1. Helen Tamiris, "Tamiris in Her Own Voice," *Studies in Dance History* 1:1 (Fall–Winter 1989–1990): 56.

2. Tamiris, "Tamiris in Her Own Voice," p. 20.

3. Tamiris, "Tamiris in Her Own Voice," p. 44.

4. Marcia B. Siegel, *The Shapes of Change*, p. 42.

5. Christena L. Schlundt, "Tamiris: A Chronicle of Her Dance Career," *Studies in Dance History* 1:1 (Fall–Winter 1989–1990): 105.

6. Joseph Arnold, "Dance Events Reviewed," *American Dancer* (October 1933): 10.

7. Gervase N. Butler, "Tamiris and Her Group," *Dance Observer* (April 1936): 42.

8. Ernestine Stodelle, *Deep Song*, p. 60.

9. Don McDonagh, *Martha Graham*, p. 6.

10. McDonagh, *Martha Graham*, p. 18.

11. Stodelle, *Deep Song*, p. 10.
12. McDonagh, *Martha Graham*, p. 19.
13. Jack Anderson, *The American Dance Festival*, p. 15.
14. Stodelle, *Deep Song*, p. 51.
15. Elizabeth Selden, *The Dancer's Quest*: first quotation, pp. 96–97; second quotation, p. 92.
16. Selma Jeanne Cohen, *Doris Humphrey*, pp. 63–64.

STRUGGLES, DISPERSALS, AMALGAMATIONS

1. Nellie C. Cornish, *Miss Aunt Nellie*, pp. 71, 172, 210; Fernau Hall, *Modern English Ballet*, pp. 140–142; Fernau Hall, "Modern Dancing at King's Cross," *Dancing Times* (January 1938): 526–528; "Dance-Mime at Dartington," *Dancing Times* (May 1932): 118–119.
2. Hall, "Modern Dancing at King's Cross," pp. 526–528.
3. Conversation with Valda Craig.
4. Jeannette Rutherston lists these dancers in "The Central European Dance in England," *Dancing Times* (December 1934): 313–316.
5. Information on Waldeen from Jacqueline Robinson, *L'Aventure de la Danse Moderne en France (1920–1970)*, p. 341; Verna Arvey, "Express Dance in America," *American Dancer* (October 1932): 8, 19.
6. Robinson, *L'Aventure de la Danse Moderne en France (1920–1970)*, p. 341; John Fealy, "The Mexican Dance Scene Today," *Dance Magazine* (March 1957): 30–33, 62–64.
7. Basic biographical information on Shankar can be found in Fernau Hall, "Honoring Uday Shankar," *Dance Chronicle* 7:3 (1984–1985): 326–344.
8. Ralph Taylor, "Harald Kreutzberg," *Dance Observer* (April 1935): 40; Frederic L. Orme, "Tamiris: The One Explorer," *American Dancer* (February 1938): 42.
9. Blanche Evan, "Barter at the Bar," *American Dancer* (February 1938): 15, 47.
10. L. Franc Scheuer, "New Ballets in Paris," *Dancing Times* (August 1935): 483.
11. Information on Theilade from undated typescript manuscript in the Dance Collection of the New York Public Library for the Performing Arts.
12. Leonard Ware, "Nina Verchinina," *American Dancer* (December 1936): 24.
13. Basic information on Ruskaja can be found in R. G. Hadfield, "An Experiment at La Scala," *Dancing Times* (July 1933): 342; "Notes from Italy," *Dancing Times* (December 1934): 361–363; Adrian H. Luijdjens, "Roman Scandal," *Dance Magazine* (February 1957): 27, 71–72.
14. Jooss's early career is described in Anna Markard and Hermann Markard, *Jooss*, pp. 29–39.
15. Markard and Markard, *Jooss*, p. 149.
16. Albertina Vitak, "Dance Events Reviewed," *American Dancer* (October 1941): 15; conversation with Agnes de Mille.

CATASTROPHE

1. Information about the Nazis and dance can be found in Horst Koegler, "In the Shadow of the Swastika," *Dance Perspectives* 57 (Spring 1974); and Valerie Preston-Dunlop, "Laban and the Nazis," *Update Dance/USA* (August–September 1989): 12–13, 19–22.

2. Preston-Dunlop, "Laban and the Nazis," p. 19.

3. J. Lewitan, "Messerer in Berlin and Other German Notes," *Dancing Times* (May 1933): 131; and Koegler, "In the Shadow of the Swastika," p. 31.

4. Koegler, "In the Shadow of the Swastika," p. 31.

5. Baird Hastings, "Concours à Copenhagen," *Dance Magazine* (September 1947): 21.

6. Anna Markard and Hermann Markard, *Jooss*, p. 9.

7. 1935 quotation in Koegler, "In the Shadow of the Swastika," p. 41; 1936 quotation in Susan A. Manning, "Reinterpreting Laban," *Dance Chronicle* 11:2 (1988): 318.

8. Preston-Dunlop, "Laban and the Nazis," pp. 13, 19.

9. J. Lewitan, "Berlin News," *Dancing Times* (December 1934): 365.

10. J.R., "Three New Books from Germany," *Dancing Times* (September 1937): 757.

11. J. Lewitan, "The Dance in Germany," *Dancing Times* (January 1935): 509–511.

12. J. Lewitan, "Olympic Dance Events," *American Dancer* (October 1936): 9, and "International Dance Festival and Olympiade in Berlin," *Dancing Times* (September 1936): 619.

13. Preston-Dunlop, "Laban and the Nazis," pp. 20–21.

14. John Foster, *The Influence of Rudolph Laban*, p. 28.

15. Theories about Wigman summarized by Hedwig Müller in "At the Start of a New Era," *Ballett International* 6:12 (December 1983): 12, and "Mary Wigman and the Third Reich," *Ballett International* 9:11 (November 1986): 18–23; see also Norbert Servos, "Whether to Resist or Conform," *Ballett International* 10:1 (January 1987): 18–21.

16. Valerie Preston-Dunlop and Susanne Lahusen, eds., *Schrifttanz*, p. 28.

17. Ernst Scheyer, "The Shapes of Space," *Dance Perspectives* 41 (Spring 1970): 145.

18. Müller, "At the Start of a New Era," p. 12.

19. Rolf Garske, "Learning to Think from an Early Age," *Ballett International* 7:2 (February 1984): 24.

20. Hans-Gerd Artus and Maud Paulissen-Kaspar, "Austria," *Ballett International* 8:3 (March 1985): 28.

21. John Martin, "The Dance: A Note on Kreutzberg," *New York Times*, 9 December 1945, and "The Dance: Returns," *New York Times*, 28 September 1947.

22. Berk's career is summarized by Fernau Hall in *Modern English Ballet*, pp. 142–145.

23. Giora Manor, *The Life and Dance of Gertrud Kraus*, pp. 22, 32–37.

24. Bodenwieser's career is discussed by Shona Dunlop MacTavish in *An Ecstasy of Purpose*; material also gained from conversations with Valda Craig and Keith Bain.

25. Dorathi Bock Pierre, "California," *American Dancer* (April 1940): 36.

26. Harold Norse, *Memoirs of a Bastard Angel*, pp. 125–126.

MODERN DANCE: AN AMERICAN ART

1. Paul Love, "Approach," *Dance Observer* (February 1934): 5; "New School Series: Martha Graham," *Dance Observer* (April 1934): 34.

2. Virginia Stewart and Merle Armitage, *The Modern Dance*, pp. 53–56.

3. Joseph Arnold and Paul R. Milton, "Modern Dance—Today and Tomorrow," *American Dancer* (March 1935): 8.

4. "In Memoriam," *American Dancer* (August 1932): 17.

5. Horst quotation from Karl Leabo, ed., *Martha Graham*, unpaginated.

6. Elizabeth Selden, *Elements of the Free Dance*, pp. 81–82.

7. Ernestine Stodelle, *Deep Song*, p. 81.

8. "New School Series: Martha Graham," pp. 32, 34.

9. John Dewey, *Art as Experience*, pp. 84, 86.

10. Dewey, *Art as Experience*, pp. 89, 109.

11. Martin first published his ideas in *The Modern Dance*; see also *The Dance in Theory* and Jack Anderson's introduction to it, pp. vi–xvi.

12. Martin, *The Modern Dance*, p. 48.

13. Koner quotation from Selma Jeanne Cohen, ed., *The Modern Dance*, p. 77.

CROSSCURRENTS

1. This artistic interchange is discussed by Susan Manning in "The Americanization of Wigman," a lecture delivered at a conference, "Mary Wigman 1886–1973," 24 September–3 October 1986, in West Berlin.

2. Marion Schillo, "Chicago's Little Concert House," *American Dancer* (February 1936): 13.

3. Albertina Vitak, "Graff Ballet," *American Dancer* (December 1941): 28; John Martin, *New York Times*, 10 January 1942.

4. S. Hurok, *Impresario*, p. 172.

5. Program for "Homage to Hanya," Manhattanville College, Purchase, New York, 21 February 1991.

6. Walter Sorell, *Hanya Holm*, p. 23.

7. Sorell, *Hanya Holm*, p. 45.

8. Sorell, *Hanya Holm*, p. 45.

9. Manning discusses this matter in "The Americanization of Wigman."

10. Walter Terry, in Sorell, *Hanya Holm*, pp. 72–73.

11. Dorathi Bock Pierre, "Los Angeles," *American Dancer* (January 1939): 46.

12. Ann Barzel, "East Meets West in Nimura," *Dance Magazine* (September 1948): 20–23; "Yeichi Nimura, Dancer, Choreographer, Teacher," *New York Times*, 5 April 1979.

13. "The Sitter Out," *Dancing Times* (December 1934): 233.

14. Gluck-Sandor's career is summarized in Sulamith Ish-Kishor, "Dancing for the Multitudes," *Jewish Tribune*, 1 February 1929, p. 11; and his obituary, "Gluck-Sandor Was Active in Modern Dance, Theater," *New York Times*, 1 March 1978.

15. Stuart Palmer, "The Month in the States," *Dancing Times* (June 1932): 238.

16. Joseph Arnold, "Dance Events Reviewed," *American Dancer* (May 1934): 24.

17. Pauline Koner discusses her life and repertoire in *Solitary Song*.

18. L. B., *New York World-Telegram*, 16 November 1936.

19. Martin, *New York Times*, 9 April 1939.

20. Larry Warren discusses Horton's career in *Lester Horton*.

1. Jane Sherman and Barton Mumaw, *Barton Mumaw*, p. 60.

2. Sherman and Mumaw, *Barton Mumaw*, p. 64.

3. Walter Terry, *Ted Shawn*, p. 143.

4. Sherman and Mumaw, *Barton Mumaw*, pp. 97–98.

5. Terry, *Ted Shawn*, p. 5.

6. Karl Leabo, ed., *Martha Graham*, unpaginated.

7. Elizabeth Selden, *The Dancer's Quest*, p. 92.

8. Joseph Arnold, "Dance Events Reviewed," *American Dancer* (June 1933): 21.

9. Ernestine Stodelle, *Deep Song*, p. 85.

10. Joseph Arnold, "Dance Events Reviewed," *American Dancer* (June 1933): 21.

11. Margaret Einert, "Bennington July 1938," *Dancing Times* (September 1938): 646; Joseph Arnold, "Dance Events Reviewed," *American Dancer* (January 1934): 9.

12. Don McDonagh, *Martha Graham*, pp. 90–94; "World's Fair Opening," *Dance Observer* (May 1939): 215.

13. Stodelle, *Deep Song*, p. 36.

14. "Editorial," *Dance Observer* (February 1934): 2.

15. Louis Horst and Carroll Russell, *Modern Dance Forms in Relation to the Other Modern Arts*, p. 39.

16. The ideas are discussed throughout Horst and Russell and in Louis Horst, *Pre-Classic Dance Forms*; Jack Anderson summarizes them in *The American Dance Festival*, pp. 69–71.

17. Marcia B. Siegel, *Days on Earth*, p. 1.

18. 1931 quotation: Siegel, *Days on Earth*, p. 80; 1932 quotation: Selma Jeanne Cohen, *Doris Humphrey*, p. 252; final quotation: Jane Sherman, "Doris and Charles and Pauline Fifty Years Ago," *Dance Magazine* (October 1978): 57.

19. Blaise Pascal, *Pensées*, p. 238.

20. Siegel, *Days on Earth*, p. 157.

21. Gervase N. Butler, "Humphrey-Weidman," *Dance Observer* (December 1938): 148.

22. Sherman, "Doris and Charles and Pauline Fifty Years Ago," p. 62.

23. Kinetic pantomime is discussed by Martin in *Introduction to the Dance*, p. 265; and Don McDonagh, *The Complete Guide to Modern Dance*, pp. 111–113.

24. Leah G. Cohen, "Tamiris," *Dance Observer* (February 1937): 18.

CHOREOGRAPHIC CONSCIENCES

1. Stacey Prickett surveys the period in "Dance and the Workers' Struggle," *Dance Research* 8:1 (Spring 1990): 47–61, and "From Workers' Dance to New Dance," *Dance Research* 7:1 (Spring 1989): 47–64.

2. Jacqueline Maskey, "The Group," *Dance Magazine* (January 1965): 45.

3. Judith Delman, "The New Dance Group," *Dance Observer* (January 1944): 8, 11.

4. "New School Series: Nadia Chilkovsky of the Workers' Dance League," *Dance Observer* (August–September 1934): 68–69.

5. Paul Love, "Workers' Dance League," *Dance Observer* (May 1934): 43–44.

6. Valuable surveys of black dance include Lynne Fauley Emery, *Black Dance from 1619 to Today*; and Gerald E. Myers, ed., *American Dance Festival 1988: The Black Tradition in American Modern Dance.*

7. Eunice Brown, "An Experiment in Negro Modern Dance," *Dance Observer* (January 1946): 4.

8. "Paris Notes," *Dancing Times* (August 1927): 527.

9. Myers, *American Dance Festival 1988*, p. 11.

10. Ralph Taylor, "Edna Guy and Group," *Dance Observer* (May 1934): 12.

11. Joseph Arnold, "Dance Events Reviewed," *American Dancer* (July 1934): 12.

12. Hampton, Karamu, and Bernice Brown are discussed in Myers, *American Dance Festival 1988*, pp. 12–14.

13. The Minneapolis scene is described by Brown in "An Experiment in Negro Modern Dance," pp. 4–5.

14. Myers, *American Dance Festival 1988*, p. 14.

15. Joyce Aschenbrenner surveys Dunham's career in *Katherine Dunham.*

16. Frederick L. Orme, "The Negro in the Dance," *American Dancer* (March 1938): 46.

17. Orme, "The Negro in the Dance," p. 46.

18. George W. Beiswanger, "Dance and the Myth of Race," *Dance Observer* (April 1943): 40.

19. Sali Ann Kriegsman, *Modern Dance in America*, p. 7 (includes Martin quotation); Dance Repertory Theatre is also discussed in Christena L. Schlundt, "Tamiris: A Chronicle of Her Dance Career 1927–1955," *Studies in Dance History* 1:1 (Fall–Winter 1989–1990): 74; and Marcia B. Siegel, *Days on Earth*, p. 113.

20. Hallie Flanagan's account of the Federal Theatre is *Arena*; the Dance Project is surveyed in Grant Code, "Dance Theatre of the WPA," *Dance Observer*, Part I (October 1939): 264–265, 274; Part II (November 1939): 280–281, 290; Part II (conclusion) (December 1939): 302; Part III (March 1940): 34–35.

21. Information on Becque can be found in "Dance Project Started by WPA," *American Dancer* (March 1936): 9.

22. Unsigned dance review, *New York Times*, 22 April 1929.

23. Flanagan, *Arena*, p. 76.

24. "Federal Dance Theatre," *Dance Observer* (October 1936): 87–88; Flanagan, *Arena*, 76.

25. Henry Gilfond, "Public Hearing: Federal Dance Theatre," *Dance Observer* (November 1936): 97.

26. "Quits WPA Dance Group," *New York Times*, 7 February 1937.

27. Schlundt, "Tamiris," p. 98.

28. Schlundt, "Tamiris," pp. 100–102.

29. A complete account of the Bennington Festivals is Kriegsman, *Modern Dance in America*; a summary of their accomplishments can be found in Jack Anderson, *The American Dance Festival*, pp. 1–6.

30. Joseph Arnold Kaye, "Dance Events Reviewed," *American Dancer* (October 1935): 10.

31. Kaye, "Dance Events Reviewed," p. 11.

32. Kriegsman, *Modern Dance in America*, p. 11.

33. Helen Caldwell, *Michio Ito*, p. 105.

AMERICAN VICTORIES

1. Cobbett Steinberg, ed., *The Dance Anthology*, p. 186.

2. George W. Beiswanger, "Doris Humphrey, Charles Weidman, and Dance Company," *Dance Observer* (April 1944): 39.

3. Humphrey's illness and teaching methods are discussed in Marcia B. Siegel, *Days on Earth*, pp. xiii, 191–193; and Pauline Koner, *Solitary Song*, p. 157.

4. Basic biographical information in Daniel Lewis, *The Illustrated Dance Technique of José Limón*; Barbara Pollock and Charles Humphrey Woodford, *Dance Is a Moment*; and Siegel, *Days on Earth*.

5. Lewis, *The Illustrated Dance Technique of José Limón*, p. 11.

6. Larry Warren, *Anna Sokolow*, p. 8.

7. Warren, *Anna Sokolow*, p. 220.

8. Warren, *Anna Sokolow*, p. 1.

9. Marjorie Church, "Anna Sokolow and Dance Unit," *Dance Observer* (April 1937): 41.

10. Selma Jeanne Cohen, *The Modern Dance*, p. 36.

11. Barnes quoted in Warren, *Anna Sokolow*, p. 230.

12. Doris Hering, "Dudley-Maslow-Bales," *Dance Magazine* (May 1946): 17.

13. George W. Beiswanger, "Dudley, Maslow, Bales," *Dance Observer* (January 1944): 3.

14. Joyce Aschenbrenner, *Katherine Dunham*, p. 56.

15. Gerald E. Myers, ed., *American Dance Festival 1988*, p. 17.

16. Aschenbrenner, *Katherine Dunham*, p. 56.

17. Lynne Fauley Emery, *Black Dance from 1619 to Today*, p. 265.

18. John Martin, *New York Times*, 27 February 1949.

19. Lois Balcom, "What Chance Has the Negro Dancer?" *Dance Observer* (November 1944): 110.

EXPLORERS AND DISSENTERS

1. Mary Emma Harris, *The Arts at Black Mountain College*, p. 196.

2. Edwin Denby, *Looking at the Dance*, p. 332.

3. Louis Horst and Carroll Russell, *Modern Dance Forms in Relation to the Other Modern Arts*, p. 142.

4. Robert Sabin, "Nina Fonaroff, May O'Donnell and Group," *Dance Observer* (June–July 1945): 71.

5. Doris Hering, "The Moderns in Concert," *Dance Magazine* (February 1946): 43.

6. Doris Hering, "Mattie Haim," *Dance Magazine* (July 1946): 26.

7. All quotations from Marsicano are from William Como, "Peril and Delight," *Dance Magazine* (May 1965): 27, 74, 25.

8. Don McDonagh, *The Complete Guide to Modern Dance*, p. 178.

9. Lillian Moore, *New York Herald Tribune*, 6 August 1962.

10. Margaret Lloyd, *The Borzoi Book of Modern Dance*, p. 239; basic information on Shearer can be found on pp. 232–243.

11. Lloyd, *The Borzoi Book of Modern Dance*, p. 236.

12. Information on Shearer's programs: John Martin, *New York Times*, 28 April 1946; Walter Terry, "World of Dance," *Saturday Review*, 7 February 1970; quotations: by Martin, *New York Times*, 19 June 1951; by Terry, *New York Herald Tribune*, 20 June 1951.

13. Shearer quotation from Martin, *New York Times*, 8 November 1953.

14. Quotations from Selma Jeanne Cohen, *The Modern Dance*, p. 39; program note in McDonagh, *The Complete Guide to Modern Dance*, pp. 298–299.

15. McDonagh calls Nikolais the Wizard of Oz in *The Rise and Fall and Rise of Modern Dance*; Nikolais quotation from Cohen, *The Modern Dance*, p. 63.

16. George W. Beiswanger, "New London: Residues and Reflections (Part III)," *Dance Observer* (January 1957): 6.

17. Marcia B. Siegel, "Nik: A Documentary," *Dance Perspectives* 48 (Winter 1971): 10.

18. Robert Sabin, "Merce Cunningham, John Cage," *Dance Observer* (May 1944): 57; "Merce Cunningham," *Dance Observer* (February 1945): 20–21.

19. Sabin, "Merce Cunningham, John Cage," p. 57.

20. Merce Cunningham, *Changes*, unpaginated.

21. Cunningham, *Changes*, unpaginated.

22. The *Aeon* scandal is discussed in Jack Anderson, *The American Dance Festival*, pp. 85–86 (includes quotations).

23. Paul Taylor, *Private Domain*, p. 29.

24. Anderson, *The American Dance Festival*, p. 231.

25. Doris Hering, "Two Concerts," *Dance Magazine* (July 1946): 23–24.

26. Walter Terry, *New York Herald Tribune*, 10 September 1961; Jon Boorstin, *The Hollywood Eye*, p. 13.

ICONOCLASTS

1. Quotations from Roni Feinstein, *The "Junk" Aesthetic: Assemblage of the 1950s and Early 60s*, p. 6.

2. Mary Emma Harris, *The Arts at Black Mountain College*, pp. 154–156, 266.

3. Harris, *The Arts at Black Mountain College*, pp. 226–227.

4. The best general survey of Happenings is Michael Kirby's *Happenings*, from which these descriptions are taken.

5. Lynnette Y. Overby and James H. Humphrey, eds., *Dance: Current Selected Research*, vol. 1, p. 99.

6. Ann Halprin, "An Interview," *Tulane Drama Review* 10:2 (Winter 1965): 143–144.

7. Susanne K. Langer, *Feeling and Form*, p. 187.

8. Langer, *Feeling and Form*, pp. 175–176, 190, 204.

9. Jack Anderson, "The Paradoxes of James Waring," *Dance Magazine* (November 1968): 64.

10. Anderson, "The Paradoxes of James Waring," pp. 66–67.

11. The early days at Judson are discussed by Sally Banes in *Democracy's Body*; Carmines quotation: conversation with the author.

12. Banes, *Democracy's Body*, pp. 38–39.

13. Banes, *Democracy's Body*, p. 44.

14. *New York Times*, 7 July 1962.

15. Banes, *Democracy's Body*, p. 208.
16. Yvonne Rainer, *Work 1961–73*, p. 8.

FERTILE GROUND, BARREN SOIL

1. A general view of Canadian modern dance is Max Wyman, *Dance Canada*.
2. Modern dance influences upon Argentina are summarized in Jacqueline Robinson, *L'Aventure de la Danse Moderne en France (1920–1970)*, p. 341.
3. John Fealy, "The Mexican Dance Scene Today," *Dance Magazine* (March 1957): 32.
4. Eleanor Rachel Luger, "Guillermina Bravo's Dances of Mexico," *Dance Magazine* (February 1982): 70.
5. Larry Warren, *Anna Sokolow*, pp. 198–199.
6. Information on Les Ballets Nègres can be found in Janet Rowson Davis, "Ballet on British Television, 1946–1947: Starting Again," *Dance Chronicle* 13:2 (1990): 134–135; Arthur H. Franks, "Ballets Nègres," *Dancing Times* (June 1946): 447–449.
7. Franks, "Ballets Nègres," p. 449.
8. The best survey of French modern dance is Robinson, *L'Aventure de la Danse Moderne en France (1920–1970)*.
9. P. W. Manchester, "Birgit Åkesson Captures New York Dance World," *Dance News* (September 1955): 13.
10. Fernau Hall, *An Anatomy of Ballet*, p. 223; Selma Jeanne Cohen, "Birgit Åkesson," *Dance Observer* (August–September 1955): 100.
11. George Beiswanger, "New London: Residues and Reflections (Part I)," *Dance Observer* (November 1956): 133.
12. Birgit Cullberg, "Ballet: Flight and Reality," *Dance Perspectives* 29 (Spring 1967): 10.
13. Cullberg, "Ballet: Flight and Reality," p. 21.
14. Cullberg, "Ballet: Flight and Reality," p. 46.
15. Hedwig Müller, "Exceeding All Bounds," *Ballett International* 6:3 (March 1983): 25.
16. Jack Anderson, "A Dance Troupe Lands and Takes Off," *New York Times*, 27 January 1989.
17. Mary Wigman, *The Language of Dance*, pp. 7–8.
18. Paul Moor, *New York Times*, 5 November 1957.
19. Horst Koegler, "Introducing Dore Hoyer," *Dance Magazine* (August 1957): 53.
20. Doris Hering, "New London: Tenth Summer," *Dance Magazine* (October 1957): 29.
21. Koegler, "Introducing Dore Hoyer," p. 25.

STABILITY AND CHANGE

1. New York City Center program for 28 December 1991, p. 40.
2. Joyce Aschenbrenner, *Katherine Dunham*, p. 61.
3. Graham quotation from Marian Horosko, "Frontier of the Mind: Martha Graham at 95," *Dance Magazine* (May 1989): 55; Agnes de Mille, *Martha*, p. x.
4. Michael Kirby, *The Art of Time*, p. 104; lecture quotation from Anne Livet, ed., *Contemporary Dance*, p. 166.

5. Sally Banes, *Terpsichore in Sneakers*, pp. xiv–xv.

6. Walter Sorell, "Louis Horst," *Dance Magazine* (March 1964): 39.

7. Hughes and Johnston quotations from Sally Banes, *Democracy's Body*, pp. 86–88.

8. Yvonne Rainer, *Work 1961–73*, p. 51; Banes, *Democracy's Body*, p. 78.

9. Jack Anderson, *The American Dance Festival*, p. 71.

10. Statement in program for *Spiral*, Brooklyn Academy of Music, 11–13 November 1977.

11. Max Wyman, *Dance Canada*, p. 140.

12. Deborah Jowitt, *Time and the Dancing Image*, p. 362.

13. This issue is discussed in Jack Anderson, *Choreography Observed*, pp. 262–265.

14. Anderson, *Choreography Observed*, p. 136.

Contemporary British Dance

1. Interview with Robin Howard. Background information on the dance scene of the 1950s and 1960s also taken from conversations with Ann Hutchinson Guest.

2. Barbara Newman, "John Ashford," *Dancing Times* (April 1989): 644.

3. Jennifer Dunning, "Robin Howard, an English Patron of Modern Dance, Is Dead at 65," *New York Times*, 14 June 1989.

4. Mary Clarke and Clement Crisp, *London Contemporary Dance Theatre*, p. 14.

5. The history of London Contemporary is told in Clarke and Crisp, *London Contemporary Dance Theatre*; also in Stephanie Jordan, *Striding Out*, pp. 13–16.

6. "Dance Study Supplement Part One—Contemporary Dance," *Dancing Times* (October 1989): i–viii.

7. Clarke and Crisp, *London Contemporary Dance Theatre*, p. 128.

8. Angela Kane, "Christopher Bruce's Choreography," *Dancing Times* (October 1991): 44.

9. Conversation with the author.

10. Kane, "Richard Alston: Twenty-one Years of Choreography," *Dance Research* 7:2 (Autumn 1989): 26.

11. Alston's style is analyzed by Jordan, *Striding Out*, pp. 117–124.

12. Jordan, *Striding Out*, p. 111.

13. Clarke and Crisp, *London Contemporary Dance Theatre*, p. 111.

14. Davies's style is analyzed by Jordan, *Striding Out*, pp. 137–145.

15. Quoted by Jordan, *Striding Out*, p. 60.

16. Jordan, *Striding Out*, p. 185.

A League of Dancing Nations

1. Sally R. Sommer, "The Lyon Biennale de la Danse: American Review and Au Revoir," *Dance Magazine* (September 1990): 46–47.

2. Jack Anderson, *The American Dance Festival*, p. 206.

3. Insert for program for Groupe Emile Dubois, City Center, New York, 22–27 January 1985.

4. Rebecca Libermann, "New Director Will Take Charge of Finnish Ballet," *Dance Magazine* (August 1991): 20.

5. Program note quoted in John Percival, "Summer Assortment," *Dance and Dancers* (August 1987): 17.

6. Auli Räsänen, "New Festival Works," *Ballett International* 8:10 (October 1990): 28.

7. Liberman, "New Director Will Take Charge of Finnish Ballet," p. 20.

8. Jack Anderson, "U.S. Dance Importing Other Ideas," *New York Times*, 15 July 1989.

9. Catalogue for "Refigured Painting: The German Image 1960–88," exhibition at Solomon R. Guggenheim Museum, 11 February–23 April 1989.

10. Norbert Servos, "Whether to Resist or Conform: Ausdruckstanz Then, and Now?" *Ballett International* 10:1 (January 1987): 20.

11. Roland Langer, "Politician of Dance Theatre: An Interview with Johann Kresnik," *Ballett International* 8:5 (May 1985): 8.

12. Horst Koegler, "Heidelberg," *Dance Magazine* (October 1987): 23; Kresnik quotation from Langer, "Politician of Dance Theatre," p. 8.

13. Norbert Servos, *Pina Bausch*, pp. 235–236.

14. Servos, *Pina Bausch*, p. 20.

15. Hedwig Müller, "The Path Is the Goal," *Ballett International* 6:4 (April 1983): 11.

16. Birgitt Kirchner, "Dancing Really Does Make Sense," *Ballett International* 6:12 (December 1983): 22, 24.

17. Kirchner, "Dancing Really Does Make Sense," pp. 24, 26.

18. Kirchner, "Dancing Really Does Make Sense," p. 26.

19. *New York Times*, 4 July 1982.

20. Ethan Hoffman, *Butoh*, pp. 8–9; see also Anderson, *American Dance Festival*, p. 205.

21. Discussions of productions taken from Hoffman, *Butoh*, pp. 11–12, 14, 88.

22. Annalyn Swan, "A Dazzling Feast from Japan," *Newsweek*, 19 July 1982, p. 61.

23. Hoffman, *Butoh*, pp. 14–15.

24. Information on China from Ou Jian-Ping, "International Reviews: Shanghai," *Dance Magazine* (May 1989): 110–111; Joseph H. Mazo, "U.S. Department of Modern Dance," *Dance Magazine* (June 1990): 43.

25. Commentary on the Canadian modern dance scene can be found in Max Wyman, *Dance Canada*.

CONCLUSION: THE UNDEFINABLE REDEFINING ART

1. Sheldon Cheney, *Expressionism in Art*, p. 5.

2. Genevieve Stebbins, *Delsarte System of Expression*, p. 161.

3. Wall caption for "Parallel Visions" exhibition, Whitney Museum of American Art, 31 July–25 October 1993; these ideas are developed in Jack Anderson, "Re-formations, Re-Formings, Modern Dances," *Dance Chronicle* 18:2 (1995): 153–161.

4. John Martin, *New York Times*, 1 July 1930.

5. Robert Henri, *The Art Spirit*, p. 4.

6. Václav Havel, "The End of the Modern Era," *New York Times*, 1 March 1992.

SELECTED BIBLIOGRAPHY

This bibliography is restricted to books and lengthy magazine articles. The sources of news items and brief newspaper and magazine reviews quoted in the text are cited in the notes to each chapter.

Adorée Villany, Phryné Moderne devant l'Aréopage. Munich: F. Bruckmann, n.d. (ca. 1913).

Allan, Maud. *My Life and Dancing.* London: Everett and Co., 1908.

Ambegaokar, Saga. "Maggie Gripenberg (1881–1976): A Finnish Pioneer in Modern Dance." In *Proceedings of the Tenth Annual Conference, Society of Dance History Scholars* (University of California, Irvine, 13–15 February 1987), pp. 75–84. Riverside, Calif.: Dance History Scholars, 1987.

Anderson, Jack. *The American Dance Festival.* Durham: Duke University Press, 1987.

———. *Ballet and Modern Dance: A Concise History* 2nd ed. Princeton: Princeton Book Co., 1992.

———. *Choreography Observed.* Iowa City: University of Iowa Press, 1987.

———. "The Paradoxes of James Waring." *Dance Magazine* (November 1968): 64–67, 90–91.

———. "Reformations, Re-Formings, Modern Dances." *Dance Chronicle* 18:2 (1995): 153–161.

———. "U.S. Dance Importing Other Ideas." *New York Times,* 15 July 1989.

Arnheim, Rudolf. "Visiting Palucca." *Dance Scope* 13:1 (Fall 1978): 6–11.

Arnold, Joseph, and Paul R. Milton. "Modern Dance—Today and Tomorrow." *American Dancer* (March 1935): 8.

———. "Technique and Subject." *American Dancer* (April 1935): 9.

Artus, Hans-Gerd, and Maud Paulissen-Kaspar. "Austria." *Ballett International* 8:3 (March 1985): 28–30.

Arvey, Verna. "Creates Jewish Dance." *American Dancer* (October 1931): 13, 30.

Aschenbrenner, Joyce. *Katherine Dunham: Reflections on the Social and Political Contexts of Afro-American Dance.* New York: CORD, Dance Research Annual XII, 1980.

Atkinson, Madge. "Blending Nature and Art in 'Natural' Dancing." *Ball Room* (December 1926): 27–28.

Au, Susan. *Ballet and Modern Dance.* New York: Thames and Hudson, 1988.

Balcom, Lois. "The Negro Dances Himself." *Dance Observer* (December 1944): 122–124.

———. "What Chance Has the Negro Dancer?" *Dance Observer* (November 1944): 110–111.

Banes, Sally. *Democracy's Body: Judson Dance Theater 1962–1964.* Ann Arbor: UMI Research Press, 1983.

———. *Terpsichore in Sneakers: Post-Modern Dance* (with a new introduction). Middletown: Wesleyan University Press, 1987.

Barber, X. Theodore. "Four Interpretations of Mevlevi Dervish Dance: 1920–1929 (Jean Börlin, George Ivanovitch Gurdjieff, Mary Wigman, Ted Shawn)." *Dance Chronicle* 9:3 (1986): 328–355.

Barel, Jacques. *La Danse Moderne (d'Isadora Duncan à Twyla Tharp).* Paris: Editions Vigot, 1977.

Barzel, Ann. "East Meets West in Nimura." *Dance Magazine* (September 1948): 20–23.

———. "European Dance Teachers in the United States." *Dance Index* 3:4–6 (April–June 1944): 56–100.

Beiswanger, George W. "Dance and the Myth of Race." *Dance Observer* (April 1943): 40.

Berghaus, Günter. "Dance and the Futurist Woman: The Work of Valentine de Saint Point (1875–1953)." *Dance Research* 11:2 (Autumn 1993): 27–42.

Bizot, Richard. "Lester Horton's *Salome,* 1934–1953 and After." *Dance Research Journal* 16:1 (Spring 1984): 35–40.

Bohlin, Peter. "Swedish Contemporary Dance—Concentrated, Effective Energy." *Ballett International* 12:3 (March 1989): 9–15.

Boorstin, Jon. *The Hollywood Eye: What Makes Movies Work.* New York: Cornelia and Michael Bessie Books, 1990.

Brandenburg, Hans. *Der Moderne Tanz.* Munich: George Müller, 1913.

Brown, Eunice, "An Experiment in Negro Modern Dance." *Dance Observer* (January 1946): 4–5.

Caffin, Caroline, and Charles H. Caffin. *Dancing and Dancers of Today: The Modern Revival of Dancing as an Art.* New York: Dodd, Mead and Co., 1912.

Caldwell, Helen. "Michio Ito: An American Pioneer." *Dance Magazine* (May 1977): 89–90.

———. *Michio Ito: The Dancer and His Dances.* Berkeley: University of California Press, 1977.

Carne, Betty, "About Angna Enters," *American Dancer* (July 1931): 14.

Cheney, Sheldon. *Expressionism in Art.* Revised ed. New York: Liveright, 1948 (original edition, 1934).

Cherniavsky, Felix. "Maud Allan." *Dance Chronicle*: I. "The Early Years, 1873–1903," 6:1 (1983): 1–36; II. "First Steps to a Dancing Career," 6:3 (1983):

189–227; III. "Two Years of Triumph, 1908–1909," 7:2 (1984): 119–158; IV. "The Years of Touring, 1910–1915," 8:1–2 (1985): 1–50; V. "The Years of Decline, 1915–1956," 9:2 (1986): 177–236.

———. *The Salome Dancer: The Life and Times of Maud Allan.* Toronto: McClelland and Stewart, 1991.

Clarke, Mary, and Clement Crisp. *London Contemporary Dance Theatre: The First Twenty-one Years.* London: Dance Books, 1989.

Cocuzza, Ginnine. "Angna Enters: American Dance-Mime." *Drama Review* 24:4 (T88) (December 1980): 93–102.

Code, Grant. "Dance Theatre of the WPA." *Dance Observer*, Part I (October 1939): 264–265, 274; Part II (November 1939): 280–281, 290; Part II (conclusion) (December 1939): 302; Part III (March 1940): 34–35.

Cohen, Selma Jeanne. *Doris Humphrey: An Artist First.* Middletown: Wesleyan University Press, 1972.

———., ed. *The Modern Dance: Seven Statements of Belief.* Middletown: Wesleyan University Press, 1966.

Como, William. "Peril and Delight." *Dance Magazine* (May 1965): 25–27, 74–75.

Constanti, Sophie. "Spotlight on Fergus Early." *Dancing Times* (April 1992): 638–640.

Cook, John D. "Raymond Duncan." *Opera and Concert* (April 1948): 22–28.

Copeland, Roger, and Marshall Cohen, eds. *What Is Dance?: Readings in Theory and Criticism.* Oxford: Oxford University Press, 1983.

Cornish, Nellie C. *Miss Aunt Nellie.* Ed. Ellen Van Volkenburg Browne and Edward Nordhoff Beck. Seattle: University of Washington Press, 1964.

Craig, Edward Gordon. *The Theatre—Advancing.* Boston: Little, Brown and Co., 1919.

Creese, Robb. "Anthroposophical Performance." *Drama Review* 22:2 (June 1978): 45–74.

Croce, Arlene. *Afterimages.* New York: Alfred A. Knopf, 1977.

Cullberg, Birgit. "Ballet: Flight and Reality." Trans. Laura de la Torre Bueno. *Dance Perspectives* 29 (Spring 1967).

Cunningham, Merce. *Changes: Notes on Choreography.* Ed. Frances Starr. New York: Something Else Press, 1968.

Curtiss, Minna. *Bizet and His World.* London: Secker and Warburg, 1959.

"Dance-Mime at Dartington." *Dancing Times* (May 1932): 118–119.

"Dance Study Supplement Part One—Contemporary Dance." *Dancing Times* (October 1989): i–viii.

"The Dance Theatre of Lester Horton." *Dance Perspectives* 31 (Autumn 1967).

Davis, Janet Rowson. "Ballet on British Television, 1946–47: Starting Again." *Dance Chronicle* 13:2 (1990): 103–153.

de Mille, Agnes. *Martha: The Life and Work of Martha Graham.* New York: Random House, 1991.

Denby, Edwin. *Dance Writings.* Ed. Robert Cornfield and William Mackay. New York: Alfred A. Knopf, 1986.

———. *Looking at the Dance.* New York: Horizon Press, 1968.

Dewey, John. *Art as Experience.* New York: Capricorn Books/G. P. Putnam's Sons, 1958 (reprint of original 1934 edition).

Dienes, Gedeon P. "Memories of Dr. Valeria Dienes." In *Proceedings of the Tenth Annual Conference, Society of Dance History Scholars* (University of California, Irvine, 13–15 February 1987), pp. 145–146. Riverside, Calif.: Dance History Scholars, 1987.

Divoire, Fernand. *Pour la Danse.* Paris: Editions de la Danse, 1935.

Duncan, Irma. *Duncan Dancer: An Autobiography.* Middletown: Wesleyan University Press, 1966.

Duncan, Irma, and Allan Ross Macdougall. *Isadora Duncan's Russian Days and Her Last Years in France.* New York: Covici-Friede, 1929.

Duncan, Isadora. *My Life.* New York: Boni and Liveright, 1927 (often reprinted).

Dunning, Jennifer. "Rediscovering a Pioneer Dance Critic." *New York Times,* 5 March 1987.

Ehrmann, Hans. "Jooss, Conquistadores, and the Wheel of Fortune." *Dance Magazine* (November 1964): 32–34.

Einert, Margaret. "Exit Romanticism." *Dancing Times* (July 1929): 325–326.

———. "Some New York Impressions, 1929." *Dancing Times* (September 1929): 525.

Emery, Lynne Fauley. *Black Dance from 1619 to Today.* 2d rev. ed. with new chapter by Brenda Dixon-Stowell. Princeton: Dance Horizons, 1988.

Engdahl, Horace. "Birgit Åkesson: A New Dimension in Dance." *Ballett International* 12:10 (October 1989): 10–15.

Estrada, Ric. "To Be a Clown." *Dance Magazine* (August 1968): 49–50.

Ettlinger, Karl. "Sent M'Ahesa." *Tanzdrama* 14 (1993): 32–34.

Evan, Blanche. "Barter at the Bar." *American Dancer* (February 1938): 15, 47.

———. "*Inquest*: Historic in Setting, Modern in Form, Timeless in Content." *Dance Observer* (January 1945): 4–5.

Fealy, John. "The Mexican Dance Scene Today." *Dance Magazine* (March 1957): 30–33, 62–64.

Feinstein, Roni. *The "Junk" Aesthetic: Assemblage of the 1950s and Early 60s.* New York: Whitney Museum of American Art, 1989.

Fiedler, Leonhard M., and Martin Lang. *Grete Wiesenthal: Die Schönheit der Sprache des Körpers in Tanz.* Salzburg: Residenz Verlag, 1985.

Findlay, Elsa. "Lessons with Monsieur Jaques." *Dance Magazine* (August 1965): 41–45.

———. *Rhythm and Movement.* Evanston: Summy-Birchard Co., 1971.

Flanagan, Hallie. *Arena: The Story of the Federal Theatre.* New York: Limelight Editions, 1985 (reprint of original 1940 edition from New York: Duell, Sloan and Pearce).

Flitch, J. E. Crawford. *Modern Dancing and Dancers.* London: Grant Richards, 1913 (originally published 1912).

Foster, John. *The Influence of Rudolph Laban.* London: Lepus Books, 1977.

Foster, Susan. *Reading Dancing: Bodies and Subjects in Contemporary American Dance.* Berkeley and Los Angeles: University of California Press, 1986.

Franko, Mark. *Dancing Modernism/Performing Politics.* Bloomington: Indiana University Press, 1995.

Franks, Arthur H. "Ballets Nègres." *Dancing Times* (June 1946): 447–449.

Fuller, Loïe. *Fifteen Years of a Dancer's Life.* London: Herbert Jenkins, 1913.

Garske, Rolf. "Learning to Think from an Early Age." *Ballett International* 6:12 (December 1983): 14–17; and 7:2 (February 1984): 24–25.

Gill, Brendan. *Many Masks: A Life of Frank Lloyd Wright.* New York: G. P. Putnam's Sons, 1987.

Ginner, Ruby. "The Art and Technique of the Revived Greek Dance." *Dancing Times,* Part I (March 1933): 662–666; Part II (April 1933): 12–16; Part III (May 1933): 118–122; Part IV (June 1933): 235–239.

———. *Gateway to the Dance.* London: Newman Neame, 1960.

———. "The Revival of the Greek Dance." *Dancing Times* (October 1935): 39–41, 44.

Goodman, Saul. "Lady from Nykoping." *Dance Magazine* (June 1960): 14–15, 58.

Gordon, Mel. "Gurdjieff's Movement Demonstrations: The Theatre of the Miraculous." *Drama Review* 22:2 (June 1978): 33–44.

Guest, Ivor. *Le Ballet de L'Opéra de Paris.* Paris: Opéra de Paris/Flammarion, 1976.

Guthrie, William Norman. *The Relation of the Dance to Religion* ("A paper read before The Club, an organization of clergymen in the Diocese of New York and from neighboring Dioceses, and reprinted from the May issue of 'The Chronicle.'"). N.p.: 1923.

Hall, Fernau. *An Anatomy of Ballet.* London: Andrew Melrose, 1953.

———. "Honoring Uday Shankar." *Dance Chronicle* 7:3 (1984–1985): 326–344.

———. "Modern Dancing at King's Cross." *Dancing Times* (January 1938): 526–528.

———. *Modern English Ballet: An Interpretation.* London: Andrew Melrose, n.d.

Halprin, Ann. "An Interview." *Tulane Drama Review* 10:2 (Winter 1965): 142–166.

Harris, Mary Emma. *The Arts at Black Mountain College.* Cambridge, Mass.: MIT Press, 1987.

Haskell, Arnold L. "The Central European Dance Viewed by a 'Balletomane.'" *Dancing Times* (September 1930): 546–547.

Havel, Václav. "The End of the Modern Era." *New York Times,* 1 March 1992.

H'Doubler, Margaret. *Dance: A Creative Art Experience.* New York: F. S. Crofts and Co., 1940.

Henri, Robert. *The Art Spirit.* Comp. Margery Ryerson. Philadelphia: J. B. Lippincott Co., 1951 (new edition of original 1930 Lippincott publication).

Hering, Doris. "Dudley-Maslow-Bales." *Dance Magazine* (May 1946): 17.

———. "Harald Kreutzberg." *Dance Magazine* (April 1953): 65.

———. "The Moderns in Concert." *Dance Magazine* (February 1946): 26–27, 40–45.

———. "Why Ohio?: A Dance Safari through the Buckeye State." *Dance Magazine* (September 1971): 48–62.

Hodgson, John, and Valerie Preston-Dunlop. *Rudolf Laban: An Introduction to His Work and Influence.* Plymouth, U.K.: Northcote House, 1990.

Hoffman, Ethan. *Butoh: Dance of the Dark Soul.* New York: Aperture, 1987.

Horosko, Marian. "Frontier of the Mind: Martha Graham at 95." *Dance Magazine* (May 1989): 51–57.

———. ed. *Martha Graham: The Evolution of Her Dance Theory and Training 1926–1991.* Pennington, N.J.: A Cappella Books, 1991.

Horst, Louis. *Pre-Classic Dance Forms.* New York: Dance Horizons, 1968.

———. "Tamiris." *Dance Observer* (April 1934): 1, 28.

Horst, Louis, and Carroll Russell. *Modern Dance Forms in Relation to the Other Modern Arts.* San Francisco: Impulse Publications, 1961.

Howard, Ruth Eleanor. "An Interview with Ruth St. Denis." *American Dancer* (February 1929): 12, 30.

———. "The Story of New York's Dance Guild." *American Dancer* (February 1929): 9, 17, 22, 30.

Howe, Dianne S. "The Notion of Mysticism in the Philosophy and Choreography of Mary Wigman, 1914–1931." *Dance Research Journal*, 19:1 (Summer 1987): 19–24.

Humphrey, Doris. *The Art of Making Dances.* New York: Rinehart and Co., 1959.

———. "Reflections on the Humphrey-Weidman Season." *Dance Observer* (May–June 1941): 76–77.

Hurok, S. *S. Hurok Presents.* New York: Hermitage House, 1953.

Hurok, S., in collaboration with Ruth Goode. *Impresario.* New York: Random House, 1946.

Ingber, Judith Brin. "The Gamin Speaks: Conversations with Gertrud Kraus." *Dance Magazine* (March 1976): 45–50.

Ish-Kishor, Sulamith. "Dancing for the Multitudes." *Jewish Tribune*, 1 February 1929, p. 11.

Jackson, George. "The Aesthetic and Political Origins of European Modern Dance." *Dance Magazine* (October 1985): 45–51.

———. "Relations and Rejections: Modern Dance in Germany and America." Translation of German version published by University of Bayreuth's summer series from the Institute for Lyric Theatre, 1986.

Jaques-Dalcroze, Emile. *Eurhythmics, Art and Education.* Trans. Frederick Rothwell. New York: Arno Press, 1976 (reprint of 1930 edition).

Jordan, Stephanie. "British Modern Dance: Early Radicalism." *Dance Research* 7:2 (Autumn 1989): 3–15.

———. *Striding Out: Aspects of Contemporary and New Dance in Britain.* London: Dance Books, 1992.

———. "Ted Shawn's Music Visualizations." *Dance Chronicle* 7:1 (1984): 33–49.

Jowitt, Deborah. *The Dance in Mind.* Boston: David R. Godine, 1985.

———. *Time and the Dancing Image.* New York: William Morrow and Co., 1988.

Kane, Angela. "Christopher Bruce's Choreography: Inroads or Retracing Old Steps?" *Dancing Times* (October 1991): 44–53.

———. "Richard Alston: Twenty-one Years of Choreography." *Dance Research* 7:2 (Autumn 1989): 16–54.

———. "Siobhan Davies: Family Connections (Dance Study Supplement Part Six)." *Dancing Times* (March 1990): i–viii.

Kendall, Elizabeth. *Where She Danced.* New York: Alfred A. Knopf, 1979.

Kirby, Michael. *The Art of Time.* New York: E. P. Dutton and Co., 1969.

———. *Happenings.* New York: E. P. Dutton and Co., 1965.

Kirchner, Birgitt. "Dancing Really Does Make Sense." *Ballett International* 6:12 (December 1983): 22–28.

Kirstein, Lincoln. *Ballet: Bias and Belief.* New York: Dance Horizons, 1983.

———. *Nijinsky Dancing.* New York: Alfred A. Knopf, 1975.

Klingenbeck, Fritz. *Die Tänzerin Rosalia Chladek.* Amsterdam: L. J. Veen's Uit-
gevers Maatschappij N.V., 1936.

Koegler, Horst. *The Concise Oxford Dictionary of Ballet.* 2nd ed. London: Oxford
University Press, 1982.

———. "In the Shadow of the Swastika: Dance in Germany, 1927–1936." *Dance
Perspectives* 57 (Spring 1974).

———. "Introducing Dore Hoyer." *Dance Magazine* (August 1957): 24–25, 52–54.

Koepke, Dorothy. "Mary Wigman." *American Dancer* (January 1931): 9, 40.

Koner, Pauline. *Solitary Song.* Durham: Duke University Press, 1989.

Kostelanetz, Richard, ed. *Merce Cunningham: Dancing in Space and Time.* Pennington, N.J.: A Cappella Books, 1992.

———. *The Theatre of Mixed Means.* New York: Dial Press, 1968.

Kraus, Richard, and Sarah Alberti Chapman. *History of the Dance in Art and Education.* 2nd ed. Englewood Cliffs: Prentice-Hall, 1981.

Kreemer, Connie. *Further Steps: Fifteen Choreographers on Modern Dance.* New
York: Harper and Row, 1987.

Kriegsman, Sali Ann. *Modern Dance in America: The Bennington Years.* Boston:
G. K. Hall and Co., 1981.

Laban, Rudolf. *A Life for Dance,* trans. Lisa Ullmann. London: Macdonald and
Evans, 1975.

Lahusen, Susanne. "Oskar Schlemmer: Mechanical Ballets?" *Dance Research* 4:2
(Autumn 1986): 65–77.

Langer, Roland. "Politician of Dance Theatre: An Interview with Johann Kresnik."
Ballett International 8:5 (May 1985): 6–8.

Langer, Susanne K. *Feeling and Form.* New York: Charles Scribner's Sons, 1953.

Layson, June. "Isadora Duncan—A Preliminary Analysis of Her Work." *Dance
Research* 1:1 (Spring 1983): 39–49.

Leabo, Karl, ed. *Martha Graham.* New York: Theatre Arts Books, 1961.

Lewis, Daniel. *The Illustrated Dance Technique of José Limón.* New York: Harper
and Row, 1984.

Lewitan, J. "International Dance Festival and Olympiade in Berlin." *Dancing
Times* (September 1936): 615–619.

———. "Olympic Dance Events." *American Dancer* (October 1936): 9, 34.

Libermann, Rebecca. "New Director Will Take Charge of Finnish Ballet." *Dance
Magazine* (August 1991): 20.

Liess, Andreas. *Carl Orff.* Trans. Adelheid Parkin and Herbert Parkin. London:
Calder and Boyars, 1966.

Linick, Etta. "Wigman School and Modern Dance." *American Dancer* (March
1932): 8, 32.

Livet, Anne, ed. *Contemporary Dance.* New York: Abbeville Press, 1978.

Lloyd, Margaret. *The Borzoi Book of Modern Dance.* New York: Alfred A. Knopf,
1978.

"Looking Back." *Hungarian Dance News* 1 (1987): 32.

Love, Paul. "Charles Weidman." *Dance Observer* (March 1934): 1, 20.

———. "Workers' Dance League." *Dance Observer* (May 1934): 43–44.

Luger, Eleanor Rachel. "Guillermina Bravo's Dances of Mexico." *Dance Magazine*
(February 1982): 68–71.

Luijdjens, Adrian H. "Roman Scandal." *Dance Magazine* (February 1957): 27, 71–72.

Luley, Waltraud. "Dore Hoyer: An Attempted Portrait." *Ballett International* 11:2 (February 1988): 4–13.

MacDonald, Anne Sprague. "The Neighborhood Playhouse." *Dance Observer* (December 1938): 144–145.

MacTavish, Shona Dunlop. *An Ecstasy of Purpose: The Life and Art of Gertrud Bodenwieser.* Dunedin, N.Z.: Shona Dunlop MacTavish, Les Humphrey and Associates, 1987.

Magriel, Paul, ed. *Nijinsky, Pavlova, Duncan.* New York: Da Capo, 1977.

Maletic, Vera. "Wigman and Laban: The Interplay of Theory and Practice." *Ballet Review* 14:3 (Fall 1986): 86–95.

Manning, Susan A. "The Americanization of Wigman." Lecture delivered at a conference, "Mary Wigman, 1886–1973," 24 September–3 October 1986, West Berlin.

———. *Ecstasy and the Demon: Feminism and Nationalism in the Dance of Mary Wigman.* Berkeley: University of California Press, 1993.

———. "From Modernism to Fascism: The Evolution of Wigman's Choreography." *Ballet Review* 14:4 (Winter 1987): 87–98.

———. "Reinterpreting Laban." *Dance Chronicle* 11:2 (1988): 315–320.

———. "Reviews" [of books about Valeska Gert, Anita Berber, and Jean Weidt]. *Dance Research Journal* 18:2 (Winter 1986–1987): 70–73.

Manor, Giora. *The Life and Dance of Gertrud Kraus.* Hakibbutz Hameuchad, Israel: Hakibbutz Hameuchad Publishing House, 1978.

"Margaret H'Doubler," *Dance Magazine* (April 1966): 33, 72.

Markard, Anna, and Hermann Markard. *Jooss.* Cologne: Ballett-Bühnen Verlag, 1985.

Marsh, Lucile. "The Music-less Dance." *Dancing Times* (April 1930): 12–16.

Martin, John. *The Dance in Theory.* Princeton: Princeton Book Co., 1989 (a reprint of pp. 31–126 of *Introduction to the Dance,* with a new introduction by Jack Anderson).

———. *Introduction to the Dance.* Brooklyn: Dance Horizons, 1965. (Reprint of original edition: New York: W. W. Norton and Co., 1939.)

———. *The Modern Dance.* Brooklyn: Dance Horizons, 1965. (Reprint of original edition: New York: A. S. Barnes and Co., 1933.)

———. *Sybil Shearer.* Privately published, 1965. Distributor: M. Yoshimasu, Box 515, Palatine, Illinois.

Marx, Henry. "Madeleine: Two Reviews." *Drama Review* 22:2 (T78) (June 1978): 27–31.

Maskey, Jacqueline. "The Group." *Dance Magazine* (January 1965): 44–49.

Mazo, Joseph H. *Prime Movers: The Makers of Modern Dance in America.* New York: William Morrow and Co., 1977.

———. "U.S. Department of Modern Dance." *Dance Magazine* (June 1990): 40–43.

McDearmon, Lacy. "Maud Allan: The Public Record." *Dance Chronicle* 2:2 (1978): 85–105.

McDonagh, Don. *The Complete Guide to Modern Dance.* Garden City: Doubleday and Co., 1976.

———. *Martha Graham: A Biography.* New York: Praeger Publishers, 1973.

———. *The Rise and Fall and Rise of Modern Dance.* New York: New American Library, 1970.

Michel, Artur. "Kate Vaughan, or the Poetry of the Skirt Dance." *Dance Magazine* (January 1945): 12–13, 29–32.

Morgan, Barbara. *Martha Graham: Sixteen Dances in Photographs.* Dobbs Ferry, N.Y.: Morgan and Morgan, 1980. (Reprint of original publication: New York: Duell, Sloan and Pearce, 1941.)

Morris, Margaret. *My Life in Movement.* London: Peter Owen, 1969.

Morris, Robert. "Notes on Dance." *Tulane Drama Review* 10:2 (Winter 1965): 179–186.

Moulton, Robert D. "Bird Larson, the Legend." *Dance Observer* (April 1959): 53–54.

Müller, Hedwig. "At the Start of a New Era." *Ballett International* 6:12 (December 1983): 6–13.

———. "Dance between Ecstasy and Death." *Ballett International* 7:12 (December 1984): 40.

———. "Emile Jaques-Dalcroze: The Beginnings of Rhythmic Gymnastics in Hellerau." *Ballett International* 8:6–7 (1985): 24–27.

———. "Exceeding All Bounds." *Ballett International* 6:3 (March 1983): 22–25.

———. "Mary Wigman and the Third Reich." *Ballett International* 9:11 (November 1986): 18–23.

———. *Mary Wigman: Leben und Werk der grossen Tänzerin.* Berlin: Quadriga, 1986.

———. "The Path Is the Goal." *Ballett International* 6:4 (April 1983): 11–19.

Mumaw, Barton, with Jane Sherman. "Ted Shawn, Teacher and Choreographer." *Dance Chronicle* 6:2 (1981): 91–112.

Myers, Gerald E., ed. *African American Genius in Modern Dance.* Durham: American Dance Festival, n.d.

———. *American Dance Festival 1988: The Black Tradition in American Modern Dance.* Durham: American Dance Festival, 1988.

Nagrin, Daniel. "Tamiris in Her Own Voice: Draft of an Autobiography." *Studies in Dance History* 1:1 (Fall–Winter 1989–1990): 1–64.

Newman, Barbara. "John Ashford." *Dancing Times* (April 1989): 643–645.

Norse, Harold. *Memoirs of a Bastard Angel.* New York: William Morrow and Co., 1989.

Novack, Cynthia J. *Sharing the Dance: Contact Improvisation and American Culture.* Madison: University of Wisconsin Press, 1990.

Ochaim, Brygida Maria. "Die Getanzten Bilder der Rita Sacchetto." *Tanzdrama* 14 (1991): 22–25.

Odom, Maggie. "Mary Wigman: The Early Years, 1913–1925." *Drama Review* 24:4 (T88) (December 1980): 81–92.

Odom, Selma Landen. "Wigman at Hellerau." *Ballet Review* 14:2 (Summer 1986): 41–53.

Orme, Frederick L. "The Negro in the Dance." *American Dancer* (March 1938): 10, 46.

Otte-Betz, Irma. "The Work of Rudolf von Laban." *Dance Observer* (December 1938): 147.

Ou Jian-Ping. "International Reviews: Shanghai." *Dance Magazine* (May 1989): 110–111.

———. "The Modern Dance in China: From 'Fierce Floods and Savage Beasts' to One of the 'One Hundred Flowers'" (unpublished essay).

Overby Lynnette Y., and James H. Humphrey, eds. *Dance: Current Selected Research.* Vol. 1. New York: AMS Press, 1989.

Page, Ruth. "Kreutzberg as I Remember Him." *Dance Magazine* (August 1968): 40, 74.

Parker, H. T. *Motion Arrested.* Ed. Olive Holmes. Middletown: Wesleyan University Press, 1982.

Parkes, Kineton. "Dancing the Emotions: The Art of Sent M'Ahesa." *Dancing Times* (November 1925): 141–143.

Partsch-Bergsohn, Isa. *Modern Dance in Germany and the United States: Crosscurrents and Influences.* Chur: Harwood Academic Publishers, 1994.

Pascal, Blaise. *Pensées.* Trans. A. J. Krailsheimer. Harmondsworth: Penguin Books, 1966.

Pelikan, Jaroslav, ed. *The World Treasury of Modern Religious Thought.* Boston: Little, Brown and Co., 1990.

Percival, John. "Summer Assortment." *Dance and Dancers* (August 1987): 16–18.

Pierre, Dorathi Bock. "This We Were and Are." *Dance Magazine* (January 1943): 12, 29.

Pollock, Barbara, and Charles Humphrey Woodford. *Dance Is a Moment: A Portrait of José Limón in Words and Pictures.* Pennington, N.J.: Dance Horizons, 1993.

Pospisil, Francis. "Rudolf von Laban." *Dancing Times* (April 1930): 18–19.

Preston-Dunlop, Valerie. "Laban and the Nazis." *Update Dance/USA* (August–September 1989): 12–13, 19–22.

Preston-Dunlop, Valerie, and Susanne Lahusen, eds. *Schrifttanz: A View of German Dance in the Weimar Republic.* London: Dance Books, 1990.

Prevots, Naima. *American Pageantry: A Movement for Art and Democracy.* Ann Arbor: UMI Research Press, 1990.

———. *Dancing in the Sun: Hollywood Choreographers, 1915–1937.* Ann Arbor: UMI Research Press, 1987.

———. "Zurich Dada and Dance: Formative Ferment." *Dance Research Journal* 17:1 (Spring–Summer 1985): 3–8.

Prickett, Stacey. "Dance and the Workers' Struggle." *Dance Research* 8:1 (Spring 1990): 47–61.

———. "From Workers' Dance to New Dance." *Dance Research* 7:1 (Spring 1989): 47–64.

Raffé, Marjorie, with Cecil Harwood and Marguerite Lundgren. *Eurythmy and the Impulse of Dance.* N.p.: Rudolf Steiner Press, 1974.

Rainer, Yvonne. *Work 1961–73.* Halifax: Press of the Nova Scotia College of Art and Design; and New York: New York University Press, 1974.

Renick, Dorothy Waties. "The Saga of an Elf-Woman." *Dance* (August 1926): 29, 64.

Robertson, Allen, and Donald Gutera. *The Dance Handbook.* Boston: G. K. Hall and Co., 1988.

Robinson, Jacqueline. *L'Aventure de la Danse Moderne en France (1920 – 1970).* Clamecy: Editions Bougé, 1990.

Roslavleva, Natalia. "Prechistenka 20: The Isadora Duncan School in Moscow." *Dance Perspectives* 64 (Winter 1975).

Rutherston, Jeannette. "The Central European Dance in England." *Dancing Times* (December 1934): 313 – 316.

Ruyter, Nancy Lee Chalfa. "The Intellectual World of Genevieve Stebbins." *Dance Chronicle* 11:3 (1988): 381 – 397.

———. *Reformers and Visionaries: The Americanization of the Art of Dance.* New York: Dance Horizons, 1979.

Rydberg, Olaf. *Die Tänzerin Palucca.* Dresden: Carl Reissner Verlag, 1935.

Sacchetto, Rita. "Symphonic Dance of the Future." *Musical America,* 12 February 1910, p. 2.

St. Denis, Ruth. "The Dance as Life Experience." *American Dancer* (August– September 1929): 9, 31.

———. *An Unfinished Life.* New York: Harper, 1939.

Satin, Leslie. "Valentine de Saint-Point." *Dance Research Journal* 22:1 (Spring 1990): 1–12.

Sayre, Henry M. *The Object of Performance: The American Avant-Garde since 1970.* Chicago: University of Chicago Press, 1989.

Scharnhorst, Gary, and Jack Bales. *The Lost Life of Horatio Alger Jr.* Bloomington: Indiana University Press, 1985.

Scheier, Helmut. "What Has Dance Theatre to Do with Ausdruckstanz?" *Ballett International* 10:1 (January 1987): 12–17.

Scheyer, Ernst. "The Shapes of Space: The Art of Mary Wigman and Oskar Schlemmer." *Dance Perspectives* 41 (Spring 1970).

Schlundt, Christena L. "Into the Mystic with Miss Ruth." *Dance Perspectives* 46 (Summer 1971).

———. *The Professional Appearances of Ruth St. Denis and Ted Shawn.* New York: New York Public Library, 1962.

———. *The Professional Appearances of Ted Shawn and His Men Dancers.* New York: New York Public Library, 1962.

———. "Tamiris: A Chronicle of Her Dance Career 1927–1955." *Studies in Dance History* 1:1 (Fall–Winter 1989–1990): 65–154.

Schneider, Ilya Ilyich. *Isadora Duncan: The Russian Years.* Trans. David Magarshack. New York: Harcourt, Brace and World, 1968.

Schuftan, Werner. *Manuel de Danse.* Paris: Encyclopédie Roret-Editions Edgar Malfère (SFELT), 1938.

Schumann, Gerhard, ed. *Palucca: Porträt einer Künstlerin.* Berlin: Henschelverlag Kunst und Gesellschaft, 1972.

Schur, Ernst. *Der Moderne Tanz.* Munich: Gustav Lammers, 1910.

Selden, Elizabeth. *The Dancer's Quest.* Berkeley: University of California Press, 1935.

———. *Elements of the Free Dance.* New York: A. S. Barnes and Co., 1930.

Seroff, Victor. *The Real Isadora.* New York: Dial Press, 1971.

Servos, Norbert. *Pina Bausch—Wuppertal Dance Theater, or the Art of Training a Goldfish: Excursions into Dance*. Trans. Patricia Stadié. Cologne: Ballett-Bühnen-Verlag, 1984.

———. "Whether to Resist or Conform: Ausdruckstanz Then, and Now?" *Ballett International* 10:1 (January 1987): 18–21.

Shanor, Rebecca Read. *The City That Never Was*. New York: Viking, 1988.

Shawn, Ted. *Every Little Movement: A Book about François Delsarte*. Brooklyn: Dance Horizons, 1968.

Shawn, Ted, with Gray Poole. *One Thousand and One Night Stands*. Garden City: Doubleday and Co., 1960.

Shelton, Suzanne. *Divine Dancer: A Biography of Ruth St. Denis*. Garden City: Doubleday and Co., 1981.

Sherman, Jane. "Doris and Charles and Pauline Fifty Years Ago." *Dance Magazine* (October 1978): 57–62.

———. *The Drama of Denishawn Dance*. Middletown: Wesleyan University Press, 1979.

Sherman, Jane, and Barton Mumaw. *Barton Mumaw, Dancer: From Denishawn to Jacob's Pillow and Beyond*. New York: Dance Horizons, 1986.

Sherman, Jane, with Christena L. Schlundt. "Who's St. Denis? What Is She?" *Dance Chronicle* 10:3 (1987): 305–329.

Siegel, Marcia B. *Days on Earth: The Dance of Doris Humphrey*. New Haven: Yale University Press, 1987.

———. "*The Green Table*—Sources of a Classic." *Dance Research Journal* 21:1 (Spring 1989): 15–21.

———, ed. "Nik: A Documentary." *Dance Perspectives* 48 (Winter 1971).

———. *The Shapes of Change: Images of American Dance*. Boston: Houghton Mifflin Co., 1979.

Smith, Wendy. *Real Life Drama: The Group Theatre and America, 1931–1940*. New York: Alfred A. Knopf, 1990.

Soares, Janet Mansfield. *Louis Horst: Musician in a Dancer's World*. Durham: Duke University Press, 1992.

Sommer, Sally R. "Loïe Fuller's Art of Music and Light." *Dance Chronicle* 4:4 (1981): 389–401.

———. "The Lyon Biennale de la Danse: American Review and Au Revoir," *Dance Magazine* (September 1990): 46–47.

Sorell, Walter. *Hanya Holm: The Biography of an Artist*. Middletown: Wesleyan University Press, 1969.

Spector, Irwin. *Rhythm and Life: The Work of Emile Jaques-Dalcroze*. Stuyvesant, N.Y.: Pendragon Press, 1990.

Sperlinger, T., J. Ehrlich, and K. Kronfield. "The Central European School of Dance." *Dancing Times* (December 1928): 317–323.

Spiesman, Mildred. "The Bird Larson School of Natural Rhythmic Expression." *Dance Magazine* (September 1951): 22, 35–36.

———. "The Natural Dance Program." *Dance Magazine* (June 1951): 16, 42–45.

Spoto, Donald. *Madcap: The Life of Preston Sturges*. Boston: Little, Brown and Co., 1990.

Stebbins, Genevieve. *Delsarte System of Expression*. New York: Dance Horizons, 1977 (reprint of 1902 edition).

Steinberg, Cobbett, ed. *The Dance Anthology*. New York: New American Library, 1980.

Stewart, Virginia, and Merle Armitage. *The Modern Dance*. New York: Dance Horizons, 1970 (republication of 1st ed. "manufactured in the plant of the Will A. Kistler Co., 1935").

Stöckemann, Patricia. "Niddy Impekoven: Geburtstag eines Wunderkind." *Tanzdrama* 11 (1990): 26–29.

Stodelle, Ernestine. *Deep Song: The Dance Story of Martha Graham*. New York: Schirmer Books, 1984.

Svetloff, Valerien. "Isadora Duncan." *Dancing Times* (December 1927): 327–329, 336.

Taylor, Paul. *Private Domain*. New York: Alfred A. Knopf, 1987.

Tembeck, Iro. "Early Modern Montreal: 1929–1970." *Dance Connection* (February/March 1991): 26–32.

Terry, Walter. "Miss Birgit." *Ballet News* (November 1982): 18.

———. *Miss Ruth: The "More Living" Life of Ruth St. Denis*. New York: Dodd, Mead and Co., 1969.

———. *Ted Shawn: Father of American Dance*. New York: Dial Press, 1976.

Thomas, F. G. "The People." *Dancing Times* (October 1932): 19–21.

Thornton, Samuel. *Laban's Theory of Movement: A New Perspective*. Boston: Plays Inc., 1971.

"Time to Walk in Space." *Dance Perspectives*, 34 (Summer 1968).

"Tribute to Irene Lewisohn." *Dance Observer* (May 1944): 55–56.

Van Loo, Anne, ed. *Akarova: Spectacle et Avant-Garde/Entertainment and the Avant-Garde 1920–1950*. Brussels: Aux Archives d'Architecture Moderne, 1988.

Veroli, Patrizia. "The Choreography of Aurel Milloss." Part I: 1906–1945, *Dance Chronicle* 13:1 (1990): 1–46; Part II: 1946–1966, *Dance Chronicle* 13:2 (1990): 193–240.

———., ed. *I Sakharoff: Un Mito della Danza fra Teatro e Avanguardie Artistiche*. Bologna: Edizioni Bara, 1991.

Visher, Joe. "Twenty Years of Rapid Development." *Dancing Times* (October 1931): 26–28.

Vuillermoz, Emile. *Clotilde et Alexandre Sakharoff*. Lausanne: Editions Centrales, 1933.

Warren, Larry. *Anna Sokolow: The Rebellious Spirit*. Princeton: Dance Horizons, 1991.

———. *Lester Horton: Modern Dance Pioneer*. New York: Marcel Dekker, 1977.

Welzien, Leonore. "Vom Rhythmus zur Bewegung—von der Bewegung zum Tanz: Interview mit Rosalia Chladek." *Tanzdrama* 11 (1990): 18–23.

West, Martha Ullman. "Frontier of Design: Isamu Noguchi 1904–1988." *Dance Magazine* (May 1989): 58–60.

Wigman, Mary. *The Language of Dance*. Trans. Walter Sorell. Middletown: Wesleyan University Press, 1966.

———. *The Mary Wigman Book.* Ed. and trans. Walter Sorell. Middletown: Wesleyan University Press, 1975.

Wolfe, Oscar. "Raymond Duncan the Executive." *Dance Magazine* (February 1930): 11, 50.

Wolff, Stéphane. *L'Opéra au Palais Garnier (1875–1962).* Paris: Editions Slatkine, 1983.

Wyman, Max. *Dance Canada.* Vancouver: Douglas and McIntyre, 1989.

INDEX

Gabriel, Onni, 82
Gainsborough, Thomas, 32
Gallotta, Jean-Claude, 275
Galsworthy, John, 27
García Lorca, Federico, 188, 263
Garden, Mary, 31
Gardener in Love, The (Kreutzberg), 66
Garnier, Jacques, 274
Garth, Midi, 199, 292
Gehry, Frank, 246
Genée, Adeline, 148
Gentry, Eve, 183
George, Henry, 131
Georgi, Yvonne, 64, 97–98, 100, 106, 107, 131, 135, 188, 189, 202, 231, 291, 292, 293
Gershwin, George, 151, 152, 265
Gert, Valeska, 67–68, 69, 70, 139, 192, 294
Gide, André, 20
Gilbert, Melvin Ballou, 8
Gillet, Ernest, 32
Gillis, Margie, 289
Ginner, Ruby, 28, 82, 83, 292
Gish, Lillian, 164
Glacial Decoy (Brown), 245
Glanternik, Toby, 209
Glass, Philip, 245, 253
Gleisner, Martin, 137
Gluck, Christoph, 21, 23, 27, 47, 75, 280
Gluck-Sandor, Senia, 149–150, 152, 175, 176
Goebbels, Joseph, 133, 136, 138
Goff, Steve, 268
Goldberg, Richard, 220
Goleizovsky, Kasian, 79
Golovine, Serge, 276
Goossens, Leon and Leslie, 124
Gordon, David, 220, 241, 252, 274
Gore, Walter, 259
Gorki, Maxim, 93, 186
Goslar, Lotte, 192–193
Gottschild, Hellmut, 232
Gough, Orlando, 266
Gould, Norma, 43–45, 119
Goya, Francisco de, 89
Graff, Grace Cornell and Kurt, 57, 145–146, 150, 175
Graham, Martha, 106, 109, 111, 112, 113, 115–118, 123, 135, 140–141, 142, 145, 156–160, 162, 174, 176, 177, 178, 184–186, 188, 189, 190, 192, 196, 197, 198, 199, 202, 205, 206, 209, 214, 216, 217, 226, 227, 230, 237, 238–239, 240, 242, 246, 250, 251,

252, 258, 259, 260, 261, 262, 263, 264, 271, 273, 278, 288, 291, 292, 293, 294
Grand Union, the, 241
GRCOP (Groupe de Recherche Chorégraphique de l'Opéra de Paris), 274
Greek influence on modern dance, 21, 26, 27, 28–29, 82–83, 184–186
Green, Ray, 197–198
Green Table, The (Jooss), 130–131, 231
Grieg, Edvard, 27, 33, 86
Griffes, Charles T., 86
Gripenberg, Maggie, 81, 117, 227, 291
Grona, Eugene von (also van), 106, 172
Grooms, Red, 213
Gropius, Walter, 70
Grossman, Daniel Williams, 288
Grosz, George, 129
Groupe de la Place Royale, Le, 224
Groupe Emile Dubois, 275
Gruenberg, Louis, 171
Guangdong Academy of Dance, 287
Guest, Ann Hutchinson, 183
Guest, Ivor, 183
Guiablesse, La (Page), 173
Günther, Dorothee, 55, 75–76, 135, 136, 254
Gurdjieff, George Ivanovitch, 94–95
Guthrie, Phoebe, 110
Guthrie, William Norman, 110
Guthrie, Woody, 191
Guy, Edna, 171
Gypsy Dances (Wigman), 62

Haim, Mattie, 198, 292
Hall, Fernau, 95, 228
Halprin, Anna (also Ann), 205, 214–216, 218, 242, 244, 247, 255, 292
Hampton Institute Creative Dance Group, 171
Handel, George Frideric, 158, 209, 251
Hangman's Dance (Kreutzberg), 66
Happenings, 212–214, 252
Happy Hypocrite, The (Weidman), 165
Harbach, Otto, 13
Harkarvy, Benjamin, 259
Harmel, Lilian, 257
Harvest 1935 (Tamiris), 166
Harvey, John, 46
Haskell, Arnold L., 95–96
Hatfield, Ruth, 172
Haupt, Walter, 278
Hauptmann, Gerhart, 39